Perspectives on Economics and Management

The world of economics and management is being reshaped in more ways than one, including rapid advancements in technology and business practices. This book weaves together a diverse set of issues such as consumption patterns, wealth disparities and the management, behaviour and financial health of businesses and consumers to analyse the effectiveness of economic and business strategies.

Rapid technological advancements along with the need for cost-effectiveness and convenience are making service providers embrace technology as a partner rather than a tool in their economic journey. Relatedly, traditional management philosophy is coming under a scanner, with an increasing emphasis on the holistic development of the organization, rather than a top-down approach, as has been the case in the past. Understanding major developments in economic and financial policymaking has perennially been a key concern of public policy, shaped by recent global and related developments, this has necessitated a relook at these issues, couched in a cross-cutting perspective. Viewed from this standpoint, the present volume, written to honour the rich academic work of the eminent economist Professor Anindya Sen intersects this triad of economics, finance and public policy that are integral to policy thinking and its formulation. The smorgasbord of research ideas, involving both theoretical analysis and empirical evidence, presented in this volume, provides useful perspectives on the drivers that are continually reshaping the dynamism in the world around us and, in the process, integrates a multidisciplinary perspective of focusing on several pertinent policy challenges.

This book will be useful to researchers and students of economics, finance and public policy, economic theorists, microeconomics, and even to those with a broader canvass such as researchers in macroeconomics, international economics, business, management and marketing.

Saibal Ghosh worked at the Reserve Bank of India (RBI) for two decades. In his final stint, he was the deputy research adviser at the Centre for Advanced Financial Research and Learning, RBI. He has over 25 years of experience in financial intermediation, financial stability and developmental issues. His research has been extensively published in leading international and national journals. He is presently working as an expert (adviser) with the Qatar Central Bank in Doha, Qatar.

Partha Ray is currently the director of the National Institute of Bank Management, Pune. Earlier for nearly a decade, he was a professor of economics at Indian Institute of Management Calcutta. His earlier stints include adviser to the executive director (India) at the International Monetary Fund and an economist at the Department of Economic & Policy Research, Reserve Bank of India. He has written extensively on issues relating to global and Indian macroeconomics and the financial sector.

Perspectives on Economics and Management

Essays in Honour of Anindya Sen

Edited by Saibal Ghosh and Partha Ray

Routledge
Taylor & Francis Group
LONDON AND NEW YORK

First published 2025
by Routledge
4 Park Square, Milton Park, Abingdon, Oxon OX14 4RN

and by Routledge
605 Third Avenue, New York, NY 10158

Routledge is an imprint of the Taylor & Francis Group, an informa business

British Library Cataloguing-in-Publication Data
A catalogue record for this book is available from the British Library

ISBN: 978-1-032-67094-2 (hbk)
ISBN: 978-1-032-83523-5 (pbk)
ISBN: 978-1-003-50972-1 (ebk)

DOI: 10.4324/9781003509721

Typeset in Sabon
by SPi Technologies India Pvt Ltd (Straive)

Contents

Figures

Tables

Contributors

Rajat Acharyya is a professor of economics, and former dean of the Faculty Council of Arts, Jadavpur University. He received his MSc (Economics) from Calcutta University (1990) and PhD (Economics) from Jadavpur University (1996). He was a Ford Foundation postdoctoral fellow at Rochester University, New York (1997–98). He received the EXIM Bank International Trade Research Award in 1997, the Global Development Network Research Medal in 2003, the Mahalanobis Memorial Medal in 2006 and the Best University Teacher Award from the Government of West Bengal in 2016.

Balram Avittathur is a professor at the Indian Institute of Management (IIM) Calcutta. He has a doctorate from IIM Bangalore and has been with IIM Calcutta since 1999. He works in the areas of supply chain management, innovations and entrepreneurship and has well-cited research articles in reputed research journals. Apart from his teaching and research, he also serves the industry through consulting and training. He is a Fulbright Post-Doctoral Fellow (2003), and his recent international assignments include teaching at HHL Leipzig (Germany) and WU Vienna.

Preetam Basu is a senior lecturer in the Department of Analytics, Operations and Systems at the Kent Business School, University of Kent, UK. Previously, he was an associate professor at the Indian Institute of Management Calcutta. He has a doctorate in operations management from the University of Connecticut, USA. Earlier, he did his MS in applied mathematics from the University of Minnesota, USA. His research interests include supply chain management, risk management, supply chain finance and revenue management.

Sanjay Basu holds a master's degree in economics from Calcutta University and a PhD in economics from IIM Calcutta. He is a professor in the Finance Group and the editor of the flagship journal *Prajnan* of the National Institute of Bank Management. His areas of interest are bond portfolio management, market risk management, asset-liability management, financial crises, applied game theory and contract theory. He has published in reputed journals, such as the *European Journal of Operational Research* and the *Journal of Economic Behaviour and Organization*, in these areas.

Saumitra Bhaduri is a professor and dean of student affairs at the Madras School of Economics. He completed his PhD from IGIDR, Mumbai and is a renowned scholar in the field of Economics and Finance, with extensive research on Indian capital markets. With over 25 years of experience, he has published extensively in top journals. His expertise spans economic policy analysis, quantitative research, corporate finance, market microstructure and risk management. He is renowned for his consultancy services in analytics for leading corporations, contributing significantly to key projects.

Subhajit Bhattacharyya is a professor at the Institute of Management Technology Ghaziabad. In the last 21 years, he has also contributed to its growth in various capacities, including as dean and director, at its sister campuses. He received his PhD in economics from Indira Gandhi Institute of Development Research, Mumbai and has research interests in game theory, digital economy and business strategy.

Anindita Chakrabarti is a teaching fellow in economics at the University of Leeds and a fellow of the Higher Education Academy. She completed her PhD in economics at the Centre for Economic Studies and Planning at JNU, New Delhi, India. Her main research interest is health economics, particularly evaluating the importance of socio-economic factors in explaining the utilisation of maternal and child health care services in India. She also is interested in the importance of health care financing, particularly the importance of community-based health insurance services as a source of financing private health care services among the rural community in India.

Manisha Chakrabarty is a professor in economics at the Indian Institute of Management (IIM), Calcutta. She has been associated with IIM Calcutta for 16 years, and earlier, she was an assistant professor at Keele University, UK. She received her PhD from the Indian Statistical Institute, Calcutta and later worked at Bonn University, Germany, as a postdoc fellow before moving to the UK. Her main focus of research is in the areas of applied econometrics, development economics, gender, labour economics and economics of households.

Indrani Chakraborty is a professor of economics and currently the director of the Institute of Development Studies Kolkata. She was formerly at the Centre for Development Studies, Thiruvananthapuram. She received her PhD in economics from the University of Calcutta and is a recipient of a CICOPS scholarship and a Liverpool–India Fellowship. She has published widely in reputed journals and contributed to many book volumes on the impact of capital inflows, the role of financial development on economic growth and the capital structure of corporate firms.

Jyoti Chandiramani is presently the director of Symbiosis School of Economics and also the dean of the Faculty of Humanities and Social Sciences at Symbiosis International (Deemed) University since 2010 and is in her fourth term. She also heads the Symbiosis Centre for Urban Studies since 2022. Her research interests are aligned with the Indian economy especially urban economic development as well as international development cooperation. She has worked on various research projects and continues to guide a number of PhD scholars, while some scholars have completed their thesis under her guidance.

Kausik Chaudhuri is a Chair Professor in Applied Economics at the University of Leeds. He also holds visiting appointments at the Indian Institute of Management in Bangalore, India, the University of New South Wales, the University of Sydney in Australia and the Madras School of Economics in Chennai, India. He has been a consultant economist for the World Bank and specialises in applied econometrics, empirical development economics and political economy.

Tasneem Chherawala is an associate professor, in the Finance Group, at the National Institute of Bank Management. She holds a master's degree in quantitative economics from the Indian Statistical Institute and a PhD in finance from Savitribai Phule Pune University. Her domain expertise is in the areas of risk modelling and management, Basel, IFRS, financial derivatives, project finance and structured finance, in which she conducts executive training and postgraduate courses.

Mousumi Dutta is currently a professor at the Economics Department, Presidency University, Kolkata. She is a Gold Medalist in MSc (Economics) from Calcutta University and completed her doctoral degree in "Economics of Conservation of Built Heritage: The Case of Kolkata" from the same university. She has been a principal or a co-principal investigator on projects funded by the International Growth Center, London School of Economics; Rosa Luxemburg Society, Berlin, ICSSR, and UGC. Professor Dutta has worked extensively on the built environment, health and gender issues.

Saibal Ghosh, co-editor of this volume, worked at the Reserve Bank of India (RBI) for two decades. In his final stint, he was the deputy research adviser at the Centre for Advanced Financial Research and Learning, RBI. He has more than 25 years of experience in financial intermediation, financial stability and developmental issues. His research has been extensively published in leading international and national journals. He is presently working as an expert (adviser) with the Qatar Central Bank in Doha, Qatar.

Saswata Ghosh is an associate professor at the Institute of Development Studies Kolkata (IDSK). He was a visiting fellow at the Asia Research Centre of the London School of Economics and the Bangladesh Institute of Development Studies. He is currently serving as a member of the International Advisory Board of the *Asian Population Studies Journal*. His areas of interest include low fertility, religious demography, family planning and son preference, family demography, field survey methods, indirect demographic estimations and econometric methods.

Zakir Husain is a professor in the Economics Department, Presidency University, Kolkata. A graduate of Presidency College, he uses econometric tools and methods to study the issues related to exclusion and discrimination in gerontology, education, demography and health. He has been a faculty in the Institute of Economic Growth and Indian Institute of Technology Kharagpur, a senior consultant in the Prime Minister's High-Level Committee to prepare a report on the status of Muslims and a member of the West Bengal Planning Board.

Tanveer Ahmad Khan is currently working as an Indian economic service officer in the Department of Expenditure, Government of India. He looks after the appraisal of the central sector and central-sponsored schemes in the department. He completed his MPhil in development studies from the Institute of Development Studies, Kolkata. He also has a master's in economics from the University of Kashmir. He has published multiple research papers mostly focused on international trade.

K.S. Kavi Kumar is a professor at the Madras School of Economics, Chennai. His research interests include environmental economics, climate change economics and development economics. He has served as a member of various committees of the Government of Tamil Nadu and the Government of India.

Arpita Kundu is currently working as a scientific assistant at the Economic Research Unit, Indian Statistical Institute, Calcutta. Earlier, she was in a doctoral program at IIM Calcutta in the Economics group. She did her postgraduation degree in economics from Jadavpur University, Kolkata, and her bachelor's degree was from Presidency University, Kolkata with economics as the major. Her research interests are primarily in the areas of gender studies, health economics and development economics in general.

Sudipa Majumdar is presently the Director of The Integrated Research and Action for Development (IRADe). Earlier, she was professor of economics at Symbiosis School of Economics, Pune and a fellow of the Higher Education Academy, UK. She completed her bachelor's degree at Presidency College Kolkata; her master's at JNU New Delhi and her doctorate from IGIDR Mumbai. She also completed her postgraduation in advanced statistical learning at Stanford University, USA, and in higher education at

Middlesex University, UK. She has been academically involved with institutions of international repute for more than two decades and has published her research work in numerous peer-reviewed journals.

Amarendu Nandy is an assistant professor in the economics area of the Indian Institute of Management Ranchi. He holds a PhD from the Lee Kuan Yew School of Public Policy, National University of Singapore. His research interests are in the areas of labour and development economics, business environment and public policy, with a focus on India. He has numerous peer-reviewed international journal publications to his credit. He regularly contributes to public debates through his op-ed articles in leading business dailies.

Parthapratim Pal is a professor in the Economics Group at the Indian Institute of Management (IIM) Calcutta. He has been with IIM Calcutta since 2006. He teaches several courses, including Macroeconomics, International Economics, and Development Economics, at IIM Calcutta. He has a master's, MPhil and PhD in economics from Jawaharlal Nehru University, New Delhi. He has also received education from Cambridge University, UK, and the Harvard Business School, USA.

Partha Ray, co-editor of this volume, is currently the director of the National Institute of Bank Management, Pune. Earlier, for nearly a decade, he was a professor of economics at Indian Institute of Management Calcutta. His earlier stints include adviser to the executive director (India) at the International Monetary Fund and an economist in the Department of Economic & Policy Research, Reserve Bank of India. He has written extensively on issues relating to global and Indian macroeconomics and the financial sector.

Runa Sarkar is a professor with the Economics Group and the coordinator of the Centre for Development and Environment Policy at the Indian Institute of Management Calcutta. She serves as an independent director on the boards of Bandhan Financial Holdings Ltd., the Climate Policy Initiative India and Basix Consulting and Technology Services Ltd. and as a jury member for the Excellence in Sustainability Steelie Award of the World Steel Association.

Santosh Kumar Shrivastav is an associate professor of business analytics at IMT, Ghaziabad, India. Dr. Santosh has 10-plus years of teaching and research experience in the field of data science. Dr. Santosh's research interest and experience include predictive analytics, natural language processing, machine learning and deep learning, survival analysis, stochastic modelling, non-linear optimization and text analytics.

Bipin Sony is currently an assistant professor at the Vidyashilp University, Bengaluru. Holding a PhD from Madras School of Economics, his research interests include corporate finance, financial economics and macroeconomics. He has published multiple papers in reputed journals and his research focuses on firm-level issues in the Indian capital market.

Abhisek Sur is an assistant professor of economics and a research fellow at IDEAS at O P Jindal Global University. He completed his PhD in economics from the Indian Institute of Management Ranchi. His research interests are primarily in the areas of open economy macroeconomics and economic policy, with reference to India and other emerging market economies. He has published in a number of peer-reviewed journals, in addition to publishing op-eds in leading business dailies.

Brinda Viswanathan is a professor at the Madras School of Economics, Chennai. Her research and teaching interests are in the broad area of development economics and applied econometrics. She regularly contributes as a resource person for workshops and training programs for government officials, college teachers and PhD students on statistical and econometric techniques.

Introduction

Saibal Ghosh and Partha Ray

Anindya Sen has been an academician throughout his life. After completing his graduation from Presidency College, Calcutta, and post-graduation from the University of Kolkata, he worked as a lecturer in economics at the University of Calcutta for about 5 years. Afterward, he went to the University of Southern California, USA, where he received his doctoral degree in 1990 in the broad area of industrial organisation. Immediately after, he joined the Indira Gandhi Institute of Development Research (IGIDR) and worked there as a faculty member. He was the dean of Graduate Studies at IGIDR. He joined the Indian Institute of Management, Calcutta (IIMC) in 1998. Prof. Sen spent the majority of his academic career at this institute, teaching courses in economics, including microeconomics and economics of business policy.

During the latter part of his career, Prof. Sen assumed additional academic-cum-administrative responsibilities including as the dean of Programme Initiatives (2005–2007) and the dean (Academic) from 2012 to 2015 at IIMC, a faculty representative to the board of governors of IIMC (2016–2018) and the chairman of the Computer Services Committee (2014–2017). As dean (Academic), he successfully carried through the various accreditation processes. Besides, he has also served as the chairman of the Fellowship Research Program Committee and served as the editor of the IIMC flagship journal *Decision* from 1999 to 2002. He also served as the director-in-charge of the newly instituted the Indian Institute of Management–Ranchi during its initial phase from 2014–2017. He was a visiting professor at the School of Business and Management, American University of Armenia, and in the Department of Economics, University of Notre Dame, USA. After his retirement from IIM Calcutta, Prof. Sen was instrumental as pro-vice-chancellor in setting up a School of Social Sciences at M. S. Ramaiah Institute of Applied Sciences in Bangalore, Karnataka.

Prof. Sen is the recipient of several awards such as the Annual Prof. Panchanan Chakraborty Memorial Award for the best teacher and researcher in economics in West Bengal for 2005. He has won various academic awards from the Government of India, an All-University Pre-Doctoral Merit Fellowship from the University of Southern California and merit certificates from the Office of International Students and Scholars, University of Southern California.

DOI: 10.4324/9781003509721-1

Prof. Anindya Sen is well known in academic circles as a gentle and affable person for his warm and mild-mannered nature and for always being attentive to the needs of his students and colleagues and in his peer community as a sharp mind with a strong intellect, able to discern the nuances of economic theory and policy. Reflecting this, Prof. Sen has co-authored several books in economics and business with several of his colleagues across institutes of higher learning where he has worked, including several of his own. His book *Microeconomics: Theory and Applications*, published by Oxford University Press in 1999, and the co-authored book *The Economics of Business Policy*, published by Oxford University Press in 2004, are well known to his students for their lucid and elegant articulation of the complexities inherent in modern-day microeconomics and business policy.

He was the general editor for a cluster of books on economics and development in the Oxford India Short Introduction series. Currently, he is the series editor for two series being published by Routledge, one titled "Contemporary Themes in Business and Management" and the other "Routledge Focus on Management and Society." He has published in both Indian and international journals and contributed chapters to a number of volumes.

This book is a collection of essays by the students and colleagues of Prof. Sen on various aspects of the triad of micro-evidence and business and macro policies, centred primarily on the Indian context but occasionally going beyond. The diversity of authors and their rich and varied background enables the integration of theoretical rigour, empirical validation and documentary evidence on a diverse set of academic and policy concerns, which were close to Prof. Sen. In terms of its key features, three elements stand out. First, being the first such volume in the post-COVID-19 world, it draws on the hands-on nature of research, with evidence being accumulated to bear on the broad themes. Second, the diversity of research ideas, both theoretical and empirical, provides useful perspectives on the drivers that are continually reshaping the economic world around us and, in the process, integrates a multidisciplinary approach to deal with economic policy challenges.

Micro-Evidence

The economies of scale in household consumption arise as the per person cost of the 'public' good decreases with household size, thereby releasing resources for the 'private' goods in larger families. The empirical evidence in support of this fact has met with limited success in the Indian context. Chapter 1 by Brinda Viswanathan and K.S. Kavi Kumar titled "Economies of Scale in Household Consumption Patterns", re-examines the public good approach to measure economies of scale in household expenditure using the Indian Human Development Survey (IHDS) data for the year 2011–2012. Preliminary analysis shows that as disposable income expands with economies of scale, consumption diversifies towards a more varied diet and from food to non-food items. As of 2019–2020, about 44% of rural and 39% of urban households in India belong to non-nuclear families. Furthermore, larger households are over-represented among the poor. The detailed findings from this study provide policy ideas as to the behaviour of households across income and social strata regarding their response towards consumption and investment and how they balance them to ensure higher living standards.

Given reduced social interactions and economic distress, concerns about mental health have gained primacy during COVID-19. In Chapter 2, Zakir Husain, Saswata Ghosh, Mousumi Dutta, Anindita Chakrabarti and Kausik Chaudhuri dwell on this issue in detail. Titled "Analyzing Mental Well-Being of Adults during the COVID-19 Pandemic Using a MIMIC Model: Evidence from Indian Metropolitan Cities", the authors estimate the prevalence of mental health problems during the first wave of COVID-19 and identify its determinants among the general population of Indian metropolitan cities. The data were collected from over 1200 adults randomly selected from the list of mobile phone users in Bengaluru, Chennai, Delhi, Kolkata, Mumbai and Hyderabad. The Depression Anxiety Stress Scale (DASS) was administered to the study participants. The study employed a multiple-indicator, multiple-cause (MIMIC) model to measure depression, anxiety and stress using observed indicators of these latent constructs and identify the socioeconomic groups at risk of these disorders. Preliminary estimates suggest that close to 50% of respondents reported anxiety symptoms, with the percentage reporting depression and stress being around similar (or slightly lower) levels. Single respondents, members of minority groups, those less educated and those from large households were identified as the most at risk. The results also indicate a positive relationship between economic stress and mental illness. Although COVID-19 increased the psychological burden of the population, all persons reporting psychological disorders may not require clinical attention. While community-based support may be sufficient, general monitoring is required to identify at-risk persons who may require clinical support.

In Chapter 3, Rajat Acharyya examines the implications a merger has for the quality of new and existing innovations. The chapter titled "Quality of Innovation and Market Access under Merger" notes that two important considerations dominate the cost implications of mergers. First, for new innovations, the sunk cost of innovation is what is of paramount importance. Once a product is innovated and developed, the marginal cost of producing the innovated product is usually low and invariant with respect to the scale of production. Second, for the choice of qualities (or products) from the set of existing innovations, what is relevant is the cost of production that increases with the choice of the quality level itself. So, does this distinction between the nature of costs – sunk development cost versus variable production cost – matter for the post-merger quality level? Another useful dimension of the analysis is the role of cost synergy – both for sunk development and marginal production costs. Apart from the quality of innovations by a merged firm, another relevant issue is the post-merger market coverage. Does a merger reduce the extent of the market coverage? These issues hold useful implications for critical industries such as pharmaceuticals. To illustrate, if a merger reduces the extent of market coverage, it could impede access to newly innovated drugs, presumably to poor patients. And if the drug in question is a life-saving vaccine such as a vaccine for COVID-19, then such denial of market access has far-reaching implications for welfare and well-being. Viewed from this standpoint, the analysis has useful public policy implications regarding the interaction between mergers and their ability to modulate market coverage, especially in industries with critical interfaces with human life.

In Chapter 4, Sudipa Majumdar and Jyoti Chandiramani focus on the wealth disparities in India. Relatedly, they also focus on the adequacy of fiscal policies to address this issue. Titled "Fiscal Interventions to Combat Wealth Disparity in India", the authors trace wealth disparity in India from 1983 to 2021. A preliminary analysis highlights a widening of the wealth gap since 1992. In this regard, they assess the relevance of various fiscal interventions within an empirical setup. The results underscore the inadequacy of tax revenues and the absence of redistributive effects and have important policy recommendations. Given the paucity of fiscal space, the findings also call for innovative financing mechanisms other than tax revenues like crowdfunding, private investments, corporate social responsibility initiatives and self-help groups, along with urban employment guarantee schemes, to tackle this issue in a comprehensive manner.

In Chapter 5, Subhajit Bhattacharyya and Santosh Kumar Shrivastav present an overview of game theory, with an application to management puzzles. Titled "The Crossroads of Management Puzzles and Game Theory", the authors affirm that game theory, having its genesis in the womb of mathematical sciences, seeks to mathematically identify the best strategic response of the players, who, in general, are assumed to be rational and have complete information about the context and circumstances, as also the outcome of the different strategies played (although may have incomplete or imperfect information about the rival players). On the contrary, the business world does not enjoy the benefit of full information or the perfectly predictable outcome of any competition. It is therefore not surprising that the literature on business strategies has not attached much reference to game theory and vice versa. Based on a bibliometric analysis, this chapter explores cross-cutting research areas, quantify the research trends, overviews the research outcomes and highlights the potential areas where game theoretic ideas could be exploited in addressing management puzzles.

Although several facets of banking have been adequately addressed, one area which has largely bypassed the attention of researchers in the Indian context is bank internationalisation. To address this shortcoming, Saibal Ghosh looks at this issue in Chapter 6. Titled "Does Internationalization Affect Bank Risk-Taking? Evidence from India", the author utilises annual data on domestic Indian banks for an extended period to assess its impact on risk-taking. In this regard, borrowing from recent research, both accounting and market-based risk measures are employed while onboarding other relevant considerations such as bank size, funding strategy and income profile, which could be relevant in explaining bank risk. The findings suggest that internationalisation increases bank risk-taking, measured in accounting or market-based measures. Relatedly, the chapter also examines the channels through which such internationalisation impacts bank riskiness and, relatedly, the effect of their expansion strategies. It is found that greater operational complexity and simultaneous expansion into multiple markets are key factors that adversely affect their riskiness. From a policy standpoint, the analysis suggests a thorough analytical assessment of the potential gains versus the consequences of alternate expansion strategies to ensure long-term viability of banks.

In Chapter 7, titled "Security Issue Decisions in Public and Private Security Markets: Evidence From an Emerging Economy", Saumitra Bhaduri and Bipin Sony examine the role of information asymmetry in capital structure decisions made in public and private security markets. Specifically, they test the contention that firms in countries with higher information premia circumvent the challenges arising from information asymmetries by choosing securities and market types with less information sensitivity. Consistent with the arguments of information-based models, the empirical findings for India suggest that firms with less information asymmetry make public issues. However, the twist in the tale comes from the private security markets, where they report the reversal of the pecking-order behaviour. In contrast to the conventional wisdom, they find that firms with higher information asymmetry issue equity over debt in the private securities market. The authors conclude with some policy discussions of the findings and correlate them with the Indian experience.

Using an extended sample of Indian manufacturing firms covering the 2000–2020 period, Tanveer Ahmad Khan and Indrani Chakraborty examine the effect of financial constraints on the extensive and intensive margins of exports in Chapter 8 titled "Financial Constraints and Export Behaviour: An Analysis of Indian Manufacturing Firms". Using two multivariate indices of financing constraints proposed by Whited and Wu (2006) and Hadlock and Pierce (2010), along with conventional measures like liquidity and leverage, they examine whether changes in firms' financial health influence the decision to export as well as the level of exports. Relatedly, they also test the learning-by-exporting hypothesis. Finally, they examine whether implementing the Insolvency and Bankruptcy Code (IBC) in 2016 helped reduce firms' financial constraints. Their findings also show that after the implementation of IBC-2016, financial constraints have declined. The findings are correlated with the recent evidence which suggests that exporting manufacturing firms have benefitted from the bankruptcy reform law.

Business and Macro Policies

In Chapter 9, Amarendu Nandy and Abhisek Sur elucidate the importance of fiscal policy in India's economic progress. Titled "Fiscal Policy in India:

A Critical Analysis", the authors discuss the contours of fiscal policy, focusing particularly on the developments in the post-liberalisation period. Describing the philosophy of expenditure and revenue management and various policy reforms, the analysis underscores the development of fiscal discipline frameworks and the move towards fiscal consolidation. In doing so, the authors emphasise and analyse the issues of persistent fiscal deficit, role of the political economy and relatedly, fiscal populism. Towards the end, the study traces the role of fiscal policy during the COVID-19 pandemic and its role in the post-pandemic recovery of the Indian economy. The chapter concludes by outlining key imperatives for fiscal policy in India.

An increase in policy rates to control inflation may lead to a credit crunch, a slowdown in economic growth and a spurt in non-performing loans. Titled "Financial Instability, Credit Growth and Optimal Monetary Policy Design", Chapter 10 by Sanjay Basu and Tasneem Chherawala employs a demand–supply framework to explore the impact of policy rate shocks on the volume and cost of bank credit. Utilising an analytically tractable framework, the authors examine the conditions under which credit growth may occur, both in corporate and retail segments, despite a rise in policy rates. Relatedly, the authors also analyse central bank monetary policy announcements within a game-theoretic setup, which considers future decisions by banks and borrowers, on the quantum and cost of credit. The authors discuss how the central bank fixes its optimal policy rates, given its dual objectives of managing price stability and safeguarding financial stability in an economy. They highlight the dilemma the central bank faces when it seeks to manage both inflation and systemic risk through its policy rate announcements. The findings gleaned from the theoretical premise are correlated with the Indian evidence.

Women's empowerment is an important indicator of a nation's economic prosperity and social development. Manisha Chakrabarty and Arpita Kundu take a fresh look at this issue in Chapter 11 titled "Evolving Nature of Women Empowerment in India". In essence, the authors address the slower pace of development in women empowerment in India by looking at two aspects: empowerment and determinants. In this regard, they construct a measure of women empowerment (WEMP) onboarding its multiple dimensions such as education, health, domestic autonomy and access to free mobility-related indicators. Second, they analyse the association of different socio-economic, demographic, and household-level characteristics with this measure of women empowerment index. In this regard, they exploit multiple rounds of National Family Health Survey data NFHS3 (2005–2006), NFHS4 (2015–2016), and NFHS5 (2019–2020) at the district level to assess the impact. The findings reveal that the districts in the southern region not only perform better in terms of empowering women but also remain in the top quintile of the distribution of the WEMP index. However, poor-performing districts in the central and eastern region have made certain improvements during this period, although they remain in the lower quintiles. The multivariate regressions separately for the two rounds indicate the dominance of demographics, in addition to educational and family structure variables in explaining WEMP as compared to socioeconomic and sociodemographic variables.

To date, climate change discussions, whether at the annual Conference of Parties (COP) or otherwise, have highlighted essentially two broad areas, mitigation and adaptation. While mitigation relates to ameliorating the stressors responsible for climate change, adaptation relates to building institutional and human capacity to live with climate change. These lines of discourse were adequate when climate change was considered as an important factor that would affect the global economy in the (near) future. However, with climate change concerns migrating from the periphery to the centre of the policy debate, it is imperative that the world wakes up to a third thread of deliberations and even more urgent action, namely assessing and compensating for loss and damage. In Chapter 12, Runa Sarkar follows the debate on loss and damage at COP 27 in the chapter titled "Should Climate Change Include a Separate Focus on Loss and Damage?" The author unravels the multiple threads of discussions around it. Ahead of COP 27, particularly after the devastating floods in some neighbouring countries, the developing world is insisting that loss and damage be on the agenda for discussion. Accordingly, it is imperative that countries discuss threadbare who should fund losses and damage, how they are measured and who the beneficiaries would be. This opens up the possibility of tensions among the advanced and emerging economies regarding how to bear the expenses of loss and damage and to what extent, especially when considering the principle of common but differentiated responsibility and climate justice.

India spends less than 1% of its gross domestic product (GDP) on research and development (R&D) activities, while no country spends more than 2% of its GDP in R&D activities and still has a per capita GDP of less than US$10,000. Much of India's R&D activities are funded by the government, and the country boasts of several reputed institutions of global stature. Indian firms, particularly in manufacturing, have not fully realised the strategic value of formal R&D-based innovations. Many still believe that their greatest advantage is to compete on cost. The degree of competition its exports face in global markets and the vital technology-based products it imports measure how innovative India is. Many educated and qualified Indians are compelled to explore employment opportunities due to the insignificant opportunities in R&D and the high-end knowledge economy. In Chapter 13, Partha Ray and Balram Avittathur delve into this issue in "India Beyond *Jugaad*: The Opportunities and Pitfalls of R&D-Based Innovations". The authors explore the evolution of the manufacturing sector in modern India and argue how R&D-based innovations could drive the next round of high growth as many global factors are expected to work favourably for India in the coming years.

India is increasing its economic and strategic presence in Southeast Asia. Over the past decade and more, India has signed a number of free-trade agreements with different members of the Association of Southeast Asian Nations. However, India has also withdrawn from the Regional Comprehensive Economic Partnership agreement, in which China is a participating country. In Chapter 14, Parthapratim Pal assesses these agreements in "India and the Recent Wave of Regionalism in Asia-Pacific". The author finds that this recent wave of regionalism involving India and other countries in South-East Asian countries may not immediately bring huge economic gains to the country but can help diversify India's export destinations. It might also prove advantageous by facilitating diversification of sources of imports. As many South-East Asian countries are active players in the global value chains, India's integration with these countries may also benefit India from that aspect. Over and above, these agreements might also be important from a geo-political standpoint and help the country to prepare itself adequately in a reconfigured world trade regime in which mega-trade blocks may dominate.

Notwithstanding China's emergence as a focal point in global value chains, recent trade-war threats and, subsequently, the COVID-19 pandemic appears to have dampened China's attractiveness. Several advanced economies are contemplating diversifying their dependence on China – a strategy known as "China-Plus-One". Preetam Basu and Partha Ray examine this phenomenon in Chapter 15, titled "Global Supply Chains: Which Way Now?" The authors propose a methodology for arriving at an aggregate ranking of the major economies of emerging Asia, built on a few standard indices such as the World Bank's Logistic Performance Index, the World Bank's Ease of Doing Business Indicator, the World Economic Forum's Global Competitiveness Index and the Economic Complexity Index from the Harvard University. In this regard, the authors rank seven key countries in the region, including India, as possible destinations for selecting the "Plus One" destination country. The results of the findings are analysed and discussed, along with gleaning the key implications.

References

Whited, T., and Wu, G. (2006). Financial constraints risk. *Review of Financial Studies* 19, 531–559.

Hadlock, C., and Pierce, J. (2010). New evidence on measuring financial constraints: Moving beyond the KZ index. *Review of Financial Studies* 23, 1909–1940.

Part I

Micro Evidence

1 Economies of Scale in Household Consumption Patterns

Brinda Viswanathan and K.S. Kavi Kumar

1.1 Introduction

The measurement and understanding of individual living standards play an important role in the formulation of a range of policies, particularly for developing countries. The inferences on individual welfare as well as comparisons across different persons or groups of persons in developing countries are typically based on the analysis of household survey data of consumption expenditure. The household-level data are, however, not suitable to measure individual welfare levels and the standard practice in such a case for welfare comparisons across individuals is to use the per capita consumption, which is obtained as a ratio of the household consumption to the household size. This approach of measuring per capita consumption implicitly assumes that the cost of maintaining a given level of well-being for an individual is independent of the household size to which the individual belongs.

This assumption precludes the general understanding of "two live as cheaply as one" (Nelson, 1988, p. 2). Considering a utility function for an individual living in an *n*-person household would mean that the total utility of this household is *n* times the utility of each individual, assuming that the preference of each household member is the same (Deaton, 1997).[1] With economies of scale in household consumption, there would be higher welfare in a larger household compared to a smaller household keeping per capita income and demographic composition of these two households as the same. Individuals in larger households could benefit by sharing certain goods which are 'public' within the household, like a house, as consumption of these goods need not increase with household size (up to the point of congestion). As a result, per person cost of the 'public' good decreases with household size, and this, in turn, releases resources for the consumption of other goods by the household members. The additional resources could lead either to an expansion of the consumption basket or the consumption of higher quality of the same set of 'private' goods or more of certain 'private' goods, particularly among poorer households (Viswanathan, 2000; Nagarajan, 2007).

As of 2019–20, about 44% of rural and 39% of urban households in India belong to non-nuclear families (IIPS, 2021). It would be important to

DOI: 10.4324/9781003509721-3

understand if poorer households tend to live as a joint family largely to gain from the public goods they share so that their per capita consumption of private goods could be higher than what they would have had if they lived a smaller nuclear family. In this context, there is significant welfare gain in living together in large families and inter-personal welfare comparisons could ignore this while ranking households with the same per capita resources but different household sizes.

There has been limited empirical support for this in the Indian context and the present study is an attempt to fill that gap in the literature. The chapter is organised as follows: Section 1.2 briefly reviews the literature on economies of scale. The next section describes the methodology and the data set used. Section 1.4 discusses the main findings from the empirical analysis, and Section 1.5 provides a discussion and conclusions from the chapter.

1.2 Economies of Scale: A Brief Review of Literature

Economies of scale in household consumption could arise from several sources. First, households consume certain commodities that could be termed as public goods, as all household members share them without any member being deprived of its consumption, for instance house rent, electricity, cooking fuel, several consumer goods and appliances. The private goods would be those consumed individually by each member, and sharing would lead to lower consumption per person. Given the consumption basket of a particular household, if the household size increases, one would normally expect the consumption expenditure to increase. Larger households could benefit by sharing certain goods which are 'public' within the household, like a house, as consumption of these goods need not increase with household size (up to the point of congestion), provided the larger and smaller households are same in all other respects (like household composition). Hence, the per person price of the 'public' good will decrease with household size, generating income and substitution effects (Deaton and Paxson, 1998). For private goods, cost savings arising from the public good would result in an income effect leading to an increase in its per capita consumption, but when the private good becomes dearer, there would be substitution effects away from it (Abdulai, 2003). The size of the increase in consumption of the private good is used as a measure of *economies of scale* (Lanjouw and Ravallion, 1995; Deaton and Paxson, 1998). Individuals in a larger household would be better off at any given level of per capita total expenditure and the same demographic composition (adults and children).

A second reason for scale economies to arise could be because larger households may be able to take advantage of promotional discounts like 'two for one' sales, in particular, or availing bulk discounts in purchases, in general. A third reason could be due to increasing returns in household production of goods and services. If the presence of an additional member in the household adds relatively little (marginally) to the time costs of cooking a meal, the total expense in terms of time and money per member will decline with household size. Decreasing the costs in household production leads to a reduced expenditure if increasing returns to the household production time cause the household to substitute purchases of more unprocessed foods for eating out.

Deaton (1997) details the challenges not only to model economics of scale within the utility framework but also to derive the demand equation to estimate the economies of scale. One strand of the empirical examination of scale economies has been to measure the scale economies in terms of the extent of increase in the per capita resources when the household size doubles, ceteris paribus. The effective per capita consumption was estimated to increase for India by 28% and for Pakistan by 13% by Deaton and Paxson (1998), while Lanjouw and Ravallion (1995) found that the per capita consumption for Pakistan increased by 40% during the 1990s.

A second strand of empirical analysis tried to understand how the gains from scale economies are channelled back into the consumption basket of the household. Deaton and Paxson (1998) predict that the expenditure share of private good, which is food consumption, would increase due to this implicit income transfer from the gains of being part of the larger household (keeping all else the same). However, analyses based on a wide range of data sets from different countries show that food expenditure share does not increase, and most often decreases, and hence consider this as a puzzle. Several studies (based on data from the early 1990s) that followed, report a similar finding among data from either developed nations like Russia, Switzerland and the US or developing nations like South Africa, Pakistan and rural India (Kochar, 2000; Gan and Vernon, 2001; Abdulai, 2003; Nagarajan, 2007). An exception to this result was for the Indian state of Bihar (rural), with a positive sign for household size based on 1993–94 consumption survey data while all other states showed a negative sign of varying magnitudes (Viswanathan, 2000). In another instance, Vernon (2004) finds that food expenditure share rises with household size vis-à-vis the share of another public good for the US, but food expenditure shares in total expenditure do not increase with household size.

An analysis of the nature of the relationship between household size and expenditure shares of different types of public and private goods is limited in the Indian context with the exception of Nagarajan (2007), compared to a few more in other country contexts (Nelson, 1988; Abdulai, 2003; and Vernon 2004). All these studies consider some broad aggregates of public and private goods and find that for the public goods, the signs are negative, while for the private goods, the signs are mixed for household size. Nagarajan (2007) based on the 1993–94 rural consumption data, examines private goods, such as cereals, milk and milk products, footwear and clothing, and public goods, such as cooking gas (liquefied petroleum gas, LPG) and firewood (for cooking) expenditure share for India. The economies of scale are analysed for each state of India by estimating the equations simultaneously (seemingly unrelated regression [SUR] model) but only for those households which report positive consumption. However, the study finds no clear pattern of the positive sign for the private goods and negative sign for the public goods.

As the results are still mixed, a re-examination of the presence of economics of scale and its variation across different disaggregates of private and public goods is considered for a more recent year, 2011–12, consumption survey for All India. We consider food expenditure shares and expenditure shares of different (private) goods within the food group, as well as dietary diversity and clothing expenditure shares. We also examine the effect of household size on the composition of fuel expenditure share and cooking fuel expenditure share and furniture purchases all of which are public goods. In India, several households are still dependent on firewood, while many also use LPG. The former is an inferior good and a source of indoor pollution (hence termed as dirty fuel), while the latter is a normal good but is not easily accessible and affordable by many poor households. We examine if the scale economies exist for the disaggregate of food items and, if so, how different are they across the set of food items as available in the data. We also examine similarly, within the fuel basket, if there is a reallocation of commodities that would reflect higher welfare, for instance a shift away from firewood towards LPG.

1.3 Methodology and Data Set

The methodology followed in this study is largely similar to that suggested by Deaton and Paxson (1998) and used in most of the later studies that examine economies of scale in household consumption. A priori, we expect a positive and significant coefficient for household size for food share (and its disaggregate), keeping the per capita income of the household fixed in a linear regression model. Unlike most of the earlier studies, we estimate several regression models with different types of dependent variables:

a. share of expenditure on either a single commodity or an aggregate of commodities in total household expenditure,
b. logarithm of per capita expenditure on either a single or groups of commodities, and
c. the choice of using a certain commodity (or not) or the preference to consume a certain commodity (or not).

When the dependent variable is continuous and there is no zero consumption, we estimate the linear regression model using ordinary least squares (OLS). When the dependent variable is continuous and there is zero consumption reported by several households, then we estimate the Tobit model for censored data. For a dichotomous (binary) variable, wherein the reported consumption value is discretised as used/consumed or not, we estimate the logit model. All these estimations are single equations (commodity) and are not estimated as a system of demand equations.

The independent variable that is the focus of this study is household size. The two important control variables are (logarithm of) monthly per capita total expenditure (used as a proxy for household income) and the household composition included as the share of household members in different age and sex groups. Two other independent variables controlled for are categorical variables – state fixed effect and income source of household head.

As mentioned earlier, three different methods of econometric techniques are used depending on the nature of the dependent variable. First is the OLS model to estimate a linear regression of the budget shares on household size (n), the logarithm of monthly per capita expenditure of the household ($\ln(X/n)$), household composition variables (n_j/n) considered as the proportion of household members in j different age and sex groups and a few other control variables represented by the vector z in the following model. These variables are discussed later in detail in the data section.

1. OLS model:

$$w_i = \beta_1 + \beta_2 n_i + \beta_3 \ln\left(\frac{X_i}{n_i}\right) + \sum_{j=1}^{k-1} \gamma_{ij}\left(\frac{n_{ij}}{n_i}\right) + \tau.z_i + \in_i$$

2. Tobit model: In this regression model the probability of censoring at $w_i = 0$ is also taken into account while estimating the regression model for the positive expenditure shares represented by

$$w_i = \beta_1 + \beta_2 n_i + \beta_3 \ln\left(\frac{X_i}{n_i}\right) + \sum_{j=1}^{k-1} \gamma_{ij}\left(\frac{n_{ij}}{n_i}\right) + \tau.z_i + \in_i; i = 1,2,\ldots,n.$$

3. Logit model for the probability of purchase: Let $Y_i = 1$ if the commodity was consumed in the last month or in the last year in the case of a durable good; $Y_i = 0$ otherwise. If $\boldsymbol{X}$ is the set of vectors for the explanatory variables that includes household size (n), the logarithm of monthly per capita expenditure of the household ($\ln(X/n)$), household composition variables (n_j/n) as in the linear model in (1) then: $F(\mathrm{X}_i\beta) = \frac{e^{\mathrm{X}_i\beta}}{1+e^{\mathrm{X}_i\beta}}$ = Probability that $(Y_i = 1) = p_i$, say. The odds ratio of this logit model is $\Omega(X) = \frac{p_i}{1-p_i} = \exp(\boldsymbol{X}_i\beta)$. If one of the explanatory variables, say, household size (n), changes by δ, then a comparison of the odds ratio before and after the change works out to[2] $\exp(\beta_h{}^*\delta)$. If $\delta = 1$, then this would simply be the exponential of the estimated coefficient of the household size.

In the preceding equations, w_i is the budget share of one of the following commodities: cereals and cereal substitutes (and its disaggregates: rice, wheat, other cereals, cereal substitutes), pulses, milk, fuel and light (and its disaggregates: firewood and kerosene), and clothing.

The Indian Human Development Survey Data (Desai and Vanneman, 2014) for 2011–12 (henceforth, IHDS-II) is used to examine the variations in scale economies across different food and non-food private goods and a few public goods. Since most of the earlier Indian studies use the National Sample Survey data on consumption, this study uses IHDS-II to examine the empirical validity of the economies of scale debate using an alternate consumer expenditure dataset. The variables extracted from the IHDS-II data set and used for the estimation are discussed next.

Dependent Variables: The private and public goods used as a dependent variable to examine the statistical significance and the estimates of household size are:

1. Expenditure Share: (a) Total Food, (b) Cereals and cereal products, (c) Milk and milk products, (d) Clothing, and (e) Total fuel. All are private goods except total fuel, and the last two are non-food items. We expect all the private (public) goods to show a positive (negative) and significant coefficient for household size, ceteris paribus, if the scale economies hold as suggested by the utility theory framework.
2. Dietary Diversity Index: This is a transformation of the Herfindahl Index. The Herfindahl index is calculated as the sum of squares of the share of different food items in total expenditure and then subtracted from one. The higher the value of this index, the higher the dietary diversity. We expect the coefficient of household size to be positive and significant, ceteris paribus, if the scale economies hold as suggested by the utility theory framework.
3. Censored Data: Some of the food and non-food items are not preferred for consumption by the households: (a) Milk products; (b) Processed food; (c) Meat, egg and fish; (d) Eating out; (e) LPG; and (f) Firewood. The results for the uncensored OLS estimates and the Tobit estimates are compared to understand if the coefficient of household size changes in significance as well as sign and magnitudes when the appropriate econometric model is used for estimation.
4. Binary Variable: Variables considered here include (a) Any milk products (excluding liquid milk) consumed in the last month or not; (b) Meat, egg and/or fish consumed in the last month or not; (c) LPG is used as primary fuel for cooking or not; (d) Firewood is used as primary fuel for cooking or not; and (e) Purchase of any furniture items in the last year or not. This binary choice model is estimated as an additional illustration that the resources gained due to scale economies are expended on food and non-food items. So accordingly, we expect the household size to increase the probability of the purchase of a private good, as well as a public good that is a normal or a luxury good.

Prime Explanatory Variable: Household size is the reported number of household members residing in the house at the time of survey.

Control Variables:

a. Logarithm of monthly per capita consumption expenditure (and its square depending on its statistical significance for some of the expenditure shares). This is an important control variable to account for the ceteris paribus effect of keeping the per capita income of two households the same so that the net effect of household size is estimated.
b. A vector of household composition variables representing each of the two sexes in the following four age groups 0–12 years (child), 13–19 years (teens), 20–60 years (adults) and greater than 60 years (older adults) – totalling to eight such variables. It is measured as the ratio of the number of members in each of these categories to the total household size and the share of adult males in the family is the omitted category. This is also an important control variable as household composition will matter for the consumption pattern as, for example, a household with three adults and one child will be different from a household with two adults and two children, even though both have the same number of household members. Thus, we consider the net effect of household size keeping the household composition as fixed.
c. Dummy variables for the main source of household income are categorised into Agriculture and allied (reference category), Agricultural labour, Non- agricultural labour, Business, Salaried and Others.
d. Dummy variables for all the states and union territories of India with Jammu and Kashmir as the reference category.

The last two dummy variables account for the variability in income, access to homegrown consumption, rural–urban differences and various food habits and preferences. The addition of many other explanatory variables, such as caste, religion, rural–urban residence, does not change the results, and hence, we estimate a parsimonious model.

The multiple regression framework used here enables us to study the effect of household size on the corresponding dependent variable keeping per capita total expenditure and household composition constant or the ceteris paribus effect of household size on consumption.

1.4 Economies of Scale: Main Findings

1.4.1 Summary Statistics

In order to examine what are the variations in the estimate of household size on household consumption, we choose a set of commodities mentioned in the previous section. These commodities are a combination of private and public goods, and among them, some of these commodities are not preferred or purchased by all households (many households report zero values). Table 1.1a presents the summary statistics of the expenditure share of these select

Table 1.1a Summary Statistics of Expenditure Share for Select Commodities, 2011–12

Variable	*Mean*	*Standard Deviation*	*Minimum*	*Maximum*	*Zero Consumption (Proportion)*
Food	0.48	0.151	0.02	1	0.00
Cereals and its Products	0.12	0.081	0.001	0.77	0.01
Meat etc.	0.05	0.049	0	0.72	0.30
Milk and its Products	0.08	0.077	0	0.67	0.14
Milk Products Only	0.01	0.023	0	0.54	0.49
Eating Out	0.01	0.021	0	0.75	0.28
Dietary Diversity	0.95	0.040	0.41	1.00	0.0
Fuel and Lighting	0.07	0.052	0	0.93	0.0
Firewood	0.01	0.04	0	0.92	0.44
LPG	0.02	0.026	0	0.47	0.59
Clothing	0.03	0.025	0	0.44	0.05
Furniture	0.002	0.01	0.0	0.87	0.86

Source: Authors' own estimation from IHDS data.

Note: The expenditure share of these variables is used as dependent variables in the regression models. LPG = liquefied petroleum gas.

commodities, and the last column reports the proportion of households that report zero consumption.

The average share of food expenditure was 48% in 2011–12 for Indian households, which is less than 50% of the total household expenditure. As mentioned before, if the price of a public good becomes cheaper due to sharing then there is a possibility of substitution away from the private good, which now becomes dearer, provided the private good is price-inelastic. Deaton (1997) argues that when the food share is large (almost two-thirds), then it is unlikely that, keeping everything else constant, food share would decline with household size. This observation was based on data from developing countries like India and Pakistan during the early 1990s. More than a decade later, with higher economic growth and poverty reduction, the food share has come down to below 50%. The interest is then to re-examine whether the decline in food expenditure share with household size is still observed, in which case it could now be justified as a substitution effect.

We expect that cereal and its products and milk and its products, along with total food, could show a decline in their expenditure share with household size. The summary statistics in Table 1.1a show that the variance, as well as the minimum and maximum values, is not large, perhaps indicating that most households may have reached close to their saturation levels. This gives scope for diversification from the staples within the food group or towards diversifying milk products within the milk group or away from coarse cereals within the food group. The average dietary diversity is substantially large and close to 1, and with values ranging from 0.41 to 1, it is likely that many households may shift within the food group when household size increases as long as it does not become dearer compared to other public goods. The average expenditure shares of most other commodities chosen for the analysis (listed in Table 1.1a) are very small perhaps due to zero expenditure share for many of these commodities (except fuel and lighting expenditure and clothing expenditure) among several households in 2011–12. The proportion of such households with zero consumption shares ranges from 0.49 to 0.86 across different commodities chosen for this study. We conjecture that within these sets of commodities, the household size coefficients will be positive (negative) and significant for private (public) goods when the zero consumption values are appropriately accounted for in the econometric estimations (for instance, the Tobit model for a censored data or the logit model for the probability of purchase and hence consumption). Furthermore, the aim is to document the range in the magnitude of household size coefficient estimates across different commodities.

The summary statistics of the explanatory variables are presented in Table 1.1b. The household size ranges between 1 and 15, with an average size of 4.7. The data set has households up to 27, but after a size of 15, the numbers have gaps and sample observations for each of those household sizes are very

Table 1.1b Summary Statistics of the Explanatory Variables, 2011–12

Variable	*Mean*	*Standard Deviation*	*Minimum*	*Maximum*
Household Size	4.72	2.200	1	15
Logarithm (monthly per capita expenditure)	7.38	0.674	5.50	10.5
Household Composition				
Share of male children (0–12 years)	0.13	0.155	0	0.8
Share of female children (0–12 years)	0.11	0.153	0	0.83
Share of male teenagers (13–19 years)	0.06	0.110	0	1
Share of female teenagers (13–19 years)	0.06	0.115	0	1
Share of adult males (20–60 years)	0.26	0.158	0	1
Share of adult females (20–60 years)	0.26	0.158	0	1
Share of elderly males (>60 years)	0.07	0.142	0	1
Share of elderly females (>60 years)	0.08	0.172	0	1
Main Income Source of the Household				
Self-Employed in Agriculture	0.26	0.438	0	1
Agricultural Labour	0.12	0.323	0	1
Non-Agricultural Labour	0.24	0.425	0	1
Business	0.12	0.320	0	1
Salaried	0.17	0.376	0	1
Others	0.10	0.299	0	1

Source: Authors' own estimation from IHDS data.

Note: The summary statistics of the proportion of households in different states and union territories are not reported here for space considerations.

small (which account for about 0.01% of the sampled households in IHDS-II). Household composition is also an important part of this analysis as age–sex composition would matter regarding the needs of the households. A household with young children may have higher milk and clothing expenditure shares compared to a household with a higher number of adults for the same household size. About 50% (with an equal share of men and women) of the household members are in the 20–60-year age group, and the next highest share is for the 0–12-year group, with a slightly higher share for boys (13%) than for girls (11%). Teenagers and older adults together constitute less than one third of the household members, on average. The sex composition may be important considering that boys/men have higher basal metabolic rate and hence would require more food intake, and quite often, there are biases in food expenditure favouring boys and men in the patriarchal socio-cultural context of India. However, we use household composition as the control variable and do not report the estimated coefficients to keep the focus of the study on household size.

The main income source of the household is used as a control variable as self-employed households could be different from salaried households and households depending on income from wage labour. Self-employed households, including those in agriculture (26% in the sample), may prefer to remain as a joint family to either carry out the economic activities by pooling household members' time so that labour costs are cheaper, and similarly family businesses (12%) are quite common in developing countries for reasons of trustworthiness. The wage-labour households are distinguished between agriculture (12%) and non-agriculture (24%) as the former may possibly have access to in-kind food items as they are producing themselves, which could affect the food availability and preferences. The salaried households (17%) are usually among the richest and more likely to be residing in urban areas as a nuclear family. Once again, the coefficients for these variables are not reported here to keep the discussions focused.

Indian states vary substantially in their level of economic development, agro-climatic conditions, religion and caste composition. All of these will have implications for food preferences and the type of local food availability, prices and per capita income. Viswanathan (2000) finds that the magnitude, and sometimes the statistical significance, varies across states for the household size coefficient, and the range of variation is more so for food expenditure shares and the type of food item (for instance, expenditures shares for rice in southern and eastern India and wheat in the northern and western states of India).

In this study also, we observe that the exclusion of these three sets of variables (either one at a time or in some combination) affects the significance, sign and magnitude of the estimated coefficient of household size directly. Similarly, the coefficient of monthly per capita expenditure is also affected which then indirectly affects the coefficient of household size. The extent of such variations differs across commodity types.

1.4.2 Findings from Econometric Estimations

Table 1.2 reports the coefficient estimates only for household size and (logarithm) of monthly per capita expenditure. The other coefficient estimates are not reported for an effective discussion of the main results. Controlling for everything else, expenditure shares for total food; cereal and cereal products decline with household size while for milk and milk products, household size has no effect, as the coefficient is not statistically significant at 1%. The dietary diversity index and clothing expenditure share increase with household size as predicted for a private good, and the expenditure share for total fuel expenditure decreases with household size as predicted for a public good.

We further explore as to why food expenditure share declines while dietary diversity improves. In the food basket, food items like milk products, other processed food and eating out are not consumed by all the households. For these items, we report (Table 1.3a) both the OLS (uncensored estimates) and the Tobit estimates accounting for the zero (censored) values so that the coefficient estimates are unbiased and consistent. The magnitude of the estimated coefficient and their significance changes across these two models. Focusing on Tobit estimates (as they are the appropriate ones), we find that except for the expenditure share for meat, eggs and fish, the coefficient estimates are positive and significant indicating that the additional resources gained by the larger households are being spent on food items that would otherwise not be possible to consume due to limited budgets in the smaller households. In the case of meat, eggs and fish (non-vegetarian food items), there is a mix of preferences as well. Many households do not consume these food items not only due to affordability reasons but also due to specific food preferences in the

Table 1.2 Ordinary Least Squares Estimates for Select 'Private' and 'Public' Goods in a Household

	Private Goods					*Public Good*
Variable	*Food*	*Dietary Diversity*	*Cereals & Cereal Products*	*Milk & Milk Products*	*Clothing*	*Fuel (Cooking, Lighting and Own Vehicle)*
Hhsz	−0.0108***	0.0019***	−0.0010***	0.0002	0.0004***	−0.0041***
	(0.0004)	(0.0001)	(0.0002)	(0.0003)	(0.00008)	(0.0002)
lnmpce	0.1407***	0.0288***	−0.0551***	−0.0040***	−0.0076***	−0.0249***
	(0.0195)	(0.0005)	(0.0009)	(0.001)	(0.0003)	(0.0007)
sqlnmpce	−0.0194***					
	(0.0012)					
Adjusted R^2	0.4690	0.3370	0.4588	0.2707	0.0977	0.2564

Source: Authors' own estimation from IHDS data.

Note: OLS = ordinary least squares; hhsz = household size; lnmpce = logarithm of monthly per capita expenditure; sqlnmpce = squared (logarithm of monthly per capita expenditure). The values in parenthesis are standard errors. The estimates for the remaining control variables are not reported here and can be made available upon request from the authors.

**p* < .05; ***p* < .01; ****p* < .00.

Table 1.3a Ordinary Least Squares and Tobit Estimates for Expenditure Shares of Select Food Items

Variable	*OLS (Uncensored[a]) Estimates*				*TOBIT (Censored[b]) Estimates*			
	Milk Products	*Meat, Egg, Fish etc.*	*Processed Food*	*Eating Out*	*Milk products*	*Meat, Egg, Fish etc.*	*Processed Food*	*Eating Out*
hhsz	0.0001	–0.001***	–0.00004	0.0003***	0.0010***	0.0007	0.0002***	0.0026***
	(0.0001)	(0.0002)	(0.00003)	(0.00006)	(0.0001)	(0.0004)	(0.00004)	(0.0001)
lnmpce	0.0018***	–0.013***	–0.0003**	0.0041***	0.0078***	0.0019	0.0007***	0.0192***
	(0.0002)	(0.0006)	(0.0001)	(0.0002)	(0.0005)	(0.001)	(0.0001)	(0.0008)
Adjusted R^2	0.2286	0.2961	0.1137	0.1038				
Uncensored Observations					22,966	26,247	30,600	11,046
Censored Observations					16,806	13,525	9,172	28,726

Source: Authors.

Note: OLS = ordinary least squares; hhsz = household size; lnmpce = logarithm of monthly per capita expenditure; sqlnmpce = squared (logarithm of monthly per capita expenditure). The values in parenthesis are standard errors. The estimates for the remaining control variables are not reported here and can be made available upon request from the authors.

*$p < .05$; **$p < .01$; ***$p < .00$.

[a] Uncensored refers to the inclusion of zero values also in the linear regression model.

[b] Censored refers to the data where zero expenditure share values have been appropriately accounted for.

Indian context. Hence, the results are different for only this commodity group. This also explains why the household dietary diversity index shows a positive coefficient for household size arising from an expanded food consumption basket for many households in the presence of economies of scale.

Similar to the food items we also consider public goods that have several zero values (censored) for many households. Results reported in Table 1.3b suggest that for the OLS estimations, all the public goods show a decline in expenditure shares with household size. Between LPG and firewood, the magnitude of decline is higher for firewood than for LPG, implying that there is a substitution between these two public goods. Larger households now allocate a higher expenditure share for LPG, a more expensive commodity and the shift occurring perhaps from an income effect (Kumar and Viswanathan, 2007). This shift away from firewood implies a greater welfare improvement from reduced indoor air pollution from using firewood due to a bigger decline in its consumption for a larger household (ceteris paribus) compared to a smaller household (Chaudhuri and Pfaff, 2002). The estimates from the (statistically appropriate) censored regression model clearly capture the substitution away from firewood (a larger negative effect here compared to uncensored estimates) to LPG (positive effect). The sign for the household size coefficient for expenditure share on furniture purchase changes from negative in the OLS model to (expected) positive in the Tobit model.

Thus, this result for the LPG and furniture expenditure shares shows that they are public goods based on the uncensored estimates as the price per person declines so expenditure shares decline. However, when these estimates

Table 1.3b Ordinary Least Squares (OLS) and Tobit Estimates for Expenditure Shares of Liquified Petroleum Gas (LPG), Firewood and Furniture

Variable	*OLS (Uncensored) Estimates*			*Tobit (Censored) Estimates*		
	LPG	*Firewood*	*Furniture*	*LPG*	*Firewood*	*Furniture*
Hhsz	−0.0004***	−0.0011***	−0.0001**	0.0014***	−0.0018***	0.0002***
	(0.0001)	(0.0001)	(0.00003)	(0.0002)	(0.0004)	(0.0002)
Lnmpce	−0.0018***	−0.0093***	−0.0029***	0.0108***	−0.0208***	0.0023***
	(0.0003)	(0.0005)	(0.0002)	(0.0007)	(0.0018)	(0.001)
	0.1837	0.0966	0.0371			
Adjusted R^2	0.1847	0.0966	0.0382			
Uncensored Observations				17,698	10,206	5,455
Censored Observations				22,074	29,566	34,317

Source: Authors.

Note: OLS = ordinary least squares; hhsz = household size; lnmpce = logarithm of monthly per capita expenditure; sqlnmpce = squared (logarithm of monthly per capita expenditure). The values in parenthesis are standard errors. The estimates for the remaining control variables are not reported here and can be made available upon request from the authors.

**p* < .05; ***p* < .01; ****p* < .00.

are adjusted for only positive consumption then LPG or furniture purchase has a higher expenditure share compared to a smaller household, ceteris paribus. Hence, such commodities that are public goods in nature could also have a positive effect of household size on their consumption due to scale economies if analysed differently.

We further examine this preference for purchasing a more expensive commodity or expanding the commodity basket by considering the odds of purchasing such goods by a larger household compared to a smaller household. For this, the logit regression model is estimated and if the calculated odds ratio on household size is greater (lesser) than one, then it implies that larger households have a higher (lower) probability of making the expenditure/purchase than a smaller household. Table 1.4 reports the odds of purchasing commodities (in the last 30 days) like milk products; meat, egg and fish; eating out; LPG as the primary fuel; firewood as the primary fuel; and any furniture purchase (within in the last year for this item). All the items chosen here have at least 30% of zero values, implying that there is a preference or a choice that households are making to consume or not.

The odds ratio on household size is greater than one for all these items, except for firewood and statistically significant at 1% for all of them. This means that the odds of purchasing the commodities, such as milk products, meat, egg and fish, LPG and the like, increase as the household size increases by one keeping all other variables constant, while for firewood, the odds of purchase decrease. Alongside the household size coefficient, if we observe the coefficient for a household's monthly per capita expenditure, then we observe that when the odds are greater (less) than 1, then the household size for those commodities has a positive (negative) effect. This implies that when the commodity is an inferior good (coefficient estimates for *lnmpce* in a regression model with per capita expenditure or expenditure share as the dependent variable has negative values – results not reported here), then the probability of purchase declines with household size and vice versa for normal goods.

Table 1.4 Odds Ratio from Logit Estimates for Select Commodities

Variable	*Milk products*	*Meat etc.*	*LPG*	*Firewood*	*Furniture*
hhsz	1.218*** (0.011)	1.055*** (0.012)	1.258*** (0.0002)	0.924*** (0.008)	1.163*** (0.0114)
lnmpce	3.249*** (0.012)	1.091* (0.045)	4.971*** (0.242)	0.429*** (0.014)	2.226*** (0.0872)

Source: Authors.

Note: OLS = ordinary least squares; hhsz = household size; lnmpce = logarithm of monthly per capita expenditure; sqlnmpce = squared (logarithm of monthly per capita expenditure). The values in parenthesis are standard errors. The estimates for the remaining control variables are not reported here and can be made available upon request from the authors.

*$p < .05$; **$p < .01$; ***$p < .00$.

1.5 Discussion and Conclusion

The measurement of economies of scale based on the public good approach proposed by Deaton and Paxson (1998) are driven by two factors: (a) the public good would have low own price elasticity, and (b) food would have high income elasticity and low substitution elasticity. Consequently, the additional resources that a larger household has due to the presence of public goods would be spent on food, thereby increasing its budget share, while the budget share of the public good declines.

The results from the analysis in this study show that though the fuel (public good) expenditure share declines with household size, the food share (private good) does not increase. However, the disaggregated commodities within the broad public and private goods can alter in terms of how the households spend the additional income in reallocating the consumption basket. This is perhaps because the public good behaves as in (a) while (b) holds only for the disaggregated food items rather than for the food group as a whole.

The larger household behaves as though an income transfer has been made and the expected outcome would be a decline in food share (Engel's law) with a more diversified diet (Bennet's law). This substantiates the fact that larger households enjoy higher welfare. Moreover, the household enjoys higher welfare from a decrease in indoor air pollution due to a shift in the cooking fuel from firewood to LPG. Wu et al. (2021) provide a different perspective on environmental sustainability, due to loss in scale economies in a country like China, where family sizes are shrinking. A larger number of smaller families increases the demand for electricity, whose production is ecologically and environmentally unsustainable, leading to an increase in environmental footprint and associated welfare reduction for society.

Earlier studies based on the National Sample Survey Organisation (NSSO) data for 1993–94 show that within the disaggregated food items, the expenditure share increases more for the normal goods with higher income elasticity (like wheat in all India data), and luxury items, such as milk products (Viswanathan, 2000). The other normal goods (rice) which have a lower income elasticity and high substitution elasticity increase less. These observations are more obvious when estimations are carried out at the state level when preference patterns are (more) homogeneous within states than between states. It should, however, be noted that in all the preceding analyses, the elasticities are not calculated but are 'inferred' based on the preference patterns (frequency of consumption and average consumption). The fact that households reallocate their budget across commodities in the presence of a public good requires that elasticities be calculated based on income and price coefficients obtained from estimating a system of demand equations rather than from a single equation for each commodity. As mentioned in the literature section, Nagarajan (2007) attempts to estimate a system of demand equation for several items in a multiple equation model using SURs for consumption data in 1993–94. This study finds that cereals, meat, egg and fish and fruits, as well as non-food items like clothing (all private goods), increase with household size, ceteris paribus, for most states in India. However, commodities like milk give mixed results across states depending on the preference pattern. In both the previously mentioned studies based on the 1993–94 Indian data, the results are based on data that comprise all (i.e., zero- and positive-consumption) households. In that respect, the results reported in the present study based on a censored regression model could be more robust. The fact that a system of demand equations is not considered in our study could be a limitation and this needs to be explored in future studies.

Future studies also need to re-examine not just expenditure shares but quantities and prices to understand the trade-off, if any, between a larger quantity versus a higher quality of the same quantity. Viswanathan (2000) and Nagarajan (2007) examine quantities and quality but the evidence across private and public goods does not provide a clear picture and hence warrants further analysis.

Other issues that require further analysis include the role of household composition. Kochar (2000) finds that the results for household size coefficient are sensitive to inclusion of household composition as well as the functional form used for capturing the same. These have also not been examined in detail in the present study and could be considered for future studies. IHDS-I and IHDS-II, provide the option of constructing a panel data set and hence facilitate tracking the households that report change in household size across the two waves. This, in turn, could enable a more thorough examination of the economies-of-scale puzzle, provided there are enough observations to carry out a ceteris paribus analysis.

Notes

1 Another important aspect of this kind of interpersonal comparison is that all members of the household have equal needs. This is usually addressed by constructing an effective household size or adult-equivalent scale (Lanjouw and Ravallion, 1995; Dreze and Srinivasan, 1997; Meenakshi and Ray, 1999; Lanjouw *et al.*, 2000).

2 $$\frac{\Omega(X, X_h + \delta)}{\Omega(X, X_h)} = \frac{\exp(X_1\beta_1)\exp(X_2\beta_2)\ldots\ldots\exp(X_h\beta_h)\exp(\delta\beta_h)\ldots\ldots\exp(X_k\beta_k)}{\exp(X_1\beta_1)\exp(X_2\beta_2)\ldots\ldots\exp(X_h\beta_h)\ldots\exp(X_k\beta_k)}$$
$$= \exp(\beta_h * \delta).$$

References

Abdulai, A. (2003, July), Economies of Scale and the Demand for Food in Switzerland: Parametric and Non-Parametric Analysis. *Journal of Agricultural Economics*, Vol. 54, no. 2, pp. 247–267.

Chaudhuri, S., and A.S.P. Pfaff (2002), 'Economic Growth and the Environment: What Can We Learn from Household Data?', *Working Paper no.0102–51*, Economics Department, Columbia University, New York. [Retrieved from: https://academiccommons.columbia.edu/doi/10.7916/D8P279C7]

Deaton, A. (1997), *A Micro-Econometric Approach to Household Level Survey Data*, Johns Hopkins: Maryland.

Deaton, A., and C. Paxson (1998), 'Economies of Scale, Household Size, and the Demand for Food', *Journal of Political Economy*, Vol. 106, No. 5, pp. 897–930.

Desai, Sonalde, and Reeve Vanneman (2014), "India Human Development Survey-II (IHDSII)." 2011–12, Inter-university Consortium for Political and Social Research [distributor]. doi:10.3886/ICPSR36151.v6.

Dreze, J.P. and P.V. Srinivasan (1997), 'Widowhood and Poverty in Rural India: Some Inferences from Household Survey Data', *Journal of Development Economics*, Vol. 54, No. 2, pp. 217–234.

Gan, Li, and V. Vernon (2001), 'Testing for Barten Model of Economies of Scale in Household Consumption: Resolving a Paradox of Deaton and Paxson', *SSRN Working Paper*. [Retrieved from: http://ssrn.com/abstract=267736]

International Institute for Population Sciences (IIPS) and ICF (2021), 'India Factsheet', *National Family Health Survey (NFHS-5), 2019–20*: Mumbai.

Kochar, A. (2000), 'Parental Benefits from Intergenerational Coresidence: Empirical Evidence from Rural Pakistan', *Journal of Political Economy*, Vol. 108, pp. 1184–1207.

Kumar, K., and B. Viswanathan (2007), 'Changing Structure of Income Indoor Air Pollution Relationship in India', *Energy Policy*, Vol. 35, No. 11, pp. 5496–5504.

Lanjouw, P., B. Milanovic, and S. Paternostro, (2000), 'Poverty and Economic Transition: How Do Changes in Economies of Scale Affect Poverty Rates of Different Households?', *World Bank Working Paper No. WPS2009*, Washington, DC: World Bank.

Lanjouw, P., and M. Ravallion, (1995), 'Poverty and Household Size', *The Economic Journal*, Vol. 105, pp. 1415–1434.

Meenakshi, J.V. and R. Ray (1999), 'Impact of Household Size, Family Composition and Socio-Economic Characteristics on Poverty in Rural India', Working papers 68, Centre for Development Economics, Delhi School of Economics.

Nagarajan D. (2007), 'Testing for the Presence of Economies of Scale in Household Consumption', *Unpublished Master's Thesis*, Madras School of Economics, Chennai.

Nelson, J.A. (1988), Household Economies of Scale in Consumption: Theory and Evidence. *Econometrica*, Vol. 56, No. 6, pp. 1301–1314.

Vernon, V.K. (2004), 'Household Economies of Scale, Food Consumption and Intra-Household Allocation of Time', Ph.D. Dissertation, The University of Texas at Austin. [Retrieved from: https://repositories.lib.utexas.edu/handle/2152/1425]

Viswanathan, B (2000), 'Household Size and Demand for 'Private' and 'Public' Goods in Household Consumption: Evidence from Rural Indian Data', Presented at *Winter School held from 28 December to 3 January, 2000, at Center for Development Economics*, Delhi School of Economics, Delhi.

Wu, W., Y. Kanamori, R. Zhang, Q. Zhou, K. Takahashi, and T. Masui (2021), 'Implications of Declining Household Economies of Scale on Electricity Consumption and Sustainability in China', *Ecological Economics*, Vol. 184, p. 106981. doi:10.1016/j.ecolecon.2021.106981.

2 Analyzing mental well-being of adults during the COVID-19 pandemic using a MIMIC model

Evidence from Indian metropolitan cities

Zakir Husain, Anindita Chakrabarti, Saswata Ghosh, Mousumi Dutta, and Kausik Chaudhuri

2.1 Introduction

Historically, pandemics have often affected social perceptions and behavior resulting in the manifestation of psychological disorders (Morganstein et al., 2017). The advent of COVID-19 is no exception. The lockdowns and measures to reduce interaction and mobility during the first year of the pandemic resulted in social isolation. Simultaneously, 'coronophobia' emerged among the general population. It was generated by various factors, such as the unpredictable character of the disease, ignorance about the treatment protocols, contradictory information disseminated by the governments, high morbidity and death rates, stigma and shortage of medical facilities (Dubey et al., 2020). The fear of COVID-19 interacted with social isolation, and economic distress was widely expected to adversely affect mental well-being.

Existing literature has reported that anxiety, stress and depression ranged between 10 to 50 per cent in both developed countries like the US, the UK, Italy, Spain, Germany, China and Japan and developing countries like Bangladesh (Banna et al., 2020; Giallonardo et al., 2020; González-Blanco et al., 2020; Kuehner et al., 2020; Liao et al., 2021; Liu et al., 2021; Paulino et al., 2021; Pierce et al., 2020; Shigemura et al., 2020). Studies in the Indian context also observed a rise in mental ill-being among the general population (Kar et al., 2021; Rehman et al., 2021; Roy et al., 2020; Varshney et al., 2020).

Most of these studies, however, have tended to state the estimated proportion of the sample reporting mental health symptoms, either among the public or among sub-samples. Such sub-samples were formed on the basis of gender, education level, marital status, and economic status. In studies that did undertake statistical analysis, the methods were limited to univariate statistical tests. The studies either reported the results of mean differences or undertook correlational analysis (Huang & Zhao, 2020; Kar et al., 2021; Paulino et al., 2021; Rehman et al., 2021). A few studies applied multivariate analysis; they have used ordinary least square, logit and multinomial models

DOI: 10.4324/9781003509721-4

(Giallonardo et al., 2020; González-Blanco et al., 2020; Varshney et al., 2020; Verma & Mishra, 2020; Y. Wang et al., 2021).

Such approaches fail to consider that anxiety, depression and stress are latent variables reflected through observed behavioral patterns. Furthermore, latent variables generally do not have scales but are measured using indicator variables. Thus, using univariate tests for differences in proportion or tests for association is methodically incorrect (Proitsi et al., 2011). Rather, structural equation models (SEMs) should be used to analyze the causal relations between observed indicators and the latent variables. The present study uses the multiple-indicator, multiple-cause (MIMIC) model, which is a special category of SEMs. MIMIC models enable us to simultaneously measure the latent constructs (in this case, of mental ill health) based on information on observed indicators and estimate the structural relationship between the latent variables and their causal determinants. Thus, MIMIC models provide better insight by examining the nature of associations between determinants of mental ill-health indicators, after controlling for the latent nature of the phenomenon being studied (Proitsi et al., 2011). Although MIMIC models are widely used in development studies, the existing studies on mental health during COVID-19 have yet to apply this method. To our knowledge, there is only one study using SEM to study the status of mental health during the COVID-19 pandemic (Morales Chainé et al., 2022).

The present study focuses on the period following the first wave of COVID-19 in India, which occurred from April to June (2020).[1] It estimates the proportion of respondents reporting mental health problems and identifies the underlying risk factors. The data for the analysis were collected through a telephonic survey of the general population undertaken in six metropolitan cities in India during the months of August and September 2020. The Depression, Anxiety and Stress Scale–21 Items (DASS-21) measure was used to measure the mental well-being of respondents (Lovibond & Lovibond, 1995), a commonly used method to measure mental health during the pandemic (Ransing et al., 2020). The choice of the period studied is primarily motivated by the nature of the lockdown in India. India experienced arguably the longest and most stringent lockdowns during the first wave; the resultant socioeconomic burden was huge, particularly on the economically vulnerable sections of the population (Dhingra & Ghatak, 2021; Ray & Subramanian, 2020). A rise in mental health issues is to be expected in such a situation. Secondly, "this period may provide a more unbiased reflection of COVID on mental ill-health as people are yet to adapt to the enforced ban on social interaction and infringement to personal freedom" (Husain et al., 2021, p. 3).

The structure of the chapter is as follows: The data and method are described in Section 2.2, followed by a presentation of results and its discussion. The final section summarizes the results and discusses their policy implications.

2.2 Method

2.2.1 Survey design and instrument

The telephonic survey was administered to 1275 adults. Their ages ranged from 21 to 60 years. Respondents were randomly selected from a list of mobile phone users residing in the six Class 1 metropolises of India – Bengaluru, Chennai, Delhi, Kolkata, Mumbai and Hyderabad. These cities had seen a high number of active cases (22.30 percent of all cases) and deaths due to COVID-19 (37.99 percent of all cases), along with a shortage of medical facilities (Table 2.A1). The respondents were normal residents of the metropolitan city (having resided there for at least 3 years preceding the survey) and belonging to the age group 21–59 years. The survey was undertaken during the months of August and September 2020, when the lockdown had ended but COVID-19 cases and deaths were rising rapidly (Husain et al., 2023a). Given the social restrictions during the pandemic, the survey was administered over the phone. Despite its limitations, including the inability to obtain written consent, this method was used by many researchers during the pandemic to avoid infection during the interview process (Shah et al., 2021). Interviewers provided information to respondents about the research objective and obtained consent verbally. The rejection rate was less than 5% of those approached.

The measurement of psychological distress is an important methodological issue. In addition to established measures—like DASS-42 (Lovibond & Lovibond, 1995) and 4-item Patient Health Questionnaire (PHQ4) (Kroenke et al., 2009)—new self-reported scales had also been developed to study COVID-19-related mental health issues. Although such scales are short and easy to administer even under self-isolation or quarantine, they have major limitations. For instance, "[such scales] have limited potential to measure outcome parameters of interventions as the findings may not be aligned with objective assessment and be more prone to response bias" (Bibi et al., 2020). Moreover, the previously mentioned new scales are uni- or, at most, bidimensional (Scholten et al., 2017). Finally, their reliability in different sociocultural settings and across different subgroups is not established (Bibi et al., 2020).

Therefore, the survey was administered using the abridged, shorter version of the DASS questionnaire, DASS-21 (Lovibond & Lovibond, 1995). This is an instrument used to measure mental health issues related to anxiety, depression and stress and has been reported to possess a high level of internal consistency (Le et al., 2017; McAlonan et al., 2007). It has been widely used in different countries and sociocultural contexts, and for different sociodemographic subsamples (Ahmad et al., 2020; National Institute of Mental Health and Neuro Sciences, 2016; C. Wang, Pan, Wan, Tan, Xu, Ho, et al., 2020a). It has been used during both COVID-19 (Hossain et al., 2020; Ozamiz-Etxebarria et al., 2020; Rehman et al., 2021; Verma & Mishra, 2020; C. Wang, Pan, Wan, Tan, Xu, McIntyre, et al., 2020b) and other health epidemics (Nazli et al., 2020). The DASS-21 is particularly appropriate for measuring mental well-being during the COVID-19 pandemic as it has three components (anxiety, stress and depression) that have all been commonly reported during the pandemic. Estimates of Cronbach's alpha for the sample used in the study are .89 for anxiety, .88 for stress, .87 for depression and .96 for the overall reliability index.

2.2.2 *Ethical Consideration*

The ethical clearance for the study was obtained from the Institutional Ethics Committee of Presidency University (Kolkata), (PU/IEC(H)/PROV CL/M-01/2020 dated 12/9/2020). Interviewers obtained informed verbal consent from respondents before starting the survey.

2.2.3 *Statistical analysis*

The analysis is based on three scores:

1. raw scores,
2. normalized scores and
3. categorical scores formed by recoding the raw scores.

Five categories of scores are formed using the cutoff values suggested by Lovibond and Lovibond (1995)—normal, mild, moderate, severe and extremely severe. There are no established cutoff values for DASS-21 scores. Moreover, the particular form of mental health ailment is more relevant for an appropriate clinical response than an ad hoc score obtained after summing up scores for the three components.

The statistical analysis of the data starts with an exploratory analysis of the raw and normalized scores and an analysis of the association between the individual scores. In the next step, the proportion of respondents distributed over the categories of mental health was estimated. The study next analyzed the variation in mean scores over subsamples formed on the basis of sociodemographic characteristics. Finally, MIMIC models were estimated for anxiety, stress, depression and the aggregate DASS-21 scores. The MIMIC model has two components:

1. *Measurement model*: confirmatory factor analysis to measure the value of latent constructs (here mental well-being)
2. *Structural model*: a model that identifies the exogenous causes of the status of mental health.

Thus, the observed variables (Y: manifested indicators of mental ill-health problems) result from the latent factors (F: the underlying mental health condition). The latter are caused by exogenous sociodemographic and economic variables denoted by X. A path diagram summarizes the structure in Figure 2.1.

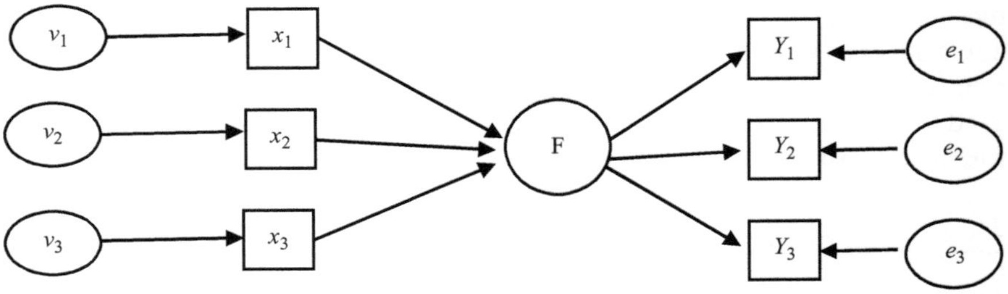

Figure 2.1 Multiple-indicator, multiple-cause model.

Source: Authors.

The model is described as follows:

$$F_{k\times 1} = \beta Y_{m\times 1} + e \tag{2.1}$$

$$F_{k\times 1} = \delta X_{n\times 1} + v \tag{2.2}$$

where β and δ are matrices of appropriate dimensions and e and v are vectors of error terms. Equation (2.1) describes the relationship between the latent variable and the observed indicators and is called the measurement model. A parametric model links the 'indicators' to the latent dimension. The choice of a parametric model is based on the nature of the observed indicators; given that they are ordered categorical variables, an ordered probit model is used (depicted on the right-hand side of Figure 2.1). The structural part is portrayed on the left-hand side of the path diagram and is described in Equation (2.2); it expresses the relationship between the exogenous determinants of the latent variables and observed indicators of the status of mental health.

The vector Y contains the responses to questions in the DASS-21 schedule. The vector X comprises the exogenous variables, whose details are provided in Appendix B. The variables are the age of the respondent, gender of the respondent, whether currently married, socioreligious identity, whether the respondent has at least a graduate level of education, household size, employment status of main earning member, whether the respondent resides in an owned house, residence type and whether they faced COVID-19 cases.

2.3 Results

2.3.1 Sample profile

Table 2.1 reports the sample profile. Most of the respondents belong to the 21–50-year age group. The gender distribution is roughly equal. About 40 and 30 percent of the respondents belong to the Hindu General and Hindu Other Backward Classes categories. The majority of the respondents are

Table 2.1 Sample profile

Variables	*Total*
Age group	
Mean age	38
21–30	26.90
31–40	39.92
41–50	21.96
51–60	11.22
Gender	
Male	48.94
Female	51.06
Socioreligious identity	
Hindu General	43.45
Hindu OBC	29.33
Hindu SC&ST	18.51
Minority	8.71
Marital status	
Currently unmarried	19.06
Currently married	80.94
Education	
Below graduate	85.18
Graduate & above	14.00
Employment status	
Self-employed	36.24
Fixed income	58.82
Variable income or part-time	4.94
Per capita monthly family expenditure	
Mean per capita monthly family expenditure	79.59
USD 25.00 or less	9.44
USD 25.01–40.00	15.18
USD 40.01–60.00	25.96
USD 60.01–80.00	17.70
USD 80.01–100.00	11.64
Above USD 100.00	20.06
Ownership of residence	
Rented	44.16
Owned	55.84
Residential pattern	
Slum	16.94
Bungalow	39.61
Standalone flat	21.33
Residential complex	22.12
Number of bedrooms in the house	
No bedroom	4.98
1 bedroom	44.38
2 bedrooms	39.56
3 or more bedrooms	11.08
Number of family members	
0–3 members	26.51

(*Continued*)

Table 2.1 (Continued)

Variables	*Total*
4 members	39.53
5 members	21.65
6 or more members	12.31
Number of family members 60 years and older	
No such member	72.94
At least one such member	27.06
Whether affected by COVID-19	
Not affected	58.43
COVID-19 cases with recovery	32.00
COVID-19 deaths	9.57
Total Sample	**1275**

Source: Estimated from primary data.

Note: USD = Rs.73.5042, the average of the exchange rate at the start and end of our survey (accessed from https://bit.ly/3zgB3ox on 18 September 2021). OBC = Other Backward Class; SC&ST = Scheduled Caste and Scheduled Tribe.

currently married. About 85 percent of the respondents do not have a college education. Most of the respondents are from families with a fixed monthly income. While 40 percent of the respondents reside in bungalow-type houses, 17 percent are slum dwellers. About 65 percent of respondents reside in households with four or fewer members. One out of three families has at least one member aged 60 years or older. Every third respondent has a family member, relative or friend who had COVID-19, while one out of 10 respondents have suffered bereavement due to COVID-19.

2.3.2 *Prevalence levels of mental health problems*

The average raw scores for anxiety, stress and depression are 10.08, 11.94 and 11.51, respectively (Table 2.2) are quite low, representing moderate, normal and mild levels of mental health, respectively. The average of the DASS-21

Table 2.2 Mean and median of mental health scores

Indicator	N	*Mean*	*Median*	*Std. Err.*	*95% Conf. Int.*	
Anxiety	1275	10.08	6.00	0.28	9.54	10.63
Stress	1275	11.94	8.00	0.29	11.38	12.51
Depression	1275	11.51	8.00	0.29	10.94	12.08
DASS-21	1275	11.18	8.00	0.27	10.65	11.71

Source: Estimated from primary data.

Note: Confidence interval is for 95% level. DASS-21 = Depression, Anxiety and Stress Scale–21 Items.

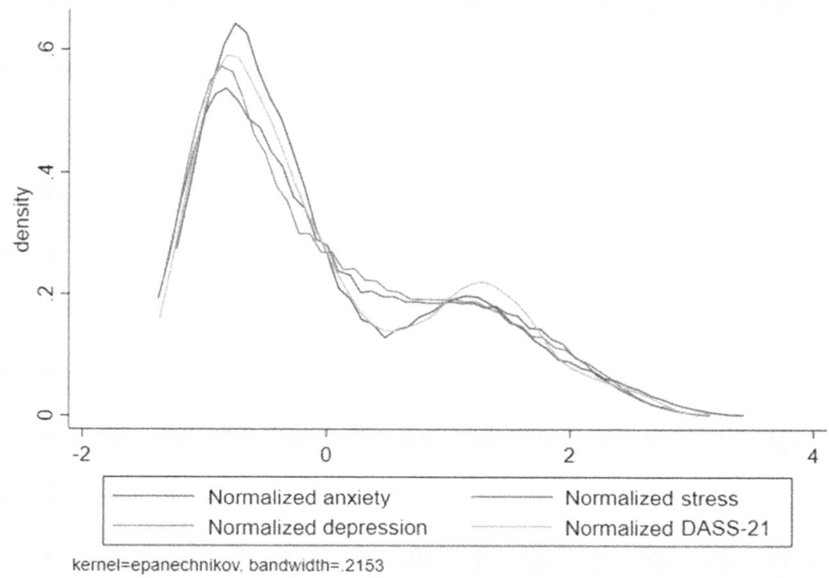

Figure 2.2 Kernel densities of normalized scores for mental health.
Source: Estimated from primary data.

score (aggregate of the raw scores) is 11.18. The median values of the scores are much lower.

The distribution of the DASS-21 scores and its components, depicted in Figure 2.2 using kernel density plots, reveal a similar pattern of distribution for all four scores. The plots reveal a bimodal distribution, with one peak occurring at a low value of the scores (representing normal scores) and the other at a higher value of the scores (at about 1.5). The latter peak, however, is much smaller than the earlier peak. It implies the presence of moderate to severe mental health issues during the COVID-19 pandemic; however, it is restricted to only a very small part of the population and is not very common. The mental health tsunami anticipated by some studies (Inkster, 2021; Torjesen, 2020) seems to be absent (Shevlin et al., 2021), at least for India.

A relevant question, in this context, is whether anxiety stress and depression are correlated with each other. Such a finding would suggest that different forms of psychological disorders reinforce each other, with a possible synergistic effect. Table 2.3 reports the Pearson correlation scores between the three components and the DASS-21 score. Results reveal a high, positive correlation, that is, statistically significant at a 1 percent level, between all four scores.

We next examine the distribution of respondents across levels of mental health status (Table 2.4). As indicated by the preceding analysis, the mental

Table 2.3 Correlation between mental health scores

	Anxiety	*Stress*	*Depression*	*DASS-21 score*
Anxiety	1.00			
Stress	0.85*	1.00		
Depression	0.85*	0.88*	1.00	
DASS-21 score	0.95*	0.95*	0.96*	1.00

Source: Authors.

Note: DASS-21 = Depression, Anxiety and Stress Scale–21 Items.

*$p < 0.01$.

Table 2.4 Distribution of respondents by severity of mental health status

Health status	*Anxiety*		*Stress*		*Depression*	
	Number	*Percentage*	*Number*	*Percentage*	*Number*	*Percentage*
Normal	687	53.88	840	65.88	664	52.08
Mild	83	6.51	102	8.00	126	9.88
Moderate	140	10.98	144	11.29	206	16.16
Severe	69	5.41	146	11.45	141	11.06
Extremely severe	296	23.22	43	3.37	138	10.82
Any symptom	588	46.12	435	34.11	611	47.92

Source: Estimated from primary data.

Note: Any symptom is the sum of mild, moderate, severe and extremely severe categories.

health scores of the majority of the respondents are 'normal'. Only 6–10 percent of the sample report mild symptoms of mental health, and 14–28 percent report concerning levels of adverse mental health (severe or extremely severe). The findings, therefore, match that of Figure 2.2.

2.3.3 Identifying groups 'at risk'

The results of the exploratory analysis indicate that, while a mental health tsunami is absent, a small subsample reports high levels of mental ill health. Such groups need to be identified so that they are reached through intervention strategies that mitigate their mental ill-being. Table 2.5 reports the mean scores of anxiety, depression and stress for sample groups grouped on the basis of sociodemographic and economic characteristics. Scores are normalized to facilitate comparison. Respondents aged between 31 and 40 years, belonging to the socially advantaged Hindu General caste, having per capita monthly expenditure levels above USD 100 and having experienced COVID-19 in their immediate social circle have lower scores. These subgroups are, therefore, relatively better off than other subgroups. Similarly,

Table 2.5 Variations in mean scores of mental health symptoms across correlates

Variables	*Depression*	*Anxiety*	*Stress*
Age group			
21–30 years	11.81	10.12	12.24
31–40 years	10.2	8.85	10.76
41–50 years	12.61	11.21	12.77
51–60 years	13.31	12.15	13.82
Gender			
Male	12.3	10.68	12.66
Female	10.76	9.51	11.25
Socioreligious identity			
Minority	21.66	18.97	20.41
Hindu General	9.94	7.81	10.65
Hindu OBC	10.74	10.4	11.41
Hindu SC&ST	11.64	10.75	11.84
Marital status			
Currently unmarried	11.65	9.28	11.78
Currently married	11.48	10.27	11.98
Education			
Below graduate	12.1	10.64	12.51
Graduate & above	8.13	6.88	8.68
Employment status			
Self-employed	12.46	10.92	12.68
Fixed income	10.8	9.39	11.4
Variable income	13.05	12.13	13.08
Per capita monthly family expenditure			
USD 25.00 or less	11.8	10.98	13.65
USD 25.01–40.00	14.69	13.45	14.72
USD 40.01–60.00	13.31	12.08	13.24
USD 60.01–80.00	12.26	10.68	13.1
USD 80.01–100.00	9.89	8.14	10.43
Above USD 100.00	7.06	5.22	7.35
Residential Pattern			
Slum	12.57	12.34	12.32
Bungalow	10.14	9.1	10.55
Standalone flat	15.6	13.07	16.93
Residential complex	9.21	7.23	9.33
Number of bedrooms in house			
No bedroom	15.11	13.68	14
1 bedroom	13.8	12.8	14.06
2 bedrooms	9.68	8.08	10.52
3 or more bedrooms	6.39	3.7	6.91
Number of family members			
0–3 members	10.72	8.28	10.57
4 members	11.53	10.61	12.35
5 members	11.43	10.36	11.83
6 or more members	13.31	11.77	13.78

(*Continued*)

Table 2.5 (Continued)

Variables	*Depression*	*Anxiety*	*Stress*
Number of family members 60 years and older			
No aged member	11.65	10.4	12.18
At least one aged man	11.14	9.23	11.31
COVID-19 cases among family, relatives or friends			
None	11.95	10.78	12.32
Had COVID-19 but recovered	10.29	8.65	10.97
Died from COVID-19	12.89	10.59	12.92
Total Sample	1275	1275	1275

Source: Estimated from primary data.

Note: USD = Rs.73.5042, the average of the exchange rate at the start and end of our survey (accessed from https://bit.ly/3zgB3ox on 18 September 2021). OBC = Other Backward Class; SC&ST = Scheduled Castes & Schedule Tribes.

respondents with fixed income, monthly per capita expenditure levels in the range of USD 25.01–40.00, residing in bungalows or residential complexes, and having at least two bedrooms are also relatively less vulnerable vis-à-vis other economic groups.

2.3.4 Results of MIMIC model

The results of the MIMIC model are reported in Table 2.6. The estimates for the measurement model are given in the top panel. All the indicators are significant at a one percent level and expectedly positive. It indicates that unobserved anxiety, stress and depression are being satisfactorily reflected through the observed indicators.

The results for the structural model, examining the association between the characteristics of respondents and their mental status, are given in the bottom panel of Table 2.6. The scores for mental health do not depend on the age of respondents or their marital status. Although anxiety scores do not vary between male and female respondents, the likelihood of females having a low depression and stress score is high. Respondents from the minority groups are significantly more likely to have higher scores vis-à-vis Hindu Scheduled Castes and Scheduled Tribes (SC&ST) and Hindu-General respondents. The only exception is stress. Depression scores are significantly higher for respondents with low levels of education, that is, with a below-graduate level of education. The probability of respondents belonging to families whose main earning member is self-employed reporting high mental health scores for all dimensions is higher compared to households whose main earner has a fixed or variable income. Higher levels of anxiety and stress are reported by respondents residing in large households relative to respondents from small households. Respondents residing in owned flats (vis-à-vis residents of rented flats), in slums or in bungalows (compared to residents of standalone flats) are more likely to have high scores for all three dimensions of maternal health

Table 2.6 Results of the multiple-indicator, multiple-cause model for anxiety, depression and stress

Variables	*Anxiety*			*Stress*			*Depression*		
	Beta	*95% CI*		*Beta*	*95% CI*		*Beta*	*95% CI*	
Measurement model									
I1	1			1			1		
I2	0.97***	0.84	1.10	1.53***	1.29	1.76	0.93***	0.82	1.04
I3	1.17***	1.01	1.33	2.00***	1.70	2.30	1.32***	1.14	1.50
I4	0.86***	0.75	0.98	1.57***	1.34	1.81	1.06***	0.90	1.21
I5	0.69***	0.58	0.79	1.58***	1.33	1.84	1.10***	0.95	1.25
I6	1.05***	0.90	1.20	2.12***	1.80	2.44	1.52***	1.29	1.75
I7	0.83***	0.70	0.96	1.77***	1.51	2.03	1.46***	1.21	1.71
Structural model									
Age groups (31–40 years)									
21–30 years	-0.09	-0.27	0.09	-0.09*	-0.18	0.01	-0.09	-0.23	0.05
41–50 years	-0.03	-0.23	0.17	-0.05	-0.16	0.07	-0.02	-0.18	0.14
51–60 years	0.03	-0.21	0.27	-0.04	-0.17	0.09	-0.04	-0.21	0.14
Marital status (currently not married)									
Currently married	-0.05	-0.25	0.15	-0.03	-0.14	0.07	-0.10	-0.25	0.05
Female	-0.07	-0.20	0.06	-0.09**	-0.16	-0.01	-0.12**	-0.23	-0.02
Socioreligious group (minorities)									
Hindu General	0.15*	-0.02	0.33	0.06	-0.05	0.16	0.14**	0.01	0.28
Hindu OBC	0.00	-0.18	0.18	-0.08	-0.18	0.02	-0.07	-0.22	0.07
Hindu SC&ST	0.68***	0.43	0.92	0.30***	0.16	0.44	0.57***	0.38	0.77
Education (below graduate)									
Above graduate	-0.09	-0.23	0.06	-0.03	-0.11	0.06	-0.10*	-0.21	0.01

(*Continued*)

Table 2.6 (Continued)

Variables	*Anxiety*			*Stress*			*Depression*		
	Beta	*95% CI*		*Beta*	*95% CI*		*Beta*	*95% CI*	
Employment status of main earner (self-employed)									
Fixed income	−0.18**	−0.31	−0.05	−0.09**	−0.17	−0.01	−0.15**	−0.25	−0.04
Variable income or part-time	−0.26*	−0.56	0.03	−0.16*	−0.32	0.00	−0.21*	−0.43	0.01
Household size	0.05*	0.00	0.10	0.03*	0.00	0.05	0.02	−0.02	0.06
Residence type (flat)									
Slum	0.04	−0.16	0.25	0.16**	0.04	0.29	0.15*	−0.02	0.32
Bungalow	0.65***	0.43	0.87	0.57***	0.44	0.71	0.61***	0.43	0.79
Residential complex	0.56***	0.31	0.80	0.35***	0.21	0.49	0.57***	0.38	0.76
House ownership (rented)									
Owned	−0.19**	−0.32	−0.05	−0.15***	−0.24	−0.07	−0.22***	−0.33	−0.11
Faced COVID-19 case (No)									
Only COVID-19 cases	0.42***	0.25	0.58	0.18***	0.09	0.28	0.19***	0.07	0.31
COVID-19 deaths	0.63***	0.34	0.92	0.25***	0.08	0.41	0.26**	0.05	0.48
City fixed effects (Bengaluru)									
Chennai	0.08	−0.15	0.30	0.14**	0.00	0.27	0.32***	0.13	0.51
Delhi	−2.37***	−2.72	−2.01	−0.78***	−0.95	−0.62	−1.14***	−1.37	−0.92
Hyderabad	−1.07***	−1.34	−0.79	−0.72***	−0.89	−0.55	−1.04***	−1.30	−0.78
Kolkata	−2.53***	−2.91	−2.15	−1.02***	−1.21	−0.82	−1.10***	−1.37	−0.83
Mumbai	0.09	−0.13	0.31	0.19***	0.06	0.32	0.26***	0.08	0.43
var(e)	0.87	0.69	1.10	0.87	0.24	0.39	0.31	0.44	0.71

Source: Estimated from primary data.

Notes: I1-I7 corresponds to questions for measuring depression, anxiety and stress in the Depression, Anxiety and Stress Scale–21 Items schedule. The category in parentheses indicates the reference group. OBC = Other Backward Class; SC&ST = Scheduled Caste and Scheduled Tribe.

$*p < 10$; $**p < .5$; $***p < .01$.

problems assessed here. Experience of COVID-19 in the form of cases and deaths due to COVID-19 in the immediate circle (comprising the immediate family, relatives or friends) increases the risk of psychological issues. Statistically significant city fixed effects are observed, indicating considerable regional variations in mental well-being during the pandemic.

The results of the MIMIC model relating DASS-21 scores to its indicators (Depression, Anxiety and Stress scores) and determinants are reported in Table 2.7. As in the earlier model, the overall mental health status is reflected adequately in the scores for depression, anxiety and stress. The structural model identifies males to be more vulnerable than females. It also reveals that respondents without a college education, currently unmarried respondents, members of minority communities, self-employed respondents, residents of standalone flats and respondents experiencing COVID-19 in their immediate social and family circle face a high level of risk of having poor mental health.

Table 2.7 Results of the multiple-indicator, multiple-cause model for the Depression, Anxiety and Stress Scale–21 Item score

Variables	*Beta*	*95% CI*	
Measurement model			
Anxiety	1		
Depression	1.10***	0.85	1.37
Stress	1.11***	0.90	1.33
Structural model			
Age groups (31–40 years)			
21–30 years	0.17	0.85	1.37
41–50 years	0.22	0.90	1.33
51–60 years	0.24		
Female	-0.24*		
Socioreligious group (minorities)		-0.53	0.12
Hindu General	-1.48***	-0.35	0.39
Hindu OBC	-1.00***	-0.42	0.45
Hindu SC&ST	-1.67***	-0.50	-0.01
Education (below graduate)			
Above graduate	-0.33*	0.14	0.81
Employment status of main earner (self-employed)			
Fixed income	-0.28**	-0.54	-0.04
Variable income or part-time	-0.51*	-1.04	0.00
Household size	0.07	-0.02	0.16
Marital status (currently not married)			
Currently married	-0.32*	-0.69	0.03
Residence type (flat)			
Slum	-1.77***	0.11	0.92
Bungalow	-1.30***	1.36	2.26
Residential Complex	-0.50**	0.81	1.75

(*Continued*)

Table 2.7 (Continued)

Variables	*Beta*	*95% CI*	
House ownership (rented)			
Owned	−0.58***	−0.84	−0.32
Faced COVID-19 case (no)			
Only COVID-19 cases	0.55***	0.27	0.87
COVID-19 deaths	0.78***	0.31	1.33
City fixed effects (Bengaluru)			
Chennai	0.66***	0.21	1.11
Delhi	−3.14***	−3.77	−2.32
Hyderabad	−2.21***	−2.78	−1.63
Kolkata	−2.86***	−3.59	−2.15
Mumbai	0.58**	0.18	1.04
var(e)	3.61	2.74	4.73

Source: Estimated from primary data.

Note: The category in parentheses represents the reference group. OBC = Other Backward Class; ST&SC = Scheduled Tribes & Scheduled Caste. See Appendix 2B for more details.

*$p < .1$; **$p < .5$; ***$p < .05$.

2.4 Discussion

The study reveals that the pandemic did lead to a deterioration in the mental well-being of the adult residents of Indian metropolitan cities. Furthermore, the levels of the different components of mental well-being, anxiety, stress and depression, were high and had a synergistic effect. But the expected tsunami did not occur; rather, the level of mental health fell to levels requiring clinical attention for only a small subsection of the population who reported severe or extremely severe symptoms of anxiety, stress and depression. The analysis also reveals that the MIMIC models revealed that the indicators were able to capture the three mental disorders and mental ill-being quite effectively.

Moreover, the impact of the pandemic on mental health status was not homogeneous but varied over socioeconomic groups. For instance, self-employed respondents were less likely to report high anxiety, stress and depression scores. Gender differences were observed for stress, depression and aggregate mental ill-being. Predictably, respondents who had experienced COVID-19, particularly if they had experienced the death of any family member, reported higher mental health scores. Furthermore, nonlinear effects of the pandemic were observed. The population segments identified to be at risk included members of both socially advantaged Hindu-General and socially marginalized Hindu SC&ST respondents. Similarly, residents of both slums and residential complexes and bungalows had higher levels of mental well-being vis-à-vis residents of standalone flats.

The findings of the present study are consistent with other studies undertaken in the Indian context, both before and during the pandemic. A national-level study undertaken in 2016 (Kalin, 2020) had reported that about one out of 10 people had some mental health disorder. Moreover, 2.7, 3.0 and 0.2 percent of the population were found to be suffering from depression, anxiety and stress, respectively. This is much lower than the results of the present study. The higher incidence of mental health problems reported during the pandemic, however, is expected and may be attributed to home isolation, economic uncertainties and fear of being infected. Other studies undertaken in India reported higher levels of mental illness during the pandemic (Badellino et al., 2021; Fenollar-Cortés et al., 2021; Kar et al., 2021; Rehman et al., 2021; Varshney et al., 2020; Verma & Mishra, 2020). A review of studies on mental health during COVID-19 (Hudson, 2005) also reports high levels of mental illness during the pandemic in other countries. Our study also corroborates the strong association between anxiety stress and depression reported in developed countries (Frasquilho et al., 2015).

In general, the findings of this study correspond to the results reported in existing studies in India and other countries. Our study indicates that male respondents, members of socially marginalized communities, less educated respondents and those currently unmarried, belonging to larger households and from less affluent households face a high risk of being psychologically affected by the pandemic. These results match those of other studies. While most Indian studies report males to be more at risk of psychological distress (Badellino et al., 2021; Fenollar-Cortés et al., 2021; Rehman et al., 2021), studies in Spain (Ridley et al., 2020), China (C. Wang, Pan, Wan, Tan, Xu, McIntyre, et al., 2020b) and the UK (Pierce et al., 2020) report otherwise. Similarly, studies report currently unmarried respondents (Fenollar-Cortés et al., 2021; Kar et al., 2021) and minorities (Fenollar-Cortés et al., 2021; Pierce et al., 2020) to be more likely to report higher mental health scores. However, in contrast to existing literature identifying age as an important predictor of mental health (Viseu et al., 2018), our analysis did not find any association between the two variables.

There are multiple pathways through which economic stress affects mental health through multiple mechanisms. Such pathways include rising unemployment, financial threat, indebtedness, economic hardship, volatility in income, deterioration in living standard and decreased levels of welfare support (Ridley et al., 2020; Viseu et al., 2018). While our study did not specifically examine the effect of economic distress on mental health directly, we found indirect evidence in support of this commonly accepted proposition (Hudson, 2005, p. 3). Households whose main earning member is self-employed or respondents residing in rented houses are more likely to report depression, anxiety and stress.

Given the difficulties in maintaining social distancing or poor hygiene standards due shared communal toilet facilities (Patranobis et al., 2020), slum dwellers are considered to be a high risk group. A possible reason may be positional objectivity (Sen, 1993). Slum dwellers had already been adversely affected by demonetization and the slowdown of the Indian economy; it may explain why the incremental impact of the pandemic was marginal. It is also possible that the extensive ties based on social networks or kinship relations may have helped the slum dwellers to adapt to the pandemic and face the resultant stress better (Das et al., 2020).

2.5 Conclusion

The study highlights the importance of tracking mental health during health epidemics and national-level disasters. It provides evidence of the deterioration in mental well-being in India at the onset of the pandemic. At the same time, we should not be alarmist but keep in mind that the proportion of people requiring clinical treatment was not substantial in the sample. Therefore, we recommend

1. using local authorities to identify and monitor subgroups who are at higher risk of facing mental health problems,
2. ensuring emergency services for such groups,
3. establishing facilities to combat posttraumatic stress disorders, and
4. furthermore, given the evidence on the psychological impact of economic distress during the pandemic (Husain et al., 2023a), providing economic support to economically vulnerable households should be made a key component of post-COVID-19 recovery programs (Pierce et al., 2020).

Finally, we point out certain limitations of our study. The survey was undertaken over the telephone. It is possible that the poorest sections of society and those who are less technically 'savvy' may have been included in the study. Furthermore, responses could not be verified. However, the survey instrument has been reported to be reliable in different sociocultural contexts, including COVID-19. Second, studies have also noted that mental well-being may improve over the course of the pandemic (Husain et al., 2023b). The present study focuses on a single point of time, ignoring such fluctuations.

In spite of these limitations, however, the present study, based on the use of rigorous econometric methods, provides valuable insights into the socioeconomic determinants of mental health status in a low-middle-income country with inadequate mental health facilities. Our study, unlike the existing literature, acknowledges that mental (ill) health is a latent variable and, by using the MIMIC model, provides a better insight into the channels through which socioeconomic covariates influence the status of mental health and its components (viz. stress, anxiety and depression).

Acknowledgment

The authors are grateful to Dr. Soumitra Sankar Datta (Tata Medical Center, Kolkata) for his comments and inputs. An early version of this study was published as a Research Square preprint:

Husain, Z., Ghosh, S., Dutta, M., Chaudhury, K. & Chakrabarti, A. (2021) *Analysing mental well-being of adults during COVID using a MIMIC model: Evidence from Indian metropolitan cities*. https://doi.org/10.21203/rs.3.rs-1044572/v1.

Data availability

Husain, Zakir; Ghosh, Saswata; Dutta, Mousumi; Chaudhuri, Kausik; Chakrabarti, Anindita (2021), "Mental Health in Indian metro cities: 2020", Mendeley Data, V1, doi: 10.17632/jtzpkhw3mk.1.

Note

1 See Kapoor and Panda (2022).

Appendix 2A: Appendix Tables

Table 2.A1 COVID-19 cases in metro cities of India as on 1 August 2021

Region	*Confirmed*	*Active*	*Recovered*	*Deceased*
Bengaluru	61,888	39,358	21,442	1087
Chennai	101,951	12,193	87,604	2154
Hyderabad	39,991	39,663	305	23
Kolkata	23,062	6597	15,666	799
Mumbai	116,436	21,394	88,299	6447
NCT of Delhi	137,677	10,356	123,317	4004
Metro cities (total)	481,005	129,561	336,633	14,514
India	1,808,322	581,001	1,188,650	38,201
Metro cities (percentage of total)	26.60	22.30	28.32	37.99

Source: Estimated from data downloaded from https://data.covid19india.org/documentation/csv/ on 2 August 2021.

Note: NCT = National Capital Territory.

Appendix 2B: Construction of control variables

1. Four age groups were constructed: 21–30 years (reference category), 31–40 years, 41–50 years and 51–60 years.
2. The respondents are divided into Hindu General Hindu Scheduled Caste or Scheduled Tribe, Hindu Other Backward Classes (OBCs), and minority groups. Scheduled castes are subcommunities within the Hindu religious community who have faced deprivation, oppression and social isolation on account of their perceived low birth status. In contrast, Scheduled Tribes are classified as marginalized communities on the basis of geographical isolation and may include groups from other religious communities also. The list of such subgroups is given in the Constitution (Scheduled Castes/Tribes) Order, 1950. OBCs are social groups that have

been traditionally marginalized in India and still face oppression and social, economic and educational isolation but do not fall into the Scheduled Castes or Scheduled Tribes list, fall into the OBC category. The list of OBCs is provided by the National Commission for Backward Classes. Religious minorities consist of Muslims, Christians, Sikhs, Jains, Buddhists and Zoroastrians.

3. The categories for employment status are fixed income, variable income or part-time and self-employed (reference category).
4. The residential categories are slums, bungalow, standalone flats (reference categories) and residential complexes.

References

Ahmad, A., Rahman, I., & Agarwal, M. (2020). Factors influencing mental health during covid-19 outbreak: An exploratory survey among Indian population. *Journal of Health Sciences*. https://doi.org/10.17532/jhsci.2020.950

Badellino, H., Gobbo, M. E., Torres, E., & Aschieri, M. E. (2021). Early indicators and risk factors associated with mental health problems during COVID-19 quarantine: Is there a relationship with the number of confirmed cases and deaths? *International Journal of Social Psychiatry*, *67*(5), 567–575. https://doi.org/10.1177/0020764020966020

Banna, M. H., Al Sayeed, A., Kundu, S., Christopher, E., Hasan, M. T., Begum, M. R., Kormoker, T., Dola, S. T. I., Hassan, M. M., Chowdhury, S., & Khan, M. S. I. (2020). The impact of the COVID-19 pandemic on the mental health of the adult population in Bangladesh: A nationwide cross-sectional study. *International Journal of Environmental Health Research*, 1–12. https://doi.org/10.1080/09603123.2020.1802409

Bibi, A., Lin, M., Zhang, X. C., & Margraf, J. (2020). Psychometric properties and measurement invariance of Depression, Anxiety and Stress Scales (DASS-21) across cultures. *International Journal of Psychology*, *55*(6), 916–925. https://doi.org/10.1002/ijop.12671

Das, M., Angeli, F., & Schayck, O. C. P. (2020). Understanding self-construction of health among the slum dwellers of India: a culture-centred approach. *Sociology of Health & Illness*, *42*(5), 1001–1023. https://doi.org/10.1111/1467-9566.13075

Dhingra, S., & Ghatak, M. (2021). *The Pandemic in Data: How Covid-19 Has Devastated India's Economy*. Scroll Blog. https://scroll.in/article/999275/the-pandemic-in-data-how-covid-19-has-devasted-indias-economy

Dubey, S., Biswas, P., Ghosh, R., Chatterjee, S., Dubey, M. J., Chatterjee, S., Lahiri, D., & Lavie, C. J. (2020). Psychosocial impact of COVID-19. *Diabetes & Metabolic Syndrome: Clinical Research & Reviews*, *14*(5), 779–788. https://doi.org/10.1016/j.dsx.2020.05.035

Fenollar-Cortés, J., Jiménez, Ó., Ruiz-García, A., & Resurrección, D. M. (2021). Gender differences in psychological impact of the confinement during the COVID-19 outbreak in Spain: A longitudinal study. *Frontiers in Psychology*, *12*. https://doi.org/10.3389/fpsyg.2021.682860

Frasquilho, D., Matos, M. G., Salonna, F., Guerreiro, D., Storti, C. C., Gaspar, T., & Caldas-de-Almeida, J. M. (2015). Mental health outcomes in times of economic recession: A systematic literature review. *BMC Public Health*, *16*(1), 115. https://doi.org/10.1186/s12889-016-2720-y

Giallonardo, V., Sampogna, G., Del Vecchio, V., Luciano, M., Albert, U., Carmassi, C., Carrà, G., Cirulli, F., Dell'Osso, B., Nanni, M. G., Pompili, M., Sani, G., Tortorella, A., Volpe, U., & Fiorillo, A. (2020). The impact of quarantine and physical distancing following COVID-19 on mental health: Study protocol of a multicentric italian population trial. *Frontiers in Psychiatry*, *11*. https://doi.org/10.3389/fpsyt.2020.00533

González-Blanco, L., Dal Santo, F., García-Álvarez, L., de la Fuente-Tomás, L., Moya Lacasa, C., Paniagua, G., Sáiz, P. A., García-Portilla, M. P., & Bobes, J. (2020). COVID-19 lockdown in people with severe mental disorders in Spain: Do they have a specific psychological reaction compared with other mental disorders and healthy controls? *Schizophrenia Research*, *223*, 192–198. https://doi.org/10.1016/j.schres.2020.07.018

Hossain, M. M., Tasnim, S., Sultana, A., Faizah, F., Mazumder, H., Zou, L., McKyer, E. L. J., Ahmed, H. U., & Ma, P. (2020). Epidemiology of mental health problems in COVID-19: A review. *F1000Research*, *9*, 636. https://doi.org/10.12688/f1000research.24457.1

Huang, Y., & Zhao, N. (2020). RETRACTED: Chinese mental health burden during the COVID-19 pandemic. *Asian Journal of Psychiatry*, *51*, 102052. https://doi.org/10.1016/j.ajp.2020.102052

Hudson, C. G. (2005). Socioeconomic status and mental illness: Tests of the social causation and selection hypotheses. *American Journal of Orthopsychiatry*, *75*(1), 3–18. https://doi.org/10.1037/0002-9432.75.1.3

Husain, Z., Datta, S. S., Ghosh, S., & Dutta, M. (2023a). Changes in mental health status during the COVID-19 pandemic: A longitudinal study of residents of Indian metropolitan cities. *Journal of Mental Health*, forthcoming. https://doi.org/10.1080/09638237.2023.2182417

Husain, Z., Datta, S. S., Ghosh, S., & Dutta, M. (2023b). Change in mental health during the COVID-19 pandemic: A longitudinal study of residents of Indian metropolitan cities. *Journal of Mental Health*, *32*(5), 879–889. https://doi.org/10.1080/09638237.2023.2182417

Husain, Z., Ghosh, S., Dutta, M., Chaudhuri, K., & Chakrabarti, A. (2021). *Analysing Mental Health Problems of Adults During COVID Using a MIMIC Model: Evidence from Indian Metropolitan Cities* (Research Square Preprint). https://doi.org/10.21203/rs.3.rs-1044572/v1

Inkster, B. (2021). Early warning signs of a mental health Tsunami: A coordinated response to gather initial data insights from multiple digital services providers. *Frontiers in Digital Health*, *2*. https://doi.org/10.3389/fdgth.2020.578902

Kalin, N. H. (2020). The critical relationship between anxiety and depression. *American Journal of Psychiatry*, *177*(5), 365–367. https://doi.org/10.1176/appi.ajp.2020.20030305

Kapoor, M., & Panda, P. K. (2022). India's second COVID wave: How is it different from the first wave? *International Journal of Infectious Diseases*, *116*, S50. https://doi.org/10.1016/j.ijid.2021.12.121

Kar, N., Kar, B., & Kar, S. (2021). Stress and coping during COVID-19 pandemic: Result of an online survey. *Psychiatry Research*, *295*, 113598. https://doi.org/10.1016/j.psychres.2020.113598

Kroenke, K., Spitzer, R. L., Williams, J. B. W., & Lowe, B. (2009). An ultra-brief screening scale for anxiety and depression: The PHQ-4. *Psychosomatics*, *50*(6), 613–621. https://doi.org/10.1176/appi.psy.50.6.613

Kuehner, C., Schultz, K., Gass, P., Meyer-Lindenberg, A., & Dreßing, H. (2020). Psychisches Befinden in der Bevölkerung während der COVID-19-Pandemie. *Psychiatrische Praxis*, *47*(07), 361–369. https://doi.org/10.1055/a-1222-9067

Le, M. T. H., Tran, T. D., Holton, S., Nguyen, H. T., Wolfe, R., & Fisher, J. (2017). Reliability, convergent validity and factor structure of the DASS-21 in a sample of Vietnamese adolescents. *PLOS ONE*, *12*(7), e0180557. https://doi.org/10.1371/journal.pone.0180557

Liao, H.-P., Pan, X.-F., Yin, X.-Q., Liu, Y.-F., Li, J.-Y., & Wang, J.-L. (2021). Decreased COVID-related adaptive behavior and increased negative affect: A multivariate latent growth curve model. *Journal of Health Psychology*. https://doi.org/10.1177/13591053211021651

Liu, L., Xue, P., Li, S. X., Zhang, J., Zhou, J., & Zhang, W. (2021). Urban-rural disparities in mental health problems related to COVID-19 in China. *General Hospital Psychiatry*, *69*, 119–120. https://doi.org/10.1016/j.genhosppsych.2020.07.011

Lovibond, P. F., & Lovibond, S. H. (1995). The structure of negative emotional states: Comparison of the Depression Anxiety Stress Scales (DASS) with the beck depression and anxiety inventories. *Behaviour Research and Therapy*, *33*(3), 335–343. https://doi.org/10.1016/0005-7967(94)00075-U

McAlonan, G. M., Lee, A. M., Cheung, V., Cheung, C., Tsang, K. W., Sham, P. C., Chua, S. E., & Wong, J. G. (2007). Immediate and sustained psychological impact of an emerging infectious disease outbreak on health care workers. *The Canadian Journal of Psychiatry*, *52*(4), 241–247. https://doi.org/10.1177/070674370705200406

Morales Chainé, S., Robles García, R., López Montoya, A., Bosch Maldonado, A., Beristain Aguirre, A. G., Treviño Santa Cruz, C. L., Palafox, G. P., Lira Chávez, I. A., Barragán Torres, L., & Rangel Gómez, M. G. (2022). Screening tool for mental health problems during COVID-19 pandemic: Psychometrics and associations with sex, grieving, contagion, and seeking psychological care. *Frontiers in Psychology*, *13*. https://doi.org/10.3389/fpsyg.2022.882573

Morganstein, J. C., Ursano, R. J., Fullerton, C. S., & Holloway, H. C. (2017). Pandemics: Health emergencies. In R. J. Ursano, S. C. Fullerton, L. Weisaeth, & B. Raphael (Eds.), *Textbook of disaster psychiatry* (2nd editio, pp. 270–283). Cambridge University Press.

National Institute of Mental Health and Neuro Sciences. (2016). *National mental health survey of india, 2015-16: Prevalence, pattern and outcomes*. NIMHANS.

Nazli, T., Grover, S., & Kishore, J. (2020). Covid 19 pandemic and "Feeling Depressed": An online survey. *Epidemiology International* *5*(2), 27–31. https://doi.org/10.24321/2455.7048.202014

Ozamiz-Etxebarria, N., Dosil-Santamaria, M., Picaza-Gorrochategui, M., & Idoiaga-Mondragon, N. (2020). Niveles de estrés, ansiedad y depresión en la primera fase del brote del COVID-19 en una muestra recogida en el norte de España. *Cadernos de Saúde Pública*, *36*(4). https://doi.org/10.1590/0102-311x00054020

Patranobis, S., Gandhi, S., & Tandel, V. (2020). Are slums more vulnerable to COVID-19 pandemic: Evidence from Mumbai. *Brookings Institute Blog*. https://www.brookings.edu/blog/up-front/2020/04/16/are-slums-more-vulnerable-to-the-covid-19-pandemic-evidence-from-mumbai/

Paulino, M., Dumas-Diniz, R., Brissos, S., Brites, R., Alho, L., Simões, M. R., & Silva, C. F. (2021). COVID-19 in Portugal: exploring the immediate psychological impact on the general population. *Psychology, Health & Medicine*, *26*(1), 44–55. https://doi.org/10.1080/13548506.2020.1808236

Pierce, M., Hope, H., Ford, T., Hatch, S., Hotopf, M., John, A., Kontopantelis, E., Webb, R., Wessely, S., McManus, S., & Abel, K. M. (2020). Mental health before and during the COVID-19 pandemic: a longitudinal probability sample survey of the UK population. *The Lancet. Psychiatry*, *7*(10), 883–892. https://doi.org/10.1016/S2215-0366(20)30308-4

Proitsi, P., Hamilton, G., Tsolaki, M., Lupton, M., Daniilidou, M., Hollingworth, P., Archer, N., Foy, C., Stylios, F., McGuinness, B., Todd, S., Lawlor, B., Gill, M.,

Brayne, C., Rubinsztein, D. C., Owen, M., Williams, J., Craig, D., Passmore, P., … Powell, J. F. (2011). A multiple indicators multiple causes (MIMIC) model of behavioural and psychological symptoms in dementia (BPSD). *Neurobiology of Aging*, *32*(3), 434–442. https://doi.org/10.1016/j.neurobiolaging.2009.03.005

Ransing, R., Ramalho, R., Orsolini, L., Adiukwu, F., Gonzalez-Diaz, J. M., Larnaout, A., Pinto da Costa, M., Grandinetti, P., Bytyçi, D. G., Shalbafan, M., Patil, I., Nofal, M., Pereira-Sanchez, V., & Kilic, O. (2020). Can COVID-19 related mental health issues be measured? *Brain, Behavior, and Immunity*, *88*, 32–34. https://doi.org/10.1016/j.bbi.2020.05.049

Ray, D., & Subramanian, S. (2020). *India's Lockdown: An Interim Report* (No. 27282; NBER Working Paper). http://www.nber.org/papers/w27282

Rehman, U., Shahnawaz, M. G., Khan, N. H., Kharshiing, K. D., Khursheed, M., Gupta, K., Kashyap, D., & Uniyal, R. (2021). Depression, anxiety and stress among Indians in times of Covid-19 lockdown. *Community Mental Health Journal*, *57*(1), 42–48. https://doi.org/10.1007/s10597-020-00664-x

Ridley, M., Rao, G., Schilbach, F., & Patel, V. (2020). Poverty, depression, and anxiety: Causal evidence and mechanisms. *Science*, *370*(6522). https://doi.org/10.1126/science.aay0214

Roy, D., Tripathy, S., Kar, S. K., Sharma, N., Verma, S. K., & Kaushal, V. (2020). Study of knowledge, attitude, anxiety & perceived mental healthcare need in Indian population during COVID-19 pandemic. *Asian Journal of Psychiatry*, *51*, 102083. https://doi.org/10.1016/j.ajp.2020.102083

Scholten, S., Velten, J., Bieda, A., Zhang, X. C., & Margraf, J. (2017). Testing measurement invariance of the Depression, Anxiety, and Stress Scales (DASS-21) across four countries. *Psychological Assessment*, *29*(11), 1376–1390. https://doi.org/10.1037/pas0000440

Sen, A. (1993). Positional objectivity. *Philosophy and Public Affairs*, *22*(2), 126.

Shah, S. M. A., Mohammad, D., Qureshi, M. F. H., Abbas, M. Z., & Aleem, S. (2021). Prevalence, psychological responses and associated correlates of depression, anxiety and stress in a global population, during the coronavirus disease (COVID-19) pandemic. *Community Mental Health Journal*, *57*(1), 101–110. https://doi.org/10.1007/s10597-020-00728-y

Shevlin, M., Butter, S., McBride, O., Murphy, J., Gibson-Miller, J., Hartman, T. K., Levita, L., Mason, L., Martinez, A. P., McKay, R., Stocks, T. V. A., Bennett, K., Hyland, P., & Bentall, R. P. (2021). Refuting the myth of a 'tsunami' of mental ill-health in populations affected by COVID-19: Evidence that response to the pandemic is heterogeneous, not homogeneous. *Psychological Medicine*, 1–9. https://doi.org/10.1017/S0033291721001665

Shigemura, J., Ursano, R. J., Morganstein, J. C., Kurosawa, M., & Benedek, D. M. (2020). Public responses to the novel 2019 coronavirus (2019-nCoV) in Japan: Mental health consequences and target populations. *Psychiatry and Clinical Neurosciences*, *74*(4), 281–282. https://doi.org/10.1111/pcn.12988

Torjesen, I. (2020). Covid-19: Mental health services must be boosted to deal with "tsunami" of cases after lockdown. *BMJ*, m1994. https://doi.org/10.1136/bmj.m1994

Varshney, M., Parel, J. T., Raizada, N., & Sarin, S. K. (2020). Initial psychological impact of COVID-19 and its correlates in Indian Community: An online (FEEL-COVID) survey. *Plos One*, *15*(5), e0233874. https://doi.org/10.1371/journal.pone.0233874

Verma, S., & Mishra, A. (2020). Depression, anxiety, and stress and socio-demographic correlates among general Indian public during COVID-19. *International Journal of Social Psychiatry*, *66*(8), 756–762. https://doi.org/10.1177/0020764020934508

Viseu, J., Leal, R., de Jesus, S. N., Pinto, P., Pechorro, P., & Greenglass, E. (2018). Relationship between economic stress factors and stress, anxiety, and depression: Moderating role of social support. *Psychiatry Research*, *268*, 102–107. https://doi.org/10.1016/j.psychres.2018.07.008

Wang, C., Pan, R., Wan, X., Tan, Y., Xu, L., Ho, C. S., & Ho, R. C. (2020a). Immediate psychological responses and associated factors during the initial stage of the 2019 coronavirus disease (COVID-19) epidemic among the general population in China. *International Journal of Environmental Research and Public Health*, *17*(5), 1729. https://doi.org/10.3390/ijerph17051729

Wang, C., Pan, R., Wan, X., Tan, Y., Xu, L., McIntyre, R. S., Choo, F. N., Tran, B., Ho, R., Sharma, V. K., & Ho, C. (2020b). A longitudinal study on the mental health of general population during the COVID-19 epidemic in China. *Brain, Behavior, and Immunity*, *87*, 40–48. https://doi.org/10.1016/j.bbi.2020.04.028

Wang, Y., Shi, L., Que, J., Lu, Q., Liu, L., Lu, Z., Xu, Y., Liu, J., Sun, Y., Meng, S., Yuan, K., Ran, M., Lu, L., Bao, Y., & Shi, J. (2021). The impact of quarantine on mental health status among general population in China during the COVID-19 pandemic. *Molecular Psychiatry*. https://doi.org/10.1038/s41380-021-01019-y

3 Quality of innovation and market access under merger

*Rajat Acharyya**

Recently there has been a growing interest among researchers regarding how mergers and acquisitions (M&A) influence the post-merger quality of innovations or the choice from the set of existing quality-differentiated innovations (or products). More precisely, the research question that has drawn attention is whether M&A induces the merged entity to select a low-quality product from the existing set or not. Similarly, for new innovations, the relevant question that crops up is whether M&A leads to low-quality innovations. A growing interest in these issues is motivated by the increasing number of incidences of M&A in industries like the aviation industry, hospital care, and the pharmaceutical industry. For example, during 2022, there were 16 deals worth almost US$1 billion in value.[1] While the basic concern in cases of M&A in the aviation industry and hospital care appears to be the quality of service being provided by the merged entity, for the pharmaceutical industry the major concern is the quality of new innovations of drugs.

In the small but growing literature, the role of the intensity of pre-merger competition – captured through the extent to which products were differentiated from each other, as well as through whether the firms were operating in the same or in different markets – and spatial dimension of distribution of heterogeneous consumers have been the focal point of analyses so far (Bauer and Matzler 2014; Chen and Gayle 2019; Brekke et al. 2017; Johnson and Rhodes 2021). However, the role of the nature of pre-merger strategic competition between oligopolistic firms has not been explored. But, since the seminal works of Gabszweicz and Thisse (1979) and Shaked and Sutton (1982), a vast literature has emerged subsequently with one focal point of analysis being how the strategic competition amongst oligopolistic firms – both incumbents and new entrants – influence their choices of product qualities (from the existing set of innovations) or the quality of their new innovations. In light of this, the present chapter focuses on how the pre-merger nature of strategic competition – price competition or quantity

* I thank Tarun Kabiraj for drawing my attention to some of the papers in the literature on merger.

DOI: 10.4324/9781003509721-5

competition – influences the post-merger quality choices. In this context, I also examine the role of costs in two ways. First, for new innovations what matters most is the sunk cost of innovations. Once a product is innovated and developed, the marginal cost of producing the innovated product is usually low and invariant with respect to the scale of production. This is more relevant, for example, for the pharmaceutical industry and the development of new medical drugs. However, for the choice of qualities (or products) from the set of existing innovations, the more relevant is the cost of production that increases with the choice of the quality level itself. So, does this distinction between the natures of costs – sunk development cost versus variable production cost – matter for the post-merger quality level? Note that this issue is essentially asking about what implications a merger has for the quality of new and existing innovations.

Second, I explore the role of cost synergy – both for sunk development cost and marginal production cost – that may be achieved through a merger. In the literature on mergers, Perry and Porter (1985) was the first paper to introduce synergy to study the profitability of a merger. Subsequently, cost-synergy effect is further considered by Chondrakis (2016), Farrell and Shapiro (1990); Davis and Wilson (2008); Devos et al. (2009), Fluck and Lynch (1999), Makri et al. (2010), Rao, Yu, and Umashankar (2016); and, more recently, Feldman and Hernandez (2022), among others. Similar in spirit this paper explores how a cost synergy achieved through merger may influence the choice of post-merger quality of innovations.

Apart from the quality of innovations by a merged firm, another relevant issue is the post-merger market coverage. Does the merger reduce the extent of the market coverage? This is an extremely important issue for mergers in the pharmaceutical industry. If the merger reduces the extent of the market coverage, that is, excludes some low-income buyers, then it actually means that the merger denies poor patients access to newly innovated drugs. If the drug in question is a lifesaving drug for a disease like AIDS or COVID-19, then such denial of market access has far-reaching implications for welfare and well-being. In the context of patent protection and parallel imports, this issue of market access to new innovations of drugs for poor patents has been analyzed by a handful of researchers (see, e.g., Acharyya and Garcia-Alonso 2012, 2014; Danzon 1998, Danzon, Mulcahy, and Towse 2011; Malueg and Schwartz, 1994; Maskus 2000). In light of this, we examine whether the merger lowers the extent of the market coverage and thus denies low-income buyers market access to new and/or existing innovation.

3.1 Existing Literature: What Do We Know From It?

Whereas the existing literature on M&A is huge, examining whether the post-merger qualities of products produced by the merged entity as well as by the other firms in the industry change or not is relatively small. There are two main focuses of this subset of literature. First is the role of the intensity of pre-merger competition. This is captured through the extent to which products were differentiated from each other and whether the firms were operating in the same or different markets. Second is how the spatial dimension of the distribution of heterogeneous consumers influences the post-merger choice of qualities.

To examine the effect of a merger on the quality of service in the aviation industry, Chen and Gayle (2019) consider the role of market operation before the merger. Their theoretical model predicts that a merger between firms that were competing with each other lowers the quality. But, if the merged firms had no pre-merger competition with each other, then the quality improves. Furthermore, in the former case, the relationship between the pre-merger competition intensity – captured through the degree of product differentiation – and the quality change is non-monotonic. To illustrate, Chen and Gayle (2019) assume that the demand functions for the two firms A and B are linear and additively separable in own quality, q_i; price of own product, p_i; and quality-adjusted price of the competing product, $p_j - q_j$:

$$x_i = q_i - p_i + \beta\left[p_j - q_j\right], i = A, B; i \neq j, \tag{3.1}$$

where $\beta \in [0, 1]$ measures the degree of product differentiation and thus the intensity of competition between the two firms. Each firm chooses its product quality and price at the same time, and firms make such decisions simultaneously. Marginal production costs are assumed to be invariant with respect to output levels but increasing in the quality levels chosen by the firms. Firms have the same technology and marginal cost, which, in the pre-merger situation, is given by the following cubic function:

$$c(q_i) = \frac{1}{3}q_i^3, \quad i = A, B. \tag{3.2}$$

Then, under a pre-merger "symmetric" equilibrium, where the competing firms were producing the "same" quality, they solve the price and quality as

$$p^d = \frac{(1-\beta)^2}{(2-\beta)^2}, q^d = \frac{(1-\beta)}{(2-\beta)}. \tag{3.3}$$

Post-merger, the merged firm continues to offer both products. Thus, it chooses prices and qualities to maximize "joint" profit. Under the merger, there is also a cost synergy:

$$c_M(q_M) = \frac{1}{3}\delta q_i^3, \quad i = A, B, \tag{3.4}$$

where δ is the extent of synergy, and Chen and Gayle assume it be in the interval $\left(\frac{1}{2}, 1\right]$.

Again, under *symmetric* equilibrium, the optimal choices are given as

$$p^M = \frac{1-\beta}{4\delta}, q^M = \frac{1-\beta}{2\delta}. \tag{3.5}$$

An inspection of (3.3) and (3.5) reveals that $q^M > q^d$ only if $\beta < 2(1 - \delta)$. Thus, the merger will improve quality only if the degree of product substitutability, and consequently, the intensity of pre-merger competition between the two firms (which have now merged) is small. Note that the critical value of the product differentiation varies positively with the extent of cost synergy achieved through merger, $1/\delta$. At the extreme, if there is no cost synergy, that is, $\delta = 1$, then post-merger quality will be lower. These rankings of pre- and post-merger qualities are shown in Figure 3.1.

Hence, for post-merger quality to be higher there must be some degree of cost synergy that is achieved through a merger. Otherwise, if there is no cost synergy that can be achieved through a merger, a merger will degrade the product quality no matter how differentiated the products of the two firms were before the merger, and what Chen and Gayle (2019) take as an indicator of the intensity of competition between them. The typical sources of synergies are combined capital stock or productive capacity of merged firms; and complementarity of their assets. There may also be financial synergies. The different types of synergies – cost synergy being among those – that can be achieved through M&A are discussed in a recent paper by Feldman and Hernandez (2022). They provide a typology of five distinct sources of synergy and show that the total value created by M&A as the sum of each of the synergy types, their co-synergies, and their dis-synergies. However, the foremost paper to talk about synergies making a merger profitable is Perry and Porter (1985). If the merged firm has access to the combined productive capacity or capital stock, it reduces the cost of production for the merged firm and makes it profitable. The cost-synergy effect is further explained by Farrell and Shapiro (1990), and they argue that unless there is a strong

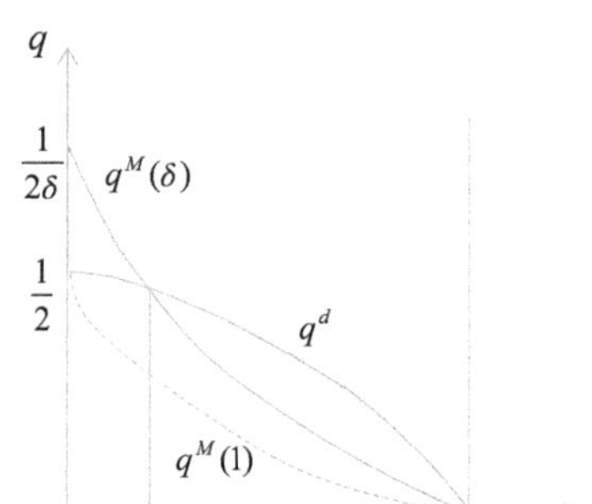

Figure 3.1 Product Differentiation, Cost Synergy, and Post-Merger Quality.

Source: Author.

countervailing synergy effect, the market-power effect of a merger leads to lower industry output and necessarily a lower consumer surplus.

Chen and Gayle (2019) empirically test their theoretical result by studying two recent airline mergers: Delta and Northwest; and Continental and United Airlines. In each case, the merging firms produce in multiple markets. Moreover, the firms did not operate simultaneously in all such markets before the mergers. They take *routing quality* as a specific measure of air travel product quality, which is measured by the ratio of nonstop flight distance to the product's itinerary flight distance for a particular origin-destination combination. Since travel by some airlines for some origin–destination combinations require intermediate airport stop(s) that are not on a straight path between the origin and the destination, this ratio is strictly less than 1 and reflects routing quality as long as passengers are most convenience if they can reach their destinations by the shortest route and with least or no stopovers. Based on this estimate of airline quality, estimates by Chen and Gayle (2019) suggest that each merger increases routing quality only in markets where the merging firms did not compete with each other prior to the merger. Moreover, the increase in quality is larger for the Continental and United Airlines merger, although exhibiting a U-shaped relationship with the two firms' pre-merger competition intensity between Continental and United Airlines. There are a few more recent studies in the airline industry that examine the effect of mergers on product quality. For example, Prince and Simon (2017) find that airline mergers have minimal negative impacts on quality. Rupp and Tan (2019), by comparison, find that the post-merger product quality is higher through a de-hubbing effect of the merger, which emerges when an airline chooses to stop operating at a particular airport as a hub in their route network structure.[2]

An earlier analysis by Brekke et al. (2017) examined the effect of a two-firm merger in a three-firm industry on the qualities provided by both the merged firms and the outside (or non-merged) firm, as well as on prices and welfare. Their analysis is couched in a horizontal differentiation framework similar to Economides (1993) and Ma and Burgess (1993). The three-firm framework enables them to analyze the role of post-merger competition between the merged firms and the non-merged firm. However, Brekke et al. (2017) consider spatial competition between firms that differ from each other in terms of their (exogenously given) locations. This spatial dimension may reflect the extent to which their products are horizontally differentiated, or geographical distance between firms. The consumers also differ in terms of the same spatial dimension: their locations along the circumference of a circular city represent their heterogeneous preferences. Each consumer is assumed to buy only one unit of the good from the most preferred firm depending on the price and quality offered by each firm and their distance from the consumer. The net utility of a consumer located at z and buying the good from firm i, located at x_i, is given by

$$u(z, q_i, p_i, x_i) = v + bq_i - p_i - t(z - x_i)^2, \tag{3.6}$$

where q_i and p_i are the quality offered and the price charged, respectively, by firm i; $b > 0$ is the marginal utility of quality; and $t > 0$ is a transportation cost parameter.

Brekke et al. assume both variable and fixed costs of quality provision and the marginal cost of output rising in quality:

$$C_i = cq_iD_i + \frac{k}{2}q_i^2 + F_i, 0 < c\langle b,k\rangle 0, \tag{3.7}$$

where D_i is the total demand for ith firm's product with quality q_i.

Like Chen and Gayle (2019), Brekke et al. (2017) also consider that each firm chooses price and quality simultaneously. At the Nash equilibrium, the qualities of the three firms in the pre-merger situation are gross strategic complements: $\frac{\partial q_i}{\partial q_j} > 0$. If firm i raises its quality, then ceteris paribus, demand for the product from firm j falls. This lowers the marginal cost of quality provision (see the first term on the right-hand side in [3.7]) and thereby induces firm j to raise the quality of its product. Note that if there had been no variable cost of production (i.e., $c = 0$), then qualities would have been independent of each other. However, when optimal price adjustments are taken into account, the qualities turn out to be (net) strategic substitutes. At the *symmetric* Nash equilibrium, qualities and prices depend on the demand parameter (or the marginal utility of quality), b, and the cost parameters, t, c, and k:

$$q^d = \frac{b-c}{3k},\ p^d = \frac{t}{9} + \frac{c(b-c)}{3k}. \tag{3.8}$$

After a merger between two firms, say, Firms 1 and 2, the outside Firm 3 chooses its quality and price by maximizing its profits, whereas the merged firms choose quality and price for each of their products by maximizing their joint profits. In the post-merger Nash equilibrium, the qualities and prices of the merged firms are the same, whereas those of the outside firm are different:

$$\begin{aligned} q_1^M = q_2^M &= \frac{(b-c)\left[5kt - 9(b-c)^2\right]}{9k\left[2kt - 3(b-c)^2\right]}, p_1^M \\ = p_2^M &= \frac{\left[2kt + 3c(b-c)\right]\left[5kt - 9(b-c)^2\right]}{27k\left[2kt - 3(b-c)^2\right]} \end{aligned} \tag{3.9}$$

$$q_3^M = \frac{(b-c)\left[8kt - 9(b-c)^2\right]}{9k\left[2kt - 3(b-c)^2\right]}, p_3^M = \frac{\left[kt + 3c(b-c)\right]\left[8kt - 9(b-c)^2\right]}{27k\left[2kt - 3(b-c)^2\right]}. \tag{3.10}$$

By comparing pre- and post-merger profits that Firms 1 and 2 get by offering qualities and charging prices as in (3.8) and (3.9), Brekke et al. (2017) observe that merger is profitable only for some high values of the transport cost parameter:

$$t > \frac{9(b-c)^2}{4k}. \tag{3.11}$$

From (3.8), (3.9), and (3.10), it can be checked that the merged firms lower their qualities, though the outside firm raises its quality. Brekke et al. (2017) also show that the outside firm gains more from the merger than the merged firms. This is known as the merger paradox in the standard literature on horizontal mergers. However, the effect of a merger on prices is ambiguous, and so is the effect on welfare.

In contrast to these two papers examining how a merger affects product-quality choices by firms in a horizontally differentiated market, Johnson and Rhodes (2021) consider a vertically differentiated market. Their focus is on the product mix and average quality that a merger results in. Consumers differ in how much they value quality and accordingly in their marginal willingness to pay (MWP) for a low-quality product and a high-quality product (denoted by 1 and 2, respectively) that are available given the state of technology or existing innovations. Each consumer buys, if at all, only one unit of the product – high quality or low quality – that gives them a higher non-negative net utility. There are infinite numbers of firms, each choosing output levels for each of the two products. Firms make such decisions simultaneously, that is, are Cournot players, and any firm *i may not offer both products at equilibrium.* Marginal costs are constant, which differ across firms and products: $c_2^i > c_1^i \geq 0$. Two or more firms merge together, and such a merger may or may not exhibit cost synergies. Let $c_2^M > c_1^M \geq 0$ be the constant marginal costs of the merged firm. Johnson and Rhodes (2021) then define cost synergy arising when both these marginal costs are lower than the marginal costs of the most efficient firm among the merged firms. But if the marginal costs of the merged firm and the most efficient firm are the same, then the merger exhibits no synergy. Following Johnson and Myatt (2003, 2006) and Anderson and Celik (2015), Johnson and Rhodes (2021) take an upgrades approach, by which they derive the price that the marginal consumer would pay to upgrade from low to high quality instead of deriving directly the price of the high-quality good. And this upgrade price depends on the type of consumer who is indifferent between buying low-quality and the high-quality product.

Johnson and Rhodes (2021) demonstrate that firms may reposition their product lines by adding or removing products of different qualities following a merger. Thus, a merger may change the equilibrium mix of products that are consumed. This is the product-mix effect of a merger. Under no synergies, the product-mix effect will be favorable, that is, aggregate (or, industry) output of high-quality products will increase if before the merger some firms in the industry were selling only high-quality products, and only some merging firms were selling low-quality products. Such a favorable product-mix effect raises the consumer surplus. They also consider how merger-induced cost synergies influence market outcomes. In some cases, synergies induce unfavorable product-mix effects and lower consumer surplus, such as in the case of a cost synergy that reduces a merged multiproduct firm's cost of low quality.

While all these analyses reviewed above shed light on how a horizontal merger affects product (or service) quality in the industry and improves our understanding of the related dimensions, they do not take into account the *nature* (not just intensity) of pre-merger strategic competition in a sequential decision-making and, most importantly, the distinction between merger affecting choices from existing innovations (and thus, from the existing set of qualities) and merger leading to new quality/product innovations. The nature of the cost of quality with its far-reaching implications (as partly evident from the analyses reviewed earlier) is also related to the latter dimension. The existing vast literature on qualities offered by monopoly and oligopoly firms emphasizes these aspects quite elaborately. Drawing from such analyses, in the next section, I explore how these two dimensions – nature of pre-merger competition, Cournot versus Bertrand, and nature of costs, sunk cost of new innovations versus variable production costs of existing innovations – update our knowledge regarding how a merger affects product quality. Furthermore, following the literature on endogenous market coverage (Wauthy, 1996), I do not impose any ex ante restriction regarding the extent of the market coverage at the pre- and post-merger equilibrium. This enables me to examine whether a merger allows market access for low-type or low-income buyers who could not buy the good earlier or pushes out of the market some of the low-income buyers who were buying the good earlier. This issue of market access, which has got almost no attention in the literature on mergers and product quality, is important in itself in the pharmaceutical and health care markets (see, Acharyya, 2013; Acharyya & Garcia-Alonso, 2008; Maskus, 2000).

3.2 Merger in a Vertically Differentiated Market

Similar to Johnson and Rhodes (2021), I also consider competition between firms in a vertically differentiated market with consumers being heterogeneous with respect to their valuations of quality and consequently with respect to their MWP. However, I closely follow Gabszweicz and Thisse (1979), Mussa and Rosen (1978), and Shaked and Sutton (1982). Consider a sequential decision of firms regarding product quality (or the level of innovated quality as the case may be) and price or quantity as the case may be, although at each stage the firms make their decisions simultaneously. This stage game is one of the main points of departure from the three papers discussed earlier and the others referred to. There is another important departure. I do not ex ante restrict the analysis to a symmetric equilibrium as in Chen and Gayle (2019) and Brekke et al. (2017). In the case of an existing set of innovations, the firms offer distinctly different qualities that characterize an asymmetric equilibrium. In the case of innovation of a new product's quality, an asymmetric equilibrium evolves once again as each firm innovates only one quality, which is distinctly different from the other. In contrast, pre-merger asymmetric equilibrium arises in Johnson and Rhodes (2021) primarily because firms have different marginal costs and thus are asymmetric. But, as we will see, the asymmetric equilibrium emerges in our case even when firms have identical costs ex ante. Considering the alternative cases of choice from (continuum of) existing innovations and choice of a new innovation also allow me to examine the role of variable cost in producing an existing innovation vis-à-vis the sunk cost of a new innovation as I elaborate later.

Consider a set of heterogeneous consumers defined by their type α and distributed uniformly over the interval $[0,\bar{\alpha}]$. The type of consumer may reflect either her taste, as in Mussa and Rosen (1978) and Acharyya (1998), or her income level, as in Gabszweicz and Thisse (1979), Shaked and Sutton (1982). Each consumer either buys only one unit of a good X or does not buy this good at all. Her purchase decision depends on the net utility that she derives from the quality of this good, indexed by q, and the price that she pays for it. More precisely, assuming that her reservation utility is zero, she buys the good if her net utility from consuming this good X is non-negative:

$$V(\alpha,q,p)=\alpha q-p\geq 0. \tag{3.12}$$

Note that the tie-breaking rule applied here is that the consumer *buys* the good when they are indifferent between buying and not buying the good, that is, their net utility from consuming the good X of quality q by paying the price is zero. However, between any two qualities, q_1 and q_2, of the good available in the market at prices p_1 and p_2, respectively, the consumer prefers to buy the higher quality of the good, say, q_2, if she derives at least the same net utility from it as she does from the low quality of the good:

$$V(\alpha,q_2,p_2)\geq V(\alpha,q_1,p_1). \tag{3.13}$$

The individual-rationality constraint (3.12) defines the relevant marginal consumers, and consequently, the total market size – consumers who buy the good. The self-selection constraint (3.13), however, indicates the segmentation of the market – consumers who buy quality q_1 offered by Firm 1 paying the price p_1 and those who buy the quality q_2 offered by Firm 2 by paying the price and p_2. More precisely, let $\alpha_1=\frac{p_1}{q_1}$ denote the marginal consumers who are indifferent between buying or not buying good X and $\alpha_2=\frac{p_2-p_1}{q_2-q_1}$ denote

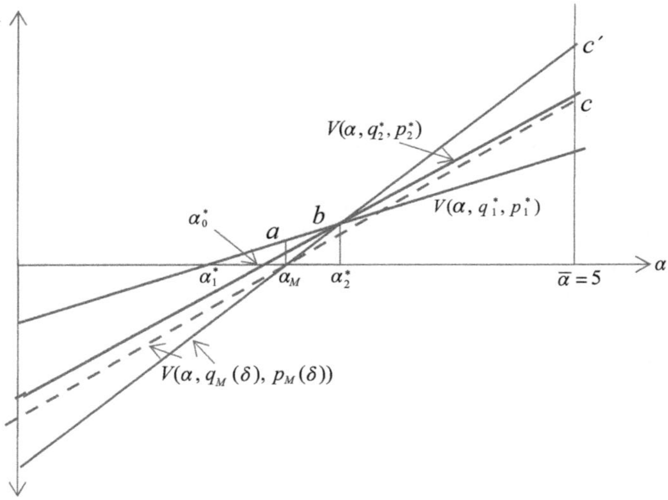

Figure 3.2 Welfare under merger.
Source: Authors.

the consumers who are indifferent between buying the low-quality good and the high-quality good. Thus, the quantity demanded for the low- and high-quality goods are given as

$$D_1 = \int_{\alpha_1}^{\alpha_2} d\alpha = \frac{p_2 - p_1}{q_2 - q1} - \frac{p_1}{q1} \tag{3.14}$$

$$D_1 = \int_{\alpha_2}^{\bar{\alpha}} d\alpha = \bar{\alpha} - \frac{p_2 - p_1}{q_2 - q1}. \tag{3.15}$$

Note that the market is partially covered – that is, all consumers are not served – as long as $\alpha_1 > 0$. Later I focus on this partial coverage at the equilibrium, which will enable me to address whether a merger lowers the extent of the market coverage and thus restricts market access to existing or new innovations for some low-type (or poorer) buyers.

There are two firms 1 and 2 in the market that offer qualities q_1 and q_2, respectively. Following the literature on vertically differentiated markets, I consider two alternative cases regarding these qualities. First, the firms choose q_1 and q_2 from an existing set of innovations, or set of qualities, that can be produced given the present state of technology and knowledge.

I denote such a set of existing innovations by the interval $[0,\bar{q}]$. In this case, the relevant cost that the firms incur is the production costs, and following the standard literature I assume only variable production costs. The marginal cost is invariant with respect to output x_i (which is equal to demand D_i) that a firm i produces but increases with the quality $q_i \in [0,\bar{q}]$ that it chooses. However, to ensure that the choice of a quality by each firm is strictly less than the maximum quality – that is, interior qualities at the sub-game perfect Nash equilibrium (SPNE) – I assume that the marginal cost is convex in quality:[3]

$$C_i = \frac{1}{2} q_i^2 x_i. \tag{3.16}$$

Note that (3.14) indicates that the two firms are ex ante identical. But, as I show later, Firm 1 chooses a quality strictly higher than the lowest one at the SPNE. Hence, the market is partially covered at the equilibrium.

Second scenario that I consider is that firms innovate qualities q_1 and q_2 by incurring sunk research and development (R&D) cost, which is again convex in the level of the new innovated quality:

$$S_i = \frac{1}{2} q_i^2 \tag{3.17}$$

Again, following the standard literature, I assume that once firm i develops the quality q_i, it incurs no further costs whatsoever to produce the good.[4]

In either of these cases of existing innovations (and set of qualities) or new innovations, before the merger, firms simultaneously make their choices about the product qualities prior to simultaneously choosing prices or quantities. That is, I consider a two-stage game in contrast to the existing literature on horizontal merger and quality as reviewed earlier: In the first stage, firms choose qualities, and in the second stage, they choose either prices or quantities. As demonstrated by Motta (1993), whether firms choose prices or quantities (i.e., the nature of competition) in the second stage matters for the extent to which firms differentiate the quality of their products in the first stage. So, it will be interesting to examine whether this has some relevance for the merger decision as well as for post-merger variation in quality.

I consider these two sets of alternatives in the following manner. In the next section, pre-merger choices of qualities from the existing set of innovations $[0,\bar{q}]$ in the first stage are considered, with the second stage being alternatively the price game or the quantity game. In the section thereafter, pre-merger choices of new innovations or qualities are considered, again in the alternative cases of the second stage being either the price game or the quantity game.

3.2.1 Existing Innovations, Merger, and Product Quality

3.2.1.1 Merger between Price-Setting Firms

Without any loss of generality, suppose Firm 1 provides the low-quality of the good and Firm 2 provides the high-quality before their merger. Given the variable production cost specified in (3.16), profits of these competing firms are given as

$$\pi_i = p_i x_i - \frac{1}{2} q_i^2 x_i, i = 1,2 \tag{3.18}$$

Given their quality choices $q_1 < q_2$ from the set $[0, \bar{q}]$ in the first stage, the profits to be realized in the second stage depend on prices that these two firms set. Substitution of (3.14) and (3.15) in (3.18) yields such profits as

$$\pi_1 = \left(p_1 - \frac{1}{2} q_1 \right) \left[\frac{p_2 - p_1}{q_2 - q_1} - \frac{p_1}{q_1} \right] \tag{3.19}$$

$$\pi_2 = \left(p_2 - \frac{1}{2} q_2 \right) \left[\bar{\alpha} - \frac{p_2 - p_1}{q_2 - q_1} \right]. \tag{3.20}$$

I solve the pre-merger quality and price competition between the two firms by backward induction. Thus, given the Nash equilibrium pair of qualities of the first stage, each firm chooses the price to maximize its profit, which is given as

$$p_1(q_1, q_2) = \frac{q_1 \left(q_2^2 + 2q_2\bar{\alpha} - 2q_1\bar{\alpha} + 2q_1q_2 \right)}{2[4q_2 - q_1]} \tag{3.21}$$

$$p_2(q_1, q_2) = \frac{q_2 \left(2q_2^2 - 4q_1\bar{\alpha} + 4q_2\bar{\alpha} + q_1^2 \right)}{2[4q_2 - q_1]}. \tag{3.22}$$

Substitution of these Nash equilibrium pair of prices, for any given $q_i \in [0, \bar{q}]$, in (3.19) and (3.20) yields the profit functions in the first stage as

$$\pi_1(q_1, q_2) = \frac{q_1 q_2 [q_2 - q_1](q_2 - q_1 + 2\bar{\alpha})^2}{4(4q_2 - q_1)^2} \tag{3.23a}$$

$$\pi_2(q_1, q_2) = \frac{q_2^2 [q_2 - q_1](2q_2 + q_1 - 4\bar{\alpha})^2}{4(4q_2 - q_1)^2}. \tag{3.23b}$$

Maximization of profits yields the following best-response functions in the two quality levels:

$$\frac{\partial \pi_1(q_1,q_2)}{\partial q_1} = \frac{q_2(q_2-q_1+2\bar{\alpha})\begin{bmatrix}4q_2^3-19q_1q_2^2+17q_1^2q_2-2q_1^3\\+(8q_2^2-14q_1q_2-8q_1^2)\bar{\alpha}\end{bmatrix}}{4(4q_2-q_1)^3}=0 \qquad (3.24a)$$

$$\frac{\partial \pi_2(q_1,q_2)}{\partial q_2} = \frac{q_2(2q_2+q_1-4\bar{\alpha})\begin{bmatrix}24q_2^3-22q_1q_2^2+5q_1^2q_2+2q_1^3\\-(16q_2^2-12q_1q_2+8q_1^2)\bar{\alpha}\end{bmatrix}}{4(4q_2-q_1)^3}=0. \qquad (3.24b)$$

Solving these we can obtain the Nash equilibrium pair of quality choices. But getting an analytical solution is rather complex without assigning specific numerical values for the highest taste (or income) parameter, $\bar{\alpha}$. However, if a solution exists then the SPNE will be the one where the firms choose distinctively different qualities: $q_1^* < q_2^*$. If the firms choose the same quality, then the subsequent (or second-stage) price competition forces them to charge prices equal to their marginal costs and earn zero profits given that they have ex ante identical costs. Thus, choosing the same qualities $q_1^* = q_2^*$ cannot be a SPNE. The firms will choose qualities far apart from each other and thus produce goods that are *quality*-differentiated so that subsequent price competition does not erode positive super-normal profits. This result was first demonstrated by Shaked and Sutton (1982): quality competition relaxes price competition. Shaked and Sutton (1982), however, assumed the sunk costs of developing qualities, which is more relevant for new innovations as I discuss in a later section. In the present context of variable cost of quality, which is more relevant for choices from an existing set of (quality) innovations, the quality-differentiation result has been formalized in Champsaur and Rochet (1989) and, subsequently, in Motta (1993). Motta (1993), for example, finds a unique pair of qualities for $\bar{\alpha} = 5$:

$$q_1^* = 1.9936, \; q_2^* = 4.0976. \qquad (3.25)$$

In the rest of this section, I confine myself to this specific equilibrium in the pre-merger situation when the firms compete in prices after committing to the qualities of their respective goods.[5]

Thus, we have an asymmetric equilibrium in which the two firms select distinctly different qualities.[6] Also note that the market is partially covered, which is similar in spirit to the argument by Wauthy (1996) and Acharyya (1998) that the extent of market coverage is endogenous. Note that the price that Firm 1 set at the equilibrium can be obtained by substitution of values from (3.25) in (3.21): $p_1 = 3.7503$. Hence, consumers having taste parameters less than $\alpha_1^* = \frac{p_1}{q_1} = 1.8811$ do not participate in the market. This partial-market-coverage result however depends on our lower bound on the consumer type.

Consider now a merger between these two firms. Post-merger, the firm achieves some cost synergy that lowers its variable cost at the rate δ:

$$c_M(q_M) = \frac{1}{2}\delta q_M^3. \tag{3.26}$$

Unlike Chen and Gayle (2019), I assume that $\delta \in (0,1)$.

The merged firm chooses a uniform quality q_M and charges a price p_M that maximizes its profit:

$$\pi_M = \left[p_M - \frac{1}{2}\delta q_M^2\right]\left[\bar{\alpha} - \frac{p_M}{q_M}\right]. \tag{3.27}$$

Note that the uniform quality-price menu defines the marginal consumer $\alpha_M = \frac{p_M}{q_M}$ and, correspondingly, the extent to which the merged firm covers the market and the demand for its product: $\bar{\alpha} - \alpha_M$. It is straightforward to check that such a quality-price menu can be obtained from solving the two first-order conditions $\frac{\partial \pi_M}{\partial q_M} = 0$ and $\frac{\partial \pi_M}{\partial p_M} = 0$ as[7]:

$$q_M^* = \frac{2\bar{\alpha}}{3\delta}, p_M^* = \frac{4\bar{\alpha}^2}{9\delta}. \tag{3.28}$$

To check whether the merger is profitable, first note that substitution of these values in (3.27) yields the profit for the merged firm as

$$\pi_M = \frac{2\bar{\alpha}^3}{27\delta}. \tag{3.29}$$

However, using (3.25), the total profit before the merger can be obtained from (3.23a) and (3.23b) as

$$\pi_1 + \pi_2 = 4.4499. \tag{3.30}$$

Since, $\pi_M = \frac{9.259}{\delta}$ for $\bar{\alpha} = 5$, so merger is profitable for all values of $\delta \in (0, 1]$. Turning now to comparisons of qualities before and after merger, note that $q_M^* = \frac{3.33}{\delta}$ for $\bar{\alpha} = 5$. Hence, the merged firm offers a quality higher than the pre-merger lower quality q_1^* regardless of the cost synergy. But, whether it offers a quality higher than the pre-merger higher quality q_2^* or not depends on the extent of cost synergy. A more precise statement is made in the following proposition:

Proposition 1

For $\bar{\alpha} = 5$, and firms first choosing qualities first and then prices in the pre-merger scenario, $q_M^* > q_2^*$ if $\delta < 0.8126$. Otherwise, $q_2^* > q_M^* > q_1^*$.

Proof: Follows from $q_M^* = \frac{3.33}{\delta}$ for $\bar{\alpha} = 5$, and the pre-merger quality levels under the second-stage price competition given in (3.25).

Therefore, even if the merged firm degrades its quality relative to q_2^*, it does not degrade the quality too much.

However, since $\alpha_M = 3.33 > 1.8811$, the merged firm restricts access to the product significantly. This has a far-reaching implication in the context of a merger in the pharmaceutical industry and access for poor patients to lifesaving drugs. Note that the extent of market coverage is invariant with respect to the degree of cost synergy.

Gains and losses for the consumers who still have the market access and can buy the good of quality $q_M^* = \frac{3.33}{\delta}$ at price $p_M^* = \frac{11.11}{\delta}$ are illustrated in Figure 3.2. The flatter bold line reflects net utility $V\left(\alpha, q_1^*, p_1^*\right)$ for all consumers when they consume the menu $\left(q_1^*, p_1^*\right)$ offered by Firm 1. It has a positive slope equal to q_1^* and a negative vertical intercept $\left(-p_1^*\right)$. The steeper bold line reflects net utility $V\left(\alpha, q_2^*, p_2^*\right)$ for all consumers when they consume the menu $\left(q_2^*, p_2^*\right)$ offered by Firm 2, which has a larger (negative) vertical intercept. $\alpha_1^* = 1.8811$ is the type of marginal consumers who are indifferent about buying and not buying the good of either quality, and $\alpha_2^* = 3.59$ is the type of marginal consumers indifferent between buying the low-quality and buying the high-quality. Thus, by the individual-rationality and self-selection constraints (3.12) and (3.13), before the merger, the consumers of lowest types $\alpha \in [0, 1.8811)$ could not participate in the market; consumers of types $\alpha \in [1.8811, 3.59)$ bought the low-quality good from Firm 1, and rest of the consumers of types $\alpha \in [3.59, 5)$ bought the high-quality good from Firm 2. However, the slope and the vertical intercept of the net utility curve under merger $V(\alpha, q_M(\delta), p_M(\delta))$ – given by $q_M = \frac{3.33}{\delta}$ and negative of $p_M = \frac{11.11}{\delta}$ respectively – depend on the extent of cost synergy $\delta \in (0, 1]$. For example, since quality is degraded when there is no cost synergy achieved through merger, $q_2^* > q_M^* = 3.33$, but the price is higher, $p_2^* < p_M$, so the $V(\alpha, q_M(\delta), p_M(\delta))$ curve will lie below $V\left(\alpha, q_2^*, p_2^*\right)$ for all consumer types and also will be flatter than $V\left(\alpha, q_2^*, p_2^*\right)$. For lower value of δ, $V(\alpha, q_M, p_M)$ gets steeper and shifts up. However, since the type of consumers who derive zero net utility and thus are indifferent between buying and not buying the good after merger is given by $\alpha_M = 3.33$, so the $V(\alpha, q_M(\delta), p_M(\delta))$ curve cuts the horizontal axis at such value of α regardless of the value of δ. Now, it can be checked that for $\delta = 0.6032$, $V(\alpha, q_M(\delta), p_M(\delta))$ curve crosses over $V\left(\alpha, q_2^*, p_2^*\right)$ -curve at $\bar{\alpha} = 5$. Thus, the highest type of consumers are indifferent. Everyone else loses. Consumers of types $\alpha \in [1.8811, 3.33)$ lose because they *now* do not have market access. Consumers of types $\alpha \in [3.33, 3.59)$ who were buying the low quality before the merger, as well as consumers of types $\alpha \in [3.59, 5)$ who were buying the high quality before the merger now lose even though the quality of the merged firm is higher. The relatively low types lose because they value higher quality less, and thus, their utility gain is less from it than their utility loss from paying a higher price. For the higher types, even though they value higher quality more, the quality offered by the merged firm is not sufficiently high to compensate for their losses from paying a higher price. For even smaller value of δ (than 0.6032), $V(\alpha, q_M(\delta), p_M(\delta))$ curve crosses over $V\left(\alpha, q_2^*, p_2^*\right)$ -curve for $\alpha < \bar{\alpha} = 5$ so that some very high-type consumers – to the right of the crossover – now gain more from the higher quality than they lose from paying the higher price. More precisely, such consumers are the ones who are of types higher than the marginal consumer α^* who derives the same net utility before and after mergers: $V\left(\alpha, q_M(\delta), p_M(\delta)\right) = V\left(\alpha, q_2^*, p_2^*\right)$. Given the quasi-linear forms of net utility functions and the values of qualities and prices, the value of α^* is given as

$$\alpha^* = \frac{p_2^* - p_M}{q_2^* - q_M} = \frac{11.30434\delta - 11.11}{4.0976\delta - 3.33}.$$

Note that the lower the value of δ, the lower the type these marginal consumers α^* who derive the same net utility by consuming $\left(q_2^*, p_2^*\right)$ before the merger and $\left(q_M^*, p_M^*\right)$ after the merger and that such consumers exist – that is, $\alpha^* < \bar{\alpha} = 5$ – for $\delta < 0.6032$. Equating α^* with $\alpha_2^* = 3.59$ gives us the critical level of cost synergy, $\delta^* = 0.2466$, for which all high-type consumers who were buying $\left(q_2^*, p_2^*\right)$ before the merger gain from consuming $\left(q_M^*, p_M^*\right)$ after the merger. All low-type consumers still lose after merger for reasons spelled out earlier. By similar logic, it follows that an even higher cost synergy, $\alpha^* < \alpha_2^*$, which, although is inconsequential for the post-merger gains for the high-type consumers who were buying $\left(q_2^*, p_2^*\right)$ before the merger, brings in gains for *some* of the low-type consumers who were buying the menu $\left(q_1^*, p_1^*\right)$ before the merger. In terms of Figure 3.2, the $V(\alpha, q_M(\delta), p_M(\delta))$ curve crosses over $V\left(\alpha, q_1^*, p_1^*\right)$ -curve for $\tilde{\alpha} \in \left(\alpha_M^*, \alpha_2^*\right]$. Algebraically, $\tilde{\alpha}$ is such that $V\left(\tilde{\alpha}, q_M(\delta), p_M(\delta)\right) = V\left(\tilde{\alpha}, q_1^*, p_1^*\right)$, and given the properties of these net utility functions, $\tilde{\alpha}$ is increasing in δ.

All these can be summarized in the following proposition:

Proposition 2

For $\bar{\alpha} = 5$, and firms first choosing qualities and then prices in the pre-merger scenario,

a. the merged firm restricts market access by pricing out some of the low-type consumers $\alpha \in \left[\alpha_1^*, \alpha_M\right)$, where the limiting values are as defined earlier;
b. gains (and losses) of other consumers who can still buy the good depends on the value of δ as follows: (i) everyone loses for all $\delta > 0.6032$; (ii) for $\delta \in (0.2466, 0.6032)$, some high-type consumers with type higher than $\alpha^* \in \left(\alpha_2^*, \bar{\alpha}\right)$ among those who were buying $\left(q_2^*, p_2^*\right)$ before merger gain from merger, whereas all low-type consumers who were buying $\left(q_1^*, p_1^*\right)$ before the merger lose; (iii) for $\delta \in (0, 0.2466)$, all high-type consumers and $\alpha \in \left(\tilde{\alpha}, \alpha_2^*\right)$ types among low-type consumers gain from the merger, whereas everyone else lose.

Proof: Follows from the previous discussion.

Referring back to Figure 3.2, the magnitudes of gains and losses are measured by the area between $V(\alpha, q_M(\delta), p_M(\delta))$ curve and the $V\left(\alpha, q_1^*, p_1^*\right)$ curve or $V\left(\alpha, q_2^*, p_2^*\right)$ -curve for the relevant range of consumer types. For example, for the level of cost synergy for which the $V(\alpha, q_M(\delta), p_M(\delta))$ curve passes through point b, the total post-merger gain for (all) consumers who were buying $\left(q_2^*, p_2^*\right)$ before the merger is given by the area *bc′c*; the total post-merger loss (all) consumers who were buying $\left(q_1^*, p_1^*\right)$ before the merger is given by the area $\alpha_1^* b \alpha_M$, of which area $\alpha_1^* a \alpha_M$ is the post-merger loss for those who cannot access the product under the merger and area $\alpha_M ab$ is the post-merger loss for those low-type buyers who can still buy the good. The overall gains or losses from the merger are thus ambiguous. However, if the good in question is a lifesaving drug to combat AIDS or a vaccine to immunize against the COVID-19 virus, then restricted market access for low-type or low-income patients is a far more serious problem than a smaller net surplus for others who can still access the drug or the vaccine.

3.2.1.2 Merger between quantity-setting firms

When the firms compete in quantities rather than in prices after choosing qualities before the merger, the second-stage Nash equilibrium choice of quantities are given as (see Motta, 1993)

$$x_1(q_1, q_2) = \frac{q_2^2 - 2q_1q_2 + 2q\bar{\alpha}_2}{8q_2 - 2q_1} \tag{3.31a}$$

$$x_2(q_1, q_2) = \frac{q_1^2 - 2q_2^2 + 4q_2\bar{\alpha} - 2q\bar{\alpha}_1}{8q_2 - 2q_1}. \tag{3.31b}$$

Using these output levels, the qualities in the first-stage game, denoted by $q_i^C, i = 1,2$, can be obtained for $\bar{\alpha} = 5$ as

$$q_1^C = 2.9278, q_2^C = 3.6904. \tag{3.32}$$

Thus, once again we have an asymmetric equilibrium in which the firms choose distinctively different qualities. However, comparing (3.25) and (3.32), it immediately follows that the two firms offer less quality-differentiated products when they compete in quantities than in prices in the second stage. This is not surprising since when less differentiated products are offered, the intensity of competition is greater and, consequently, profits are lower in the latter case than in the former. Thus, firms have larger incentives to quality-differentiate their products from each other under subsequent price competition than under subsequent quantity competition. Given the quality choices (3.32), the total profit of the two firms is given as

$$\pi_1^C + \pi_2^C = 8.7749. \tag{3.33}$$

When the firms merge, the merged firm chooses the same price and quality as specified in (3.28) with the realized profit as given in (3.29). Thus, again the merger is profitable regardless of the cost synergy. However, a similar result as in Proposition 1 holds. However, since $q_2^C < q_2^*$, so the merged firm will offer higher quality than the pre-merger qualities even for a smaller cost synergy (i.e., even for a higher value of δ) achieved through a merger. A more precise statement is made in Proposition 3:

Proposition 3

For $\bar{\alpha} = 5$, and firms first choosing qualities and then quantities in the pre-merger scenario, $q_M > q_2^*$ if $\delta < 0.9024$. Otherwise, $q_2^* > q_M > q_1^*$.

Proof: Follows from $q_M = \frac{3.33}{\delta}$ for $\bar{\alpha} = 5$, and the pre-merger quality levels under the second-stage quantity competition given in (3.32).

To check the market access, note that the following prices are charged by the two firms before the merger:

$$p_1^C = 7.8743, p_2^C = 10.857. \tag{3.34}$$

Thus, consumers lower than the type $\alpha_1^C = 2.6895$ could not access the good before the merger. Since post-merger, consumers who can just buy the good are the type $\alpha_M = 3.33$, so again the merged firm restricts access to the product though to a lesser extent than when the firms were competing in prices before the merger. This result that a smaller number of buyers are now denied market access by the merged firm compared to the previous case is due to the fact that under quantity competition before the merger, the firms serve a smaller number of buyers than when they compete in prices ($\alpha_1^* < \alpha_1^C$). Hence, the further reduction of market coverage under the merger now is less.

Gains and losses for other consumers depends on the extent of cost synergy similar to what I have spelled out in the case of price competition and illustrated in Figure 3.2. In particular, following similar logic, it is straightforward to derive the critical values as stated in Proposition 4:

Proposition 4

For $\bar{\alpha} = 5$, and firms first choosing qualities and then quantities in the pre-merger scenario,

a. the merged firm restricts market access by pricing out some of the low-type consumers $\alpha \in \left[\alpha_1^C, \alpha_M\right)$, where the limiting values are as defined earlier;
b. gains (and losses) of other consumers who can still buy the good depends on the value of δ as follows: (i) everyone loses for all for $\delta > 0.9024$; (ii) for $\delta \in (0.534, 0.9024)$, some high-type consumers with type higher than $\alpha^* \in \left(\alpha_2^C, \bar{\alpha}\right)$ among those who were buying $\left(q_2^*, p_2^*\right)$ before the merger gain from the merger, whereas all low-type consumers who were buying $\left(q_1^*, p_1^*\right)$ before the merger lose; (iii) for $\delta \in (0, 0.534)$, all high-type consumers and $\alpha \in \left(\tilde{\alpha}, \alpha_2^C\right)$ types among low-type consumers gain from the merger, whereas everyone else loses.

However, again the cause of concern may be restricted market access for some poorer patients under the merger between pharmaceutical firms.

3.2.2 Merger and New Innovations

Consider now the case of new innovations. Suppose that, in the pre-merger situation, two firms independently and simultaneously develop qualities by incurring the R&D cost specified in (3.17). After developing the qualities, they produce the good without incurring any other cost. Once again, the second-stage competition between these two firms is modeled alternatively as the price competition or quantity competition. Note that during the second stage, the quality development cost becomes sunk. Before considering these alternative second-stage games, it is worthwhile to mention that due to the

R&D cost increasing at an increasing rate with the target level of new innovation, each firm will target only one innovation. In fact, even when a firm is the sole provider of the good, and thus does not face any competition in the market whatsoever either from any other incumbent firms or from any potential entrant, it will still innovate only one quality and offer a pooling menu despite consumer heterogeneity generating scope for quality discrimination. This is unlike the case of existing innovations and variable costs of producing qualities in which a monopolist may offer separating menus (the case of quality discrimination). See Acharyya (2013) for details.

3.2.2.1 Merger between Price-Setting Firms

Given the sunk R&D cost, the profits of these competing firms are given as

$$\pi_i = p_i x_i - \frac{1}{2} q_i^2 \ , i = 1,2. \tag{3.35}$$

To solve the two-stage game by backward induction, note that in the second stage with the R&D costs becoming sunk since qualities have been already innovated or developed and with no variable cost of quality by assumption, firms maximize revenues $R_i = p_i x_i$, $i = 1, 2$:

$$R_1 = \left[\frac{p_2 - p_1}{q_2 - q1} - \frac{p_1}{q1}\right] p_1 \tag{3.36}$$

$$R_2 = \left[\bar{\alpha} - \frac{p_2 - p_1}{q_2 - q1}\right] p_2. \tag{3.37}$$

Given the Nash equilibrium pair of qualities of the first stage, the profit-maximizing choice of prices is given as

$$p_1(q_1, q_2) = \frac{q_1(q_2 - q_1)\bar{\alpha}}{4q_2 - q_1} \tag{3.38a}$$

$$p_2(q_1, q_2) = \frac{2q_2(q_2 - q_1)\bar{\alpha}}{4q_2 - q_1}. \tag{3.38b}$$

Given these prices contingent upon qualities developed in the first stage, the subgame perfect innovation levels by maximizing profits specified in (3.35) are given as (Motta, 1993)

$$\tilde{q}_1 = 0.0482\bar{\alpha}^2, \tilde{q}_2 = 0.2533\bar{\alpha}^2. \tag{3.39}$$

Again, an asymmetric equilibrium with the innovated qualities being distinctively different is obtained, which is not surprising for reasons explained earlier. Prices charged and profits realized at the sub-game perfect equilibrium are given as:

$$\tilde{p}_1 = 0.0102\bar{\alpha}^3,\ \tilde{p}_2 = 0.1076\bar{\alpha}^3 \tag{3.40}$$

$$\pi_1 + \pi_2 = 0.02612\bar{\alpha}^4 \tag{3.41}$$

Before I move to the case of a merger, it is interesting to observe that for $\bar{\alpha} = 5$, the innovated qualities under sunk R&D cost are smaller than qualities chosen from existing set of the innovations under the variable cost of quality: $\tilde{q}_1 = 0.241 < q_1^*$, $\tilde{q}_2 = 1.2665 < q_2^*$. The extent of quality differentiation is also smaller: $(\tilde{q}_2 - \tilde{q}_1) < (q_2^* - q_1^*)$. This brings out the role of sunk versus variable costs of quality.

Now consider the merger between these two firms. The merged entity has two options: It can continue to offer either both the qualities innovated by the firms before the merger at the prices given in (3.40) or only the higher quality $\tilde{q}_2 x$ at a price that maximizes its profit. Note that for both these options, there will be no additional costs that the merged firm has to incur and thus the case of cost synergy does not arise. Of course, there is a third option, which is to undertake a new innovation by incurring a sunk R&D cost. Before considering this, let me examine which of the first two options will be more profitable for the merged firm. In either case, what matters is the total revenue earned. When the merged firm continues to offer the pre-merger menus $\{(\tilde{q}_1, \tilde{p}_1), (\tilde{q}_2, \tilde{p}_2)\}$, the total revenue that it earns is what the two firms earned in the pre-merger scenario. The substitution of (3.38a) and (3.38b) into (3.36) and (3.37) gives such a total revenue as

$$\begin{aligned} R_M(\tilde{q}_1, \tilde{q}_2) &= R_1(\tilde{q}_1, \tilde{q}_2) + R_2(\tilde{q}_1, \tilde{q}_2) \\ &= \frac{\tilde{q}_2(\tilde{q}_2 - \tilde{q}_1)(4\tilde{q}_2 + \tilde{q}_1)\bar{\alpha}^2}{(4\tilde{q}_2 - \tilde{q}_1)^2} = 0.05920\bar{\alpha}^4. \end{aligned} \tag{3.42}$$

However, if only the high-quality $\tilde{q}_2$ is offered by the merged firm, it chooses a price $p_M(\tilde{q}_2)$ that maximizes its revenue. Note that the marginal consumers $\alpha_M(\tilde{q}_2) = \frac{p_M(\tilde{q}_2)}{\tilde{q}_2}$ indifferent between buying this menu $\{\tilde{q}_2, p_M(\tilde{q}_2)\}$ and not buying define the demand for the merged firm: $x_M = \bar{\alpha} - \frac{p_M(\tilde{q}_2)}{\tilde{q}_2}$. The revenue-maximizing price is then given as

$$p_M(\tilde{q}_2) = \frac{\bar{\alpha}}{2}\tilde{q}_2 = 0.12665\bar{\alpha}^3. \tag{3.43}$$

Note that the merged firm charges a higher price than Firm 2 in the pre-merger case. Moreover, the corresponding revenue is large than what the merged firm can get from offering both qualities. This result is summarized in Lemma 1:

Lemma 1

When the firms that were competing in prices decide to merge their operations, then merged firm will offer the pre-merger high-quality $\tilde{q}_2$ at the price $p_M(\tilde{q}_2) = 0.12665\bar{\alpha}^3$ instead of offering both qualities $(\tilde{q}_1, \tilde{q}_2)$.

Proof: Note that $R_M(\tilde{q}_2) = \left[\bar{\alpha} - \frac{p_M(\tilde{q}_2)}{\tilde{q}_2}\right] p_M(\tilde{q}_2) = 0.0633\bar{\alpha}^4$. So, from (3.42), it follows that $R_M(\tilde{q}_2) > R_M(\tilde{q}_1, \tilde{q}_2)$.

Consider now the other option for the merged firm: innovate a different quality $\tilde{q}_M$. Suppose cost synergy is realized through lower R&D cost:

$$S_M = \frac{\delta}{2} q_M^2 \tag{3.44}$$

It can be easily checked that the merged firm will innovate a quality and will earn profit as

$$\tilde{q}_M = \frac{0.25\bar{\alpha}^2}{\delta}, \pi_M(\tilde{q}_M) = \frac{0.03125\bar{\alpha}^4}{\delta}. \tag{3.45}$$

Thus, both the level of new innovation and the profit increase with the degree of cost synergy achieved through the merger. But the extent of market coverage does not depend on such synergy:

$$\alpha_M(\tilde{q}_M) = 0.5\bar{\alpha}. \tag{3.46}$$

Comparing values in (3.43) with $\tilde{q}_2$ in (3.38) and $R_M(\tilde{q}_2) = 0.0633\bar{\alpha}^4$, it follows that

$$\tilde{q}_M > \tilde{q}_2 \forall \delta \langle 0.9869, \pi_M(\tilde{q}_M) \rangle R_M(\tilde{q}_2) \forall \delta < 0.4936. \tag{3.47}$$

All these results are summarized in the following proposition:

Proposition 5

When the firms compete in prices before the merger, and the cost synergy achieved by the merged firm is very high in the sense that $\delta < 0.4936$, then through a new innovation it offers a higher quality. Otherwise, it does not undertake a new innovation and offers the higher of the two pre-merger qualities. In either case, the merged firm lowers the market access.

Proof: Follows from the earlier discussion and Lemma 1.

So, unlike the case of choice from existing innovations and corresponding variable costs, the merged firm does not degrade the quality. Note that Proposition 5 also tells us that the merger is profitable. Suppose that the two firms were already operating in the market in period t and earned profits $\tilde{\pi}_1$ and $\tilde{\pi}_1$, given their innovation levels as specified in (3.39). In the next period, suppose, they decide whether to merge their operations or not. If they decide to merge, then either they continue to produce the good of higher quality $\tilde{q}_2$ – selling it at a price $p_M(\tilde{q}_2)$ – and get $R_M(\tilde{q}_2)$ by Lemma 1, or they make a new innovation $\tilde{q}_M$ and earn $\pi_M(\tilde{q}_M)$ as in (3.45). However, if the firms decide not to merge with each other and continue to offer their existing innovations at the (SPNE) prices they charged in the previous period, $\{(\tilde{q}_1, \tilde{p}_1), (\tilde{q}_2, \tilde{p}_2)\}$, then they together earn $R_1(\tilde{q}_1, \tilde{q}_2) + R_2(\tilde{q}_1, \tilde{q}_2)$. Hence, by Proposition 3, the merger is profitable for both the incumbent firms. Later, I consider the decision about the merger when the two firms are not incumbent firms already operating in a market or, alternatively, the decision about a merger between two potential entrants in a new market.

3.2.2.2 Merger between Quantity-Setting Firms

If in the pre-merger scenario, the two firms compete in quantities in the second stage, then given the Nash equilibrium pair of qualities of the first stage, the sub-game perfect innovation levels are given as (Motta, 1993)

$$\tilde{q}_1^C = 0.0902\overline{\alpha}^2, \tilde{q}_2^C = 0.2519\overline{\alpha}^2. \tag{3.48}$$

Two comments are warranted at this point. First, as in the case of choice from existing innovations, firms offer less quality-differentiated products through new innovations when they compete in quantities rather than in prices in the second stage. This follows from comparing (3.39) and (3.48). Second, quality distortion at the top, $\tilde{q}_2^C < \tilde{q}_2$, is marginal. This has some far-reaching implications for the merger decision, as can be seen later.

The prices charged by the two firms and their total profit are given as

$$\tilde{p}_1^C = 0.0247\overline{\alpha}^3, \tilde{p}_2^C = 0.1135\overline{\alpha}^3 \tag{3.49}$$

$$\tilde{\pi}_1^C + \tilde{\pi}_2^C = 0.1015\overline{\alpha}^4. \tag{3.50}$$

Again, after the merger, if the merged firm continues to offer the pre-merger menus $\{(\tilde{q}_1^C, \tilde{p}_1^C), (\tilde{q}_2^C, \tilde{p}_2^C)\}$, the total revenue earned by it equals

$$R_M(\tilde{q}_1^C, \tilde{q}_2^C) = R_1(\tilde{q}_1^C, \tilde{q}_2^C) + R_2(\tilde{q}_1^C, \tilde{q}_2^C) = 0.05799\bar{\alpha}^4. \tag{3.51a}$$

By comparison, if only the high quality $\tilde{q}_2^C$ is offered by the merged firm at a revenue-maximizing price $p_M(\tilde{q}_2^C)$, the revenue it earns is given as

$$R_M(\tilde{q}_2^C) = 0.06298\bar{\alpha}^4. \tag{3.51b}$$

Hence,

Lemma 2

When the firms that were competing in quantities decide to merge their operations, then the merged firm will offer the pre-merger high-quality $\tilde{q}_2^C$ instead of offering both the qualities $(\tilde{q}_1^C, \tilde{q}_2^C)$.

Proof: Follows by comparing (3.51a) and (3.51b).

However, comparing (3.51b) with (3.43), it follows that the merged firm will undertake a new innovation only if $\delta < 0.4961$. Note that this critical value of cost synergy for which the merged firm innovates a new quality is almost the same as in the case of price competition. This is not surprising since under Cournot competition in the second-stage game before the merger, the high-quality firm innovates almost the same (high) quality as it would under the second-stage price competition. Therefore,

Proposition 6

When the firms compete in quantities before the merger and the cost synergy achieved by the merged firm is very high in the sense that $\delta < 0.4961$, then, through a new innovation, it offers a higher quality. Otherwise, it does not undertake a new innovation and offers the higher of the two pre-merger qualities. In either case, the merged firm lowers market access.

Proof: The first part of the proposition follows from the earlier discussion and Lemma 2. Regarding the market access, it is sufficient to note that the marginal consumers who are indifferent between buying and not buying the good are of a higher type under the merger than those before the merger:

$$\alpha_M(\tilde{q}_2^C) = \alpha_M(\tilde{q}_M^C) = 0.5\bar{\alpha} > \alpha_1^C = 0.27\bar{\alpha}.$$

3.2.3 Entry Decision in a New Market

As a digression to the preceding cases, consider the merger decision between two firms *before* their innovation decisions. An example of this may be entry decisions of firms in a potential market for new drugs or vaccines to be innovated for combating a new infectious disease. The firms make a three-stage decision. In the first stage, they decide whether to pull their resources together as a merged unit to innovate potential drug or vaccine or not. If they decide to merge and operate in the market by producing and selling the innovated drug or the vaccine, the game ends. But if they decide to operate separately, then in the second stage, they simultaneously undertake new innovations, and in the third and final stage, they simultaneously decide prices or quantities. The SPNE of this three-stage sequential game can be derived using the backward induction method as follows.

Consider the third stage of the game, given that the firms have decided to operate separately and non-cooperatively in the first stage and innovated qualities q_1 and q_2 in the second stage, they charge prices $p_1(q_1, q_2)$ and $p_2(q_1, q_2)$ as in (3.38a) and (3.38b). Given such Nash equilibrium choices in the third stage, they innovate qualities $\tilde{q}_1 = 0.0482\bar{\alpha}^2, \tilde{q}_2 = 0.2533\bar{\alpha}^2$ as in (3.39) by incurring the (convex) sunk R&D costs. The total profit realized by the firms is as given in (3.40): $\pi_1 + \pi_2 = 0.02612\bar{\alpha}^4$.

However, if the firms had decided about merging and pooling their resources together, then the innovation level and profit earned are as given in (3.43): $\tilde{q}_M = \dfrac{0.25\bar{\alpha}^2}{\delta}$, $\pi_M(\tilde{q}_M) = \dfrac{0.03125\bar{\alpha}^4}{\delta}$. Comparing profits when they operate non-cooperatively and when they merge, it emerges that they will decide to merge regardless of the degree of cost synergy. But, given (3.46), they will innovate a higher quality only for $\delta < 0.9869$.

Proceeding similarly when the firms compete in quantities in the third stage in case they decide to act non-cooperatively, and using $\tilde{\pi}_1^C + \tilde{\pi}_2^C = 0.1015\bar{\alpha}^4$ as in (3.50), it appears that merger will be preferred over non-cooperation and competition only for a sufficiently high level of cost synergy:

$$\delta < 0.3073 \tag{3.52}$$

Thus,

Proposition 7

Two firms pull their resources together, innovate a new product (or drug), and enter a new market as a merged entity if while acting non-cooperatively, the firms would have competed in terms of prices after innovating different variants of the product. But, in the case of post-innovation quantity competition when they act non-cooperatively, the firms would enter the market as a merged entity only if a significantly large cost synergy is achieved through merger as defined in (3.52).

Proof: Follows from the previous discussions.

Again, as in the case of a merger between two incumbent firms, the merged firm restricts market access for a larger set of low-type buyers than if the firms had acted non-cooperatively.

3.3 Conclusion

In this chapter I have discussed how the pre-merger nature of strategic competition – price competition or quantity competition – influences the post-merger quality choices. This aspect is analyzed in the alternative contexts of choice from an existing set of innovations or undertaking new innovations with focus on variable production cost in the former and sunk quality-development cost in the latter. The main difference in the results that are derived in these alternative contexts is that the merged firm will offer a higher quality through a new innovation only when the extent of cost synergy achieved through the merger is almost thrice as large as the cost synergy for which the merged firm chooses a higher quality from the existing set of innovations.

I also have considered merger decisions between two firms already operating in a market, and between two firms entering into a new market. The main difference between these cases is that while a merger is always profitable in the former case regardless of the nature of post-innovation (or post-quality-choice) competition, its profitability in the latter case depends on the nature of such competition. More precisely, in the case of post-innovation quantity competition when they act non-cooperatively, the firms would enter the market as a merged entity only if a significantly large cost synergy is achieved through the merger.

Notes

1 Interesting observation is that the Indian pharmaceutical firms producing generic drugs are the more aggressive acquirers, and a majority of such acquisitions are part of diversification in overseas markets snapping up brands of locals MNCs there.

2 Regarding the impact of competition on service quality, Mazzeo (2003) and Rupp et al. (2006) find that airlines provide better on-time performance on more competitive routes.

3 See Acharyya (1998).

4 The marginal cost of production is again constant, and now with respect to quality as well, and thus can be normalized to zero. See, for example, Shaked and Sutton (1982) and Motta (1993).

5 Motta (1993) did not impose any upper bound on the quality level. Here, with an upper bound for the existing set of innovations or quality levels, two cases arise. Either the upper bound is sufficiently high so that $\overline{q} > 4.0976$ and Firm 2 offers a strictly less than the maximum quality or $\overline{q} < 4.0976$, in which case Firm 2 offers the maximum quality given the set of existing innovations. Even in the latter case,

the quality-differentiation result holds as argued earlier. See also Shaked and Sutton (1982). To keep things simple, I here assume that the upper bound is sufficiently high so that the pair of qualities in (3.25) is the SPNE pair.

6 See Motta (1993) for a formal proof that q_1^* is the optimal response from below to the choice q_2^* for Firm-1, and q_2^* is the optimal response from above to the choice q_1^* for Firm 2.

7 Between the two menus that satisfy these two first-order conditions, the menu in (28) satisfies the second-order condition for profit maximization.

References

Acharyya, R. 1998. Monopoly and Product Quality: Separating or Pooling Menu? *Economics Letters*, 61: 187–194.

Acharyya, R. 2013. Market Coverage, Price and National Welfare Under International Exhaustion of Patents. *Trade and Development Review*, 6(1–2): 29–63.

Acharyya, R. and Garcia-Alonso, M. D. C. 2008. Parallel Imports, Innovations and National Welfare: Role of the Sizes of the Income Classes and National Markets for Health Care. *The Singapore Economic Review*, Special Issue on Health Economics, 53(1): 1–23.

Acharyya, R. and Garcia-Alonso, M. D. C. 2012. Parallel Imports, Drug Innovation and International Patent Protection: A Policy Game. *Journal of International Trade and Economic Development*, 21(6): 865–894.

Anderson, S. and Celik, L. 2015. Product Line Design. *Journal of Economic Theory*, 157: 517–526.

Bauer, F. and Matzler, K. 2014. Antecedents of M&A Success: The Role of Strategic Complementarity, Cultural Fit, and Degree and Speed of Integration. *Strategic Management Journal*, 35: 269–291.

Brekke, K. R., Siciliani, L. and Straume, O. R. 2017. Horizontal Mergers and Product Quality. *Canadian Journal of Economics*, 50(4): 1063–1103.

Champsaur, P. and Rochet, J.-C. 1989. Multiproduct duopolists. *Econometrica*, 57: 533–557.

Chen, Y. and Gayle, P. G. 2019. Mergers and Product Quality: Evidence from the Airline Industry. *International Journal of Industrial Organization*, 62: 96–135.

Chondrakis, G. 2016. Unique Synergies in Technology Acquisitions. *Research Policy*, 45: 1873–1889.

Danzon, P. M. 1998. The Economics of Parallel Trade. *Pharmacoeconomics*, 13: 293–304.

Danzon, P. M., Mulcahy, A. W. and Towse, A. 2011. Pharmaceutical Pricing in Emerging Markets: Effects of Income, Competition and Procurement. NBER Working Paper 17174.

Davis, D. D. and Wilson, B. J. 2008. Strategic Buyers, Horizontal Mergers and Synergies: An Experimental Investigation. *International Journal of Industrial Organization*, 26(3): 643–661.

Devos, E., Kadapakkam, P. R., Krishnamurthy, S. 2009. How Do Mergers Create Value? A Comparison of Taxes, Market Power, and Efficiency Improvements as Explanations for Synergies. *Review of Financial Studies*, 22(3): 1179–1211.

Economides N. Mixed Bundling in Duopoly. Discussion Paper 1993. EC-93-29, Stern School of Business, N.Y.U.

Farrell, J. and Shapiro, C. 1990. Horizontal Mergers: An Equilibrium Analysis. *American Economic Review*, 80: 107–126.

Feldman, E. R. and E. Hernandez. 2022. Synergy in Mergers and Acquisitions: Typology, Lifecycles, and Value. *Academy of Management Review*, 47(4): 549–578.

Fluck, Z. and Lynch, A. W. 1999. Why Do Firms Merge and Then Divest? A Theory of Financial Synergy. *Journal of Business*, 72(3): 319–346.
Gabszweicz, J. J. and Thisse, J. F. 1979. Price Competition, Quality and Income Disparities. *Journal of Economic Theory*, 20: 340–359.
Johnson, J. P. and D. P. Myatt. 2003. Multi-Product Quality Competition: Fighting Brands and Product Line Pruning. *American Economic Review*, 93(3): 748–774.
Johnson, J. P. and D. P. Myatt. 2006. Multi-Product Cournot Oligopoly. *RAND Journal of Economics*, 37(3): pp. 583–601.
Johnson, J. and Rhodes, A. 2021. Multiproduct Mergers and Quality Competition. Available at SSRN: https://ssrn.com/abstract=3243848 or http://doi.org/10.2139/ssrn.3243848
Ma, C. A. and Burgess Jr, J. F. 1993. Quality Competition, Welfare and Regulation. *Journal of Economics*, 58: pp. 153–173.
Makri, M., Hitt, M. A. and Lane, P. J. 2010. Complementary Technologies, Knowledge Relatedness, and Invention Outcomes in High Technology Mergers and Acquisitions. *Strategic Management Journal*, 31: 602–628.
Malueg, D. A. and Schwartz, M. 1994. Parallel Imports, Demand Dispersion and International Price Discrimination. *Journal of International Economics*, 37: 167–196.
Maskus, K. 2000. Parallel Imports. *The World Economy: Global Trade Policy* 2000, 23: 1269–1284.
Mazzeo, M. 2003. Competition and Service Quality in the U.S. Airline Industry. *Review of Industrial Organization* 22: 275–296.
Motta, M. 1993. Endogenous Quality Choice: Price vs. Quantity Competition. *The Journal of Industrial Economics*, 41(2): 113–131.
Mussa, M. and Rosen, S. 1978. Monopoly and Product Quality. *Journal of Economic Theory*, 18: 301–317.
Prince, J. T. and Simon, D. H. 2017. The Impact of Mergers on Quality Provision: Evidence from the Airline Industry. *Journal of Industrial Economics*, 65(2): 336–362.
Perry, M. K. and Porter, R. H. 1985. Oligopoly and the Incentive for Horizontal Merger. *American Economic Review*, 75: 219–227.
Rao, V. R., Yu, Y. and Umashankar, N. 2016. Anticipated vs. Actual Synergy in Merger Partner Selection and Post-Merger Innovation. *Marketing Science*, 35(6): 934–952.
Rupp, N. G. and Tan, K. M. 2019. Mergers and Product Quality: A Silver Lining from De-Hubbing in the U.S. Airline Industry. *Contemporary Economic Policy*, 37(4): 652–672.
Rupp, N. G., Owens, D. and Plumly, L. 2006. Does Competition Influence Airline On-Time Performance? In: Lee, D. (Ed.), *Advances in Airline Economics: Competition Policy and Antitrust, 1*. Elsevier.
Shaked, A. and Sutton, J. 1982. Relaxing Price Competition through Product Differentiation. *Review of Economic Studies*, 49: 3–13.
Wauthy, X. 1996. Quality Choice in Models of Vertical Differentiation. *Journal of Industrial Economics*, 65: 345–353.

4 Fiscal interventions to combat wealth disparity in India

Sudipa Majumdar and Jyoti Chandiramani

4.1 Introduction

The World Inequality Database (WID) defines wealth as the net value of all assets (financial and non-financial) owned by an individual. Assets include stocks of economic resources in the form of non-financial assets such as real estate, vehicles, equipment, and financial assets such as bank deposits and share capital (Eilers, 2012). Past researchers studied income inequality by considering sources of earnings like wages, salaries, profits, dividends, interest, rents, and the like (Piketty and Saez, 2003; Rubin and Segal, 2015; Garbinti et al., 2018). However, wealth disparity is a broader and wider concept of economic well-being than income inequality, since a lack of wealth has long-term socio-economic ramifications and wealth disparity holds deeper relevance in the aftermath of the financial crisis, when assets were considered safety nets against income losses (Rodems and Pfeffer, 2021).

According to the World Inequality Report (2022), the poorer half of the world population owned 2% of total net wealth, while the top 10% owned three-quarters of it. This disparity was aggravated during the COVID-19 pandemic as 2020–21 marked the steepest increase in the share of wealth of global billionaires (World Inequality Report, 2022) as the wealth of billionaires in the Asia Pacific region alone increased by USD 1.46 trillion in 2020-21 (Seery, 2022). At the same time, the pandemic pushed 77 million people into extreme poverty (Sumner et al., 2022). In India, the wealth of the poorer 50% of the population stood at INR 0.07 million in 2021 while the top 1% owned INR 32.45 million (World Inequality Report, 2022).

Widening wealth gap has been a crucial global issue and central governments have been trying to manage the disparity through various fiscal policies. Taxation is the common fiscal intervention as progressive taxes are assumed to have strong positive linkages through the redistribution of wealth, which not only reduces the skewness of wealth accumulation but also grants economic opportunities to the underprivileged, bringing in efficiencies in the allocation of resources (Mallick et al., 2021). Fiscal interventions also include direct transfer schemes for the poor as well as public funds for social infrastructure in rural areas, which assumed importance during the COVID-19

DOI: 10.4324/9781003509721-6

pandemic (Karim et al., 2022). Countries like Mexico, Brazil and India have adopted nationwide transfer programs through targeted cash benefits, subsidies, scholarships, public distribution systems, unemployment benefits and so on (Lambert and Park, 2019). Despite such initiatives, the existing studies present mixed results on the association between fiscal interventions and wealth gaps.

This study makes an important contribution, by investigating the long-term causality association between the wealth gap and fiscal interventions in India. A multivariate analysis is carried out by taking wealth indices extracted from the World Inequality Database (WID) series, which overcomes the earlier shortcomings of income-based variables. Wealth gap based on the WID distributional indices is an important improvement over the Gini coefficient used in previous studies. The rest of the article is proceeds as follows: The next section presents a review of the literature, while Section 4.3 discusses the scenario in India. Section 4.4 elucidates the research methodology and reports the findings. Section 4.5 of the study highlights the discussion and implications of the results. In Section 4.6, the conclusions of the chapter are presented.

4.2 Literature Review

4.2.1 Taxation and Wealth Disparity

The predominant method of fiscal intervention has been taxation, in an effort to mobilize government revenues to enhance public spending for the poor (Musgrave, 1959; Anderson et al., 2017). Although a progressive rate of direct taxation is assumed to help reduce disparity (Atkinson, 2015; Piketty, 2015), the effectiveness of such redistribution is ambiguous (Auerbach, 2012; Tcherneva, 2014; Arestis et al., 2022) since causal effects depend crucially on the fiscal space (Bird and Zolt, 2008). The effectiveness of policies may be eroded due to high tax rates that discourage consumption and investment decisions (Feldstein, 2012), as well as due to high evasions when rich individuals siphon off their incomes to undeclared offshore accounts (Alstadsæter et al., 2018; Andersen et al., 2022). Therefore, the effect of tax policies on reducing wealth disparity remains unclear and we propose the first null hypothesis as follows:

> **Null Hypothesis 1 Ho1:** *Taxation has no impact on wealth disparity in India.*

4.2.2 Subsidies and Wealth Disparity

Government subsidies include price rebates on food, financial transfers, direct assistance, welfare grants and in-kind benefits such as free government education, health care services and so on. India has directed support to the poor through subsidies for fertilizers, electricity, housing, and subsidized food through the public distribution system (Bhalla et al., 2022). However, identifying and targeting high-priority beneficiaries has been the prime issue (Bigman and Fofack, 2000). Prior studies highlighted regressive distribution in the absence of optimally targeted transfers, such as Fillmore and McMahon (2022) for student scholarships, Meckel (2020) for food assistance programs, Collinson and Ganong (2018) for housing vouchers and others. Izadi (2020) opined that subsidies may lead to undesirable resource allocation by distorting market prices and cost of production, while Lee et al. (2007) found no effect of subsidies on wealth inequality for a panel of 60 counties. Earlier, Atkinson (1999) pointed out that overreliance on subsidy programs tends to generate poverty traps and welfare dependency that might prove counterproductive. Thus, there is no consensus about the effect of government subsidies on inequality, and our second null hypothesis is formulated as:

> **Null Hypothesis 2 Ho2:** *Government subsidies have no impact on wealth disparity in India.*

4.2.3 Fiscal Deficits and Wealth Disparity

According to Stiglitz (2012), policymakers tend to focus on controlling fiscal deficits in an effort to rein in external deficits and the accumulation of public debt. In emerging nations, when tax revenues fail to achieve fiscal balance, interventions to control fiscal deficits get translated into government expenditure cuts (Pal and Ghosh, 2007). Managing fiscal deficits, therefore, leads to a vicious trap as, on one hand, governments cut back on their social investments, which widens the wealth gap, while high inequalities force fiscal spending resulting in high deficits, on the other hand (Woo, 2003; Larch, 2012). Fiscal deficits also tend to mount due to the existence of shadow economies, as in the case of Pakistan, that do not contribute to the government reserves (Khan and Padda, 2021). In contrast, Namibia maintained its fiscal discipline through targeted intervention programs and achieved satisfactory reduction in inequality levels (Eita et al., 2021) as did countries in the European Union that successfully lowered disparity levels without incurring high fiscal deficits (Aksman, 2017). The ambiguity in the findings lead to the third null hypothesis:

> **Null Hypothesis 3 Ho3:** *Fiscal deficit has no impact on inequality in India.*

Prior research in India measured economic disparity through income levels (Vakulabharanam and Motiram, 2012; Tagade et al., 2018; Mishra and Bhardwaj, 2021). First, income is not considered a true representation of well-being; second, data on income is highly skewed and underreported in order to avoid tax compliance (Alm et al., 1992); and third, data from the

National Sample Survey Office surveys have been criticized due to their inaccuracies and inconsistencies (Atkinson and Piketty, 2007; Natrajan and Jacob, 2018; Chunekar and Sreenivas, 2019). Moreover, the Gini index adopted in earlier studies has also faced criticisms regarding being a subjective measure that depended crucially on the underlying distributions (Atkinson, 2015; Alvaredo et al., 2018; Liu and Gastwirth, 2020). Our data, extracted from the WID wealth series, ensure the series' consistency, accuracy and continuity and enriches the literature by overcoming the earlier shortcomings. To the knowledge of the authors, this is the first attempt to investigate causality associations between disparity and fiscal interventions using long-term multivariate data in the Indian context.

4.3 Inequality in India

Poverty has been an overriding issue in India. Up to the 1980s, the Indian government adopted a middle path of moderate inequality with satisfactory economic growth (Chakravarty, 1987). Market-oriented reforms began in the mid-1980s that were intensified into comprehensive economic liberalization in the 1990s when major disinvestments resulted in the accumulation of wealth in the hands of few private businessmen (Banerjee and Piketty, 2005; Chancel and Piketty, 2019).

Figure 4.1 shows the wealth gap in India as the difference between the wealth index of the top 1% of the population and that of the bottom 50%, based on the WID for 2022. The top 1% of the population shows a strong upward trajectory since 1992, highlighting the widening gap and increasing inequality. The trend encountered a significant dip in 2020 when the top echelon was hit by the stock market crash, with the Bombay Stock Exchange Sensitive Index falling by 13.2% on March 23, 2020, recording the highest single-day fall since 1991. Concurrently, the lower half of the population faced the brunt as India went into lockdown from March 25, 2020, and thousands of informal workers were rendered jobless. Thereafter, as the stock market bounced back, the wealth of Indian billionaires went up from USD 312.6 billion in March 2020 to USD 719 billion in November 2021,

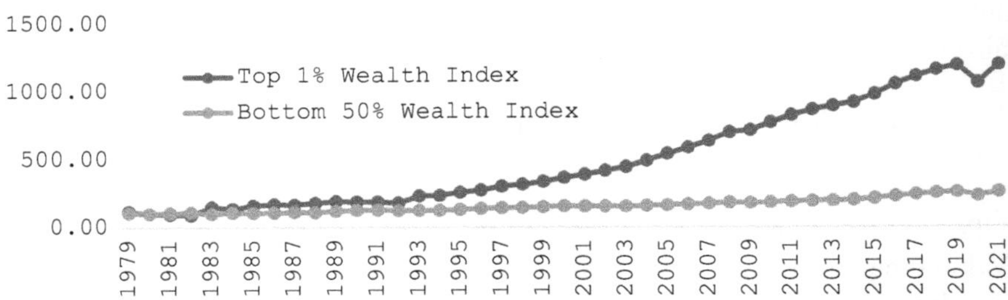

Figure 4.1 Wealth index of the top 1% and bottom 50% of the Indian population.
Source: World Inequality Report 2022.

according to the Forbes World's Billionaires List; the number of Indian billionaires grew from 102 to 142 (Hurun Research Institute, 2021).

At the other end of the spectrum, the Government of India used the Public Financial Management System to make direct transfers into the bank accounts of 160 million beneficiaries during the pandemic period, along with fiscal stimuli of loan assurances and credit extensions through financial institutions (Alok et al., 2021). The public distribution system was used for the provision of cooking gas and supply of essentials through 2 million 'Suraksha Store' retail outlets across India (KPMG, 2020). Despite these efforts, the Global Hunger rank for India worsened from 94 in 2020 to 101 in 2021 (out of 116 countries); the number of poor (with per day incomes of USD 2 or less) increased by 75 million in India with the poverty rate rising to 9.7% in 2020–21 (Kochhar, 2021). So, there is a strong need to investigate the effectiveness of fiscal interventions in India with respect to causal effects on wealth disparities across the strata of the population.

4.4 Analysis and Findings

Wealth disparity (GAP) has been calculated as the difference between the wealth index of the top 1% of the population and that of the bottom 50%, based on the WID, following Banerjee and Piketty (2005), Chancel and Picketty (2019), Blanchet et al. (2019) and others. The time series analysis was based on data from 1983 to 2021. The other variables used in this study have been defined as shown in Table 4.1.

The presence of unit root is tested using the Augmented Dickey–Fuller (ADF) test and Phillips–Perron (PP) test was used to correct for autocorrelation and heteroscedasticity. The results obtained from ADF and PP (Table 4.2) reveal the presence of unit roots at levels but stationarity at their first differences, both in terms of the ADF and PP test statistics, confirming that the series is I (1).

Optimal lags were selected by applying the lag length selection criteria, Akaike information criterion (AIC), Schwartz Bayesian criterion (SBC) and Hannan Quinn information criterion (HQIC). Table 4.3 shows a sequence of likelihood-ratio (LR) test statistics for all the full Vector Auto Regression VARs

Table 4.1 Variables and Definitions

Variable Name	*Definition*	*Unit*
GAP	Difference between wealth index of top 1% of population and wealth index to bottom 50%	
TX_GDP	Tax revenue as a percentage of gross domestic product (GDP)	%
SUB_EXP	Government subsidies as a percentage of total government expenditures	%
FD_GDP	Fiscal deficit as a percentage of GDP	%

Table 4.2 Unit Root Tests for Stationarity

Variable	*Level*		*FIRST Difference*	
	ADF	*PP*	*ADF*	*PP*
GAP	1.583 (.9978)	1.832 (.9984)	*−6.201*** (.0000)*	*−6.274*** (.0000)*
TX_GDP	−2.152 (.2240)	−2.290 (.1752)	*−5.163*** (.0000)*	*−5.085*** (.0000)*
SUB_EXP	−2.618 (.0894)	−2.503 (.1147)	*−8.225*** (.0000)*	*−8.308*** (.0000)*
FD_GDP	−2.717 (.0712)	−2.727 (.0694)	*−6.471*** (.0000)*	*−6.591*** (.0000)*

Source: Authors.

Note: *** denotes significant at 1% using the *t*-statistic approach. Figures in parentheses denote *p*-values.

Table 4.3 Selection-Order Criteria

Lag	*LL*	*LR*	df	p	*FPE*	*AIC*	*HQIC*	*SBC*
0	−504.755				5.0e+07	29.0717	29.1331	29.2495
1	−363.671	282.17	16	.000	39356.3*	21.924*	22.2309*	22.8128*
2	−351.595	24.152	16	.086	51225.5	22.1483	22.7005	23.7481
3	−343.21	16.769	16	.401	87653.6	22.5835	23.3811	24.8943
4	−327.959	30.502	16	.016	112702	22.6262	23.6694	25.6481

Source: Authors.

Note: LL = Log Likelihood; LR = likelihood ratio; FPE = final prediction error; AIC = Akaike information criterion; HQIC = Hannan Quinn information criterion; SBC, explained in the text.

*Optimal lag length.

of order less than or equal to the highest lag order, along with the final prediction error (FPE). The asterisk '*' indicates the optimal lag which is confirmed to be '1' by all the selection order criteria.

Johansen's cointegration rank test was carried out for an optimal lag length of 1, based on the maximum eigenvalue and the trace statistics (Engle and Yoo, 1987). The optimal choice involves a sequential procedure from ($r = 0$) up to ($r = k - 1$) until we fail to reject the null hypothesis. Optimality has been denoted by the asterisk in Table 4.4, where both the maximum eigenvalue and the trace statistics indicate that there does not exist any long-term cointegration relationships.

Our data set included an interaction between wealth gap (GAP), tax revenue (TX_GDP), government subsidies (SUB_EXP) and government fiscal deficit (FD_GDP) from 1983 to 2021. This was modeled as a four-variable VAR, and the time-series model can be written in functional form as:

$$\Delta GAP_t = f(\Sigma\Delta GAP_{t-n}, \Sigma\Delta TX\_GDP_{t-n}, \Sigma\Delta SUB\_EXP_{t-n}, \Sigma\Delta FD\_GDP_{t-n})$$
$$\Delta TX\_GDP_t = f(\Sigma\Delta GAP_{t-n}, \Sigma\Delta TX\_GDP_{t-n}, \Sigma\Delta SUB\_EXP_{t-n}, \Sigma\Delta FD\_GDP_{t-n})$$
$$\Delta SUB\_EXP_t = f(\Sigma\Delta GAP_{t-n}, \Sigma\Delta TX\_GDP_{t-n}, \Sigma\Delta SUB\_EXP_{t-n}, \Sigma\Delta FD\_GDP_{t-n})$$
$$\Delta FD\_GDP_t = f(\Sigma\Delta GAP_{t-n}, \Sigma\Delta TX\_GDP_{t-n}, \Sigma\Delta SUB\_EXP_{t-n}, \Sigma\Delta FD\_GDP_{t-n})$$

Table 4.4 Johansen Test for Cointegration

Max Rank	*Parameters*	*Lag Length*	*Eigenvalue*	*Statistics*	*5% Critical Value*
TRACE STATISTICS					
0	20	−396.48964	.	43.4825*	47.21
1	27	−386.7625	0.40891	24.0282	29.68
2	32	−379.36435	0.32961	9.2319	15.41
3	35	−374.94512	0.21249	0.3935	3.76
4	36	−374.7484	0.01058		
MAX STATISTICS					
0	20	−396.48964	.	19.4543*	27.07
1	27	−386.7625	0.40891	14.7963	20.97
2	32	−379.36435	0.32961	8.8385	14.07
3	35	−374.94512	0.21249	0.3935	3.76
4	36	−374.7484	0.01058		

Source: Authors.

*Statistically significant at 1%.

Table 4.5 Pre-Estimation Tests

Stability Condition		*Lagrange Multiplier Test*		
Eigenvalue	*Modulus*	*Lag*	*Chi2*	p-*value*
.9840538	.984054	1	18.7669	.28094
.9628018	.962802	2	15.5187	.48703
.6631383	.663138			
.2853702	.28537			

Source: Authors.

In order to run the VAR, pre-estimation tests were carried out to ensure stability such that the eigenvalues of a companion matrix for the system would be less than 1, such that no roots of the autoregressive system lie outside the unit circle. The Lagrange multiplier test was also carried out to check for presence of autocorrelation in the residual at the specified lag order. Table 4.5 confirms the stability condition and the absence of autocorrelation. Table 4.6 presents the estimates of the VAR model, which describes the joint generation process of variables over time and represents the Granger causality type of relationship between the multivariate time series.

Table 4.6 VAR Model Estimates

	VAR Model		
Dependent Variable	*Regressors*	*Coefficient*	*z-statistics*
GAP	GAP.L1	.9438496***	37.90
	TX_GDP.L1	.1878917	0.30
	SUB_EXP.L1	7.73795***	4.05
	FD_GDP.L1	7.73795***	-2.13
	constant	-12.72711	-0.27
TX_GDP	GAP.L1	.0060718	1.51
	TX_GDP.L1	7.73795***	7.49
	SUB_EXP.L1	-.3314302	-1.08
	FD_GDP.L1	.9872985*	1.84
	constant	12.55706	1.64
SUB_EXP	GAP.L1	.0051002**	2.36
	TX_GDP.L1	.0492066	0.89
	SUB_EXP.L1	.3682649**	2.22
	FD_GDP.L1	-.0813925	-0.28
	constant	1.92256	0.47
FD_GDP	GAP.L1	.0020159*	1.89
	TX_GDP.L1	.0394132	1.45
	SUB_EXP.L1	-.232587***	-2.84
	FD_GDP.L1	.8141635***	5.72
	constant	-.0496614	-0.02

Source: Authors.

Note: VAR = ; GAP = wealth gap; TX_GDP = tax revenue; SUB_EXP = government subsidies; FD_GDP = government fiscal deficit.

$*p < .01$; $**p < .05$; $***p < .10$.

4.5 Discussions and Recommendations

4.5.1 Taxation

There is no Granger causality between tax revenues and wealth disparity, indicating that taxation in India had no effect and was not influenced by the wealth gap. This result is in line with the case in Latin America (Cornia et al., 2011) and a panel of developing countries (Bird and Zolt, 2005).

India suffers from limited fiscal space due to inadequate direct taxes, as personal income taxes account for only 2–2.5% of gross domestic product (GDP; Datt et al., 2021) as exclusion of the agricultural sector–constrained government revenues. India also suffered from low average tax rates, whereby efforts to introduce a high degree of progressivity result in widespread avoidance and evasion (Zucman, 2019; Alstadsæter et al., 2018). In fact, contrary to expectations, direct taxation in India became pro-rich due to the abolition of wealth tax in 2016, along with steep cuts in corporate taxes. Consumption tax was levied in the form of the Goods and Services Tax (GST) in 2017, which had further adverse consequences. First, any indirect consumption tax tends to be regressive because the poor spend a larger proportion of their income on consumption. Second, in an attempt to counter the regressive nature, eight different GST rates were introduced, the highest being 28% on luxury goods (Rajagopalan, 2022), which made the system extremely complex and failed to achieve its objective of inclusivity.

Our results indicate the need for restructuring the fiscal framework to deepen and widen the tax base. A plausible recommendation would be to follow the example of countries in the Organisation for Economic Co-operation and Development to impose inheritance taxes (Cole, 2015; Niemann and Anderwald, 2022) and/or progressive wealth taxes (Malik, 2020), targeted at billionaires. According to the Oxfam Report 2022, a mere 1% additional surcharge on the richest 1% of the population would be adequate to fund all government subsidies and ensure investments in primary education, healthcare, basic social infrastructure like housing and sanitation for all, in accordance with the United Nations Sustainable Development Goals (Oxfam, 2022).

4.5.2 Government Subsidies

The significant positive bidirectional coefficient of subsidies indicates that inequality has prompted the government to give higher subsidies, but higher subsidies have also resulted in higher inequality.

The Government of India has been proactive with welfare schemes for the poor, which include price rebates for agriculture and energy, especially for kerosene and diesel. Subsidies also include tax exemptions on export income in special economic zones, tax holidays for start-ups and tax benefits for businesses in the northeastern and Himalayan states. India also has a huge network of targeted public distribution systems for subsidized food grains, through the Antyodaya Anna Yojana program involving additional subsidies for the poorest families. Monetary benefits are also credited to bank accounts through direct benefit transfers (DBTs) to farmers under the Pradhan Mantri Jan Dhan Yojana. Thus, government subsidies in India went up manifold through major fiscal interventions (NITI Aayog, 2018).

However, despite all efforts, the subsidies and transfers have aggravated wealth disparity in India, which was also reported in African studies (Odedokun and Round, 2001; Bouincha and Karim, 2018; Suratman and Mayudi, 2022). DBTs in India have been plagued with asymmetric information and administrative bottlenecks (Aiyar, 2019) since the process has been complex and time-consuming, requiring many layers of approvals and paperwork (Nirgude et al., 2019). Even the public distribution system in India has been afflicted with corruption and poor targeting (George and McKay, 2019) and did not achieve the objective of reducing wealth disparity.

Table 4.7 Selected Central Government Schemes for Tackling Wealth Disparity in India

Government Scheme	*Launch*	*Reducing Inequality through*
Food for Work Programme	2004	Wage employment for manual unskilled work.
Mahatma Gandhi National Rural Employment Guarantee Act	2006	Offering minimum wage with 100 days of annual employment to rural inhabitants.
National Rural Livelihood Mission	2011	Providing the impoverished with stable monthly income
National Food Security Act	2013	Eradicating hunger for the extreme poor
Urban Livelihoods Mission	2013	Access to employment opportunities for the urban poor
Saansad Aadarsh Gram Yojana	2014	Providing villages with basic amenities, livelihood opportunities and overall quality of life
Prime Minister People's Wealth Scheme	2014	Ensuring access to financial services like savings bank accounts, needs-based credit, remittances facility, insurance and pension to low-income groups
Swachh Bharat Mission	2014	Providing basic infrastructure, water supply, sewerage schemes, sanitation facilities for the rural and urban poor
Prime Minister's Awas Yojana	2015	Providing 'Housing for All' by 2022.
Stand-Up India Scheme	2016	Providing credits for entrepreneurs, particularly women, scheduled castes and scheduled tribes.

Source: Authors.

4.5.3 Fiscal Deficits

Bidirectional causality of wealth disparity with fiscal deficits indicate that higher inequality caused fiscal deficits and vice versa. Inequality would prompt fiscal deficit deterioration through higher interventions, as explained by Woo (2003), Tujula and Wolswijk (2004), Larch (2012), Miyazaki (2018), etc. In India, fiscal deficits mounted up to INR 18.5 trillion in 2020–21 owing to various government initiatives to reduce wealth disparity (Table 4.7). But mounting fiscal deficits would also push up wealth disparities as government revenues would be directed toward debt servicing.

4.6 Conclusion and Recommendations

Wealth disparity has been a persistent issue in India, and the Government of India has undertaken numerous initiatives to bring about inclusive and equitable growth. Our study investigates the effectiveness of such fiscal interventions in reducing the wealth gap, which has been measured by adopting wealth indices from 1983 to 2021 extracted from the WID. Our findings indicate that, in the face of budgetary constraints, fiscal interventions in India have only widened the wealth gap in the past decades. The results evidence the inadequacy of taxation revenues and the absence of redistributive effects of government subsidies, tax concessions and direct benefit transfers. Such aggressive fiscal interventions, like subsidies, concessions and transfers, have only resulted in mounting fiscal deficits that have only widened the wealth disparity even further.

India has a sound evaluation framework in place through the Bare Necessities Index and the National Multidimensional Poverty Index (NITI Aayog, 2018). The indices need regular monitoring along with fresh initiatives toward fiscal consolidation and restructuring of the taxation framework. A shift toward progressive direct taxes would imply levying a combination of real estate taxes, agricultural taxes, inheritance taxes and wealth taxes that would directly address the issues of wealth disparity. New innovative financing mechanisms are required to enhance investments in social infrastructure for the poor, like crowdfunding, public–private partnerships, corporate social responsibility initiatives as well as self-help groups (SHGs). The effectiveness of such social investments would still depend crucially on the support from local governments.

India needs to adopt innovative financing mechanisms to push up investments in social infrastructure. The Maharashtra State Council of Education Research and Training provides an example whereby schoolteachers in Maharashtra raised INR 2160 million through crowdfunding platforms to revamp classrooms and introduce digital initiatives for students (FE Online, 2017). Crowdfunding could also finance small-scale start-ups, through the Stand-Up India Scheme of the Government of India. Examples of private-sector involvement could be found in the village councils of Maharashtra, where corporate funding was successfully utilized to adopt Clean Village Campaigns (Kumar, 2014), and in Nagaland, where private capital was used to promote education, energy and sanitary infrastructure under the Village Development Boards (Shimray, 2014). Such case studies should be emulated in other States of India. The microfinance example of SHGs highlights the example in which 10–20 villagers, primarily women, accumulate small savings to form a corpus that is utilized to take loans for developing petty businesses. These poor groups need an active role by the local governments to create a supportive environment, skill them and monitor their activities. Commercial banks and National Bank for Agriculture and Rural Development (NABARD) need to innovate and design new financial products for such poor groups that would be focused exclusively on the rural poor and aim to improve their livelihoods.

India's progress in alleviation of poverty and hunger would also largely influence global outcomes in achieving the Agenda 2030 of the Sustainable Development Goals. The 2022 Economic and Social Survey of Asia and the Pacific by the United Nations Economic and Social Commission for Asia and the Pacific discusses how the COVID-19 pandemic brought forth disparities in livelihoods and health and education levels and highlights that governments need to focus on rebuilding their economies by creating knowledge economies through private-sector investments in entrepreneurial education, vocational training and technical workshops for the poorest households. The future lies in prioritizing education and creating an empowered labor force, especially among the lower socioeconomic strata of the population.

References

Aiyar, Y., 2019. The opportunities and challenges confronting India's welfare architecture. Retrieved from https://www.cprindia.org/policy-challenge/7950/economy-%26-the-welfare-state

Aksman, E., 2017. Do poverty and income inequality affect public debt? *Gospodarka Narodowa. The Polish Journal of Economics*, *292*(6), pp. 79–93.

Alm, J., McClelland, G.H. and Schulze, W.D., 1992. Why do people pay taxes? *Journal of Public Economics*, *48*(1), pp. 21–38.

Alok, V.N., Jatoliya, M. and Pareek, A., 2021. Governance and economic impact of COVID-19 in Indian federation. *Indian Journal of Public Administration*, *67*(3), pp. 452–469.

Alstadsæter, A., Johannesen, N. and Zucman, G., 2018. Who owns the wealth in tax havens? Macro evidence and implications for global inequality. *Journal of Public Economics*, *162*, pp. 89–100.

Alvaredo, F., Atkinson, A.B. and Morelli, S., 2018. Top wealth shares in the UK over more than a century. *Journal of Public Economics*, *162*, pp. 26–47.

Andersen, J.J., Johannesen, N. and Rijkers, B., 2022. Elite capture of foreign aid: Evidence from offshore bank accounts. *Journal of Political Economy*, *130*(2), pp. 388–425.

Anderson, E., Jalles D'Orey, M.A., Duvendack, M. and Esposito, L., 2017. Does government spending affect income inequality? A meta-regression analysis. *Journal of Economic Surveys*, *31*(4), pp. 961–987.

Arestis, P., Ferrari-Filho, F., Resende, M.F.D.C. and Bittes Terra, F.H., 2022. A critical analysis of the Brazilian 'expansionary fiscal austerity': Why did it fail to ensure economic growth and structural development? *International Review of Applied Economics*, *36*(1), pp. 4–16.

Atkinson, A.B., 1999. The contributions of Amartya Sen to welfare economics. *The Scandinavian Journal of Economics*, *101*(2), pp. 173–190.

Atkinson, A.B., 2015. Inequality. In *Inequality*. Harvard University Press.

Atkinson, A.B. and Piketty, T. eds., 2007. *Top Incomes Over the Twentieth Century: A Contrast Between Continental European and English-Speaking Countries*. OUP Oxford.

Auerbach, A.J., 2012. The fall and rise of keynesian fiscal policy. *Asian Economic Policy Review*, *7*(2), pp. 157–175.

Banerjee, A. and Piketty, T., 2005. Top Indian incomes, 1922–2000. *The World Bank Economic Review*, *19*(1), pp. 1–20.

Bhalla, S., Bhasin, K. and Virmani, A., 2022. Pandemic, Poverty, and Inequality: Evidence from India. International Monetary Fund, 069. Retrieved from https://www.elibrary.imf.org/view/journals/001/2022/069/article-A001-en.xml

Bigman, D. and Fofack, H., 2000. Geographical targeting for poverty alleviation: An introduction to the special issue. *The World Bank Economic Review*, *14*(1), pp. 129–145.

Bird, R.M. and Zolt, E.M., 2005. The limited role of the personal income tax in developing countries. *Journal of Asian Economics*, *16*(6), pp. 928–946.

Bird, R.M. and Zolt, E.M., 2008. Tax policy in emerging countries. *Environment and Planning C: Government and policy*, *26*(1), pp. 73–86.

Blanchet, T., Chancel, L. and Gethin, A., 2019. How unequal is Europe? Evidence from distributional national accounts, 1980–2017. *WID. World Working Paper*, *6*.

Bouincha, M. and Karim, M. 2018. Income inequality and economic growth: An analysis using a panel data. *International Journal of Economics and Finance*, *10*(5), pp. 242–253.

Chakravarty, S., 1987. *Development Planning: The Indian Experience*. Clarendon Press.

Chancel, L. and Piketty, T., 2019. Indian income inequality, 1922–2015: From British Raj to Billionaire Raj? *Review of Income and Wealth*, *65*, pp. S33–S62.

Chunekar, A. and Sreenivas, A., 2019. Towards an understanding of residential electricity consumption in India. *Building Research & Information*, *47*(1), pp. 75–90.

Cole, A., 2015. Estate and inheritance taxes around the world. *Fiscal Fact*, *458*.

Collinson, R. and Ganong, P., 2018. How do changes in housing voucher design affect rent and neighborhood quality? *American Economic Journal: Economic Policy*, 10(2), pp. 62–89.

Cornia, G.A., Gómez-Sabaini, J.C. and Martorano, B., 2011. A new fiscal pact, tax policy changes and income inequality: Latin America during the last decade (No. 2011/70). WIDER Working Paper.

Datt, G., Ray, R. and Teh, C., 2021. Progressivity and redistributive effects of income taxes: evidence from India. *Empirical Economics*, *63*, pp. 1–38.

Eilers, T., 2012. The Rise of Wealth Disparity in the United States and its Effects on Democracy: An Evaluation of the Great Recession and the Dodd-Frank Act. Senior Comprehensive Project, Occidental College.

Eita, J.H., Manuel, V., Naimhwaka, E. and Nakusera, F., 2021. The impact of fiscal deficit on inflation in Namibia. *Journal of Central Banking Theory and Practice*, *1*, pp. 141–164.

Engle, R.F. and Yoo, B.S., 1987. Forecasting and testing in co-integrating systems, *Journal of Econometrics*, *35*, pp. 143–159.

FE Online, 2017. After crowd funding generates Rs 216 cr, Maharashtra government schools access latest learning tools. Retrieved from https://www.financialexpress.com/india-news/after-crowd-funding-generates-rs-216-cr-maharashtra-government-schools-access-latest-learning-tools/632120/

Feldstein, M., 2012. The Mirrlees review. *Journal of Economic Literature*, *50*(3), pp. 781–790.

Fillmore, I. and McMahon, S., 2022. The Effect of Federal Grants on Student Outcomes Working Paper No. 2022-011, The University of Chicago.

Garbinti, B., Goupille-Lebret, J. and Piketty, T., 2018. Income inequality in France, 1900–2014: evidence from distributional national accounts (DINA). *Journal of Public Economics*, *162*, pp. 63–77.

George, N.A. and McKay, F.H., 2019. The public distribution system and food security in India. *International Journal of Environmental Research and Public Health*, *16*(17), p. 3221.

Hurun Research Institute, 2021. Hurun Global Rich List. Retrieved from https://www.hurun.net/en-US/Rank/HsRankDetails?pagetype=global

Izadi, H., 2020. An investigation on the share of rural and urban households' expenditure as a basis to determine economic policies for Iran. *Zagreb International Review of Economics & Business*, *23*(2), pp. 41–53.

Karim, A., DeWit, A. and Shaw, R., 2022. Fiscal policies and post-COVID-19 development challenges: An OVERVIEW. *Global Pandemic and Human Security*, pp. 61–82 Springer.

Khan, S. and Haq Padda, I.U., 2021. The impact of fiscal policy on income inequality: A case study of Pakistan. *The Lahore Journal of Economics*, *26*(1), pp.57–84.

Kochhar, R., 2021. In the pandemic, India's middle class shrinks and poverty spreads while China sees smaller changes. Pew Research Center.
KPMG, 2020. India: Measures in response to COVID-19. Retrieved from https://home.kpmg/xx/en/home/insights/2020/04/india-government-and-institution-measures-in-response-to-covid.html
Kumar, V., 2014. Whose cleanliness? *Economic and Political Weekly*, *49*(43/44), pp. 13–15.
Lambert, F. and Park, H., 2019. *Income inequality and government transfers in Mexico*. International Monetary Fund.
Larch, M., 2012. Fiscal performance and income inequality: Are unequal societies more deficit-prone? Some cross-country evidence. *Kyklos*, *65*(1), pp. 53–80.
Lee, C.S., Nielsen, F. and Alderson, A.S., 2007. Income inequality, global economy and the state. *Social Forces*, *86*(1), pp. 77–111.
Liu, Y. and Gastwirth, J. 2020. On the capacity of the Gini index to represent income distributions. *METRON* 78, 61–69.
Malik, A., 2020. Scope of inheritance tax in India. *Supremo Amicus*, *21*, pp. 727–732.
Mallick, L., Behera, S.R. and Murthy, R.R., 2021. Does the twin deficit hypothesis exist in India? Empirical evidence from an asymmetric non-linear cointegration approach. *The Journal of Economic Asymmetries*, *24*, p. e00219.
Meckel, K., 2020. Is the cure worse than the disease? unintended effects of payment reform in a quantity-based transfer program. *American Economic Review*, *110*(6), pp. 1821–1865.
Mishra, A.K. and Bhardwaj, V., 2021. Wealth distribution and accounting for changes in wealth inequality: empirical evidence from India, 1991–2012. *Economic Change and Restructuring*, *54*(2), pp. 585–620.
Miyazaki, T., 2018. Regional inequality in fiscal capacity and allocation of tax sources: Do local allocation taxes correct the inequality? *Public Policy Review*, *14*(2), pp. 347–368.
Musgrave, R.A., 1959. *The theory of public finance; a study in public economy*. Kogakusha Company.
Natrajan, B. and Jacob, S., 2018. Provincialising vegetarianism putting Indian food habits in their place. *Economic and Political Weekly*, *53*(9), pp. 54–64.
Niemann, R. and Anderwald, A.M., 2022. Policy note: Is the inheritance and gift tax a reasonable alternative for the net wealth tax? A legal and economic analysis across OECD countries. *Intertax*, *50*(6/7), pp. 512–520.
Nirgude, A.S., Kumar, A.M., Collins, T., Naik, P.R., Parmar, M., Tao, L., Akshaya, K.M., Raghuveer, P., Yatnatti, S.K., Nagendra, N. and Nagaraja, S.B., 2019. Coverage, delays and implementation challenges of direct benefit transfer – A mixed-methods study from South India. *Global Health Action*, *12*(1), pp. 1633725.
NITI Aayog, 2018. Strategy for New India @ 75. Retrieved from https://innovate.mygov.in/wp-content/uploads/2022/01/mygov1641275714362306.pdf
Odedokun, M.O. and Round, J.I. 2001. Determinants of income inequality and its effects on economic growth: Evidence from African countries. *African Development Review*, *16*(2), pp. 287–327
Oxfam, 2022. Inequality kills: India Supplement 2022. Retrieved from https://www.oxfamindia.org/knowledgehub/workingpaper/inequality-kills-india-supplement-2022
Pal, P. and Ghosh, J., 2007. *Inequality in India: A Survey of Recent Trends. Flat World, Big Gaps: Economic Liberalization, Globalization, Poverty and Inequality*. UN Publications, New York.
Piketty, T., 2015. Capital and wealth taxation in the 21st century. *National Tax Journal*, *68*(2), pp. 449–458.

Piketty, T. and Saez, E., 2003. Income inequality in the United States, 1913–1998. *The Quarterly Journal of Economics*, *118*(1), pp. 1–41.
Rajagopalan, S., 2022. The equity-complexity tradeoff in tax policy: Lessons from the goods and services tax in India. *Social Policy and Philosophy*, *39*, pp. 139–187.
Rodems, R. and Pfeffer, F.T., 2021. Avoiding material hardship: The buffer function of wealth. *Journal of European Social Policy*, *31*(5), pp. 517–532.
Rubin, A. and Segal, D., 2015. The effects of economic growth on income inequality in the US. *Journal of Macroeconomics*, *45*, pp. 258–273.
Seery, E., 2022. Rising to the challenge: The case for permanent progressive policies to tackle Asia's coronavirus and inequality crisis. Retrieved from https://policy-practice.oxfam.org/resources/rising-to-the-challenge-the-case-for-permanent-progressive-policies-to-tackle-a-621343/
Shimray, R.A., 2014. Decentralization from below: A case study of Nagaland, India. *International Journal of Scientific and Research Publications*, *4*(3), pp. 1–6, March 2014.
Stiglitz, J.E., 2012. Stimulating the economy in an era of debt and deficit. *The Economists' Voice*, *9*(2), pp. 1–6.
Sumner, A., Ortiz-Juarez, E. and Hoy, C., 2022. Measuring global poverty before and during the pandemic: A political economy of overoptimism. *Third World Quarterly*, *43*(1), pp. 1–17.
Suratman, E. and Mayudi, G., 2022. Impact of inflation and exchange rate on ASEAN income inequality. *International Journal of Business and Society*, *23*(1), pp. 390–403.
Tagade, N., Naik, A.K. and Thorat, S., 2018. Wealth ownership and inequality in India: A socio-religious analysis. *Journal of Social Inclusion Studies*, *4(2)*, pp. 196–213.
Tcherneva, P.R., 2014. Reorienting fiscal policy: A bottom-up approach. *Journal of Post Keynesian Economics*, *37*(1), pp. 43–66.
Tujula M. and Wolswijk G. 2004. What Determines Fiscal Balances? An Empirical Investigation in Determinants of changes in OECD Budget Balances. Working paper series No.422. European Central Bank.
Vakulabharanam, V. and Motiram, S., 2012. Understanding poverty and inequality in urban India since reforms. *Economic and Political Weekly*, *47*(47 and 48), pp. 44–52.
Woo, J., 2003. Social polarization, industrialization, and fiscal instability: Theory and evidence. *Journal of Development Economics*, *72*(1), pp.223–252.
World Inequality Report, 2022. World Inequality Lab. United Nations Development Programme.
Zucman, G., 2019. Global wealth inequality. *Annual Review of Economics*, *11*, pp. 109–138.

5 The crossroad of management puzzles and game theory

Subhajit Bhattacharyya and Santosh Kumar Shrivastav

5.1 Introduction

The second half of the twentieth century witnessed the development of a new field of study that analysed the strategic behaviour of players having conflicting interests. In the last few decades, the field has seen so much intensive research activity that it earned fifteen Nobel Prizes, beginning with the 1994 prize to John Nash, Reinard Selten, and John Harsanyi. Although not really a creation of the second half of the last century, the field has grown by leaps and bounds during this period. John von Neumann is the father of modern mathematical analyses of game theory. In a 1928 article, von Neumann, one of the greatest mathematicians of all time, used Brouwer's fixed-point theorem and provided a mathematical proof of the minimax theorem in a two-player zero-sum game with perfect information (von Neumann, 1928). He and Oskar Morgenstern extended this work to a multiple-player contest under imperfect information and published it in their book titled *Theory of Games and Economic Behaviour* (Von Neumann and Morgenstern, 1944). This von Neumann–Morgenstern analysis formed the foundation of the analyses in non-cooperative game theory.

This was followed by path-breaking work by another stalwart in the mathematics field. In 1950, John Nash, in his PhD thesis, which was later published in the *Annals of Mathematics* (Nash, 1951), proved that any n-player non-zero-sum game has a mixed-strategy equilibrium, now known as the Nash equilibrium, where no player has an incentive to deviate when the other players do not deviate from their respective equilibrium strategies. During this decade, the game theoretical framework was strengthened through extensive work on cooperative games also, including the conceptualization of the Shapley (1951) value, an optimal surplus distribution formula in a cooperative game. The thought of applying game theory in management practices was initiated around this time as well (viz. Shubik, 1955).

The decades that followed saw game theory being applied in a wide range of fields, including political science, psychology, biology, and various forms of industrial structures. This led to the development of new ideas, such as evolutionary games that provided a framework for modelling Darwinian

DOI: 10.4324/9781003509721-7

competition in the form of contests and strategies (viz. Maynard-Smith et al. (1973); repeated games, which study how players' strategies change over multiple rounds of a game (viz. Benoit et al. (1985); behavioural game theory (viz. Camerer, 1997); mechanism design theory (viz. Myerson et al. (1983); networks (viz. Jackson, 2004); and others. Today, game theory is a widely used tool in economics, political science, computer science, and other fields. It has been used to study everything from voting behaviour to international conflict and has led to important insights into decision-making and strategic behaviour.

A substantial part of research on game theory focuses on the strategic behaviour of firms in different contexts of competition or cooperation. Some key areas in which game theory is applied in business include pricing strategies, market-share rivalry, bargaining, advertising, product differentiation, moral hazard issues, auctions, cartels, and others. It also captures strategic interactions between different economic agents, such as firms, consumers, and governments.

Over the decades, the field of game theory has undergone significant advancements and has continued to be an active area of research. So much development in game theory has helped expand its applications and helped improve the understanding of strategic interactions in a wide range of domains.

The digital era has presented new challenges and opportunities for the application of game theory in this field as well. Some of the key evolutions in game theory in the digital era include "algorithmic game theory", "networked game theory", "mechanism design for digital markets", and "behavioural game theory in digital contexts". Game theory and analytics are closely related, as game theory provides a theoretical foundation for many analytical techniques used in various fields, including business, economics, finance, and political science. Some of how game theory and analytics intersect include "predictive analytics", "optimization", "simulation", and "data-driven decision-making".

Interestingly, the literature on management science does not reflect much of the application of game theoretic techniques in their optimization processes or strategic decisions. The fundamental difference between the two fields may be the nomenclature of "strategy". In game theory, *strategy* means a short-term action leading to a single-stage game outcome, wherein multiple strategies in one round of a game are called a set of strategies for that round. The set of strategies for a player could be different in different rounds of a game in a multiple-round game structure, whereas in management science, strategy has a much bigger perspective with usually a much longer horizon of decision space, both longitudinally and latitudinal. Strategy for business involves multiple decision options on many factors, which may be difficult to formalize in a game-theoretic framework. Apart from this, the ways of dealing with information sets are quite different in these two fields, particularly, the games with perfect information are, in a way, misfits for real-life business situations. There are many such differences between the two fields in terms of the treatment of various contexts in their respective analyses.

However, efforts have been made by game theorists to bridge this gap by considering many real-life business situations and inventing appropriate game structures that, in a way, resemble reality. Shubik (1955) presents a few examples of such business situations in which game theories can be utilized. Particularly interesting is his example in which a mining company finds land rich in mineral deposits. The company's dilemma lies in whether to buy the land up front and explore the resources at a later period, which has a high holding cost, or postpone the purchase to minimize the holding cost but have a potential threat of its competitors buying the land. In the mid-1990s, Brandenburger et al. (1996) suggested exploring the synergy between game theory and business strategies through a combination of competition and cooperation, commonly referred to as "coopetition". This is a perfect possibility, for example, in the automobile sector (Kukkamalla et al., 2021). In the face of competition from Silicon Valley's artificial intelligence (AI)–driven autonomous driving system, many big automakers are collaborating to provide their customers with an advanced information service on live traffic conditions based on the network of sensor-based feedback mechanisms fitted to their vehicles on the road. Here, while they compete to have a bigger share of the road in terms of the number of vehicles sold, they collaborate on sharing live traffic data to fight a common enemy. BMW, Daimler, and Volkswagen are working on one such collaboration; General Motors, Nissan, and Volkswagen are collaborating on experiments with camera-based sensor systems to invent a mechanism that offers the precision mapping required in driverless cars. One can explore similar scopes of coopetition. These are the cases in which game-theoretic tools can be used to identify the best sets of business action plans.

This chapter presents an overview of the literature focused on possible synergies between management science and game theory. We first present a bibliometric analysis of the literature in which game-theoretic tools have been used to find answers to management problems. This is followed by a brief discussion and overview of the work done under each of the dominant sub-topics emerging through the bibliometric analysis. However, this chapter does not attempt to present a critical survey of the literature. It presents glimpses of the contexts considered and of how game theory is applied to find business solutions.

The overall aim of the study is to gain a better understanding of the field's foundational concepts, publication trends, notable articles contributing to the field, the models and techniques, and potential areas in which game theory is used to solve management puzzles. This study consists of five sections. In Section 5.2, the methodology is presented. Section 5.3 provides descriptive bibliometric analyses. In Section 5.4, the key term *co-occurrence analysis* is explained along with the main topics investigated in the data set and the different clusters identified. Section 5.5 provides an overview of the literature in each of the clusters identified in Section 5.4, and this is followed by concluding remarks.

5.2 Methodology

This study utilizes a literature review approach that incorporates a descriptive bibliometric method, data analysis visualization via VOSViewer software, and keyword analysis to comprehend intensively the literature on the application of game theory across various domains of management. By applying a bibliometric method, we aim to quantify research trends and provide a detailed overview of publications in this field, as suggested in Ikpaahindi (1985). Through this bibliometric study, we attempt to uncover significant insights that are of value to both scholars and practitioners in the business domain.

Keyword analysis examines and analyses keywords in scientific publications, revealing themes, trends, and connections in a field. It informs about past literature by identifying main themes, research trends, and gaps. It helps understand the future scope through emerging keywords, interdisciplinary connections, and predictions of research trends. Overall, bibliometrics help uncover the literature through a quantitative analysis of published research. It maps the research landscape, assesses productivity, identifies seminal works, reveals trends, discovers gaps, and supports systematic reviews. By analysing publication patterns, citations, and bibliographic data, bibliometrics provides scope for a comprehensive understanding of existing knowledge.

5.3 Data collection and exploratory analysis

We have collected the literature on "game theory applications in management" using the Scopus database. The Scopus database, introduced by Elsevier in 2004, is highly valuable for literature reviews as it is the largest database that includes various types of papers and provides extensive coverage across disciplines and analysis tools and access to high-quality sources (Chadegani et al., 2013).

To ensure accuracy in identifying scientific products, we developed a research protocol, which is illustrated in Figure 5.1. Per the research protocol, the initial stage involved setting up the data set. To collect the data, the first step is to use the Scopus database as the source for this study. To conduct literature searches, we utilized a step-by-step filtering approach. We chose appropriate keywords ("Game theory applications in management") to conduct the search, resulting in 1916 documents, which include articles, conference papers, book chapters, and conference reviews.

The subsequent step involved identifying the exclusion criteria. We narrowed our research area by only considering articles that were published in the Scopus subject areas of business management and economics and decision sciences. This filter was crucial for our analysis as our goal was to generate new knowledge about the specific impact and relevance of game theory in the business management literature. Additionally, we only included papers written in English. After obtaining the raw data, we conducted preliminary

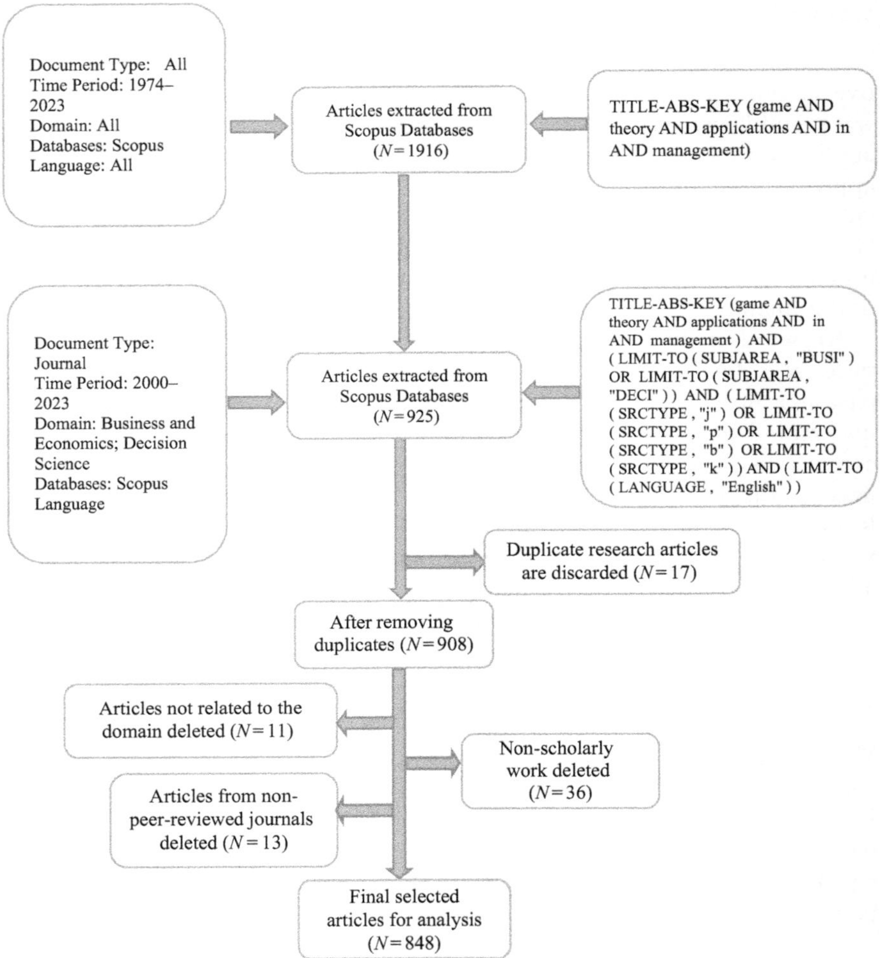

Figure 5.1 Flow chart of articles collection.

Source: Academic database.

data analysis, removing any duplicates and refining the data set manually. As a result, finally, we had 848 relevant research articles that are consistent with prior samples used in bibliometric studies.

5.3.1 Descriptive bibliometric analysis

The objective of the descriptive analysis is to present the key characteristics of our data set with a focus on six aspects that are relevant to scholars interested in the development and issues of game theory in the field of business management. This analysis aims to provide an accurate representation of the scientific works in this area. The six aspects considered are (a) publication trends, (b) types of documents and journals, (c) the different topics that researchers have studied within the realm of application of game theory in addressing business management issues, (d) publishing activity by country, (e) citations over time, and (f) the most cited papers.

5.3.1.1 Publication descriptive information

Publication descriptive information (PDI) refers to the descriptive information associated with a published work, such as a book, a journal article, or a research report, and includes information about the author(s), the title, the publisher, the date of publication, the subject or topic, the total citations, the citations over year, the citation per paper, and the citation year. This information is important because it helps readers and researchers identify, locate, and access relevant publications. It is also used by libraries, indexing and abstracting services, search engines, and other information providers to organize and retrieve publications from various databases and systems. A significantly large number of publications (1916, as reported in Table 5.1) in the literature on the topics under consideration, with an average annual citation of 906 show growing interest, progress, and development in the area. The citation of a published article represents acknowledging the source of information used in a particular piece of work, thereby allowing readers to locate and refer to the original source of information and assign due credit to the original authors.

5.3.1.2 Publications by year

Following the publication of the book by Brandenburger et al. (1996), the possibility of applying game theory to the management domain got attention from both game theorists and scholars of management science. As presented in Figure 5.2, starting from 1959, publications capturing the application of game theory to management started expanding and have significantly increased in the last 20 years.

More than 70% of the papers in our data set are from the last two decades (for 2023, the data are through April 2023). This signifies the importance of

Table 5.1 Descriptive information of research articles collected from the Scopus database

Publication years	1959–2023
Citation years	63 years (1959–2023)
Total papers	1916
Papers/year	63
Citations	57,079
Citations/year	906
Citations/paper	29.79

Source: Scopus database.

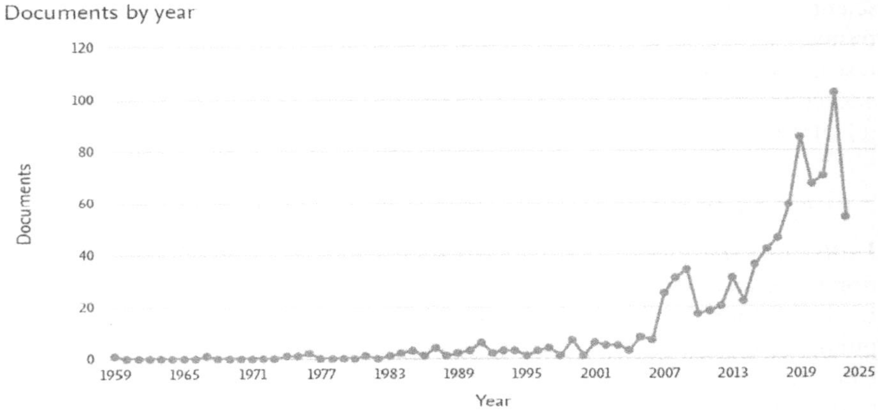

Figure 5.2 Publication by year.

game theory as a tool for solving puzzles in business and economics; analysing complex interactions, including strategic decision-making, risk analysis, complex systems, collaboration and cooperation, technology advancements, and policy and regulation; and making more informed decisions in an increasingly interconnected world.

5.3.1.3 Publications by article types

The literature collected from the Scopus database includes research articles, reviews, and conference papers. Most of the literature comprised research articles (95%), with 2% conference papers and the remaining being review papers (Table 5.2). The publications from 1959 to 2023 are included.

It is evident from Table 5.2 that the majority of papers selected for this study were published in peer-reviewed journals, confirming the unbiased selection of literature for analysis. We excluded articles that were not published in peer-reviewed journals before proceeding with the analysis.

Table 5.2 Proportion of research, review, and conference articles in the Scopus database

Documents type	*Frequency (%)*
Article	95
Book	1
Book Chapter	1
Conference Paper	2
Review	1

Source: Scopus database.

Table 5.3 Proportion of documents published in various journals subject-wise

Documents by Subject Area	*Frequency (%)*
Business, Management, and Accounting	29.10
Decision Sciences	22.90
Computer Science	13.70
Engineering	11.20
Mathematics	7.60
Social Sciences	4.70
Economics, Econometrics, and Finance	4.50
Others	2.30
Energy	1.60
Environmental Science	1.30
Arts and Humanities	1.10

Source: Scopus database.

5.3.1.4 *Publications by domain*

Articles from the social sciences, business management and accounting, economics, econometrics and finance, decision sciences, agriculture, and environmental science have all been included (Table 5.3). Since the study aims to investigate the applications of game theory in management, we have included only those articles in the analysis which were published in the domain of business and economics and decision science.

This study is focused on collecting literature or published articles from management and related areas that help achieve the study's objective. Approximately 52% of papers are listed under business management and economics and decision sciences (Table 5.3). So, we do not include other academic fields, such as law. Also, we have only considered articles available in English. Based on the previously mentioned inclusion criteria, 848 articles were selected for analysis, and information about search terms and articles is given in Figure 5.1.

5.3.1.5 *Publications by country*

The majority of game theory literature comes from the United States, China, and the United Kingdom due to renowned academic institutions, ample funding, strong academic culture and collaboration, thriving economies, and English-language dominance in publishing (Figure 5.3). Contributions in this field, however, come from scholars worldwide.

5.3.1.6 *Citations by year*

The number of citations is a valuable metric for assessing the significance of documents within a specific field of study. Figure 5.4 provides a clear depiction of the total citation count per year, allowing for a comprehensive

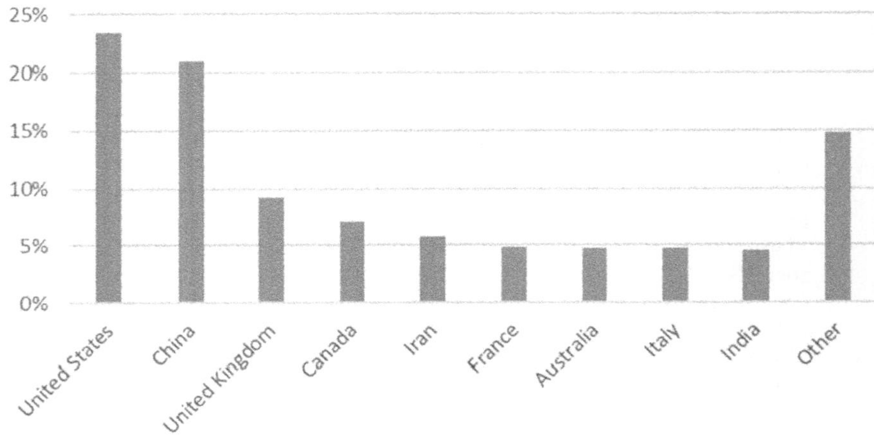

Figure 5.3 Journal publication country-wise (in percentages).

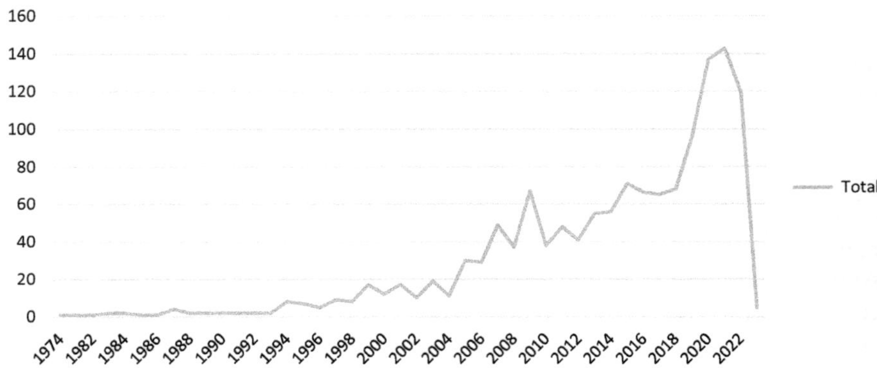

Figure 5.4 The number of citations each year.

understanding of the papers' impact. Notably, the figure prominently showcases a substantial upward trend in citations over the past two decades, underscoring the increasing recognition and influence of game theory applications. This observation highlights the enduring relevance and growing importance of research within the field over time.

5.3.1.7 Most cited documents

Many studies in this domain have received a good number of citations. Appendix Table 5.A1 presents the articles having more than 500 citations each. A notable observation is that the majority of these papers have attempted to apply game theory to find solutions to problems related to various management functionalities, reaffirming the significance and widespread utilization of game theory in this field. The high citation counts further reflect the impact and recognition these articles have garnered within the academic community. This highlights the increasing importance of game theory as a valuable tool in the business domain over time.

5.4 Keyword analysis and themes from published articles

Keyword analysis in bibliometrics examines and explores keywords used in scientific publications, revealing main themes and trends. Clusters of related keywords represent thematic areas, unveiling subfields and connections. Techniques like co-occurrence analysis visualize these clusters, aiding researchers in identifying gaps and collaboration opportunities. It organizes the knowledge landscape based on shared terminology and content. The keyword analysis of selected articles shows four clusters, as presented in Figure 5.5.

The information and dominant keyword of each cluster are given in the following sub-sections.

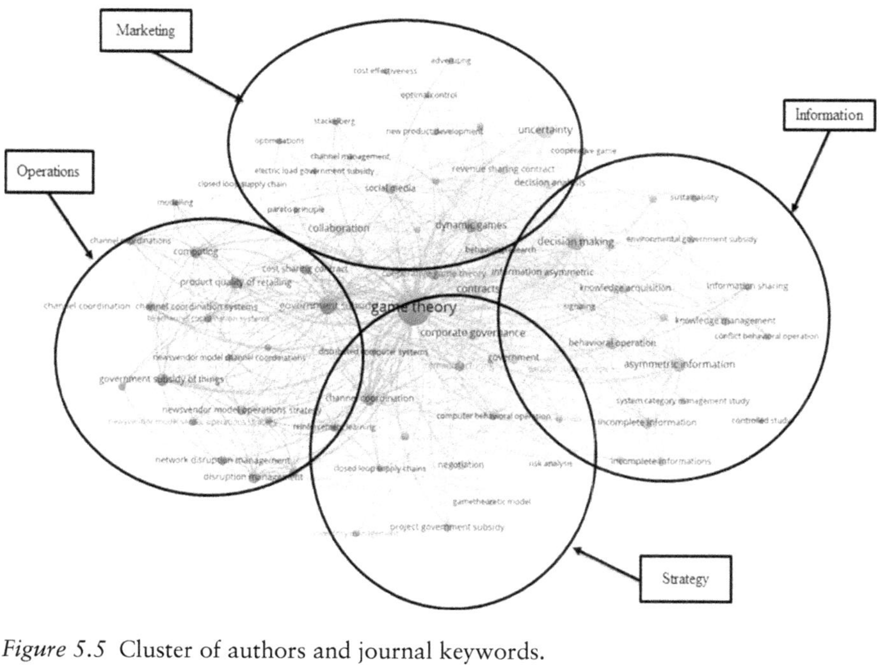

Figure 5.5 Cluster of authors and journal keywords.

Source: Authors.

5.4.1 Cluster 1: Marketing

Advertising; customer relationship management (CRM); decision-making; dynamic games; category management; channel management; consumer behaviour; dual channel pricing; dynamic pricing; marketing; inventory; non-cooperative games; new product development; retailing; store brand; social media.

5.4.2 Cluster 2: Operations

Channel coordination; channel leadership; closed-loop supply chain; contract; cost-sharing contract; disruption management; inventory management; new vendor model; operations strategy; power structure; product differentiation; quality; remanufacturing; supply chain management.

5.4.3 Cluster 3: Information

Asymmetric information; behavioural operation; incomplete information; information acquisition; information sharing; knowledge acquisition; knowledge management; knowledge sharing; moral hazard; product quality; quality management; signalling; system dynamics

5.4.4 Cluster 4: Strategy

Collaboration; contracts; cooperation; cooperative game theory; corporate governance; decision analysis; decision-making; decision support; government; government subsidy; information asymmetric; innovation; revenue sharing contract; uncertainty.

Based on the keywords of each cluster, Cluster 1 can be termed "Applications of Game theory in Marketing Management", Cluster 2 can be termed "Applications of Game Theory in Operations Management", Cluster 3 can termed "Applications of Game Theory in Information in Business Context", and Cluster 4 can be termed "Applications of Game Theory is Strategic Management". A discussion of these four clusters and related contributions are explained in Section 5.5.

5.5 Literature overview of the identified clusters

5.5.1 Cluster 1: Applications of game theory in marketing management

The cluster of Marketing covers topics related to advertising, pricing, channel management, retailing, consumer behaviour, CRM, category management, new product development, store brand, and others. Several studies have used game-theoretic tools to find optimal solutions to various problem setups in the marketing field. Choi et al. (2013), in a Nash framework, attempted to identify profit-maximizing prices to be charged in a supply chain with two retailers and one national brand (NB) manufacturer. They found that, when the retailers are allowed to come up with their respective own store brands, to maximize profit, retailers will offer differentiated products with respect to each other yet offer a product closer to the national brand. In a similar problem setup with a single retailer, a different game structure was used by Yang et al. (2018). They considered four different game structures. The first game considered the NB manufacturer as the Stackelberg leader and the retailer as the follower. This is possible in cases in which the manufacturer is a very big brand. In this game, the manufacturer decides national advertising expenditure, as well as its share in cooperative advertising cost in the local-level promotion. The retailer decides on local cooperative advertising expenditure, as well as its individual-level advertising expenses. Both are profit maximizers. They find conditions under which the manufacturer's marginal profit will be higher than that of the retailer and vice versa, as well as the conditions under which a manufacturer will share the cooperative advertising costs with the retailer. This study also considered three different game structures: (1) when a retailer is a Stackelberg leader (more relevant in organized retailing scenarios with large retailers), (2) a Nash game in which the manufacturer decides the cost-sharing formula for cooperative advertising with the retailer, and (3) a Nash game in which the retailer decides the cost-sharing formula for cooperative advertising. They find conditions for such cost-sharing depending on the value of the ratio manufacturer's marginal profit and that of retailers out of such cooperative advertising. Assarzadegan et al. (2021), using a Stackerberg leadership framework between the manufacturer of an NB and a retailer with store loyalty, its own generic store brand (GSB) product, and the premium store brand (PSB) product, attempted to understand the strategic behaviour of the two players under two scenario – first with the manufacture of NB as the leader and then the retailer as the leader. The study shows that the manufacturer of NB will have to maintain the qualitative gap with PSB through innovation and advertising. The PSB has the potential to compete with NB. Interestingly, the study finds that the retailer could be a leader if it offers both the GSB and the PSB simultaneously. In a game of choosing selling channels between an online travel agency (OTA) and a dual-channel distribution system (both OTA and self), as well as the choice between the agency model and merchant model by the OTA, Liao et al. (2019) found that in the dual-channel system, the OTA prefers the agency model if the hotel's capacity is small. The study also proposes a revenue-sharing contract to achieve channel coordination under both models.

Considering both a cooperative game and a non-cooperative Stackelberg manufacturer game in a supply chain problem involving a manufacturer and a retailer, Yuan et al. (2015) examined the impact of demand and production cost disruptions on advertising, pricing, and production quantity levels. They found that the cooperative game suggests better channel profit and higher social surplus than the non-cooperative game when retail prices are lower and advertising is at a higher level. When, in a similar framework, the retailer has an option of offering a store brand to compete with the national brand, Al-Monawer et al. (2021) found that the retailer can offer a store brand with substantially lower quality and price compared to the national brand. It also suggests that such offerings by the retailer are possible when the manufacturer's national brand has a large consumer base.

In the context of online merchandising, Xu et al. (2022) considered a strategic game between an online retailer (e-tailer) and a cashback website in having channel leadership for a manufacturer, the study examines the rebate and commission format selection strategy of both players. Interestingly, the study finds that an e-tailer's rebate has different impacts on the wholesale price depending on the commission-sharing format, but under both formats, sharing or fixed commission, such a rebate hurts the manufacturer. However, when the manufacturer is a Stackelberg leader, the e-tailer's rebate strategy benefits both, as well as the consumers. However, contrary to the literature, it has been found that for a monopolist retailer, it may not always be optimal to offer a store brand in a market with two competing NBs. But, when the two NBs are marginally differentiated, the store brand can be offered a quality lying between the two (Du et al. 2005).

Avinadav et al. (2014) considered a two-player supply chain game with a manufacturer and a retailer of digital products to evaluate optimal strategies for pricing and digital rights protection. Considering three scenarios, manufacturer–Stackelberg, retailer–Stackelberg, and vertical integration, the study finds the conditions under which the manufacturer is better off by giving up leadership to the retailer. Under both the profit criteria – expectation versus target – it establishes the dependence between pricing and protection investment. In a market with the possibility of fake products being supplied by the retailer, Zhou et al. (2022) examined the optimality of anti-counterfeiting investment by the manufacturer. It is found that the pay-off of such an investment would be negative when the proportion of fakes is sufficiently low.

Naik et al. (2008) pointed out that there was a gap in marketing literature on creating brand awareness through advertising in not considering the impact of competition. Their study derives closed-loop Nash equilibrium strategies in an *N*-brand awareness formation model to address this issue, and they suggest that contrary to practice, large brands should spend, as a proportion to sales, less in advertising than small brands. Carter et al. (1999) explore an application of game theory in strategizing for a solution to the dilemma of negative impression owing to supplier interaction and procurement cost management. Creating a positive impression resulting from a customer interaction is found to be a balancing act.

In an application to the energy market, Salyani et al. (2023) consider a cooperative game theoretic framework to capture coordination among multiple micro-grids (MGs) at the local energy market in the face of long-duration power cuts from the main grid. The MGs have two operational modes. The first is "normal operation mode" (NOM), and the second is "resiliency operation mode" (ROM) during power cuts from the main grid. The study finds that the market clears for NOM at a price less than the wholesale prices, whereas, for ROM, the prices are higher. In an interesting work, Cousins (2002), using a game-theoretic model, presented an alternative viewpoint about relationship management in the context of sales of products. Relationships are presented here to be a process rather than entities, which should be at the product, service, or commodity levels rather than at the company level.

Cachon et al. (2007) considered the category management problem of a retailer managing multiple merchandise categories. In a duopolistic retail framework, the retailers choose prices and consumers choose between retail stores and have an option of not purchasing. It is shown that, under the centralized decision in category management, no optimal solution exists and the retailer ends up offering less variety and charging higher-than-optimal prices. However, when each category is treated as a profit centre, near-optimal solutions are obtained.

5.5.2 Cluster 2: Applications of game theory in operations management

The functionality of operations management relates to production, procurements, processes, inventory, stock, transportation, and the like. In all these activities, firms face one or another conflicting situation that puts them into a dilemma regarding the best action to be chosen. Such circumstances become an appropriate domain for the application of game-theoretic analyses. The following are some such studies indicating the scope of applying game theory to the domain of operations management.

In an interesting work, Veldman et al. (2014) examined the outcome of shifting performance incentives from sales performance to product quality and process improvement in a firm. The study found that a firm can improve its profit by offering incentives to its managers for product quality and process improvement when the rival does not. But, when both offer the same incentive, the game turns out to be a prisoner's dilemma game, in which both firms are worse off compared to the situation in which they offer incentives for sales performance.

Small and medium-sized enterprises (SMEs) usually do not give importance to safety aspects in their production processes. However, they tend to hide such laxity when they strive to be a key supplier to a core enterprise that attaches high importance to such safety measures. This study by Mei et al. (2020) builds a signalling model between core enterprises and these potential suppliers and finds that adverse selection can be avoided by adjusting the signal cost parameters of the SMEs that stop them from concealing or exaggerating their safety measures in production processes.

Usually, the designing of product family architecture does not give any consideration to supply chain issues. However, in another very interesting work, Wang et al. (2016) examined the criticality of integrating a downstream supply chain (DSC) network into the designing of product family architecture (PFA) for a firm. In a Stackelberg game-theoretic structure with PFA as the upper-level player and DSC as the lower-level player, the study formulates a joint optimization problem. For the PFA, the objective is to maximize customer utility per unit of cost, while that of DSC is to minimize implementation cost. Considering the business of power transformers, this study shows the appropriateness of such joint optimization models in the Stackelberg setup.

A study by Otero-Palencia et al. (2019) explores the scope of benefitting from a collaborative replenishment program by many buyers. In the two-stage game, the first stage determines a cost-efficient replenishment frequency based on stochastic demand faced by the buyers, as well as storage and transport considerations, the second stage determines the Shapley value function for evaluating and distributing gains out of such collaborative replenishments. In a simulation of the model with 30 items, the study shows average cost savings of 32.3%, 28.2%, and 32.7% for 3, 4, and 5 players, respectively.

There is usually a conflict of interest between the project manager of a construction project and the subcontractor. The objective of the project manager is to stick to the budget and planned schedules, while the subcontractor allocates resources across multiple projects in a way that maximizes its benefits. In a game-theoretic model based on a unit-price contract between the project manager of a construction project and its subcontractor, Sacks et al. (2006) examined the influence of the reliability of a planned schedule on the behaviour of the subcontractor. The study shows that the reliability of the planned schedule is key to ensuring the success of cooperative behaviour.

Game theory has been applied in several different contexts related to operations management. Independent decisions by resource users to exploit a common pool of resources lead to a situation equivalent to the prisoner's dilemma. However, Mamada et al. (2022) show that institutional arrangements to manage the common pool of resources result in the entanglement of strategies of the resource users, which eventually results in a cooperative outcome. In a Stackelberg game model with the manufacturer as the leader, Wang et al. (2019) analysed the impact of various regulatory policies on the rate of recycling in a product market. Four scenarios are considered: "business as usual", "penalty", "reward–penalty", and "reward" for recycling used products. Interestingly, the study finds that the "reward" scenario has a negative correlation with the rate of recycling, while in all the other scenarios, it is positive.

To address water shortages in the north, China has created man–water transfer projects. Two such projects, from south to north, are through the eastern corridor and central corridor. In a game-theoretic framework, Du et al. (2019) attempted to derive optimal pricing and ordering strategies. The study found that the members of the supply chain are better off when they are under a two-part pricing contract rather than one wholesale pricing system when competition among suppliers is weak and vice versa. Song et al. (2016) designed a game theoretic framework for maritime logistics that captures horizontal and vertical interactions between liners and ports. Applying Bertrand's game and multinomial logit model, the study determines the choice of port and the pricing strategies of the players. The findings are supported by a numerical example.

In consideration of the service industry, where contracting is gradually moving to performance-based from the erstwhile material-based system, a study by Jin et al. (2015) applied the game-theoretic framework to capture the optimization problem in a "multi-party, multi-criteria and multi-item service delivery mechanism". The study shows that the supplier's actions on various aspects of its service delivery are observable to the customer, thereby avoiding any moral hazard issues. In the context of the COVID-19 pandemic, Salarpour et al. (2021) modelled a stochastic generalized Nash equilibrium framework for countries facing limited supplies of essential medical items like personal protection equipment (PPE) kits, ventilators, and so on. The study finds that the success of the countries in managing the pandemic crisis depends not only on their preparedness before the declaration of the pandemic but also on their agility to adapt to changing circumstances. Fang et al. (2010) consider a market where the products are partially complementary in the sense that one part of the demand base treats these products as complementary, while the other part treats them as a substitute, primarily demands by individuals. In a non-cooperative game framework to analyse the strategic interactions of the firms and their impact on the supply chain performance, the study found that the game may have multiple equilibria. However, they find that there exists one unique equilibrium that maximizes the profits of each of the manufacturers.

5.5.3 Cluster 3: Applications of game theory in information in a business context

Information related to product quality decisions and costs is private to a firm. Consumers attempt to decipher this information, particularly related to quality and justification of price, either through consumption or through shared experiences by other consumers, as well as price. Because of this, customers' decisions about purchasing a product depend on their perception of the product quality and the probable cost efficiency of the firm. Jiang et al. (2019) found an equilibrium at which a firm's product quality decision is positively related to its cost efficiency. However, they also show that the firm may reduce quality when its high-cost efficiency is known to the consumers.

In the prevalent distributed forms of organizations and the impending relationships among them, knowledge transfer has been necessitated to eliminate existing information asymmetry and incompleteness. However, because of this information asymmetry and incompleteness, it may not be possible to identify the qualified knowledge providers, thereby leading to an adverse selection issue. Lihui et al. (2005) considered this problem and applied game-theoretic models aimed at providing a framework to alleviate this anomaly.

In today's business era, people are flooded with information. Most of this information is based on perception rather than verifiable authentic information, particularly in the context of selling a product. In such confusing circumstances, a retailer of a product may not share information that has a probability of impacting its sales. Allon et al. (2011) analysed the impact of creating asymmetric information by a retailer on the behaviour of its customers and found conditions under which the customer's behaviour can be influenced by the retailer through such action.

A downstream buyer in a supply chain usually avoids revealing its demand preferences to the supplier owing to a threat that such action may shift a share of its profit to the supplier. However, Matsui (2021) has shown that the buyer can strategically share such information and is better off when there is a threat of entry into the upstream market of the supply chain.

Hu et al. (2021) aimed to identify the reasons behind manufacturers usually preferring to use retailers for distribution purposes rather than direct sales. They propose that information asymmetry between the manufacturer and the retailer regarding consumer quality preferences is the key reason for such a choice of manufacturer as retailers may play strategically with their advantage in acquiring information on consumer preferences.

5.5.4 Cluster 4: Applications of game theory in strategic management

The subject of industrial organization fundamentally deals with the application of game theory in the strategic decisions of firms. The literature is very rich and advanced. However, the contexts covered in that literature are very generic and very rarely specific to a particular type of company or a particular industry. Here, we present a glimpse of the literature that considers contexts related to a variety of industries and applies game theory to finding appropriate solutions.

In a two-period game with an endogenous decision on the incentive to a manager in a potential threat of entry, Sen (1993) established the linkage between this incentive and the mode of output decision. It is shown that the owner of the incumbent firm will link the manager's incentive to the profit earned when the output decision is taken through a Nash bargaining game between the managers of the incumbent and the entrant. This is not the case, however, with the owner of the entrant. The entrant will never link such an incentive to profit. Also, a high cost of entry may allow the incumbent owner to deter entry by offering appropriate incentives to the manager.

Building information modelling (BIM) is helpful in designing, planning, building, and maintaining physical infrastructure. While inter-firm cooperation may result in better BIM benefits, the self-interests of individual firms may give rise to certain moral hazard problems. A study by Zheng et al. (2017) addressed the moral hazard problem of various stakeholders in the implementation of BIM in a construction project. Using an evolutionary game in a principal–agent framework, this study finds that extending incentives to the designers/contractors may result in the expected cooperative framework that results in better BIM benefits than costs.

In the face of competition from low-cost carriers (LCCs), the full-service carriers (FSCs) in Korea started offering low-cost services as well to maintain market share. However, the objective view needs to be taken by an FSC as to whether to compete or collude with its low-cost subsidiary. What are the possibilities of a leadership equilibrium for the FSC? This study by Ko (2016) analysed the strategies of three categories of players – an FSC, its low-cost subsidiary, and an LCC. In comparison to a duopolistic framework considered in Brueckner et al. (2007), this study considers, among strategies, airfare, flight frequency, and the number of aircraft in operation for each player, with profit maximization as an objective. It considers different game structures: repeated game under competition, repeated game when the FSC and its LCC collude, a Stackelberg leader game when FSC and its LCC collude and so on. Using numerical examples, the study shows that the FSC makes more profit when it colludes with its LCC and plays a Stackelberg leader game. Various such possibilities are explained in a numerical simulation.

In line with the concept of coopetition emphasized by Brandenburger et al.(1996), a two-stage game framework was proposed by Brandenburger et al. (2007) that considers competition and cooperation at two different stages. The first stage of the game comprises competition in building "strategic capabilities" like capacity, R&D, positioning, branding, and so on, and this strategic positioning leads to the second stage of the game where a cooperative game determines the shares of value for each of the players. This form of the game has been named a "biform game". A few examples have been used to elucidate the solution process of such games. In a bargaining game between a private-sector and a public-sector agent in transport infrastructure agreements, Medda (2007) has shown that there could be a moral hazard problem in which guarantee values exceed financial loss.

Van Witteloostuijn (1998) considers a Cournot duopoly and attempts to identify the reasons behind organizational failures. The study finds that the "pure profit maximization motive" of firms may pose a threat to organizational survival. Syed et al. (2008) analyse fare-pricing competition between two airlines. Considering various deterministic and stochastic demand conditions, it finds a unique Nash equilibrium based on booking limits and pricing decisions.

Nair et al. (2012) analyse the competitive dynamics and interdependence of strategies between Coke and Pepsi. The volatility in this relationship has not been found to reduce over time. In addressing the issues related to management succession in a corporate or a family-owned business, Mathews et al. (2015) design a tournament-style game wherein two siblings compete for the CEO position. Among the factors, they consider the founder's preference for one sibling over the other, the value of winning to each of the siblings, the cost of the competition, and the first-mover advantage.

Bai et al. (2019) apply evolutionary game theory to understand the behaviour of a taxi company, a taxi driver, and a passenger in their mode of choice between dispatching and online car-hailing. Using a replicator dynamic system to capture the evolutionary process and stable state, the authors analyse different scenarios using a numerical simulation. They find that the stable state is found when both the driver and the passenger, the key players in the game, choose either dispatching or online car-hailing. A study addresses the strategic choice of channel structure and product durability by a firm. The manufacturer has a choice of direct selling through its e-channel and a retailer. The conflict of choice for the manufacturer is whether to encroach on the retailer's market through direct sales. Yan et al. (2018) find that the optimality of this choice depends on product durability. Using US x86 computer server market data, the study show that both parties gain the most when product durability is either low or sufficiently high and that the same is low when product durability is moderate.

5.6 Conclusion

The literature on industrial organization generally captures many of the aspects discussed earlier. However, bringing strategic contexts into analysis from the perspective of management functionalities is roughly about two decades old. Hence, the number of studies is relatively less than that of the entire domain of game theory and industrial organization, which is also more than seven decades old. This study attempts to present an overview of the application of game theory in various management functional contexts. The idea is not to present a literature survey on these studies but, rather, to present a glimpse of studies done in the practical domain. In addition to the previously discussed, there are studies related to finance and human resource management, which are not presented here as they have not emerged as prominent domains of work in the bibliometric analysis. These are also areas offering excellent opportunities for game theory applications.

Appendix 5A

Table 5.A1 List of articles with more than 500 citations each

Article	*Citation*	*Brief Description*
Dellarocas C., 2003, The digitization of word of mouth: Promise and challenges of online feedback mechanisms, *Management Science*, 49(10), 1407–1424.	2117	The topic of reputation in game theory and economics is presented in a comprehensive manner by reviewing the relevant research.
Chiang W.-Y.K., Chhajed D., Hess J.D., 2003, Direct marketing, indirect profits: A strategic analysis of dual-channel supply-chain design, *Management Science*, 49(1), 1–20.	1290	This study presents a game between a manufacturer and its retailer, who independently set prices. The author shows that direct marketing improves overall profitability by reducing inefficient double marginalization, benefiting both parties when combined with wholesale price reduction.
Tsay A.A., Agrawal N., 2004, Channel conflict and coordination in the E-commerce age, *Production and Operations Management*, 13(1), 93–110.	755	Internet commerce and logistics advancements prompt manufacturers to encroach on retailers' markets. This model shows that adding a direct channel does not harm retailers if the manufacturer adjusts pricing benefiting both parties. Adjusting manufacturer–reseller relationships through wholesale pricing changes, paying commissions to resellers for directing customers to the direct channel, or handing over demand fulfillment to resellers. These approaches leverage each channel's competitive advantage.
Rivkin J.W., 2000, Imitation of complex strategies, *Management Science*, 46, no. 6 (June 2000): 824–844.	717	This paper shows that complexity makes finding an optimal strategy difficult, falling under the NP-completeness theory. Copycats must rely on heuristics or learning rather than algorithmic solutions to match superior firms. However, complexity hinders heuristics and learning. Simple heuristics get trapped on local peaks, and mimicking a high performer's strategy leads to penalties for small errors. Management science and managerial choice play essential roles in a complex strategic environment.

(*Continued*)

Table 5.A1 (Continued)

Article	*Citation*	*Brief Description*
Cachon G.P., Lariviere M.A., 2001, Contracting to assure supply: How to share demand forecasts in a supply chain, *Management Science*, 47(5), 629–646.	690	This study focuses on forecast sharing in a supply chain involving a manufacturer and a supplier and explores contracts that enable credible demand forecast sharing under both compliance regimes.
Ivanov D., Dolgui A., 2020, Viability of intertwined supply networks: extending the supply chain resilience angles towards survivability. A position paper motivated by COVID-19 outbreak, *International Journal of Production Research*, 58(10), 2904–2915.	662	Interconnected supply network (ISNs) ensure the provision of goods/services. Resilience is crucial for survival and analysing survivability requires a large-scale perspective. This study examines ISN viability, and decision-making using game-theoretic models, opening avenues for future research.
Lorenz J., Rauhut H., Schweitzer F., Helbing D., 2011, How social influence can undermine the wisdom of crowd effect, *Proceedings of the National Academy of Sciences*, 108(22), 9020–9025.	580	Collective intelligence in social groups can surpass individual judgment (wisdom of crowds). However, this study challenges this, showing mild social influence undermines crowd wisdom in simple tasks. Effects include reduced diversity, truth distortion, and increased confidence without accuracy improvement. Implications range from misguided elites to financial crises.

Source: Authors.

References

Allon G., Bassamboo A., 2011, Buying from the babbling retailer? The impact of availability information on customer behaviour, *Management Science*, Volume 57, Issue 4, April 2011, Pages 713–726.

Al-Monawer N., Davoodi M., Qi L., 2021, Brand and quality effects on introduction of store brand products, *Journal of Retailing and Consumer Services*, Volume 61, Article number 102507.

Assarzadegan P., Hejazi S.R., 2021, A game theoretic approach for analyzing the competition between national and store brands by considering store loyalty, *Journal of Retailing and Consumer Services*, Volume 60, Article number 102449.

Avinadav T., Chernonog T., Perlman Y., 2014, Analysis of protection and pricing strategies for digital products under uncertain demand, *International Journal of Production Economics*, Volume 158, 1 December 2014, Pages 54–64.

Bai Z., Huang M., Bian S., Wu H., 2019, A Study of Taxi Service Mode Choice Based on Evolutionary Game Theory, *Journal of Advanced Transportation*, Volume 2019, Article number 8607942.

Benoit, J.P. & Krishna, V., 1985, Finitely Repeated Games, *Econometrica*, 53 (4): 905–922

Brandenburger A., Stuart H., 2007, Biform games, *Management Science*, Volume 53, Issue 4, Pages 537–549.

Brandenburger, A.M., Nalebuff, B.J., 1996, *Co-opetition: A Revolution Mindset that Combines Competition and Cooperation*, New York: Crown Business.

Brueckner, J.K., Flores-Fillol, R., 2007. Airline schedule competition. *Review of Industrial Organisation*, Volume 30, Issue 3, Pages 161–177.

Cachon, G.P., Kök, A.G., 2007, Category management and coordination in retail assortment planning in the presence of basket shopping consumers, *Management Science*, Volume 53, Issue 6, June 2007, Pages 934–951.

Camerer, Colin F., 1997, Progress in Behavioural Game Theory. *Journal of Economic Perspectives*, Volume 11, Issue 4, 01 November 1997, Pages 167–188.

Carter, S.M., Deephouse, D.L., 1999, 'Tough Talk' and 'Soothing Speech': Managing reputations for being tough and for being GoodCorporate. *Reputation Review*, Volume 2, Issue 4, 1 October 1999, Pages 308–332.

Chadegani, A.A., Salehi, H., Yunus, M.M., Farhadi, H., Fooladi, M., Farhadi, M., & Ebrahim, N.A., 2013, A comparison between two main academic literature collections: Web of Science and Scopus databases. arXiv preprint arXiv:1305.0377.

Choi, S., Fredj, K., 2013, Price competition and store competition: Store brands vs. national brand. *European Journal of Operational Research*, Volume 225, Issue 1, Pages 166–178.

Cousins, P.D., 2002, A conceptual model for managing long-term inter-organizational relationships. *European Journal of Purchasing and Supply Management*, Volume 8, Issue 2, 2002, Pages 71–82.

Du, R., Lee, E., Staelin, R., 2005, Bridge, focus, attack, or stimulate: Retail category management strategies with a store brand. *Quantitative Marketing and Economics*, Volume 3, Issue 4, Pages 393–418.

Du W., Fan Y., Liu X., Park S.C., Tang X., 2019, A game-based production operation model for water resource management: An analysis of the South-to-North Water Transfer Project in China. *Journal of Cleaner Production*. Volume 228, 10 August 2019, Pages 1482–1493.

Fang X., Wang Y., 2010, A model for partial product complementarity and strategic production decisions under demand uncertainty. *Production and Operations Management*, Volume 19, Issue 3, May 2010, Pages 322–342.

Hu H., Sun S., Zheng X., Chen L., Huang T., 2021, Committed or contingent? The retailer's information acquisition and sharing strategies when confronting manufacturer encroachment. *International Journal of Production Economics*, Volume 242, December 2021, Article number 108294.

Ikpaahindi, Linus, 1985, An overview of bibliometrics: Its measurements, laws and their applications. *Libri*, 35: 163.

Jackson, M.O., 2004, A survey of models of network formation: stability and efficiency. In: G. Demange and M. Wooders (Eds.), *Group Formation in Economics. Networks, Clubs and Coalitions*. Cambridge, UK: Cambridge University Press, pp. 11–57.

Jiang, B., Yang, B., 2019, Quality and pricing decisions in a market with consumer information sharing. *Management Science*, Volume 65, Issue 1, Pages 272–285.

Jin, T., Tian, Z., Xie, M., 2015, A game-theoretical approach for optimizing maintenance, spares and service capacity in performance contracting. *International Journal of Production Economics*, Volume 161, March 2015, Pages 31–43.

Ko Y.D., 2016, An airline's management strategies in a competitive air transport market. *Journal of Air Transport Management*, Volume 50, 01 January 2016, Pages 53–61.

Kukkamalla, Prasanna, Bikfalvi, Andrea, Arbussa, Anna, 2021, Collaborative partnerships in the automotive industry: Key motives and resource integration strategy.

International Journal of Business Innovation and Research, Volume 24. DOI. 10.1504/IJBIR.2021.114117

Liao, P., Ye, F., Wu, X., 2019, A comparison of the merchant and agency models in the hotel industry. *International Transactions in Operational Research*, Volume 26, Issue 3, May 2019, Pages 1052–1073.

Lihui, L., Xianjun, G., Whinston, A.B., 2005, A sender-receiver framework for knowledge transfer. *MIS Quarterly: Management Information Systems*, Volume 29, Issue 2, Pages 197–219.

Mamada, R., Perrings, C., 2022, "Entanglement" and the exploitation of common pool resources: A quantum solution to the prisoner's dilemma. *International Game Theory Review*, Volume 24, Issue 1, Article number 2150009.

Mathews, T., Blumentritt, T., 2015, A sequential choice model of family business succession, *Small Business Economics*, Volume 45, Issue 1, 1 June 2015, Pages 15–37.

Matsui, K., 2021, Buyer's strategic demand information sharing with an upstream echelon for entry promotion. *International Journal of Production Economics*, Volume 242, December 2021, Article number 108286.

Maynard-Smith, J., Price, G.R., 1973, The logic of animal conflict. *Nature*, Volume 246, Issue 5427, Pages 15–18.

Medda, F., 2007, A game theory approach for the allocation of risks in transport public-private partnerships, *International Journal of Project Management*, Volume 25, Issue 3, April 2007, Pages 213–218.

Mei, Q., Zhou, Q., Liu, S., Wang, Q., 2020, A safety signaling game for small and medium-sized manufacturing enterprises in the supply chain, *International Journal of Information Systems and Supply Chain Management*, Volume 13, Issue 1, January–March 2020, Pages 118–135.

Myerson, Roger B., Satterthwaite, Mark A., 1983, Efficient mechanisms for bilateral trading. *Journal of Economic Theory*, Volume 29, Issue 2, Pages 265–281.

Naik, P.A., Prasad, A., Sethi, S.P., 2008, Building brand awareness in dynamic oligopoly markets, *Management Science*, Volume 54, Issue 1, January 2008, Pages 129–138.

Nair, A., Selover, D.D., 2012, A study of competitive dynamics. *Journal of Business Research*, Volume 65, Issue 3, Pages 355–361.

Nash, John, 1951. Non-cooperative games. *Annals of Mathematics. Second Series*, Volume 54, Issue 2, Pages 286–295.

Otero-Palencia, C., Amaya-Mier, R., Yie-Pinedo, R., 2019, A stochastic joint replenishment problem considering transportation and warehouse constraints with gain-sharing by Shapley Value allocation. *International Journal of Production Research*, Volume 57, Issue 10, 19 May 2019, Pages 3036–3059.

Sacks R., Harel M., 2006, An economic game theory model of subcontractor resource allocation behaviour. *Construction Management and Economics*, Volume 24, Issue 8, August 2006, Pages 869–881.

Salarpour, M., Nagurney, A., 2021, A multicountry, multicommodity stochastic game theory network model of competition for medical supplies inspired by the COVID-19 pandemic, *International Journal of Production Economics*, Volume 236, June 2021, Article number 108074.

Salyani, P., Nourollahi, R., Zare, K., Razzaghi, R., 2023, A cooperative game approach for optimal resiliency-oriented scheduling of transactive multiple microgrids. *Sustainable Cities and Society*, Volume 89, February 2023, Article number 104358.

Sen, A., 1993, Entry and managerial incentives. *International Journal of Industrial Organization*, Volume 11, Issue 1, Pages 123–137.

Shapley, Lloyd S., 1951, *Notes on the n-Person Game – II: The Value of an n-Person Game*, (August 21, 1951), Santa Monica, CA: RAND Corporation.

Shubik, Martin, 1955, The uses of game theory in management science. *Management Science*, Volume 2, Issue 1, October 1955, Pages 40–54.
Song, L., Yang, D., Chin, A.T.H., Zhang, G., He, Z., Guan, W., Mao, B., 2016, A game-theoretical approach for modeling competitions in a maritime supply chain. *Maritime Policy and Management*, Volume 43, Issue 8, 16 November 2016, Pages 976–991.
Syed, Raza A., Akgunduz, A., 2008, An airline revenue management pricing game with seat allocation, *International Journal of Revenue Management*, Volume 2, Issue 1, 2008, Pages 42–62.
Van Witteloostuijn, A., 1998, Bridging behavioural and economic theories of decline: Organizational inertia, strategic competition, and chronic failure. *Management Science*, Volume 44, Issue 4, April 1998, Pages 501–519.
Veldman, J., Gaalman, G., 2014, A model of strategic product quality and process improvement incentives. *International Journal of Production Economics*, Volume 149, March 2014, Pages 202–210.
Von Neumann, J., Morgenstern, O., 1944, *Theory of Games and Economic Behaviour, copyright 1944, 1953*, Princeton, NJ: Princeton University Press.
Von Neumann, John, 1928, Zur Theorie der Gesellschaftsspiele [On the Theory of Games of Strategy]. *Mathematische Annalen* [*Mathematical Annals*] (in German), Volume 100, Issue 1, Pages 295–320.
Wang, D., Du, G., Jiao, R.J., Wu, R., Yu, J., Yang, D., 2016, A Stackelberg game theoretic model for optimizing product family architecting with supply chain consideration. *International Journal of Production Economics*, Volume 172, 1 February 2016, Pages 1–18.
Wang, M., Li, Y., Li, M., Wan, L., Miao, L., Wang, X., 2019, A comparative study on recycling amount and rate of used products under different regulatory scenarios. *Journal of Cleaner Production*, Volume 235, 20 October 2019, Pages 1153–1169.
Xu, P., Xiao, T., 2022, Analysis of online rebates and commission formats in a retailer-Stackelberg supply chain with cashback website. *Decision Sciences*. DOI: 10.1111/deci.12586
Yan, W., Xiong, Y., Chu, J., Li, G., Xiong, Z., 2018, Clicks versus Bricks: The role of durability in marketing channel strategy of durable goods manufacturers, *European Journal of Operational Research*, Volume 265, Issue 3, Pages 909–918.
Yang, L., Ji, J., Chen, K., 2018. Advertising games on national brand and store brand in a dual-channel supply chain. *Journal of Industrial and Management Optimization*, Volume 14, Issue 1, Pages 105–134.
Yuan, L., Yang, C., Li, T., 2015, Advertising and pricing decisions in a manufacturer-retailer channel with demand and cost disruptions. *International Journal of Information Systems and Supply Chain Management*, Volume 8, Issue 3, Pages 44–66.
Zheng, L., Lu, W., Chen, K., Chau, K.W., Niu, Y., 2017, Benefit-sharing for BIM implementation: Tackling the moral hazard dilemma in inter-firm cooperation. *International Journal of Project Management*, Volume 35, Issue 3, Pages 393–405.
Zhou, Y., Gao, X., Luo, S., Xiong, Y., Ye, N., 2022, Anti-counterfeiting in a retail platform: A game-theoretic approach. *Transportation Research Part E: Logistics and Transportation Review*, Volume 165, September 2022, Article number 102839.

6 Does internationalization affect bank risk-taking?

Evidence from India

Saibal Ghosh

6.1 Introduction

In recent years, countries have put a lot of emphasis on financial sector reforms to improve the overall functioning of the financial sector. The International Monetary Fund (IMF) has also been emphasizing the need for financial sector repair as one important component of reforms for countries affected by the recent financial crisis. Central to this process of reform has been the infusion of competition. Such competition, however, is a double-edged sword. On one hand, competition is seen as a stimulus to exert downward pressure on costs, engender efficient allocation of resources between firms and act as a spur to innovation (Nickell, 1996; Aghion and Schankerman, 2004). On the other hand, competition can engender excessive risk-taking by banks, thereby necessitating a role for prudential regulation in ensuring systemic stability (Carletti and Hartmann, 2002).

To address the competitive challenges and presumably diversify their asset base, banks have explored several options. One option that has found favour is internationalization. Several reasons have been advanced as to the reasons behind this trend. For example, profit opportunities could be one driver (Focarelli and Pozollo, 2005). Having a diversified customer base could be an alternative driver (Berger et al., 2005). It is also possible for banks to augment their revenue streams to overcome the high degree of domestic competition (Correa and Goldberg, 2022). Whether and to what extent such diversification affects bank risk-taking remains an open question.

To contribute to this debate, this chapter investigates the interlinkage between internationalization and risk-taking in the context of Indian banks during 2005–2018. To be more specific, we address three questions. First, does internationalization affect risk-taking by banks? In this regard, we construct a measure of internationalization akin to Berger et al. (2017) and correlate it with accounting and market risk-taking measures while controlling for other confounding factors. Second, does the impact differ across ownership? Without loss of generality, the impact of such internationalization on risk is likely to manifest more prominently for state-owned banks. This is because domestically, they cater to a combination of profit and social

DOI: 10.4324/9781003509721-8

objectives, whereas when they operate overseas, profitability overwhelms other considerations, which they might not be adequately equipped to handle. And third, what are the mechanisms through which internationalization affects bank risk? Borrowing from relevant literature, we posit three channels and correlate them with bank risk in the presence of internationalization to ascertain their relevance.

India provides a compelling case among emerging markets to test the nexus among these variables in some detail. First, during the 1990s, India underwent significant liberalization with the objectives of enhancing the efficiency, productivity and profitability of banks. One aspect of this liberalization has been an improvement in the overseas outreach by Indian banks. In 2008, the *LiveMint* made the following observation:

> Braving a bleak outlook for the financial industry globally, India's banks are proceeding with plans to expand their overseas networks, seeking to tap the estimated three crore people of Indian origin living abroad.
>
> (LiveMint, December 3)

During the period of Great Moderation, Indian banks significantly expanded their overseas presence, with their branches increasing from fewer than 100 to nearly 160 by 2018. There was a subsequent rationalization of operations wherein close to 70 branches across banks were closed. Second, India is one of the largest and fastest-growing economies, with a gamut of banks across different ownership categories. It would be of interest to examine the interrelationships between internationalization and risk-taking across ownership groups. Third, India is one of the few emerging economies with a comprehensive banking database. Akin to several countries in the region and elsewhere, the supervision of banks rests with the central bank. Accordingly, per the extant regulatory guidelines, banks have to submit their audited annual financials comprising balance sheet details and profit and loss statements within 3 months after the end of the accounting year in a structured template prescribed by the central bank. This provides reliable data with sufficient variation, both over time and across banks, to make it conducive to careful analytical research.

The analysis makes three useful contributions to the literature. First, it expands the literature on bank internationalization in the context of an emerging economy. Early studies (Buch and DeLong, 2004; Goldberg and Johnson, 1990) utilize either cross-sectional data or small time series of banks and uncover a significant role of foreign direct investment (FDI) in driving the overseas expansion strategy. For example, Goldberg and Johnson (1990) showed that among bank-specific factors, domestic deposits and macroeconomic factors, exports, per capita income and exchange rate are significant drivers of bank FDI. Mulder and Westerheuis (2015) affirm the importance of macroeconomic variables such as the size of the home country, export to gross domestic product (GDP) and per capita income and level of financial development as key drivers of internationalization. We contribute to this evidence by examining the impact of internationalization on bank risk for a leading emerging economy with banks across different ownership categories. The findings reveal that internationalization leads to an increase in bank risk, judged in terms of either accounting or market-based measures.

Second, this chapter is a contribution to the literature on bank stability. Recent research has extensively employed the *Z*-score as a measure of bank stability (Barry et al., 2011; Bertay et al., 2013; Bouwens & Verriest, 2014; Hakenes et al., 2015; Lepetit and Strobel, 2015; Shim, 2019). It could well happen that internationalization exerts a discernible impact on market-based measures of risk (as compared with accounting measures) based on the premise that the market internalizes the impact of a bank's internationalization at a much quicker pace. To onboard this fact, following Correa and Goldberg (2022), we include a market *Z*-score as well. We correlate internationalization with both measures of *Z*-scores to ascertain its relevance for bank stability. Prior evidence in this regard is mixed. While Faia et al. (2019) have found a positive impact of internationalization on bank stability in their cross-country sample of European banks, evidence for US banks suggests this association to be negative (Berger et al., 2017). Our findings appear consistent with evidence that shows that greater internationalization leads to a decline in bank stability.

Third, the analysis focuses on the interlinkage of ownership and bank risk-taking. Extant theories provide conflicting predictions regarding this linkage. On one hand, although state ownership of banks can lower risk-taking since profitability is not a compelling concern, it can also increase fragility given limited risk assessment skills and misaligned incentives (La Porta et al., 2002; Barth et al., 2004). Bertay et al. (2015) uncovered lower procyclicality of lending by state-owned banks in their multicountry sample, a fact confirmed subsequently by Duprey (2015) in their study of the largest 20 banks during 1990–2010 covering more than 80 countries. Cull and Martinez Peria (2013) also have shown that lending by state-owned banks was countercyclical in Latin America in the aftermath of the global financial crisis. On the other hand, the risk appetite of private banks depends, among others, on their ownership profile: more concentrated ownership might reduce agency problems between managers and owners, as the latter are better able to monitor and discipline the former and lead to more risk-taking. For a large sample of European banks, Ianotta *et al.* (2007) found that government-owned banks are the least stable, followed by privately owned banks, while cooperative banks are the most stable banking group. Similarly, Hesse and Cihak found that cooperative banks are more stable than commercial banks in Organisation for Economic Co-operation and Development countries. Our study finds that the adverse effect of internationalization on bank risk is much more pronounced for state-owned banks compared with their private peers.

Finally, our chapter also identifies which strategy of bank internationalization exerts a more perceptible impact on stability. In this regard, we distinguish between a *sprinkler* versus a *waterfall* strategy. The former refers to the simultaneous entry by a bank in different country markets (Kalish et al., 1995). To the extent that large banks can overcome the regulatory and cultural barriers of internationalization, a sprinkler strategy could be more appropriate (Berger et al., 2003). In contrast, smaller banks could be more inclined to pursue a waterfall strategy, wherein they open multiple branches over time within a single country. This accords with their desire to minimize risk and advantageously exploit the experience gained. Resource constraints could also be a consideration (Backhans et al., 2000; Stremersch and Tellis, 2004). The findings reveal that a sprinkler strategy exerts a dampening impact on bank risk-taking.

The rest of the chapter continues as follows: Section 6.2 discusses the relevant literature. This is followed by a discussion regarding the internationalization of Indian banks and the institutional environment (Section 6.3). Subsequently, we discuss the data (Section 6.4) and the empirics (Section 6.5), which is followed by a discussion of the results (Section 6.6) and the concluding remarks (Section 6.7).

6.2 Received literature

Studies on banking globalization are limited, especially in the context of emerging markets. Berger et al. (2017) have proposed two hypotheses that investigate the linkage between internationalization and bank risk.

Under the *diversification hypothesis*, greater overseas expansion leads to a diversification of bank portfolios. Provided asset returns across countries are not highly correlated, this makes bank portfolios less susceptible to domestic shocks, leading to a lowering of risk (Crystal et al., 2001; De Nicolo et al., 2004; Meon and Weill, 2005; Laeven and Levine, 2009). Consistent with this fact, find that greater geographic diversification lowers US bank riskiness. Cross-country studies also arrive at similar conclusions. Using data from European banks, Meon and Weill (2005) simulated cross-border mergers on bank risk and found that it leads to a potential lowering of risk. Using data from European banks, Faia et al. (2019) showed that opening of a foreign branch by a bank improves the *Z*-score by close to 1%. Yet, other studies show that international mergers do not exert any discernible impact on bank risk (Amihud, 2002).

As compared to this, the *market risk hypothesis* contends that overseas expansion might make domestic banks more susceptible to the international climate. First, foreign operations involve huge licence fees, specific to the particular jurisdiction. Cultural barriers can also prove daunting. There are additional complexities such as regulatory and legal challenges, including high operating expenses (Alibux, 2007) Violations for non-compliance with banking laws are often quite overwhelming. Coupled with that, high competition leads to longer break-even periods (Buch and DeLong, 2004), compelling banks to take higher risks.[1] In line with this argument, several studies show that higher internationalization leads to an increase in bank risk-taking (Berger et al., 2017)

Other studies have focused on the role and relevance of foreign banks on domestic economies. By way of example, Haas and Lelyveld (2014) found that lending by foreign banks improves systemic stability. Claessens and Van Horen (2014) showed that foreign banks do not immediately withdraw after crises, but instead rebalance their lending portfolio in favour of low-risk clientele. This evidence is consistent with research with supports the fact that multinational banks act as a stabilizing force during periods of exigencies, either by transmitting illiquidity shocks across borders (Cetorelli and Goldberg, 2012), by curtailing lending to opaque firms (Berger et al., 2001; Mian, 2012; Gormley, 2010) or even by penalizing opaque firms (Giannetti and Ongena, 2012) and exert positive real effects (Bruno and Hauswald, 2014).

An important concern is whether internationalization is exogenous to bank risk. On one hand, banks' internationalization drive could influence their risk-taking behaviour. On the other, it could happen that banks with a higher proportion of risky assets expand overseas in order to diversify their risks, raising endogeneity concerns. We address this challenge by employing an instrumental variable (IV) approach. Even after accounting for this fact, internationalization is observed to exert a statistically significant impact on bank risk.

6.3 Internationalization of Indian banks

The initial interest of Indian banks in expanding abroad has been driven by their desire to have a share in the growing foreign exchange business of India (Kulkarni, 1980). As India's foreign trade expanded, banks expanded by opening new offices. During 1976–84, domestic banks expanded significantly overseas: 13 Indian banks had 141 offices abroad in 1984 (Verghese, 1988). There was an ebb during the subsequent period, reflecting partly the banks' adjustments to the new norms ushered in by the financial sector reforms of the 1990s and a conservative policy stance.

The desire to tap a large pool of expatriates led to an expansion spree by Indian banks, especially 2005–11. During this period, banks' overseas representation (e.g., branches, subsidiaries, representative offices) increased at an annual average of 7.3% per year. The liberalization of policy guidelines by the Indian central bank to fund domestic Indian firms with overseas operations was also a contributory factor.[2] Reflecting this fact, overseas branches of Indian banks expanded rapidly, from fewer than 100 branches in 2000 to 119 branches on the eve of the global financial crisis in 2007 and thereafter to 185 branches by 2018, the intermittent fluctuations reflecting the adjustments shaped by the global financial crisis and country-specific considerations. Over the 2005–18 period, bank branches have increased at an annual average of roughly 5%. Indian banks had cut back their overseas branches during 2017 and 2018, primarily by state-owned banks. Commenting on this aspect, the *Business Line* (May 3, 2018) remarked:

> The immediate trigger for this pull back has been the poor performance of public sector banks during the past few years. Mounting losses, the problem of bad loans, the need for fresh capital and tightening budgetary support with a number of strings, poor valuations at the stock market and the recent cases of huge frauds, have contributed to an environment where the government has had to crack down on banks. There are about 159 branches of Indian banks operating outside and about a quarter of them are loss-making.

At the same time, banks' expansion strategy has also varied markedly. To exemplify, several banks adopted a sprinkler strategy by expanding simultaneously across multiple jurisdictions. Others, especially the smaller ones, adopted a waterfall approach, focusing on multiple branches in one country over time. We onboard this aspect as part of our empirical strategy.

6.4 The database and sample

6.4.1 The sample

To analyse the impact of internationalization on bank risk-taking, we construct a dataset for the banking sector covering the 2005–2018 period. The sample covers a total of 45 banks, including state-owned and private banks, including new private banks. Taken together, these banks, on average, accounted on average for close to 90% of total commercial banking sector assets during the period.

6.4.2 The data

The disaggregated data on the bank balance sheet and profit and loss accounts are obtained from multiple issues of *Statistical Tables Relating to Banks in India* (hereafter, *Statistical Tables*), a yearly publication of the Indian central bank. The financial year for banks starts on the first day of April of a particular year and ends on the last day of March of the subsequent year. Accordingly, the year 2005 corresponds to the period 2004 (April)–2005 (March) and so on for the other years.

The key dependent variable is bank risk. Following related prior research (Laeven and Levine, 2009; Bhagat et al., 2015; Mohsni and Otchere, 2018; Correa and Goldberg, 2022), we employ two measures. The first is an accounting measure, proxied by the Z-score and is defined as

$$Z \text{ score} = \frac{\text{RoA} + \left(\dfrac{\text{Equity}}{\text{Asset}}\right)}{SD(\text{RoA})}, \tag{6.1a}$$

where RoA is return on asset (i.e., the ratio of net profit to total asset) and *SD*(RoA) is the standard deviation of return on asset for the years $t - 2$, $t - 1$ and t. The *Z*-score measures the distance to insolvency by combining measures of leverage, profitability and volatility: higher values for the variable indicate that the bank is more stable (or less risky).

The second is a market-based measure and is defined as

$$\text{Market } Z \text{ score} = \frac{(1 + \text{Average returns})}{SD(\text{Market returns})}. \tag{6.1b}$$

The average returns are calculated based on daily stock price data of the year for any given year, and likewise, the standard deviation is calculated in a similar manner. Data on this variable are obtained from *Prowess* (akin to the US *Compustat* database). Given the potential skewness of both these variables, akin to Laeven and Levine (2009), we employ the natural logarithm of (1+) *Z*-score (respectively, market *Z*-score) in the analytical exercise.

Regarding the independent variable, akin to Berger et al. (2017), we use the ratio of foreign assets to total assets (FA). Foreign asset is proxied by the sum of balances of banks outside India, investments outside India and credit outside India. Information on the relevant variables is obtained from the *Statistical Tables*.

It may be mentioned that this measure is likely to be an underestimate. To illustrate, there is no information on the extent of fixed assets or other assets outside India. The extent of such underestimate is, however, likely to be small. This is because the excluded items (i.e., fixed assets abroad and other assets abroad) account for, on average, less than 5% of total bank assets.

Figure 6.1 provides the year-wise evolution of bank internationalization, separately by ownership. Without loss of generality, we find that the average levels of internationalization are uniformly higher for state-owned banks as compared with their private counterparts. To illustrate, on the eve of the global financial crisis, internationalization was 2.71% for state-owned banks as compared with 1.45% for private banks. In 2018, the final year of the sample, private banks had approximately 2.5% of their assets abroad on average and this figure was more than double for state-owned banks. For the period as a whole, FA for state-owned banks averaged 4.2% (*SD* = 6.16) vs. 3% (*SD* = 3.90) for private banks. These differences across years and for the period as a whole were found to be statistically significant at conventional levels.

In addition, we include several other bank-specific and, in certain cases, macroeconomic variables. These include total bank assets, total equity, fee income, cost to income and a dummy for bank's listing status. Except for the listing bank status (obtained from Prowess), the remaining variables are obtained from the *Statistical Tables*.

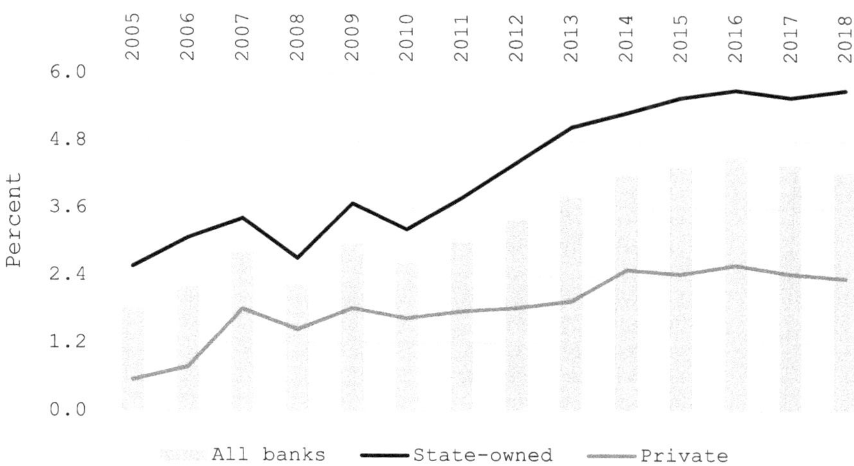

Figure 6.1 Evolution of bank internationalization.
Source: RBI.

As part of the channels behind internationalization, we employ three variables. These include bank profitability, loan diversity and business complexity. The former two variables are extracted from the *Statistical Tables*, the final one is constructed based on data extracted from *Prowess*.

The banking industry witnessed several consolidation activities during this period. We take this into account by inserting a dummy, which equals one for the acquirer bank in the year of the merger, else zero. This is obtained from the *Statistical Tables*. In addition, we also control for the fact that several new private banks became operative at different months in a given year, leading to non-standard reporting months. Given these developments, the number of bank-year varies: we have a maximum of 498 bank-years for an average of 11.1 years of observations per bank. To limit the influence of outliers, we winsorize all bank-specific variables at the 1% and 99% levels.

Table 6.1 provides the variable definitions and summary statistics. The average value of the *Z*-score was 4 compared to a global average of 2.6 in 2017 (World Bank, 2019). The average value of the market *Z*-score was 3.6, lower than the value of 4 reported for US banks for 1996–2018 (Correa and Goldberg, 2022). Just over three-fifths of the banks are state-owned; the remaining are domestic private banks.

Among the independent variables, the measure of bank internationalization is low: foreign assets on average comprise 3.3% of total bank assets. Average asset equals INR 1760 billion (≈ US $22 billion at current exchange rates), equity levels are moderate and the share of fee income at about the

Table 6.1 Variable definition and summary statistics

Variable	*Definition*	*Data source*	*N. Obs*	*Mean (SD)*
Dependent				
Z-score	Ln(1 + *Z*), where *Z* = [(Equity/Asset) + (RoA)]/*SD* (RoA), where *SD*(RoA) is based on periods *t*, *t* – 1 and *t* – 2	Author calculations based on STRBI	514	3.929 (1.087)
Market Z-score	(1 + Average returns)/*SD* (Returns), where returns are based on daily stock price data in any given year	Prowess	509	3.683 (0.307)
Independent: Key				
Foreign Asset (FA)	Foreign asset/ Total asset (%), where foreign asset is the sum of balances of banks outside India, credit outside India and investment outside India	Author calculations based on STRBI	604	3.296 (5.515)
Independent: Controls				
LTA	Ln (Total asset)	STRBI	604	15.928 (1.25)
Equity	Total equity/Total asset	As above	604	0.064 (0.021)
Fee	Fee income/Total income	As above	604	0.102 (0.042)
Cost/Income	Total expense/(Total income – interest expense)	As above	594	0.502 (0.107)
Listed	Dummy = 1 beginning from the year a bank is listed, else zero	Prowess	544	0.947 (0.225)
Channels				
RoA	Net profit/Total asset	STRBI	604	0.006 (0.007)
Divers	Herfindahl Index of loan diversity	STRBI	604	0.063 (0.112)
Complex	Herfindahl Index of business complexity, based on four segments (corporate/ wholesale, treasury, retail and others)	Prowess	574	0.587 (0.109)
Strategy				
Sprinkler	Dummy = 1 if a bank adopted a sprinkler expansion strategy, else zero	STRBI	630	0.013 (0.112)

(*Continued*)

Table 6.1 (Continued)

Variable	*Definition*	*Data source*	*N. Obs*	*Mean (SD)*
Waterfall	Dummy = 1 if a bank adopted a waterfall expansion strategy, else zero	STRBI	630	0.022 (0.148)
Ownership				
SOB	Dummy = 1, if a bank is state-owned, else zero	RTPB	630	0.622 (0.485)
PVT	Dummy = 1 if a bank is private, else zero	As above	630	0.378 (0.485)
Macroeconomic & others				
GDP	Real GDP growth in a year	World Bank	630	0.069 (0.015)
OFDI	Overseas foreign direct investment/GDP (%)	Dep. of Econ Affairs, Government of India	630	0.773 (0.397)
Others				
Merger	Dummy = 1 for the acquirer bank in the year of merger, else zero	STRBI	630	0.017 (0.131)
ARM	Dummy = 1 if annual reporting months is different from 12, else zero	Prowess	630	0.006 (0.079)
Local	Dummy = 1 if a bank is local, else zero	Based on STRBI	630	0.422 (0.494)
STRBI	Statistical tables relating to banks in India			
RTPB	Report on Trend and Progress of banking in India			

Source: Author.

10% mark. Inefficiency levels are high; to an extent, they are reflective of high operating costs.

Among the channels of influence, banks have low profitability, moderately high levels of business complexity and low levels of loan diversity.

Table 6.2 shows the correlation matrix among the key variables of interest. Both the *Z*-score and the market *Z*-score bear a negative and significant association with FA, possibly indicative of the fact that greater asset internationalization increases bank risk. The raw correlations do not incorporate bank-specific factors. Nor does it control for the economic environment or other relevant factors. To account for this fact, we resort to an econometric specification.

Table 6.2 Correlation matrix of key variables

	1	*2*	*3*	*4*
1. Z-score				
2. Market Z-score	0.133***			
3. FA	-0.078*	-0.079*		

Source: Author.

Note: ***$p < .01$; **$p < .05$; *$p < .10$.

6.5 Empirical design

To investigate the impact of internationalization on bank risk-taking, we run regressions for bank *i* at time *t* of the following form:

$$y_{i,t} = \alpha_o + \alpha_1 \text{FA}_{i,t-1} + \alpha_2 \text{Controls}_{i,t-1} + \alpha_3 \text{Merger}_{i,t} + \alpha_4 \text{ARM}_{i,t} + \theta_i + \eta_t + \varepsilon_{i,t}. \tag{6.2}$$

In Equation (6.2), *y* is the outcome variable of interest, which is either accounting (Z-score) or market-based (market Z-score) measure of risk and FA is the measure of internationalization, as discussed earlier.

The other variables include natural logarithm of total asset (as a control for size), equity-to-asset ratio (as a control for funding structure), cost to income (to account for bank inefficiencies), fee income to total income (to control for income diversity) and, finally, a dummy for the listing status of the bank. These are lagged one period to account for endogeneity concerns. Following prior evidence (Demirguc Kunt and Huizinga, 2010; Stiroh, 2006; Laeven and Levine, 2009; Barry et al., 2011), bigger, well-capitalized banks with higher fee income and efficiency levels and subject to market discipline by virtue of their listing status are likely to be less prone to risk-taking. We also include dummies to account for mergers and for non-standard reporting months.[3] θ_i captures unobserved bank-specific heterogeneity and η_t captures time-variant factors, such as changes in regulation or market structure; ε denotes the random error term.

The coefficient of interest is α_1: it identifies the impact of internationalization on bank risk-taking while onboarding other relevant factors. Provided internationalization exerts a perceptible impact on bank risk-taking, the coefficient would be statistically significant. Standard errors across all specifications are clustered by bank (Bertrand et al., 2004).

Subsequently, we examine the channels through which internationalization can influence bank risk-taking. To do this, we estimate the following specification, as given by (6.3):

$$y_{i,t} = \gamma + \gamma_0 \text{FA}_{i,t-1} + \gamma_1 \text{Channel}_{i,t-1} + \gamma_2 \left(\text{FA}_{i,t-1} * \text{Channel}_{i,t-1}\right) + \gamma_3 \text{Controls}_{i,t-1} + \gamma_4 \text{Merger}_{i,t} + \gamma_5 \text{ARM}_{i,t} + \theta_i + \eta_t + \varepsilon_{i,t}, \tag{6.3}$$

where the notations are as earlier and the coefficient of interest is γ_2. This coefficient examines the importance of a particular channel on bank risk-taking driven by internationalization.

From an economic standpoint, there are several channels through which internationalization can affect bank risk-taking. First, banks might internationalize to increase profits. We proxy profitability by return on asset (Berger et al., 2005; Merciera et al., 2007; Garcia-Herroro et al., 2009; Elsas et al., 2010). Second, internationalization can raise business complexities and along with lead to an increase in revenues. The impact of such complexities on risk-taking is not obvious, *a priori*. We proxy business complexity by the Herfindahl Index, using four business lines: corporate, wholesale/retail, treasury and others. Finally, internationalization can lead banks to increase credit diversification so as to lower risk. We proxy credit diversification by the Herfindahl Index between credit extended domestically and that provided abroad.

Finally, we focus on bank expansion strategies and their impact on bank riskiness. To do this, we estimate the following specification, as given by (6.4):

$$\begin{aligned} y_{i,t} &= \mu + \mu_0 \text{FA}_{i,t-1} + \mu_1 \text{Strategy}_{i,t} + \mu_2 \left(\text{FA}_{i,t-1} * \text{Strategy}_{i,t-1}\right) \\ &\quad + \mu_3 \text{Controls}_{i,t-1} + \mu_4 \text{Merger}_{i,t} + \mu_5 \text{ARM}_{i,t} + \theta_i + \eta_t + \varepsilon_{i,t} \end{aligned} \tag{6.4}$$

where the notations are as earlier and the coefficient of interest is μ_2. This coefficient examines the importance of a given expansion strategy on bank risk-taking driven by internationalization. Following on from the previous discussion, we focus on two expansion strategies, sprinkler versus waterfall, and examine which of these influence bank riskiness.

6.6 Results and discussion

6.6.1 Main findings

The baseline results are set out in Table 6.3. The first three columns focus on accounting *Z*-score and the subsequent columns look at market *Z*-score.

In terms of asset internationalization, the evidence in column 1 shows that the coefficient on FA is negative and statistically significant with a point estimate of –0.095. In other words, higher asset internationalization leads to increased bank risk-taking. The evidence is consistent with the *market risk hypothesis* which supports an increase in bank risk-taking, consequent upon higher internationalization (Berger et al., 2017), although evidence from European banks suggests otherwise (Faia et al., 2019). Based on the point estimates, we can infer that a one standard deviation increase in internationalization lowers *Z*-score by 0.52 or 13% (relative to the sample mean).

The next two columns disaggregate the findings by ownership. The estimates reveal that internationalization raises risk-taking by state-owned banks, although there is no such evidence for domestic private banks. Based

Table 6.3 Regression analysis – Impact of internationalization on bank risk-taking

	Z-score			*Market Z-score*		
	All banks	*State-owned*	*Domestic private*	*All banks*	*State-owned*	*Domestic private*
	(1)	*(2)*	*(3)*	*(4)*	*(5)*	*(6)*
FA	−0.095***	−0.073***	−0.017	−0.025***	−0.017***	−0.029***
	(0.025)	(0.028)	(0.057)	(0.005)	(0.005)	(0.012)
Controls	Yes	Yes	Yes	Yes	Yes	Yes
Merger	Yes	Yes	Yes	Yes	Yes	Yes
ARM	Yes	Yes	Yes	Yes	Yes	Yes
Bank FE	Yes	Yes	Yes	Yes	Yes	Yes
Year FE	Yes	Yes	Yes	Yes	Yes	Yes
Obs.	453	285	168	494	297	197
Adj. R-sq.	0.4484	0.4170	0.4242	0.4164	0.5174	0.3704

Source: Author.

Note: Standard errors (clustered by bank) within brackets.

***$p < .01$; **$p < .05$; *$p < .10$.

on the point estimates, a one standard deviation increase in internationalization by state-owned banks increases risk-taking by 0.45 or 12% relative to the sample mean. The possible reasons include steep competition, which leads to wafer-thin margins that elongate the break-even periods for operations, leading banks to assume higher risks. Often branches are opened for diplomatic and strategic reasons, and provided diplomatic ties weaken or become volatile, the business of these branches also takes a backseat, further burdening these banks. It is also possible that these banks might lack the management bandwidth or even the technological sophistication to compete with global banks.

The subsequent three columns focus on market Z-score. The evidence is fairly unequivocal: higher internationalization increases risk for both state-owned and private banks. A one standard deviation increase in internationalization raises risk by 14% for the banking sector, with the magnitude being higher for domestic private (11%) as compared with state-owned (10%) banks. The higher magnitude in the case of the former can be explained by the fact that shareholders view the weak performance of these banks as a credit negative, which is reflected in their market-based financials. The implicit government guarantee for state-owned banks would suggest that the impact on their market-based financials is relatively lower. Eichengreen and Gupta (2013) for example show that during the global financial crisis, there was a movement of deposits towards state-owned banks and away from private banks of comparable risks.

Summing up, the findings indicate a perceptible and statistically negative impact of internationalization on bank risk-taking.

6.6.2 Channels

We next examine the relevance of the channels through which internationalization affects bank risk-taking (Table 6.4). As mentioned earlier, we consider three channels, profitability, complexity and loan diversity and interact each of these channels with internationalization to ascertain the effect on bank risk-taking.

The evidence suggests that internationalization typically increases risk-taking, whereas the impact of the other variables is mixed: profitability lowers risk (i.e., increases stability), the impact of the other two variables is less compelling. The coefficient of interest is the interaction term. In columns 2 and 5, the coefficient is negative.

The coefficient is economically relevant as well. To see this, note that an increase in complexity from 0.42 to 0.68 – that is, from the 10th to the 90th percentile of the distribution – lowers *Z*-score by roughly 1% and market

Table 6.4 Regression analysis – Impact of internationalization on bank risk-taking – Channels

	Z-score			*Market Z-score*		
	(1)	*(2)*	*(3)*	*(4)*	*(5)*	*(6)*
FA*RoA	-0.089			-0.521		
	(1.278)			(0.313)		
FA*Complex		-0.166**			-0.045*	
		(0.081)			(0.025)	
FA*LD			-0.155			-0.025
			(0.110)			(0.031)
RoA	1.057***			0.119***		
	(1.436)			(0.035)		
Complex		0.769			-0.267***	
		(0.676)			(0.104)	
LD			-1.883			0.002
			(1.679)			(0.499)
FA	-0.080***	-0.031	-0.050	-0.017***	-0.052***	-0.030**
	(0.025)	(0.074)	(0.053)	(0.006)	(0.022)	(0.015)
OFDI	-0.104	-0.249	-0.299*	-0.205***	-0.195***	-0.201***
	(0.156)	(0.179)	(0.167)	(0.046)	(0.049)	(0.047)
Controls	Yes	Yes	Yes	Yes	Yes	Yes
Merger	Yes	Yes	Yes	Yes	Yes	Yes
ARM	Yes	Yes	Yes	Yes	Yes	Yes
Bank FE	Yes	Yes	Yes	Yes	Yes	Yes
GDPGR	Yes	Yes	Yes	Yes	Yes	Yes
Obs.	453	435	453	494	474	494
Adj. *R*-sq.	0.4435	0.3718	0.3490	0.1832	0.1667	0.1637

Source: Author.

Note: Standard errors (clustered by bank) in parentheses.

***$p < .01$; **$p < .05$; *$p < .10$.

Z-score by 0.3%. Thus, higher levels of complexity, by making business operations unwieldy to handle in the face of stiff competition, increases bank risk-taking and is therefore detrimental to banks.

6.6.2.1 Expansion strategy

In this section, we focus on how banks' expansion strategy affects their risk-taking behaviour. Following on from our previous discussion, we categorize the expansion strategy as sprinkler versus waterfall. More specifically, if a bank has opened branches/offices across multiple jurisdictions in a given year, we dummy code it as 1 and label this as the sprinkler strategy. By comparison, if a bank has opened multiple branches in a single jurisdiction over time, we label it a waterfall strategy by dummy coding it as 1 and zero otherwise. The table on summary statistics shows that 1% of the bank-years are premised on sprinkler strategy; as compared to this, the use of a waterfall strategy has been much higher, nearly double the proportion of bank-years.

In Table 6.5, we interact the expansion strategy with bank internationalization and ascertain the impact. The findings in column 1 show that a sprinkler strategy dampens banks' accounting *Z*-score by 8.5%, on average.

Table 6.5 Internationalization and bank risk-taking – Sprinkler versus waterfall strategy

	Z-score		*Market Z-score*	
	(1)	*(2)*	*(3)*	*(4)*
FA	−0.052***	−0.063***	−0.032***	−0.032***
	(0.024)	(0.025)	(0.006)	(0.006)
Sprinkler	1.599**		0.045	
	(0.746)		(0.205)	
Waterfall		0.282		0.051
		(0.546)		(0.160)
FA*Sprinkler	−0.085*		0.0009	
	(0.049)		(0.014)	
FA*Waterfall		−0.019		−0.002
		(0.040)		(0.012)
Controls	Yes	Yes	Yes	Yes
Merger	Yes	Yes	Yes	Yes
ARM	Yes	Yes	Yes	Yes
Bank FE	Yes	Yes	Yes	Yes
Year FE	Yes	Yes	Yes	Yes
Obs.	452	452	498	498
Adj. *R*-sq.	0.5278	0.5224	0.4439	0.4436

Source: Author.

Note: Standard errors (clustered by bank) within parentheses.

***$p < .01$; **$p < .05$; *$p < .10$.

Several factors can explain this finding. First, entry into multiple jurisdictions involves significant entry costs (e.g., capital, fixed assets), which vary across countries. Second, although banks might be lured by the expatriate population in these countries, more often than not, 'anchor customers' who offer a certain minimum volume of business to these banks, might face high switching costs and as a result, the resultant gains might not be compelling. In addition, most of these are reputed international financial centres where competition for business is steep and, resultantly, margins are quite narrow. All of these raise the break-even period for these banks to achieve profitability. This is ultimately reflected in higher risk-taking manifesting in terms of lower *Z*-scores.

6.6.3 Robustness

As observed earlier, several factors are likely to drive the internationalization in the banking sector. Thus, it is possible to argue that internationalization of banks is exogenous. Notwithstanding this argument, endogeneity concerns are not completely eliminated. To tackle this concern, we utilize an IV approach.

A valid instrument should satisfy the twin conditions of relevance and exclusion (Roberts and Whited, 2013). Accordingly, we employ a dummy is a bank is national versus local. Following previous research (Ghosh, 2022), we consider the share of total bank branches in the state where the bank is headquartered. We designate banks as local if at least 65% of the branches during these years are in the headquarters state (the median value of the share of bank branches in the headquarters state across years is much lower); otherwise, it is designated as national. This instrument is likely to satisfy the twin conditions of exclusion and relevance. It is a relevant instrument since such a strategy is likely to directly influence bank internationalization. At the same time, the largely local nature of a bank's operations would enable it to better procure and process 'soft information' on its clients and make it less likely to directly affect bank risk-taking other than its impact on internationalization.

The estimation findings are reported in Table 6.6. We find that on average, internationalization leads to an increase in bank risk-taking. As per the diagnostics, the instrument has a moderate first-stage *R*-squared and the *F*-test rejects the null hypothesis of a weak instrument. The Wu–Hausman score also rejects the null hypothesis of exogeneity at conventional levels. The Wu–Hausman test supports the fact that the chosen instrument is valid.

6.7 Concluding remarks

Using yearly data on domestic Indian banks, this chapter assesses the role of internationalization on bank risk-taking. We find strong evidence that suggests that internationalization leads to an increase in riskiness, measured in

Table 6.6 Regression results: Impact of internationalization on bank risk-taking – IV results

	Z-score	*Market Z-score*
FA (Instrumented)	−0.087*	−0.207*
	(0.048)	(0.127)
Observations	452	498
Adj. R^2	.2385	.3303
Test of endogeneity		
Wu–Hausman F-test	12.82	13.59
	(0.00)	(0.00)
First stage statistics		
Partial R-sq.	.0012	.0026
F-test (p-value)	16.19	12.26
	(.00)	(.00)

Source: Author.

Note: All equations include the full set of control variables, including dummies for mergers and non-standard reporting periods as well as bank-fixed effects, but these are not reported for brevity. Standard errors in parentheses.

$***p < .01$; $**p < .05$; $*p < .10$.

terms of not only accounting but also a market-based measure of risk. Robustness checks also lend support to these findings.

We also explored the channels owing to which there is an increase in bank risk-taking and found that by increasing the complexity of operations, internationalization increases riskiness. Relatedly, we also assess which of the two strategies of bank expansion – sprinkler versus waterfall – raises such riskiness and find evidence that it is the former that primarily contributes to an increase in riskiness.

It is possible to extend the research ideas in several directions. First, it would be useful to extend the sample to a longer time frame, encompassing additional points. Also, the relevance of internationalization for other measures of risk such as banks' non-performing loans is an interesting issue that deserves attention. Finally, the empirical analysis does not focus on the impact of internationalization on bank returns, which could be addressed in subsequent research.

Our findings provide three useful insights from a policy standpoint. First, the findings would suggest that the inclination of banks towards overseas expansion needs to be backed by thorough research which assesses the potential gains against the attendant adverse consequences, or else it might ultimately affect the bottom lines of banks. Second, the strategy of branch expansion abroad also needs careful assessment, given the costs involved in some such strategies might outweigh the returns, leading banks to increase risk-taking. And finally, typically profitability considerations dominate while expanding abroad, although the findings suggest that such expansion might lead to an increase in business complexity that can put an undue burden on banks, leading them to increase riskiness. In all, the overall results point to the fact that there is a need for further research regarding the impact of internationalization on bank risk-taking to better assess the possible linkages in order to adequately inform the policy debate in this regard.

Notes

1 In 2001, the State Bank of India was fined US$7.5 million by the Federal Reserve (the US banking regulator) for violating banking laws and failing to maintain accurate records. In 2013, the Monetary Authority of Singapore (Singapore banking regulator) stepped up vigilance of Indian banks on concerns of their deteriorating asset quality.

2 In May 2007, banks in India were allowed to extend funded and non-funded credit facilities to Indian Joint Ventures (where the holding by the Indian company is more than 51%)/Wholly Owned Subsidiaries abroad to 20% of unimpaired capital funds and subsequently to wholly owned step-down subsidiaries of subsidiaries of Indian companies.

3 The ARM is applicable primarily for new private banks, which became operational at different points in time during the financial year.

References

Aghion, P., and Schankerman, M. (2004). On the welfare effects and political economy of competition-enhancing policies. *Economic Journal* 114, 800–824.

Alibux, A. N. (2007). Cross-border mergers and acquisitions in the European banking sector. Dissertation, Erasmus University of Rotterdam.

Amihud, Y. (2002). Illiquidity and stock returns: Cross-section and time-series effects. *Journal of Financial Markets* 5, 31–56.

Backhans, I., Buschken, J., and Voeth, M. (2000). *International Marketing*. Stuttgart: Schaffer-Poeschel.

Barry, T.A., Lepetit, L., and Tarazi, A. (2011). Ownership structure and risk in publicly held and privately owned banks. *Journal of Banking and Finance* 35, 1327–1340.

Barth, J.E., Caprio, G., Jr., and Levine, R. (2004). Bank regulation and supervision: What works best? *Journal of Financial Intermediation* 13, 205–248.

Berger, A. Klapper, L., and Udell, G. (2001). The ability of banks to lend to informationally opaque small business. *Journal of Banking and Finance* 25, 2127–2167.

Berger, A.N., Clarke, G., Cull, R., Klapper, L., and Udell, G (2005). Corporate governance and bank performance: A joint analysis of the static, selection, and dynamic effects of domestic, foreign, and state ownership. *Journal of Banking and Finance* 29, 2179–2221.

Berger, A.N., Dai, Q., Ongena, S., and Smith, D.C. (2003). To what extent will the banking industry be globalised/A study of bank nationality and reach in 20 European nations. *Journal of Banking and Finance* 27, 383–415.

Berger, A.N., El Ghoul, S., Guedhami, O., and Roman, E. (2017). Internationalization and bank risk. *Management Science* 63, 2283–2301.

Bertay, A.C., Demirguc-Kunt, A., and Huizinga, H. (2013). Do we need big banks? Evidence on performance, strategy and market discipline. *Journal of Financial Intermediation* 22, 532–558.

Bertay, A. C., Demirguc-Kunt, A., and Huizinga, H. (2015). Bank ownership and credit over the business cycle: Is lending by state banks less procyclical? *Journal of Banking and Finance* 50, 326–339.

Bertrand, M., Duflo, E., and Mullainathan, S. (2004). How much should we trust differences-in-differences estimates? *Quarterly Journal of Economics* 119, 249–275.
Bhagat, S., Bolton, B., and Lu, J. (2015). Size, leverage, and risk-taking of financial institutions. *Journal of International Money and Finance* 15, 577–597.
Bouwens, J., and A. Verriest (2014). Putting skin in the game: managerial ownership and bank risk taking. Harvard Business School Working Paper 70, Cambridge, MA.
Bruno, V., and Hauswald, R. (2014). The real effect of foreign banks. *Review of Finance* 18, 1683–1716.
Buch, C., and DeLong, G. (2004). Cross-border bank mergers: What lures the rare animal? *Journal of Banking and Finance* 28, 2077–2102.
Carletti, E., and Hartmann, P. (2002). Competition and stability: What's special about banking? European Central Bank (ECB) Working Paper No. 146. ECB: Frankfurt.
Cetorelli, N., and Goldberg, L. (2012). Banking globalization and monetary transmission. *Journal of Finance* 67, 1811–1843.
Claessens, S., and van Horen, N. (2014). Foreign banks: Trends and impact. *Journal of Money, Credit, and Banking* 46(s1), 295–326.
Correa, R., and Goldberg, L.S. (2022). Bank complexity, governance and risk. *Journal of Banking and Finance* 134. No.106013.
Crystal, J., Dages, B., and Goldberg, L. (2001). *Does foreign ownership contribute to sounder banks in emerging markets? The Latin American experience*. Paper presented at the 3rd Annual World Bank, IMF and Brookings Financial Markets and Development Conference, New York, April.
Cull, R., and Martinez Peria, M.S. (2013). Bank ownership and lending patterns during the 2008–2009 financial crisis: Evidence from Latin America and Eastern Europe. *Journal of Banking and Finance* 37, 4861–4878.
De Nicolo, G., Bartholomew, P., Zaman, J., and Zephirin (2004). Bank consolidation, internationalization and conglomeration: Trends and implications for financial risk. *Financial Markets, Institutions and Instruments* 13, 173–217.
Demirguc-Kunt, D., and Huizinga, H. (2010). Bank activity and funding strategies: The impact on risk and returns. *Journal of Financial Economics* 98, 626–650.
Duprey, T. (2015). Do publicly-owned banks lend against the wind? *International Journal of Central Banking* (March), 11, 65–112.
Eichengreen, B., and Gupta, P. (2013). The financial crisis and Indian banks: Survival of the fittest. *Journal of International Money and Finance* 39, 138–152.
Elsas, R., Hackethal, A., & Holzhauser, M. (2010). The anatomy of bank diversification. *Journal of Banking and Finance* 34, 1274–1287.
Faia, E., Laffitte, S., and Ottaviano, G. I. P. (2019). Foreign expansion, competition and bank risk. *Journal of International Economics* 118, 179–199.
Focarelli, D., and Pozollo, A. (2005). Where do banks expand abroad? An empirical analysis. *Journal of Business* 78, 2435–2464.
Garcia-Herrero, A., Gavila, S., and Santabarbara, D. (2009). What explains the low profitability of Chinese banks? *Journal of Banking and Finance* 33, 2080–2092.
Ghosh, S. (2022). Elections and provisioning behaviour: Assessing the Indian evidence. *Economic Systems* 46, No. 100943.
Giannetti, M., and Ongena, S. (2012). Lending by example: Direct and indirect effects of foreign banks in emerging markets. *Journal of International Economics* 86, 167–180.
Goldberg, L., and Johnson, D. (1990). The determinants of US banking activity abroad. *Journal of International Money and Finance* 9, 123–137.
Gormley, T. (2010). The impact of foreign bank entry in emerging markets. *Journal of Financial Intermediation* 19, 26–51.

Haas, R., and Lelyveld, I. (2014). Multinational banks and the global financial crisis: Weathering the perfect storm? *Journal of Money, Credit and Banking* 46(s1), 333–364.
Hakenes, H., Hasan, I., Molyneux, P., and Xie, R. (2015). Small banks and local economic development. *Review of Finance* 19, 653–683.
Iannotta, G., Nocera, G., and Sironi, A. (2007). Ownership structure, risk and performance in the European banking industry. *Journal of Banking and Finance* 31, 2127–2149.
Kalish, S., Mahajan, V., and Muller, E. (1995). Waterfall and sprinkler new-product strategies in competitive global markets. *International Journal of Research in Marketing* 12, 105–119.
Kulkarni, G. (1980). International dimensions of Indian banking. *Economic and Political Weekly* 15, M127–M134.
La Porta, R., Lopez De Silanes, F., and Shleifer, A. (2002). Government ownership of banks. *Journal of Finance* 57, 265–301.
Laeven, L., and Levine, R. (2009). Bank governance, regulation and risk taking. *Journal of Financial Economics* 93, 259–275.
Lepetit, L., and Strobel, F. (2015). Bank insolvency risk and Z-score measures: A refinement. *Finance Research Letters* 13, 214–224.
Meon, P.-G., and Weill, L. (2005). Does better governance foster efficiency? An aggregate frontier analysis. *Economics of Governance* 6, 75–90.
Merciera, S., Schaeck, K., and Wolfe, S. (2007). Small European banks: Benefits from diversification? *Journal of Banking and Finance* 31, 1975–1998.
Mian, A. (2012). Distance constraints: The limits of foreign lending in poor economies. *Journal of Finance* 61, 1465–1505.
Mohsni, S., and Otchere, I. (2018). Does regulatory regime matter for bank risk taking? A comparative analysis of US and Canada. *Journal of International Financial Markets, Institutions and Money* 53, 1–16.
Mulder, A., and Westerheuis, G. (2015). The determinants of bank internationalization in times of financial globalization: Evidence from the world's largest banks 1980–2007. *Business History* 57, 122–155.
Nickell, S. (1996). Competition and corporate performance. *Journal of Political Economy* 104, 724–746.
Roberts, M.R., and Whited, T.M. (2013). Endogeneity in empirical corporate finance. In G.M. Constantinides, M. Harris and R.M. Stulz (Eds.) *Handbook of the economics of finance*. North Holland: Elsevier. pp. 493–572.
Shim, J. (2019). Loan portfolio diversification, market structure and bank stability. *Journal of Banking and Finance* 104, 103–115.
Stiroh, K., (2006). A portfolio view of banking with interest and noninterest activities. *Journal of Banking and Finance* 38, 1351–1361.
Stremersch, S., and Tellis, G.J. (2004). Understanding and managing international growth of new products. *International Journal of Research in Marketing* 21, 421–438.
Verghese, S. (1988). Establishing an offshore financial centre in India: Proposal revisited. *Economics and Political Weekly* 24, 1653–1661.
World Bank (2019). *Global Financial Development Database* (October). The World Bank: Washington DC.

7 Security issue decisions in public and private security markets

Evidence from an emerging economy

Saumitra Bhaduri and Bipin Sony

7.1 Introduction

The role of asymmetric information in security choice decisions is one of the main themes of contemporary corporate finance literature. The main proponents of information-based capital structure theories (e.g., pecking order theory; Myers, 1984; Myers and Majluf, 1984) argue that a better-quality firm is often compelled to avoid relatively more information-sensitive securities under information asymmetry. This behaviour is primarily attributed to the dilution cost stemming from the wedge between the market value and the value attributed by insiders.

The empirical literature has extensively tested these arguments and singled out information asymmetry as a key determinant of capital structure decisions across time and various financial market conditions, including both emerging and developed markets (Bharath et al., 2008; Leary and Roberts, 2010; Bessler et al., 2011; Gao and Zhu, 2015; Sony and Bhaduri, 2018). Notably, these studies tend to focus on capital structure decisions involving organized financial markets including debt, equity or both. Of late, the role of private markets in capital structure decisions has received much attention in corporate finance literature. In fact, few studies have analysed the role of private markets in security issue decisions, particularly in the context of information asymmetry.

The interest in the role of private markets has gained further impetus in the context of phenomenal growth in the private security markets across the globe in the last decade (Dai 2011; Klonowski, 2012; Tuli, 2016). For example, the capital raised through private equity transactions has increased from US$2 billion in 1995 to US$88 billion in 2006 in the US market (Chen et al., 2010). Private equity transactions account for 56% to 75% of all follow-on-equity issues by value in countries like Canada, the UK and Australia (Dahiya et al., 2013). India is no exception to this trend, and the private security market has grown over the years to become the second-largest source of capital for Indian firms (Shukla and Prabu, 2015). Remarkably, the amount raised by Indian firms through private security markets increased from INR 834 billion in 2004–05 to INR 6800 billion in 2017–18.[1] Therefore, India is

DOI: 10.4324/9781003509721-9

a natural ground to test the security issue decisions involving the private security market.

Furthermore, the exceptional growth of private markets can be attributed to the several potential advantages to the firms in placing securities privately, particularly in the context of emerging markets. Specifically, private placements are often seen as a security issue method alleviating the information asymmetry problems by poor quality firms (Wu, 2004; Kale and Meneghetti, 2011; Shen, 2014). Since access to information is different in private and public markets, fund providers pay different prices for the securities in these markets. The firms facing information problems often choose private security issues as they involve a few selected investors and lower information production costs. Furthermore, managers also contemplate private placements as a route to raise capital without diluting the control of the firm. Some studies suggest that in private placements, management chooses investors who protect their interests (Wu, 2004).

Given this backdrop, this study looks at the role of information asymmetry in the security issue decisions involving public and private security markets, from an emerging market, India.[2] While most of the existing capital structure studies on Indian markets examine the broad debt–equity framework, this is one of the first studies to examine the impact of information asymmetry in public and private security market using a novel approach of incorporating analyst-specific variables to capture the degree of information asymmetry.[3] Specifically, this chapter tests the contention that firms from countries with higher information premium like India circumvent the information challenges by choosing securities and market type with less information sensitivity. This chapter takes a step towards filling this gap in the literature by focusing on two specific security issue scenarios involving public and private security markets.

First, this study examines the security issue decisions between the public and private markets. It is often argued that the management can convince the quality of the firm to a selected set of investors through direct conversations – a nearly impossible task in a public offering with a large set of investors (Hertzel and Smith; 1993). However, the private security markets behave inherently differently when compared to public security markets as they demand no public disclosure of information (Petrova et al., 2008; Gomes and Phillips, 2012). As discussed earlier, the securities are sold to sophisticated investors capable of producing their own information, thereby reducing the dilution costs arising out of information asymmetry in private markets. Consequently, firms with higher information asymmetry have strong incentives to reduce information costs by issuing securities privately (Wu, 2004; Chen et al., 2010; Dai 2011; Dhaliwal et al., 2011, Kale and Meneghetti, 2011; Abidin et al., 2012; Marshall et al., 2016). Therefore, we argue that firms facing a higher degree of information asymmetry would issue more securities in the private markets than the public markets.

Second, we analyse the debt and equity issues within the private security market. In contrast to the conventional information-based theories, which often assume that the quantum and quality of information between the insiders and outsiders of the firm is fixed and no additional information production is possible, an alternative strand of literature argues that given the nature of private market involving specialized investors with superior information production possibilities, the firm has more incentives to sell more information-sensitive securities through private placements (Boot and Thakor, 1993; Klein et al., 2002; Fulghieri and Lukin, 2001; Gomes and Phillips, 2012; Abidin et al., 2012). For example, Fulghieri and Lukin (2001) argue that if outsiders are allowed to generate information on their own, then the degree of information asymmetry between the firm and outside investors becomes endogenous. Consequently, information asymmetry would depend on the degree of information sensitivity of the security used. Hence, a firm has more incentives to issue more information-sensitive security like equity in private markets, thereby encouraging information production by outside investors. Therefore, in contrast to conventional wisdom, we argue that a firm with higher information asymmetry issues equity over debt in the private security market.

Apart from the contribution to the literature on asymmetric information and security issue decisions according to the market type, this study also adds value by introducing three proxies based on the analyst forecast data – number of analysts following the firm, surprise in analyst forecast and dispersion in analyst forecast – to account for asymmetric information in the Indian context (Chang et al., 2006; Li and Zhao, 2008; Kovacs, 2010; Chen et al., 2015). For instance, if the number of analysts covering a firm is higher, it shows more focus given to the various aspects of firms by a specialized set of people capable of producing more information about the firm's quality (Bowen et al., 2008). Similarly, if the surprise and dispersion among the analyst forecast tends to be minimal, then the analysts are able to make accurate predictions about the firm performance with the available information (Li and Zhao, 2008; Gomes and Phillips, 2012).

The main findings emerging from this study show that asymmetric information plays an important role at all levels of security issue decisions of Indian firms. To begin with, this study shows that the decision to issue security in the public or private markets is driven by information asymmetry. Similar to the arguments of the information-based models, only the firms facing lesser information problems issue securities in the public market.

In contrast to conventional wisdom, whereby informationally challenged firms issuing securities are less sensitive to information problems, this study finds a reversal in the role of information asymmetry in the private security market. Importantly, we observe a reversal of pecking order behaviour in the private security market in which firms with higher levels of information problems issue equity over debt contrary to the popular narrative. We observe that Indian firms facing information problems issue equity using the private placement route. These findings are important in the context of emerging markets in which severe information problems are reported due to controlled family ownership, poor corporate governance norms, and inadequate investor protection measures combined with a weak legal framework that obstructs information disclosure (Sony and Bhaduri 2021). This finding also suggests that the dominance of private security markets in the Indian context is largely driven by higher information problems. Furthermore, the results show that the reversal of the pecking order pattern when the information sensitivity of the security is lower is not just limited to developed economies but applicable in emerging economies as well (Fulghieri and Lukin, 2001; Gomes and Phillips, 2012).

The next section discusses the previous literature and a brief overview of the private security markets in India.

7.2 Prior literature

Pecking order theory, one of the most influential capital structure theories put forward by Myers (1984), proposes a hierarchical form of financing whereby firms prefer internal financing to external sources. Myers and Majluf (1984) argue that the choice of external funds is driven by adverse selection costs arising out of the information asymmetry between managers with superior information and outside investors with less information. While the relevance of the information-based theories for understanding the capital structure in different countries is contentious, the key driving force–information asymmetry has been widely accepted key factor in determining the financing and investment decisions of corporations (Chang et al., 2006; Bharath et al., 2008; Leary and Roberts, 2010; Seifert and Gonenc, 2008; Bessler et al., 2011; Gao and Zhu 2015: Bhaduri, 2015; Sony and Bhaduri, 2018).[4]

Emerging economies, known for complex information problems, deserve a special mention in this context. While empirical studies discuss in detail the issues accentuating information problems in emerging markets economies, the Indian market is often cited as a classic example in which a complex institutional structure, a weak legal enforcement mechanism and family controlled–business ownership, among others, amplify information problems (Young et al. 2008; Sarkar and Sarkar, 2012; Claessens and Yurtoglu, 2013; Bhaduri, 2015). In fact, the market regulator, the Securities and Exchange Board of India (SEBI), has recognized the widespread agency problems and the need to improve corporate governance norms. Specifically, the Uday Kotak Committee of 2017 set up by the SEBI also highlights the need to improve the information disclosure norms and retail–investor protection measures. Therefore, the intricate information environment in the security market makes India a perfect setting to test for the role of information asymmetry.

However, the predictions made by the pecking order model assume that the level of information asymmetry between the insiders and outsiders of the firm is fixed and remains so. According to Myers and Majluf (1984), there is no case for outsiders to produce any additional information, thereby virtually closing any case for additional information acquisition by investors. Conversely, it has been argued that information dissemination mechanisms are inherently different in private and public markets due to the presence of different classes of investors.

Furthermore, the public issue of security always faces a threat of underpricing in the market because the investors assume superior information in the hands of the managers and react negatively. This demands the disclosure of a lot more information much beyond a comfortable level of many firms (Chen et al., 2010). However, the information dissemination mechanism in the private market bestows an opportunity in the hands of firms to selectively disclose information to a few investors, thereby alleviating the possibility of its competitors gaining insights (Gomes and Phillips, 2012). Fulghieri and Lukin (2001) outline two sets of investors in capital markets. The first group is the specialized investors who have the ability to generate information internally through superior information-production techniques. The second group consists of investors who are largely uninformed. It is argued that informed investors would be willing to pay more for a security than a less-informed investor, and firms prefer funds from an informed investor (Saa-Requejo, 1996). Accordingly, asymmetric information models argue that firms are sensitive to who provides funds and the type of security issued, debt or equity.

Interestingly, Gomes and Phillips (2012) report a reversal of the pecking order model of financing within the private security markets in which the firms are issuing equity relative to debt with an increase in the degree of information asymmetry. The theoretical underpinnings of this behaviour can be traced to the work of Fulghieri and Lukin (2001). They show that the two principal factors that influence information production by private investors are the sensitivity of securities to information asymmetry and the costs of information production. Conditional on private markets and the lower cost of information production, the incentives are higher for the private investors when more information-sensitive security like equity is issued. Information disclosed privately to investors motivates further information production and the investors have more insider insights directly from the management.

Fulghieri and Lukin (2001) propose a critical value of information production cost and when the cost of information production is below this threshold, firms issue equity. Furthermore, they postulate that threshold information production cost increases with the level of information asymmetry. Gomes and Phillips (2012) extend these propositions to the private security markets and hypothesize that the probability of issuing equity relative to debt increases with the degree of information asymmetry. Their results confirm the argument that information sensitivity in the private security markets is lower and that firms with a higher degree of information asymmetry choose equity over debt.

7.2.1 Security markets in India

Now, we turn our focus to the security markets in India. The liberalization policy in 1991 and the subsequent reforms in the capital market opened up various avenues to raise capital. The stock market and credit market boom in the liberalized regime witnessed firms raising capital through various alternatives. However, even after 25 years' post-liberalization, banks still remain the most preferred source of capital (Chauhan, 2017)

The listed Indian companies issue securities predominantly through two market types: private and public. Several features of the Indian capital markets make it unique when compared to the developed and emerging economies. The most striking feature of the Indian market is the near absence of a vibrant public debt market (Raghavan et al., 2014). Notably, almost all firms issuing public debt are government-controlled entities or financial institutions. However, over the period, private placement of debt and equity has gained popularity among Indian firms (Sophastienphong et al. 2008, Handbook of Statistics of Indian Economy, 2018). Security issues are considered to be private if the transaction involves a selected set of investors instead of targeting a large set of public investors.

The guiding principles of private placements in India initially fell under the purview of the Companies Act, 1956 and regulations put forward by the SEBI, the apex market regulator from time to time. However, a systematic change in the various provisions regarding private security markets was incorporated into the new Companies Act adopted in 2013 to address the increasing complexity of security markets and malpractice by manager-owners and enhance shareholder rights. The Companies Act, 2013 (GOI, 2013) widened the scope of private placements by avoiding misspecifications and included securities of all forms like debentures, bonds, shares and other marketable securities. The act defines a private placement as a security offer or invitation to purchase securities to a selected set of investors by a company through a private placement offer letter and other conditions specified. Furthermore, the act caps the maximum number of investors in a private placement offer at 50, and anything above is treated as a public issue.

As discussed earlier, the near absence of a public corporate debt market and the prevalence of the private debt market can be attributed to the non-requirement of detailed compliance formalities in private placements (Shukla and Prabu, 2015). Firms are not required to make any general announcements or advertisements and are exempted from making a filing to SEBI. All the issue sizes above INR 5 billion have to mandatorily follow an electronic book mechanism to increase transparency and enhance price discovery. Unique to India, relaxed norms on public disclosure of information and the fast pace of the process make the private placement of bonds and debentures a preferred route for raising funds instead of a public issue.

Furthermore, similar to the corporate debt market, private placements remain the most popular equity-issuing instrument owing to their lower sensitivity to information problems. As per the SEBI guidelines, listed firms can issue equity privately in two ways: preferential allotments and qualified institutional investors. Preferential allotments remain a popular mechanism among owner-managers for acquiring more equity (or convertible warrants), holding off firms due to the non-requirement of sending a private placement offer letter. However, in order to prevent malpractices, there is a 3-year lock-in period for transacting on the equity issued to the owner-manager. The pricing of the private placements is also regulated by the SEBI, which mandates that the issue price should be above the 6-month average price prior to the issue date.

In qualified institutional placement (QIP), firms issue equity, convertible debentures, or any securities other than warrants, which are convertible to a qualified institutional buyer (QIB). QIP was introduced in India in 2006 and regulated by the SEBI (Issue of Capital and Disclosure Requirements) Regulations, 2009. Mutual funds, venture capital funds, public financial institutions, scheduled commercial banks, insurance companies and pension funds listed with a recognized national stock market are considered QIB. Similar to preferential allotments, there is no requirement to make a pre-issue filing with the SEBI. Moreover, it is mandatory for the company to ensure that there are at least two buyers if the size of the issue is up to INR 2.5 billion and at least five buyers if the company is issuing securities above INR 2.5 billion.

Two major observations emerge from the existing literature. First, information asymmetry plays a major role in the security issues decisions in public and private markets, as well as within the private markets. However, contrary to the standard information asymmetry models, the literature suggests a reversal in the impact of information asymmetry in private markets. Second, in an emerging market like India, where information problems are rampant, firms prefer issuing securities privately. Given the fact that Indian firms are facing more information-asymmetry problems and the substantial growth of the private security markets gives us a unique opportunity to test for the role of information asymmetry in capital structure decisions according to security market type.

7.3 Data and Methodology

7.3.1 Data

This study uses data from non-finance Indian companies obtained from the Prowess database maintained by the Centre for Monitoring Indian Economy (CMIE). The cash flow statements became mandatory for Indian firms in 2002, and hence, our sample covers a period from 2002 to 2014.[5] We include firms listed in either the Bombay Stock Exchange (BSE) or the National Stock Exchange, the two prominent stock exchanges in India. Following the conventional practices in capital structure literature, utility, service and government-controlled entities are excluded from the sample. We also remove low-quality firms by choosing only those firms with an asset size of more than INR 1 million and choosing firms reporting a profit for at least 6 years.[6] After excluding the firms with missing values of all explanatory variables, a sample of 1372 firms with 16,919 firm-year observations has been selected.

From the initial sample, we identify the private placement of debt and equity and public issues from a dedicated section in the CMIE Prowess database and match it with the other balance sheet variables. The sample consists of only those issues with a size of more than INR10 million. Even though bank borrowings are identified as a form of private debt in some capital structure literature, we stick to the definition given in the Companies Act, 2013 to identify the private placements debt as the issue of bonds and debentures alone. Following the criteria mentioned in the Companies Act, 2013, a private placement is equity is the combination of preferential allotment and qualified institutional placement. It is also important to note that public debt markets in India are in a nascent stage and dominated by government-controlled firms and financial institutions. In the absence of listed non-finance firms in the public debt segment, our sample does not include any public debt issues of securities. Hence, the public issue of securities includes only equity issues through follow-on public offers, depository receipt issues and rights issues. Based on this we identify 595 private debt issues, 728 private equity issues and 241 public issues.

If the firm has issued private security and public security, we classify it as a public issue following the logic of the financing hierarchy suggested by Myers (1984). Similarly, if the firms have issued both equity and debt in a private market, we treat it as an equity issue. Finally, analyst coverage data are hand-collected from the pages of each company on the *Financial Times* website, which is publicly available for the 2010–2014 period. Therefore, the analysis using the analyst-specific variables is for only this period during which there are 460 private placements and 59 public issues. Within the private security market, there are 200 instances of private debt issues and 260 instances of private equity issues.

7.3.2 Determinants of capital structure

The extent of information asymmetry is captured in the capital structure literature using conventional variables like age, size, dividend issue and nature of assets of the firm. Since these variables are often subjected to multiple interpretations, we use three variables derived from the financial analyst's behaviour – analyst coverage, analyst forecast surprise and analyst forecast dispersion – to capture information asymmetry.

Financial analysts are intermediaries who generate more private information, thus exposing any mismanagement by the managers. Empirical evidence suggests that increased analyst coverage reduces adverse selection costs

(Brennan and Subrahmanyam, 1995; Kovacs, 2010; Chen et al., 2015). Chang et al. (2006) confirm that analyst coverage and information asymmetry have a negative correlation because analysts give more coverage to more transparent firms. Therefore, we argue that firms with better analyst coverage face less information asymmetry.

The surprise and dispersion element in the earnings forecast by analysts when compared to the actual earnings value reported by the firm is a better measure of the degree of asymmetric information. When the firms make more disclosures, the dispersion and surprises significantly reduce (Lang and Lundholm, 1996; Li and Zhao, 2008). Gomes and Phillips (2012) suggest a positive correlation between information asymmetry and surprises in analysts' forecasts. Thus, we treat a firm with less forecast surprise as a firm with lower levels of information problems. Dispersion among analysts forecasts increases when there is less information in the market on the financial performance of the firm (Halov and Heider, 2011). Like Gomes and Phillips (2012), we expect the dispersion measures to increase when the degree of information asymmetry.

The literature also raises concerns about using the analyst-specific data as the correlation between analysts following and firm-specific characteristics leads to potential endogeneity issues (Chang et al., 2006). In order to circumvent the potential endogeneity, this study adopts two specific strategies suggested in the literature. The first strategy re-estimates the model by adding analyst coverage variable with sufficient lags and control for prior equity issues by the firm in order to address concerns such as firms receiving more analyst coverage because analysts anticipate more equity issues. Therefore, this study uses a two-period lagged analyst coverage and accounts for past equity issues in the last 3 years.

The second strategy adopts a two-stage estimation procedure similar to Chang et al. (2006). The first step develops a negative binomial regression model to predict the number of analysts covering a firm (lagged 1 year) using factors that could potentially influence the analyst coverage (Frank and Goyal, 2009; Kurshev and Strebulaev, 2015; Kumar et al., 2017). The analyst coverage variable is lagged by 1 year, and all explanatory variables are lagged by 2 years. The second step re-estimates the model by incorporating the predicted number of analysts derived from the first step.

Apart from the analyst-specific variables, we use a set of conventional variables. Which are widely accepted as potential determinants of capital structure decisions (Bhaduri, 2002; Frank and Goyal, 2009; Delcoure, 2007; Chakraborty, 2010). Additionally, we also control for governance aspects as well. The construction of all these variables is described in Appendix A.

7.3.3 Methodology

This study tests the role of information asymmetry in two specific scenarios. The first model analyzes the impact of information asymmetry on a firm's decision to choose between the private security market and the public security market. To test our hypothesis, we use a binary logistic regression, where firms making public issues take the value 1 and 0 if private markets are chosen for security issues. The main model is described as follows:

$$P(y) = \frac{e^{\alpha+\beta X}}{1+e^{\alpha+\beta X}} \tag{7.1}$$

where y is the binary variable described earlier and X is a vector of firm-level variables, which determines the security issue behaviour.

In the second model, we specifically focus on private security markets. Here firms make a choice between debt and equity through private placement to selected investors. The base equation remains the same as Equation (7.1). The binary dependent variable takes the value of 1 if the firm issue equity and 0 if the firm issue debt. The independent variables remain the same in both the models. We incorporate year and industry-specific dummies in both models to capture time and industry-specific effects.

7.4 Empirical analysis

7.4.1 Trends and descriptive statistics

Table 7.1 summarizes the trends and patterns of security issues in the Indian markets. Panel A reports the percentage of security issues made in public and

Table 7.1 Trends in the public and the private security market

	Panel A		*Panel B*	
Year	*Private (%)*	*Public (%)*	*Private Debt (%)*	*Private Equity (%)*
2002	95.146	4.854	66.000	34.000
2003	89.109	10.891	68.817	31.183
2004	89.320	10.680	46.316	53.684
2005	59.155	40.845	40.206	59.794
2006	77.381	22.619	30.075	69.925
2007	83.688	16.312	31.148	68.852
2008	80.952	19.048	37.500	62.500
2009	87.500	12.500	50.806	49.194
2010	81.560	18.440	42.500	57.500
2011	88.462	11.538	55.789	44.211
2012	92.632	7.368	35.556	64.444
2013	91.667	8.333	50.562	49.438
2014	93.902	6.098	35.065	64.935
Overall	85.421	14.579	45.411	54.589

Note: Authors own calculation based on Centre for Monitoring India Economy Prowess data. Panel A shows the percentage of securities issued in private and public markets in a year. Panel B shows the security percentage of debt and equity issued with the private market.

private markets. We observe that public issues are less common when compared to private placements. Overall, 85.4% of the security transactions took place through private placement. The pattern observed here follows the a priori logic of the hierarchical model of financing by Myers (1984), where only those firms successfully overcoming the information problems issuing securities publicly, which are few in number.

Interesting observations emerge from the pattern of security issues within the private security markets reported in Panel B of Table 7.1. Contrary to the pecking order models, equity seems more common than debt issues. On average 54.4% of the security issues are equity issues in the private markets. Equity issues were typically high during 2005–2008, 2012 and 2014 when the equity markets were booming.

Next, we move on to analyse the size of the securities issued in the private and the public market. Even though the frequency of public issues is less, the size of the issues is much bigger. Panel A of Table 7.2 reports the average issue size as a percentage in private and public markets. We see that during the booming phase of 2005–2008, firms raised more funds from public markets. Panel B of Table 7.2 compares the average issue size of debt and equity in private markets. Although private equity is more in number, the funds raised through private issues of equity are much less when compared to the private placement of debt. This trend is more evident after 2009, and we see more funds raised through debt instruments in the private market.

Table 7.2 Size of the security issues in public and private markets

	Panel A		*Panel B*	
Year	*Private (%)*	*Public (%)*	*Private debt (%)*	*Private equity (%)*
2002	45.240	54.760	68.229	31.771
2003	39.604	60.396	74.508	25.492
2004	44.168	55.832	68.018	31.982
2005	33.084	66.916	45.638	54.362
2006	37.879	62.121	47.532	52.468
2007	17.769	82.231	51.487	48.513
2008	16.652	83.348	55.118	44.882
2009	49.401	50.599	56.223	43.777
2010	42.359	57.641	79.500	20.500
2011	47.003	52.997	91.164	8.836
2012	33.747	66.253	79.191	20.809
2013	51.930	48.070	87.782	12.218
2014	58.716	41.284	82.790	17.210
Overall	38.900	61.100	68.245	31.755

Note: Authors own calculation based on Centre for Monitoring India Economy Prowess data. Panel A reports the percentage of issue size in private and public markets in a year. Panel B shows the issue size of the issue within the private security markets.

Table 7.3 Security issues according to industry

Industry	*Panel A*		*Panel B*	
	Private (%)	*Public (%)*	*Private debt (%)*	*Private equity (%)*
Automobiles	9.422	12.974	5.042	5.769
Chemicals & Pharmaceuticals	10.410	7.888	19.832	24.451
Construction & Allied Activities	10.244	8.744	20.840	12.912
Consumer Goods	9.555	12.291	4.874	4.670
Diversified	10.778	5.996	8.068	6.593
Food & Agro	9.537	12.383	7.563	9.478
Machinery & Equipment	10.475	7.556	7.227	9.478
Metals	9.994	10.028	17.143	14.835
Mining	9.555	12.291	1.008	0.275
Textiles	10.029	9.849	8.403	11.538

Note: Authors own calculation based on Centre for Monitoring India Economy Prowess data. Panel A demonstrates the industry-wise classification of firms choosing private and public securities. Panel B reports industry-wise choice of debt or equity within the private security market.

Additionally, we analyse the security issue decisions based on industrial classification. Panel A of Table 7.3 does not show much industry-wise variation in the private markets. However, the differences are evident in public issues, which are common among automobiles, consumer goods, food and agro and mining.

Interestingly, the difference becomes more prominent within the private security markets. As shown in Panel B, most of the private placement of debt comes from firms belonging to construction, chemicals and pharmaceuticals and metals. Moreover, the same segments use more private placement of equity as well. However, while chemicals and pharmaceuticals use more private equity, metals and construction segments use more private debt. It is also worth noting that food and agro, machinery and textiles also use more privately placed equity.

Table 7.4 summarizes the major firm-specific variables examined in this study. Panel A presents the summary statistics of firms issuing securities privately and publicly. We find firms issuing public securities are older firms with more tangible assets. However, the firms issuing private securities are smaller, hold more cash, are affiliated with business groups and have a higher institutional shareholding. We do not find any significant difference in means among the analyst-specific variables in these two categories.

Panel B of Table 7.4 presents the summary statistics of debt- and equity-issuing firms within the private security market. We find evidence for higher information asymmetry faced by the firms issuing private equity. Equity-issuing firms have less analyst coverage and higher analyst forecast surprise

Table 7.4 Summary statistics

	Panel A					*Panel B*				
	Private		*Public*			*Private Debt*		*Private Equity*		
	Mean	*Std. dev.*	*Mean*	*Std. dev.*	*Mean difference*	*Mean*	*Std. dev.*	*Mean*	*Std. dev.*	*Mean difference*
Age	32.534	25.000	35.116	26.000	–2.582*	38.371	24.441	28.096	16.609	10.275***
Size	6.409	6.463	6.117	6.066	0.292**	7.358	1.69	5.706	1.717	1.652**
Dividend	0.009	0.017	0.010	0.018	0.000	0.011	0.017	0.008	0.016	0.003***
Profitability	0.129	0.119	0.128	0.120	0.001	0.128	0.096	0.13	0.178	–0.002
Tangibility	0.352	0.344	0.330	0.319	0.023*	0.356	0.181	0.348	0.189	0.009
Tobin's Q	1.038	0.811	1.089	0.861	–0.051	1.065	0.740	1.012	0.775	0.053
Slack	0.125	0.072	0.103	0.055	0.022**	0.039	0.053	0.047	0.064	–0.008**
R&D	0.008	0.001	0.006	0.001	0.002	0.003	0.008	0.002	0.007	0.001
Growth	0.611	0.143	0.328	0.203	0.283	0.244	0.371	0.898	17.262	–0.654
Group affiliation	0.633	1.000	0.556	1.000	0.077**	0.778	0.416	0.518	0.500	0.260***
Promoter shareholding	47.16	47.54	46.326	46.73	0.834	45.39	17.51	48.278	17.654	–2.888***
Institutional shareholding	14.918	10.505	11.921	7.21	2.997***	19.934	14.929	11.04	13.878	8.894***
Analyst following	2.617	7.142	1.482	6.554	1.135	3.577	8.775	0.361	2.006	3.216***
Analyst surprise	0.810	0.380	0.852	0.347	–0.043	0.780	0.382	0.925	0.247	–0.145***
Analyst dispersion	0.824	0.357	0.872	0.307	–0.048	0.797	0.342	0.919	0.260	–0.122***

Note: Authors own calculation based on CMIE Prowess data. All the variables are defined in Appendix A. Panel A summarizes the private versus public markets and Panel B describes the security issues within the private market for 2002–2014. The analyst-specific variables are summarized for 2010–2014. ***, ** and * indicate significantly different from zero at the 1%, 5% and 10% levels of significance, respectively. R&D = research and development.

and dispersion, all suggesting a higher level of information asymmetry. Private debt issuing firms are older, larger, dividend-paying group-affiliated firms and have higher institutional shareholding, suggesting lower information problems.

The relation between all these variables and the security choice indicates that firms choosing the private placement of debt face lower information asymmetry. This is quite contrary to the claims of the pecking order, which envisages a lesser degree of information asymmetry faced by equity issuers. The firms issuing private equity have more cash holdings and are higher promoters of shareholding.

The general picture emerging from the summary statistics shows that the relationship between information asymmetry and security issues in private and public markets is similar to the arguments of information-based models. However, within private markets, we see evidence of firms with higher information asymmetry issuing equity contrary to the information-based models.

7.4.2 Security choice in public versus private markets

In this section, we discuss the results of the logistic regression where the firms choose between public security markets and private security markets. Model 1 of Table 7.5 shows the results of the full sample from 2002 to 2014 without the analyst-specific variables. Our results show that firms issuing public securities are older and dividend payers indicating a lower level of information asymmetry. The public issuers are also characterized by lower institutional shareholding, a stand-alone nature of business, lower cash holding and higher growth. However, the information emerging from this analysis does not give a clear picture of the role of information asymmetry.

Table 7.5 Choice between public and private security issue decision

Variables	*Model 1*	*Model 2*	*Model 3*	*Model 4*
Analyst coverage		1.210**		
		(2.282)		
Analyst forecast surprise			−1.121**	
			(−2.002)	
Analyst forecast dispersion				−0.886*
				(−1.695)
Age	0.551***	−0.575*	−0.567*	−0.553*
	(3.777)	(−1.853)	(−1.896)	(−1.847)
Size	−0.0384	0.182	0.178	0.193
	(−0.568)	(1.393)	(1.367)	(1.517)
Dividend	0.447**	−41.84*	−40.18*	−38.63*
	(2.334)	(−1.778)	(−1.700)	(−1.666)
Profitability	−0.293	−1.525	−1.368	−1.391
	(−0.432)	(−1.317)	(−1.183)	(−1.191)

(*Continued*)

Table 7.5 (Continued)

Variables	*Model 1*	*Model 2*	*Model 3*	*Model 4*
Tangibility	−0.468	0.221	0.194	0.222
	(−0.859)	(0.221)	(0.188)	(0.213)
Tobin's Q	−0.0423	−0.601	−0.591	−0.571
	(−0.378)	(−1.230)	(−1.207)	(−1.154)
Slack	−1.696**	1.091	1.382	1.361
	(−2.140)	(1.041)	(1.301)	(1.290)
Growth	0.397***	0.338**	0.287*	0.292*
	(2.716)	(2.075)	(1.736)	(1.784)
Promoter shareholding	−0.00363	−0.0212*	−0.0216*	−0.0213*
	(−0.772)	(−1.869)	(−1.892)	(−1.866)
Institutional shareholding	−0.0168**	−0.0485***	−0.0477***	−0.0466***
	(−2.316)	(−2.708)	(−2.699)	(−2.632)
Group affiliation	−0.380*	−0.445	−0.479	−0.473
	(−1.954)	(−1.186)	(−1.261)	(−1.240)
Constant	−2.605***	−0.980	0.753	0.467
	(−3.613)	(−0.697)	(0.459)	(0.296)
Pseudo-*R*-square	.118	.154	.152	.148
Observations	1,391	516	516	516

Source: Authors.

Note: This table presents the results of the logistic regression testing the role of information asymmetry on public and private security choices. The dependent variable equals one for public issues and zero for private issues. Definitions of variables are given in Appendix A. All the dependent variables are lagged by one year. Industry and time dummies are incorporated into the model, but not reported. ***, ** and * indicates significantly different from zero at the 1%, 5% and 10% levels of significance, respectively.

To test exclusively for information asymmetry, we incorporate the analyst-specific variables into the model. The results of the logistic regression with three analyst-specific variables are reported in Models 2–4. The benchmark model reported in Model 2 uses the number of analysts following the firms to capture information asymmetry. We find that firms choosing public security issues have higher analyst coverage. As discussed earlier, a higher analyst following is associated with a lower level of information asymmetry. Therefore, this finding confirms the arguments of the information-based models that only those firms facing higher information asymmetry issue securities privately.

Furthermore, the result of the model that incorporates the other two analyst-specific variables reported in columns 3 and 4 strengthens the case for information asymmetry operating in the issue decision. We find that the forecast-surprise element has a negative association with public security issues, suggesting that the analysts could accurately predict the earnings of the firm with the available information.

The result of the model that incorporates the other two analyst-specific variables reported in columns 3 and 4 strengthens the case for information asymmetry operating in the issue decision. We find that the forecast surprise element has a negative association with public security issues, suggesting that the analysts could accurately predict the earnings of the firm with the available information.

Our results show that the firms issuing public securities have fewer forecast surprises and consequently fewer information problems. Similarly, the next asymmetric information-specific variable – analyst forecast dispersion – also shows that as the dispersion increases the probability of issuing public security reduces implying that firms with lower dispersion measure (lower information asymmetry) issue more public securities.

Additionally, it is interesting to observe that the firms issuing public issues are high-growth firms. Furthermore, firms making public issues have less promoter shareholding. We also find that firms with higher institutional shareholding and business group affiliation issue securities privately. Interestingly, we also observe that the firms issuing public securities are younger. Concerning other conventional variables, the relationship is not found to be significant to make any meaningful conclusions. Overall, the three information-asymmetry-specific variables suggest that the probability of issuing in the public market decreases with the degree of information asymmetry. However, the conventional information asymmetry variables do not provide any significant insights into the role of information asymmetry.

7.4.2.1 Robustness check

Two empirical strategies are used to test the robustness of the findings. As discussed in Section 7.3, the endogeneity between the analyst coverage and the security issue decision is a potential concern. We address this endogeneity issue by following two approaches. The first approach re-estimates the model using analyst coverage with a lag of 2 years and a control for the past equity issues. Model 5 of Table 7.6 reports the findings of this model. The results show that despite controlling for this, the results remain invariant confirming the claims in the earlier estimations.

The final approach involves a two-stage procedure outlined in Section 7.3. Similar to Chang et al. (2006), this study uses a count data methodology to predict the number of analysts lagged one period using two period-lagged dependent variables. Table 7.7 reports the results of the negative binomial regression. An interesting observation emerging from this regression is large firms (represented by size and big player dummy) firms with a higher Tobin's Q and firms that are a part of the BSE Sensex and Nifty 50 receive more analyst coverage. This is consistent with the argument that analysts typically follow firms with more information available in the market.

Table 7.6 Robustness test – choice between private and public security issue decision

Variables	*Model 5*	*Model 6*
L2. Analyst coverage	1.167**	
	(1.984)	
Predicted number of analysts		0.0667**
		(2.348)
Age	-0.564*	-0.332
	(-1.828)	(-0.892)
Size	0.0137	0.0226
	(0.0627)	(0.105)
Dividend	-35.48	-40.47*
	(-1.603)	(-1.760)
Profitability	-1.393	-0.947
	(-1.247)	(-0.943)
Tangibility	0.105	0.516
	(0.105)	(0.524)
Tobin's Q	-0.608	-0.867*
	(-1.435)	(-1.666)
Slack	1.295	1.211
	(1.210)	(1.132)
Growth	0.281	0.244
	(1.490)	(1.270)
Promoter shareholding	-0.0152	-0.0170
	(-1.372)	(-1.473)
Institutional shareholding	-0.0302**	-0.0271*
	(-2.244)	(-1.913)
Group affiliation	-0.297	-0.491
	(-0.804)	(-1.314)
Prior equity issues	2.100	1.131
	(0.922)	(0.556)
Constant	0.0803	-0.292
	(0.0673)	(-0.219)
Pseudo-*R*-square	.147	.150
Observations	515	504

Source: Authors.

Note: The dependent variable equals one for public issues and zero for private issues. Definitions of variables are given in Appendix A. All the dependent variables are lagged by 1 year. ***, ** and * indicates significantly different from zero at the 1%, 5% and 10% levels of significance, respectively. Industry and time dummies are incorporated into the model but are not reported. Z-statistics are calculated from heteroscedastic robust standard errors, which are adjusted for within-firm clustering.

Next, the result of the analysis using a predicted number of analysts is reported in Model 6 in Table 7.6. The result obtained from the two-stage procedure is very similar to the model using one period-lagged analyst (in Model 2 of Table 7.5). The predicted number of analysts also shares a positive association with public issues, suggesting that such firms face lower information problems. Overall, these three robustness measures confirm the arguments put forward in the earlier regression analysis.[7]

Table 7.7 Determinants of analyst coverage

Variables	*Analyst Coverage*
Age	-0.136
Size	0.365***
Profitability	2.061
Tobin's Q	0.336**
Past equity issues	-1.782
Index constituent	1.354***
Big player	1.584***
Sales growth	0.135
Constant	-4.617***
Year & Industry dummy	Yes
Pseudo *R*-square	.2989

Source: Authors.

Note: This table presents the results of a negative binomial regression to predict the number of analysts following a firm. All the dependent variables are lagged one period with respect to the number of analysts following the firm (which is lagged by 1 year). The variables are defined in Section 7.3. ***, ** and * indicate significantly different from zero at the 1%, 5% and 10% levels of significance, respectively. Industry and time dummies are incorporated into the model but not reported.

7.4.3 Security choice within the private security market

Next, we present the results of logistic regression, where the dichotomous outcome variable takes the value of 1 if the firms issue private equity and 0 if they issue private debt. Model 1 of Table 7.8 shows the results sample from 2002 to 2014 without the analyst-specific variables. We observe that equity-issuing firms are smaller firms. They also pay fewer dividends and have lower institutional shareholding. These characteristics are associated with firms facing higher information problems. Furthermore, the firms issuing private equity are less profitable, have a higher market-to-book ratio, have more cash holdings and have large promoter shareholding. The association of some of the conventional variables with equity issues in the private markets suggests that these firms face higher information problems.

The next models, 2–4, incorporate the three analyst-specific variables to specifically capture information asymmetry. Model 2 in Table 7.8, the benchmark model in this analysis, uses analyst coverage as a proxy, and the results demonstrate that equity-issuing firms face higher information problems. We find that firms issuing private equity typically receive lower analyst coverage. The lower visibility accentuates the information problems for these firms. Furthermore, equity issuing firms are younger, issue fewer dividends, have lower institutional ownership and are stand-alone firms –features typically associated with higher levels of information asymmetry. Moreover, the equity-issuing firms also have lower market valuations expressed by Tobin's Q. Additionally, we observe that the private equity–issuing firms are larger firms.

Table 7.8 Choice between private debt and private equity

Variables	*Model 1*	*Model 2*	*Model 3*	*Model 4*
Analyst coverage		−0.952** (−2.433)		
Analyst forecast surprise			0.890** (2.032)	
Analyst forecast dispersion				0.941** (2.126)
Age	−0.180 (−1.441)	−0.599** (−2.378)	−0.688*** (−2.677)	−0.671*** (−2.627)
Size	−0.530*** (−9.043)	0.679** (2.099)	0.670** (2.101)	0.635** (2.009)
Dividend	−20.45*** (−3.578)	−0.837*** (−2.767)	−0.801*** (−2.628)	−0.843*** (−2.734)
Profitability	−0.739* (−1.795)	0.510 (0.524)	0.223 (0.229)	0.584 (0.611)
Tangibility	−0.690 (−1.473)	−0.653 (−0.897)	−0.667 (−0.925)	−0.809 (−1.109)
Tobin's Q	0.235** (2.142)	−0.402** (−2.334)	−0.327** (−1.971)	−0.339** (−2.006)
Slack	3.965*** (2.887)	0.298 (0.276)	0.242 (0.227)	0.112 (0.106)
Growth	−1.613 (−0.190)	0.176 (0.805)	0.229 (1.044)	0.222 (1.016)
Promoter shareholding	0.0924 (0.510)	−0.00881 (−0.833)	−0.0107 (−1.042)	−0.0101 (−0.967)
Institutional shareholding	0.302*** (3.158)	−0.0593*** (−4.605)	−0.0618*** (−4.660)	−0.0623*** (−4.729)
Group affiliation	−0.149*** (−3.118)	−0.534* (−1.783)	−0.486 (−1.639)	−0.478 (−1.596)
Constant	−9.477 (−0.013)	5.518*** (3.952)	4.199*** (2.994)	4.217*** (3.006)
Pseudo-R-square	.2184	.314	.298	.299
Year & Industry dummies	Yes	Yes	Yes	Yes
Observations	1,204	459	459	459

Source: Authors.

Note: This table shows the results of the logistic regression testing the role of information asymmetry in choosing between debt and equity in private security markets by 1,372 listed Indian companies. The dependent variable equals 1 for equity issues and 0 for debt issues. The definitions of the variables are given in Appendix A. All the dependent variables are lagged by 1 year. Industry and time dummies are incorporated into the model but not reported. ***, ** and * indicate significantly different from zero at the 1%, 5% and 10% levels of significance, respectively.

The next models incorporate the two other analyst-specific variables – analyst forecast surprise and analyst forecast dispersion variables – into the estimation. Findings reported in Model 3 of Table 7.8 show that forecast surprises are higher for the private equity–issuing firms, suggesting that they are facing more information asymmetry. In other words, the private debt issuers have more information available in the markets enabling the analysts to make accurate predictions about earnings thereby reducing information asymmetry.

The third analyst variable, forecast dispersion also confirms that private equity issuers face higher information asymmetry (see Model 4 in Table 7.8). The forecast dispersion or the variance between the different analysts is higher for private equity issuers. On the contrary, the private debt issuers have lower levels of dispersion measure confirming the lower degree of information asymmetry faced by them. The association of other variables used in this study remains consistent across models.

All three models with the analyst-specific variable and the generic model demonstrate the reversal of pecking order behaviour in the private security markets, contrary to the claims of the information-based models. In private security markets where investors are capable of producing private information, firms prefer debt to equity violating the arguments of the pecking order model. This is partially enabled by the superior information production techniques of the sophisticated investors involved. We attribute this behaviour to the lower information production cost and the presence of higher incentives for choosing informationally sensitive security in private markets.

7.4.3.1 Robustness check

As a robustness check, we repeat the estimation with two alternate specifications that address the endogeneity issues discussed earlier. Model 5 of Table 7.9 re-estimates our model using a 2-year-lagged analyst coverage variable and volume of equity issues in the last 3 years. The result shows that even after using 2-year lags on analyst coverage, our results remain invariant. Furthermore, it is observed that past equity issues do not have any significant impact on security issues.

The final approach involves the two-stage procedure described earlier. Similar to Chang et al. (2006), this study uses a count data methodology to predict the number of analysts lagged one period using two-period lagged independent variables. Table 7.10 reports the results of this negative binomial regression. The findings suggest that large firms (represented by size and big player dummy), firms with a higher Tobin's Q and higher profitability and firms which are a part of the BSE Sensex and Nifty 50 receive more analyst coverage. This is consistent with the argument that analysts get attracted to firms with more information available in the market.

In the final estimation, the predicted number of analysts from a count data model is used as a proxy to capture the information asymmetry, and the results are reported in Model 6 of Table 7.9. The results obtained from the two-stage procedure are very similar to the model using one-period-lagged analyst coverage (in Model 2 of Table 7.8). The predicted number of analysts shares a negative relationship with equity issues, suggesting that in private

Table 7.9 Robustness test – choice between private debt and private equity

Variables	*Model 6*	*Model 7*
L2.Analyst coverage	−0.866* (−1.710)	
Predicted number of analysts		−0.118** (−2.020)
Age	−0.651** (−2.499)	−0.658*** (−2.578)
Size	0.659** (2.113)	0.731** (2.385)
Dividend	−0.930*** (−3.048)	−0.966*** (−3.135)
Profitability	0.506 (0.509)	0.295 (0.324)
Tangibility	−0.733 (−1.010)	−0.450 (−0.605)
Tobin's Q	−0.332* (−1.902)	−0.211 (−1.279)
Slack	0.0172 (0.0158)	0.531 (0.495)
Growth	0.245 (1.089)	0.173 (0.790)
Promoter shareholding	−0.0120 (−1.154)	−0.0181* (−1.775)
Institutional shareholding	−0.0637*** (−−4.701)	−0.0566*** (−4.025)
Group affiliation	−0.470 (−1.584)	−0.620** (−2.114)
Past Equity Issues	0.704 (0.266)	−0.446 (−0.179)
Constant	4.704*** (4.114)	4.851*** (4.134)
Pseudo-*R*-square	.294	.297
Observations	457	449

Source: Authors.

Note: This table shows the results of the logistic regression testing the role of information asymmetry in choosing between debt and equity in private security markets by 1372 listed Indian companies. The dependent variable equals 1 for equity issues and 0 for debt issues. The definitions of variables are given in Appendix A. All the dependent variables are lagged by 1 year. Industry and time dummies are incorporated into the model but not reported. ***, ** and * indicates significantly different from zero at the 1%, 5% and 10% levels of significance, respectively.

security markets, firms with higher information-asymmetry issues equity. Overall, we find that our results remain invariant with alternative measures of information asymmetry as well and uphold the arguments put forward in the earlier regression.

Table 7.10 Determinants of analyst coverage in private security markets

Variables	*Analyst coverage*
Age	–0.209
Size	0.370***
Profitability	2.551*
Tobin's Q	0.216*
Past equity issues	–1.137
Index constituent	1.239***
Big player	1.574***
Sales growth	0.142
Constant	–4.021***
Observations	449

Source: Authors.

Note: Variables are derived from the data collected from Centre for Monitoring Indian Economy's Prowess database. All the dependent variables are lagged one period with respect to the number of analysts following the firm (which is lagged by 1 year). The variables are defined in Appendix A. All the dependent variables are lagged by one year. "***", "**" and "*" indicate significantly different from zero at the 1%, 5% and 10% levels of significance, respectively. Industry and time dummies are incorporated into the model but not reported.

7.5 Conclusion

The study adds to a wide body of corporate finance literature arguing for the importance of information asymmetry in capital structure decisions by analysing the role of information asymmetry in the security issue decisions of Indian firms in public and private markets. First, we find that the decision to issue security in public or private markets is driven by information asymmetry. Only those firms with less information asymmetry choose to issue a public security. The firms facing higher information asymmetry place securities privately with investors who have superior information production capacity. The second and the most important finding of our study comes from the private security markets, where firms issue debt and equity to selected investors. The private security markets exhibit a reversal of the pecking order model of financing. Contrary to the claims of information-based models that firms with fewer information problems issue equity, we find evidence for firms facing higher information asymmetry issuing equity over debt in private markets. Our results are similar to the arguments presented in the works of Fulghieri and Lukin (2001) and Gomes and Phillips (2012), who found evidence in developed economies. Our findings gain significance in the context of higher information problems persisting in several emerging economics. Our findings suggest that firms from emerging markets with higher information problems like India circumvent the information challenges by choosing securities and market types with less information sensitivity.

Our findings also suggest that the increasing popularity of the private security market in India can be attributed to the lower sensitivity to different securities, lower cost of information production and higher incentives for sophisticated investors to produce information. Furthermore, these findings are relevant to Indian firms for two reasons. First, they outline the need for firms to address information issues if capital has to be raised from external sources – either public or private. Second, the severe distress in the banking sector (the main source of capital for the Indian firms) due to the non-performing assets is drying up the banking credit.[8] The increased monitoring and the cautious approach followed by the banks after the recent crisis have created more hurdles in the bank-lending process. Naturally, firms need to raise capital from alternate sources like public and private markets for bonds and equity, and our study makes a strong case for addressing the information problems for tapping funds from these sources. Our study also points to the need for further research into the poor information-dissemination mechanism among Indian corporates.

Notes

1 See *Handbook of Statistics on Indian Economy*, 2018.
2 For more readings, see Bertrand et al. (2002), Sarkar and Sarkar (2012); Claessens and Yurtoglu (2013), Bhaduri (2002, 2015), Bandyopadhyay and Barua (2016), and Sony and Bhaduri (2021).
3 This study specifically focus on the non-banking financing modes chosen by the Indian firms.
4 See Shyam-Sunder and Myers (1999), Bhaduri (2002, 2015), Chirinko and Singha (2000), Fama and French (2002), Delcoure (2007), Bharath et al. (2008), Seifert and Gonenc (2008); Komera and Lukose (2015), Chauhan (2016), and Bhama et al. (2016) for more pecking order tests.
5 The number of firms in the sample making public issues of equity was minimal and, in a few subsequent years, were less. Hence, these years are not included. The hand-collected information on analyst coverage was limited to 2014 as the subsequent information went behind a paywall. Therefore, the sample size had to be limited to 2014.
6 Access to external security market is limited to smaller and loss-making entities. In order to avoid bias, we have excluded smaller and non-profitable entities.
7 We constructed an information asymmetry index using all three analyst-specific variables using an additive method similar to the work of Sony Bhaduri (2021). An atheoretical index information asymmetry has been constructed in such a way that a firm with higher information problems takes the value close to 1 and a firm with fewer information problems takes values close to 0. As the variables used to construct the index are closely related, incorporating them simultaneously in the model would lead to multicollinearity issues. Due to the lack of any obvious methods to assign weights, different combinations of weights for each of these variables were assigned and tested. However, the results remained invariant to the various combinations of weights. As argued the information asymmetry index shares a negative relationship with public issues, indicating that the probability of firms issuing security in public markets increases with lower levels of information asymmetry. Another approach used by us to incorporate all three variables was to find the orthogonal components of these variables and incorporate the

orthogonalized components into the model. The findings remained invariant; however, some of the variables were insignificant.

8 The rise in nonperforming assets in the Indian banking sector led to stress in the banking sector affecting the lending process. Banks turned cautious while lending and therefore the flow of funds from banking sector to private firms also has reduced significantly. Refer to the *Financial Stability* report published by the Reserve Bank of India (https://rbi.org.in/Scripts/PublicationReportDetails.aspx?UrlPage=&ID=852).

Appendix 7A

Table 7.A1 Definitions

Variables	*Definition*
Analyst coverage	Number of analysts providing the annual revenue estimates of a company
Analyst surprise	Absolute difference between the actual revenue reported and the analyst consensus value divided by the reported revenue value. Firms that do not receive analyst coverage are marked one, which essentially consider them as facing higher degree of asymmetric information.
Analyst dispersion	Absolute difference between the highest value of revenue forecast and the lowest value revenue forecast and divided by the highest analyst forecast value. Firms that do not receive analyst coverage are marked one implying that they have greater asymmetric information.
Age	Difference between the year under consideration and year of listing in stock market
Size	Natural logarithm of total book assets
Dividend	Dividend paid/Total assets.
Profitability	Net profit/Total assets
Tangibility	Net fixed assets/Total assets
Tobin's Q	Tobin's Q is calculated as the sum of book value of debt and market value of common stock to book value of assets.
Slack	Cash and bank balance + investments/Total assets
Growth	Growth of total assets
Promoter Shareholding	Promoter shareholding in percentage
Institutional Shareholding	Non-promoter institutional shareholding in percentage
Group affiliation	Dummy = 1, for business group firms, 0 for standalone firms
Sales growth	Ratio of sales at t minus sales in $t - 1$ divided by sales in $t - 1$
Past equity issues	Equity issues in the last 3 years
Index constituent	Dummy = 1 if the firm is a part of BSE Sensex or Nifty 50 at time t, 0 otherwise
Big player	Dummy = 1 if the size of the firm is in the highest quartile, 0 otherwise

Source: Authors.

Reference

Abidin, S., Reddy, K., and Chen, L. (2012), "Determinants of ownership structure and performance of seasoned equity offerings", *International Journal of Managerial Finance*; Vol. 8 No. 4 pp. 304–331.

Bandyopadhyay, A., and Barua, N.M., (2016), "Factors determining capital structure and corporate performance in India: Studying the business cycle effects", *The Quarterly Review of Economics and Finance*; Vol. 61, pp. 160–172.

Bertrand, M., Mehta, P., and Mullainathan, S., (2002), "Ferreting out tunneling: An application to Indian business groups", *Quarterly Journal of Economics*; Vol. 117 No. 1, pp. 121–148.

Bessler, W., Drobetz, W., and Grüninger, M. C. (2011), "Information asymmetry and financing decisions", *International Review of Finance*; Vol. 11 No. 1, pp. 123–154.

Bhaduri, S. (2015), "Why do firms issue equity? Some evidence from an emerging economy, India", *Journal of Emerging Market Finance*; Vol. 14 No. 1, pp. 59–85.

Bhaduri, S. N. (2002), "Determinants of corporate borrowing: some evidence from the Indian corporate structure", *Journal of Economics and Finance*; Vol. 26 No. 2, pp. 200–215.

Bhama, V., Jain, P. K., and Yadav, S. S. (2016), "Testing the pecking order theory of deficit and surplus firms: Indian evidence", *International Journal of Managerial Finance*; Vol. 12 No. 3, pp. 335–350.

Bharath, S. T., Pasquariello, P., and Wu, G. (2008), "Does asymmetric information drive capital structure decisions?", *The Review of Financial Studies*; Vol. 22 No. 8, pp. 3211–3243.

Boot, A. W., and Thakor, A. V. (1993), "Security design", *The Journal of Finance*; Vol. 48 No. 4, pp. 1349–1378.

Bowen, R. M., Chen, X., and Cheng, Q. (2008), "Analyst coverage and the cost of raising equity capital: Evidence from underpricing of seasoned equity offerings", *Contemporary Accounting Research*; Vol. 25 No. 3, pp. 657–700.

Brennan, M. J., and Subrahmanyam, A. (1995), "Investment analysis and price formation in securities markets", *Journal of Financial Economics*; Vol. 38 No. 3, pp. 361–381.

Chakraborty, I. (2010), "Capital structure in an emerging stock market: The case of India", *Research in International Business and Finance*; Vol. 24 No. 3, pp. 295–314.

Chang, X., Dasgupta, S., and Hilary, G. (2006), "Analyst coverage and financing decisions", *The Journal of Finance*; Vol. 61 No. 6, pp. 3009–3048.

Chauhan, G. S. (2016), "Reconciling theory and evidences for corporate financing in India", *Journal of Emerging Market Finance*; Vol. 15 No. 3, pp. 295–309.

Chauhan, G. S. (2017), "Corporate financing and deleveraging of firms in India", *IIMB Management Review*; Vol. 29 No. 3, pp. 170–187.

Chen, H. C., Dai, N., and Schatzberg, J. D. (2010), "The choice of equity selling mechanisms: PIPEs versus SEOs", *Journal of Corporate Finance*; Vol. 16 No. 1, pp. 104–119.

Chen, T., Harford, J., and Lin, C. (2015), "Do analysts matter for governance? Evidence from natural experiments", *Journal of Financial Economics*; Vol. 115 No. 2, pp. 383–410.

Chirinko, R. S., and Singha, A. R. (2000). "Testing static tradeoff against pecking order models of capital structure: A critical comment", *Journal of Financial Economics*; Vol. 58 No. 3, pp. 417–425.

Claessens, S., and Yurtoglu, B. B. (2013), "Corporate governance in emerging markets: A survey", *Emerging Markets Review*; Vol 15, pp. 1–33.

Dahiya, S., Klapper, L., Parthasarathy, H., and Singer, D. (2013), "The role of private equity investments in public firms: International evidence", *The World Bank*, June 2013 https://doi.org/10.1596/1813-9450-6484

Dai, N. (2011), "Monitoring via staging: Evidence from Private investments in public equity", *Journal of Banking & Finance*; Vol. 35 No. 12, pp. 3417–3431.
Delcoure, N. (2007), "The determinants of capital structure in transitional economies", *International Review of Economics & Finance*; Vol. 16 No. 3, pp. 400–415.
Dhaliwal, D. S., Khurana, I. K., and Pereira, R. (2011), "Firm disclosure policy and the choice between private and public debt", *Contemporary Accounting Research*; Vol. 28 No. 1, pp. 293–330.
Fama, E. F., and French, K. R. (2002). "Testing trade-off and pecking order predictions about dividends and debt", *Review of Financial Studies*; Vol. 15 No. 1, pp. 1–33.
Frank, M. Z., and Goyal, V. K. (2009), "Capital structure decisions: which factors are reliably important?", *Financial Management*; Vol. 38 No. 1, pp. 1–37.
Fulghieri, P., and Lukin, D. (2001), "Information production, dilution costs, and optimal security design", *Journal of Financial Economics*; Vol. 61 No. 1, pp, 3–42.
Gao, W., and Zhu, F. (2015), "Information asymmetry and capital structure around the world", *Pacific-Basin Finance Journal*; Vol. 32, pp. 131–159.
GoI. (2013), *Companies Act 2013*. Ministry of Corporate Affairs, Government of India.
Gomes, A., and Phillips, G. (2012), "Why do public firms issue private and public securities?", *Journal of Financial Intermediation*; Vol. 21 No. 4, pp. 619–658.
Halov, N., and Heider, F. (2011), "Capital structure, risk and asymmetric information", *The Quarterly Journal of Finance*; Vol. 1 No. 4, pp. 767–809.
Handbook of Statistics on Indian Economy. (2018), Reserve Bank of India.
Hertzel, M., and Smith, R. L. (1993), "Market discounts and shareholder gains for placing equity privately", *The Journal of Finance*; Vol. 48 No. 2, pp. 459–485.
Kale, J. R., and Meneghetti, C. (2011), "The choice between public and private debt: A survey", *IIMB Management Review*; Vol. 23 No. 1, pp. 5–14.
Klein, L. S., O'Brien, T. J., and Peters, S. R. (2002), "Debt vs. equity and asymmetric information: A review", *Financial Review*; Vol. 37 No. 3, pp. 317–349.
Klonowski, D. (2012), *Private equity in emerging markets: The new frontiers of international finance*. Springer.
Komera, S., and Jijo Lukose, P.J. (2015), "Capital structure choice, information asymmetry, and debt capacity: evidence from India", *Journal of Economics and Finance*; Vol. 39 No. 4, pp. 807–823.
Kovacs, T. (2010), "Equity issues and temporal variation in information asymmetry", *Journal of Banking and Finance*; Vol. 34 No. 1, pp. 12–23.
Kumar, S., Colombage, S., and Rao, P. (2017), "Research on capital structure determinants: a review and future directions", *International Journal of Managerial Finance*; Vol. 13 No. 2, pp. 106–132.
Kurshev, A., and Strebulaev, I. A. (2015), "Firm size and capital structure", *Quarterly Journal of Finance*; Vol. 5 No. 3, p. 1550008.
Lang, M. H., and Lundholm, R. J. (1996), "Corporate disclosure policy and analyst behaviour", *Accounting Review*; Vol. 71 No. 4, pp. 467–492.
Leary, M. T., and Roberts, M. R. (2010), "The pecking order, debt capacity, and information asymmetry", *Journal of Financial Economics*; Vol. 95 No. 3, pp. 332–355.
Li, K., and Zhao, X. (2008), "Asymmetric information and dividend policy", *Financial Management*; Vol. 37 No. 4, pp. 673–694.
Marshall, A., McCann, L., and McColgan, P. (2016), "The choice of debt source by UK firms", *Journal of Business Finance and Accounting*; Vol. 43 No. 5–6, pp. 729–764.
Myers, S. C. (1984), "The capital structure puzzle", *The Journal of Finance*; Vol. 39 No. 3, pp. 574–592.

Myers, S. C., and Majluf, N. S. (1984), "Corporate financing and investment decisions when firms have information that investors do not have". *Journal of Financial Economics*; Vol. 13 No. 2, pp. 187–221.

Petrova, M. T., Yang, Y. W., and Yildirim, Y. (2008), "The choice of public vs. private equity: evidence from the SEO and PIPE markets". available at SSRN: https://doi.org/10.2139/ssrn.1100902 (Accessed 02 December 2018).

Raghavan, S., Sahoo, A., Hait, A., and Ghosh, S. (2014). *A study of corporate bond market in India: theoretical and policy implications*. Development of Economic and Policy Research, Reserve Bank of India, available at: https://rbidocs.rbi.org.in/rdocs/Publication/PDFs/DR40040314FS.pdf (Accessed 15 December 2018).

Saa-Requejo, J. (1996), "Financing decisions: Lessons from the Spanish experience". *Financial Management*; Vol. 25 No. 3, pp. 44–56.

Sarkar, J., and Sarkar, S. (2012), *Corporate governance in India*. SAGE Publications, India.

Seifert, B., and Gonenc, H. (2008), "The international evidence on the pecking order hypothesis". *Journal of Multinational Financial Management*, Vol. 18 No. 3, pp. 244–260.

Shen, C. H. H. (2014), "Pecking order, access to public debt market, and information asymmetry", *International Review of Economics and Finance*; Vol. 29, pp. 291–306.

Shukla, A. K., and Prabu, A. E. (2015), "Choice of private placement as an instrument for raising debt resources: Evidence from Indian firms", *Reserve Bank of India Occasional Papers Vol. 35 and 36, No. 1 and 2: 2014 and 2015*. https://www.rbi.org.in/Scripts/bs_viewcontent.aspx?Id=3280

Shyam-Sunder, L., and Myers, S. C. (1999), "Testing static tradeoff against pecking order models of capital structure", *Journal of Financial Economics*; Vol. 51 No. 2, pp. 219–244.

Sony, B., and Bhaduri, S. (2018), "Information asymmetry and debt–equity choice: Evidence from an emerging market, India", *Review of Market Integration*; Vol. 10 No. 3, pp. 228–252.

Sony, B., and Bhaduri, S. (2021), "Information asymmetry and financing choice between debt, equity and dual issues by Indian firms", *International Review of Economics & Finance*; Vol. 72, pp. 90–101.

Sophastienphong, K., Mu, Y., and Saporito, C. (2008), *South Asian bond markets: developing long-term finance for growth*, World Bank Publications.

Tuli, A. (2016), "Firms' choice of seasoned equity issuance method-taking private or non-private route". *Global Business Review*; Vol. 17 No. 2, pp. 400–410.

Wu, Y. (2004), "The choice of equity-selling mechanisms", *Journal of Financial Economics*; Vol. 74 No. 1, pp. 93–119.

Young, M. N., Peng, M. W., Ahlstrom, D., Bruton, G. D., and Jiang, Y. (2008), "Corporate governance in emerging economies: A review of the principal–principal perspective", *Journal of Management Studies*; Vol. 45 No. 1, pp. 196–220.

8 Financial constraints and export behaviour

An analysis of Indian manufacturing firms

Tanveer Ahmad Khan and Indrani Chakraborty

8.1 Introduction

Export promotion and integration with the global economy through the calibrated use of various policy instruments have shaped the economic fortunes of the last four decades.[1] The liberalization of world trade through tariff reduction, currency convertibility and quota removal led to an increase in allocative efficiency, facilitated technological change and improved firm-level productivity (Topalova and Kandelwal, 2011). Thanks to the widespread availability of unit-level data, the focus of trade economists recently has shifted to firm-level determinants of trade flows (Tybout et al., 1991; Harrison, 1994; Tybout and Westbrook, 1995; Pavcnik, 2002; Fernandes, 2003).

Beginning with the Ricardian general equilibrium model of international trade to the new trade theory of Melitz (2003), free trade has been the perfect guide for trade economists. Melitz (2003) made a breakthrough in the literature by recognizing firm-level heterogeneity as the main unit of analysis. The model recognized the existence of sunk costs and productivity to be the important determinants of firm-level exports. The existence of sunk costs brings into focus the role of financial constraints in determining the export status of a firm and the relevant policy of export promotion. Credit constraints will be all pervasive in a developing country characterized by imperfect capital markets and information asymmetry. Bernini (2014) shows that in transition economies where information asymmetries are prevalent, firms exposed to greater domestic or foreign competitive pressure are more likely to report serious financial constraints. Beck and Levine (2002) argue that financial constraints assume greater significance under financial globalization. In an emerging economy like India, the risk in financing under informational asymmetry and imperfect capital markets is all pervasive.

Given the institutional structure of India, most of the lending is done by public-sector banks (PSBs), with a market share of 70% in the national banking market. The market share of PSBs is declining owing to the growing presence of "new private banks" (NPBs), which were licensed in the early 1990s after the liberalization of licensing rules (Economic Survey, 2020). Despite the huge presence of PSBs, the Indian banking sector is characterized

DOI: 10.4324/9781003509721-10

by under-lending or sub-optimal lending on account of regulatory overburden, less strategic and operating freedom, distorted incentive structure of loan officers and general dwarfism of the banking sector compared to other emerging economies (see Banerjee et al., 2004). PSBs in pre–global financial crisis of 2008 advanced huge loans, especially to infrastructure projects, without proper monitoring and evaluation mechanisms in place which ultimately culminated into growing non-performing assets (NPAs). In 2019, PSBs account for 85% of bank frauds, their gross NPAs stood at ₹7.4 lakh crores or 12% of total advances and a collective loss of more than ₹66,000 crores due to bad loans (for more on PSBs, see Economic Survey, 2020). These developments contributed greatly to the recent decline in the credit growth of PSBs affecting the overall growth of the Indian economy. In order to address the problem of bourgeoning NPAs and other structural inefficiencies (especially with Non-Banking Financial Companies NBFCs), the government introduced the Insolvency and Bankruptcy Code 2016 (IBC-2016). The law aims at strengthening the bargaining position of creditors and thus shifting the pendulum away from borrowers to creditors in the process of liquidation. Under the IBC, a creditor with just a 1-lakh default can roll the company into liquidation. The IBC provides a 180-day timeframe for recovering an insolvent firm, with the creditor enjoying the discretion of whether to restructure the loan or sell a firm's assets to recover the amount. The IBC-2016 was comprehensive in scale, surpassing the Debt Recovery Tribunal Act of 1993 (DRT Act) and the Securitization and Reconstruction of Financial Assets and Enforcement of Security Interests Act of 2002 (SARFAESI Act).[2] Using this exogenous change, we try to analyse the effect of IBC-2016 reforms on financial constraints faced by Indian firms.

More specifically, in this study, we try to analyze the impact of financial constraints on the intensive and extensive margin of exports of Indian firms. The debate on causality is still in its nascent stage. In this context, we test the relevant hypotheses of learning by exporting with respect to exports and financial constraints. We utilize IBC-2016 as a natural experiment and try to analyze its impact on the financial health of firms. The study period of our analysis covers 2000–2020 based on 4434 manufacturing firms. We expect that IBC will improve the financial positions of the firms which in turn will lead to improved export participation and performance.

This study makes several contributions to the literature. First, we extend earlier studies on the relationship between financial constraints and exports in Indian manufacturing by considering the recent-year data by systematically examining the role of financial constraints in this regard. The existing literature shows that the relationship is inconclusive in terms of causality. An extension of the earlier studies by including a long period of data spanning a 20-year period and analyzing a rich panel of 4434 manufacturing firms by using novel techniques adds further rigour to the earlier studies. Second, to the best of our knowledge, there are no Indian studies that have examined a learning-by-exporting hypothesis in this context. Third, no studies have considered the role of the IBC-2016 in reducing credit constraints of exporting firms, as we study in this chapter. Fourth, we use two multivariate indices along with traditional measures like liquidity and leverage, and it distinguishes our study from most of the existing empirical research on this topic. Finally, we use the difference-in-difference (DID) methodology, along with the propensity score matching (PSM) technique, to analyse the impact of the IBC-2016 on financial constraints of exporting firms, which deal with selection and endogeneity issues, is a novel one.

The major finding of our analysis shows that an increase in the degree of financing constraints adversely affects the decision to export. Moreover, as the financing constraints increase, the level of exports decreases. These results are consistently observed for alternative measures of financing constraints. We also observe that export starters display better financial health than their non-exporting competitors, even before they start to export. Moreover, we also found that exports lead to faster improvements in the financial health of starters, possibly through a signalling effect in financial markets by reducing informational asymmetries (Ganesh-Kumar et al., 2001; Greenaway et al., 2007). Our findings also show that after the implementation of IBC-2016, financial constraint was decreased for the measure Whited and Wu Index (WWI) whereas it increased for Hadlock–Pierce Index HPI. It indicates that the findings are sensitive to the choice of the measures of financing constraints.

The remainder of the chapter is organized as follows: In Section 8.2, we present a survey of the existing literature. In Section 8.3, we discuss the empirical strategy. In Section 8.4, we discuss the data and descriptive statistics. In Section 8.5, we present the empirical analysis. Finally, we conclude in Section 8.6 with policy implications.

8.2 Literature review

Theoretical literature linking financial constraints and firm-level export determinants was kick-started with the Melitz (2003) model. Chaney (2005, 2016), Muûls (2008) and Manova (2013) extended the Melitz model to account for firm-level heterogeneity in terms of financial constraints. Chaney (2005) accounted for internal finance, while Manova (2010) included the external credit constraint in her extension. Chaney (2016) developed a model of international trade with liquidity constraints. He shows that only the most productive firms that generate enough liquidity from their domestic sales and wealthier firms are more likely to export. Manova (2010) focused on heterogeneous firms across different countries and sectors and found that firms with better financial conditions are more likely to export. Manova (2013) showed that financial constraints can hurt export volumes (intensive margin) to the extent of a firm's financial dependence on external finance. Muûls (2008) built an extended model based on Melitz (2003) to account for both internal and external finance and found that financially constrained firms are less likely to export. She found that financially constrained firms either are prevented from exporting or serve few destinations. While testing her model on Belgian firms, she found that a firm's productivity and liquidity constraints are important determinants of firm-level exports for both intensive and extensive margins. Furthermore, Li and Yu (2009) extended Melitz's (2003) model and considered credit constraints across different types of firms. They found that independent firms are more likely to be affected by external credit constraints than the affiliates of multi-national corporations (MNCs). These theoretical models posit financial constraints to be an important determinant of both extensive and intensive margins of exports.

The theoretical literature was followed by huge empirical work on the nexus between financial constraints and exports beginning with Greenaway et al. (2007). Kiendrebeogo and Minea (2012, 2017), using a panel of Egyptian manufacturing firms, found that unlike financial liquidity, financial constraints reduce the export participation of Egyptian firms. Bellone et al. (2010) found that firms enjoying better financial health are more likely to become exporters. They argue that financial constraints act as a barrier to entry into export markets and ex post export status has no effect on the financial health of a firm. Jarreau and Poncet (2014) investigated the influence of credit constraints on the export performance of Chinese firms. They found that credit constraints affect the sectoral composition of exports and provide an advantage to foreign-owned firms over private domestic firms. Paravisini et al. (2012) found that in the case of Peruvian firms, financial constraint has a negative impact on the intensive margin of exports but no effect on the extensive margin. Qasim et al. (2020) studied the relationship between financial constraints and the export entry decision of the firms in the context of Pakistan. Using the WWI and assets tangibility as measures of financial constraints, they found that being less financially constrained is a vital determinant of Pakistani firms' export participation decisions irrespective of the high firm leverage before entry. In a survey of related literature and analysis of comparable data across 25 European countries, Wagner (2014, 2019) argued that contrary to the big picture revealed by a comprehensive literature survey, a statistically significant negative relationship between financial constraints and exports is only rarely found. Egger and Kesina (2013) assessed the role of credit constraints for exports at the firm level using Chinese data. Their empirical results support the negative relationship between exports and credit constraints suggested by previous theoretical work.

In the case of India, Kapoor et al. (2012) looked at the causal impact of credit constraints on exporting firms by utilizing a natural experiment provided by two policy changes in India. First, the introduction of a subsidized direct credit scheme for small-scale firms in 1998 and its subsequent reversal in 2000. Using a suitable control group, they found that the expansion of subsidized credit increased bank borrowing by 20% and export earnings by about 22%. However, when the policy was reversed, there was no noticeable decline in either of the two indicators. Nagaraj (2014), using liquidity and leverage ratios as measures of financial constraints and multiple estimation techniques, found a strong correlation between financial health and export participation decision, that is, extensive margin of exports. Padmaja and Sasidharan (2020) examined the impact of financing constraints on the extensive and intensive margins of exports using the Prowess database. Using a liquidity ratio and a leverage ratio as financial constraint variables and controlling for initial conditions, endogeneity and selection bias, they found that financial constraints have a significant impact on the extensive margin of exports. They also tested the learning by exporting hypothesis using PSM and DID approaches and found significant positive post-entry effects of exports on firm financial performance. Mukherjee and Chanda (2020) examine the relationship between external financing constraints and the intensive margin of exports for manufacturing firms in India. Using a multivariate index proposed by Musso and Schiavo (2008) for external financing constraints, they found that an increase in the degree of external financing constraints is associated with lower firm-level exports. They looked at different types of firms and found that financing constraints are a significant binding factor even for firms with access to internal capital markets, that is, business group firms.

Financial factors also affect the firm's capability to import. Bas and Berthou (2012) developed a theoretical model linking financial constraints to the import of capital goods and then empirically tested their model using Indian data. They found an important role played by financial factors in the decision to import. They found that an improvement of liquidity or leverage ratio by 10% increases the probability of importing capital goods by 3%–5%, respectively, independent of productivity. Muûls (2015) analyzed the interaction between credit constraints and trading behaviour. He found that firms are more likely to be exporting or importing if they enjoy lower credit constraints. However, the impact varies across margins, that is, in the case of exports; both intensive and extensive margins are associated with credit constraints, whereas for imports, it is only the extensive margin that is affected by credit constraints.

The issue of causality assumes great significance in this context, especially for policymaking. On one hand, if causality runs from financial constraints to exports, then financial reforms promoting easy access to credit will promote exports. On the other hand, if causality runs from exports to financial constraints, then direct intervention to promote exports will lead to better financial performance of firms. Bernini (2014) argues that the relationship between a firm's financial attributes and export behaviour is likely to be characterized by bidirectional causation. Silva (2011) analysed the links between financial constraints and firm export behaviour using data on Portuguese manufacturing enterprises. Using the PSM and DID methodologies, he found a positive impact of exports on the financial health of firms. He further argues that such positive effects are especially important for small firms. Padmaja and Sasidharan (2020) also found support for a positive effect of exports on the financial health of firms.[3] A few studies, such as Bellone et al. (2010) and Manole and Spatareanu (2010), found no impact of exports on the financial health of a firm.

There are also some studies which have addressed the impact of bankruptcy laws on the financial health of firms. Evidence on bankruptcy laws is mostly country-specific. Rodano et al. (2016), using the 2005–2006 Italian bankruptcy law reforms, found that bankruptcy reforms that strengthen creditor rights in liquidation lead to a significant reduction in the cost of bank financing and spur firm-level investment while reforms that increase borrower rights do the opposite. La Porta et al. (1998) showed that countries with poorer investor protections have smaller and narrower capital markets, both equity and debt markets. They argue that because of a creditor-friendly ecosystem, financiers are more willing to surrender funds in exchange for securities which expands the scope of capital markets. Managers under strong creditor rights tend to be more risk-averse, that is, engage in harmful diversifying mergers and have lower cash flow risk and lower leverage (Acharya et al., 2011), than under weak creditor rights.

In the case of India, Vig (2013) showed evidence that stronger creditor rights induced a lower use of secured debt. Acharya and Subramaniam (2009) and Acharya et al. (2011) have shown that firms operating under more creditor-friendly bankruptcy codes tend to reduce corporate risk-taking and invest less in innovative activity. Chatterjee et al. (2017) looked at how creditors and firms as debtors respond to the new bankruptcy law. They found significant behavioural changes among the participants in the credit market. Bose et al. (2020) investigate how the IBC has supported financially distressed firms in mitigating their intrinsic vulnerability during the post-IBC period. Using the DID methodology, they found that due to the expanded credit availability and a lower cost of debt financing during the post-IBC period, distressed firms are able to improve their performance relative to non-distressed firms.

8.3 Empirical strategy

8.3.1 The measure of financial constraints

A firm is considered financially constrained if it does not have access to sufficient external finance and its productivity is not enough to generate sufficient internal liquidity. Financial constraint can be a measure of a firm's financial health or its balance sheet conditions, such as cash flow, leverage and size (Silva and Carreira, 2012). It is very difficult to define an objective and quantitative measure of financial constraints due to its unobservable and multidimensional character. However, a long list of proxy measures has been suggested in trade and corporate finance literature. The most common proxy is investment-cash flow sensitivity, which builds on Fazzari et al. (1988). Later, Kaplan and Zingales (1997) questioned the usefulness of investment-cash flow sensitivity as a measure of financial constraints.[4] McVanel and Perevalov

(2008) discussed various potential measures of financial constraints, such as size (Almeida et al., 2004; Acharya et al., 2007), dividend payment (Fazzari et al., 1988; Cleary, 1999), age (Schaller, 1993; Hovakimian and Titman, 2006), leverage and cash flow (Cleary, 1999). A good measure of financial constraint should satisfy the following three characteristics. First, it should be firm-specific; second, time-varying; and, finally, not necessarily binary in nature; that is, it should consider that there are different degrees of constraints (Silva and Carreira, 2012). Musso and Schiavo (2008) built a time-varying and firm-specific index to measure financial constraints based on size, profitability, liquidity, cash flow, solvency and trade credit. The other two popular measures of financial constraints are liquidity ratio and leverage ratio as employed by Greenaway et al. (2007).

We have used three measures of financial constraints that are very popular in the financial literature (and not so popular in trade literature),[5] such as the WW index, Hadlock–Pierce (HP) index and asset tangibility index. WW constructed an index based on the structural intertemporal investment model. This index is an improvement over the Kaplan and Zingales index (henceforth, KZ index) and is constructed as

$$\begin{aligned}\text{WW index} = &-0.091\text{CFit} - 0.062\text{DIVPOSit} + 0.021\text{TLTDit}\\ &- 0.044\text{LNTAit} + 0.102\text{ISGit} - 0.035\text{SGit},\end{aligned}$$

where CF is the ratio of cash flow to total assets (with a negative loading); DIVPOS is a dummy variable that takes the value of 1 if a firm pays cash dividends and 0 otherwise (negative loading); TLTD is the ratio of long-term debt to total assets (positive loading); LNTA is natural log of total assets or size (negative); ISG is the two-digit industry sales growth (positive); and SG is firm sales growth (Whited and Wu, 2006). The coefficients are taken from the original WW (2006) paper following a number of studies mentioned in Farre-Mensa and Ljungqvist (2016), which used the out-of-sample extrapolation of index coefficients. The higher the WW index, the more the firm is financially constrained.

In an attempt to reevaluate KZ index, HP (2010) estimated an ordered logit model in which financial constraint is modelled as a function of five variables used in the KZ index. They found that only two of the five components of the KZ index, cash flow and leverage, are consistently significant with the KZ index. The index is constructed as[6]

$$\textbf{HP Index} = -0.737\text{Size} + 0.043\text{Size}^2 - 0.040\text{Age},$$

where Size equals the log of the inflation-adjusted log of total assets and Age is equal to year minus the incorporation year. The higher the value of HP index, the more the firm is financially constrained. Following this tradition, we ranked firms based on the HP index into terciles in which the top tercile is classified as ‘constrained’ firms and the bottom as ‘unconstrained’ firms.

In addition to the preceding two measures, we have also used the two standard measures of financial constraints: liquidity and leverage ratio (Greenaway et al. 2007; Padmaja and Sasidharan, 2020). These indicators mostly reflect the status of a firm's internal funds. The higher the liquidity of the firm, the better its financial condition, and the higher the leverage of a firm, the more financially constrained it is. We expect liquidity to have a positive effect and leverage to have a negative effect on both the extensive and intensive margin of exports.

8.3.2 Extensive margin and financial constraints: An econometric model

We begin with the comparison of the financial health of exporters and non-exporters by following Bernard and Jensen (1999). We estimate the following model:

$$\text{LnFin}_{\text{it}} = \beta_0 + \beta_1\text{Expdum}_{\text{it}} + \beta_2\text{TFP}_{\text{it}} + \beta_3\text{Size}_{\text{it}} + +\beta_4\text{Lnlab} + \text{e}_{\text{it}}, \tag{8.1}$$

where 'Fin' is one of the four measures of financial constraints. 'Expdum' is a dummy variable that equals 1 if firm exports and zero otherwise. Size is calculated as the natural log of assets. TFP is the log of the total factor productivity obtained from the Cobb–Douglas production function following Olley and Pakes (1996), following a non-parametric approach. Lnlab is the log of total employees. We also include time and industry dummy variables to control for time and industry-specific effects.

In order to test the ex ante financial health of new exporters and non-exporters as it might be the case that financially sound firms self-select into the export market, we compare the financial health of export starters and non-exporters a year before the former starts to export. Following Wagner (2007), we write the preceding specification with a slight modification:

$$\text{LnFin}_{\text{i,t-s}} = \beta_0 + \beta_1\text{Expdum}_{\text{it}} + \beta_2\text{Z}_{\text{i;t-s}} + \text{e}_{\text{it}}, \tag{8.2}$$

where it is the beginning year of exporting in the case of export starters and the median year in the case of non-starters. This will tell us about the ex ante performance of new exporters before they start to export. $\text{Z}_{\text{it-s}}$ represents the control variables.

Second, we test for the impact of financial constraints on the extensive margin of exports. Following Qasim et al. (2020) and Bharat (2019), our main specification is given as

$$\begin{aligned}\text{Expdum}_t &= \alpha + \beta_1\text{Expdum}_{\text{i,t-1}} + \beta_2\text{Size}_{\text{I,t-1}} + \beta_3\text{Lnlab}_{\text{i,t-1}} \\ &\quad + \beta_4\text{TFP}_{\text{i,t-1}} + \beta_5\text{Age}_{\text{it}} + \beta_6\text{Fin}_{\text{i,t-1}} + \beta_7\text{Foreign dummy}_{\text{i}} \\ &\quad + \text{Control variables} + \text{e}_{\text{it}}.\end{aligned} \tag{8.3}$$

Here we have included a lagged dependent variable as one of the explanatory variables as firms that were already exporting in the previous year will not incur sunk costs in the current year. This makes the current year's exporting decision a function of the previous year's export status. Size, age and productivity are used as control variables (Greenaway et al., 2007). Foreign dummy is a dummy variable which equals 1 for foreign ownership and zero otherwise. We also introduced time and industry-specific dummy variables. 'Fin' is a measure of financial constraints that is introduced in its lagged form. We expect the WW index and the HP index to have a negative impact on export decisions and asset tangibility to have a positive impact (Almeida and Campello, 2007; Whited and Wu, 2006). Since our dependent variable is binary in nature, the estimation suffers from the issue of endogeneity. To address the issue, we lagged all the time-variant explanatory variables once (e.g., Nagaraj, 2014; Greenaway et al., 2007; Bernard & Jensen, 1999, 2004; Qasim et al., 2020). We use the logit estimation technique given the binary nature of our dependent variable.

8.3.3 Learning by exporting hypothesis: PSM-DID methodology

According to the learning by exporting (LBE) hypothesis, exporting improves the firm's financial condition. The literature suggests various reasons in support of the argument that exports reduce financial constraints such as more stable cash flow due to international diversification (Campa and Shaver, 2002), export participation as a signal of efficiency under information asymmetry (Ganesh-Kumar et al., 2001), opening up of international financial markets to firms (Tornell and Westermann, 2003) and exporters tend to be young and more efficient and, as a result, get easy access to external finance (Bernard and Jensen, 1999). On the other hand, studies like Bellone et al. (2010), Manole and Spatareanu, (2010) find no such evidence.

In order to test the ex-post effect of exports on the financial health of firms, we employed the PSM with the DID estimation technique (Rosenbaum and Rubin, 1983). This technique is useful to deal with endogeneity and unobserved effects. Silva (2011) adopted the PSM-DID method to test the ex post effect of exports on financial health of Portuguese firms. He found a significant effect of exports on financial constraints. Serti and Tomasi (2008) adopted the PSM-DID approach to find the effect of exporting on the size and productivity of firms in the context of Italian manufacturing firms. The ideal situation for evaluation studies is to have a 'control' and a 'treatment' group to look at the differential impact, in this case the differential impact of exporting on the financial health of exporters and non-exporters. However, such a group is not available. The matching technique tries to artificially create such a scenario (comparison group) based on some observable variables. This model helps in solving the problem of selection bias and provides valid estimates of average treatment effects (Guo and Fraser, 2014).[7] The use of this technique rests on the appropriate selection of covariates. We included the following firm-specific covariates such as size, age, productivity and ownership. We use the Stata command psmatch2 (Leuven and Sianesi, 2003) for matching. Guo and Fraser (2014) argued that propensity score is a balancing measure (*the coarsest score*); we performed the balancing test proposed by Becker and Ichino (2002) and a standard *t*-test for equality of means. Both tests ensure the quality of the matching performed.

8.3.4 Bankruptcy reforms and credit constraints

We also examined the effect of IBC-2016 on the credit constraints of firms by employing the PSM-DID methodology. We estimate the following model:

$$\begin{aligned} \mathrm{FC}_{\mathrm{int}} &= \alpha + \beta_0 \mathrm{Constrained}_{\mathrm{int}} + \beta_1 \mathrm{IBC} + \beta_2 \mathrm{Constrained}_{\mathrm{int}} * \mathrm{IBC}_{\mathrm{t}} \\ &+ \beta_3 \mathrm{X}_{\mathrm{int}} + \gamma_{\mathrm{i}} + \left[\delta n * \theta t\right] + \varepsilon_{\mathrm{int}}, \end{aligned} \tag{8.4}$$

where i is a cross-sectional unit, t is the time dimension and n is the industry and FC represents any of the previously mentioned measures of financial constraint of a firm. In order to create the control and treatment group, we employed the PSM technique based on some of the covariates, such as firms' size, liquidity, age and ownership. Constrained is a dummy variable that takes the value of 1 if the firm is financially constrained and zero otherwise. IBC is a time dummy variable that takes the value of 1 for period post-2016 and zero before the implementation of IBC-2016. γ_i, δn and θt denote the firm-, industry- and time-specific effects, respectively. ε_{int} is the disturbance term. Our variable of interest is β_2, which measures the causal impact of IBC-2016 implementation on the financial constraints of the firms in different industries. In order to identify the treatment effect, we have followed Vig (2013) and Thapa et al. (2020) and introduced an interaction term $[\delta n * \theta t]$, which is a non-parametric way of accounting for time- and industry-specific effects. Finally, we have also controlled for size, liquidity and ownership.

8.3.5 Intensive margin of exports and financial constraints: Empirical model

In order to analyze the impact of financial constraints on the intensive margin of exports, we estimated the following model:

$$\mathrm{Exp}_{\mathrm{it}} = \beta_1 + \beta_2 \mathrm{FC}_{\mathrm{i,t-1}} + \beta_3 \mathrm{X}_{\mathrm{i,t-1}} + \mathrm{u_i} + \mathrm{n_t} + \varepsilon_{\mathrm{it}} \tag{8.5}$$

Here, Exp is the value of exports; FC represents the measure of financial constraints; X denotes the vector of control variables; and u_i, n_t and ε_{it} represent firm fixed effects, year fixed effects and the idiosyncratic error term, respectively. We estimate the preceding model using generalized method of moments (GMM) estimation technique in order to account for possible endogeneity.

8.4 Data

Our sample is drawn from Prowess, a database provided by the Centre for Monitoring Indian Economy (CMIE). This database has been widely used in reputable studies on Indian firms (e.g., Khanna and Palepu, 1999; Khanna and Palepu, 2000; Padmaja and Sasidharan, 2020; Mukherjee and Chanda, 2020; and many others). The database includes all Indian firms listed on the Bombay Stock Exchange (BSE) and the National Stock Exchange (NSE) during the 2000–2020 period. Our sample consists of 4434 manufacturing firms, of which 2469 firms are exporters, and we are considering an unbalanced panel covered during the period 2000–2020. For the DID analysis of the IBC, we have restricted the study period to 2010–2020 to get the same number of years pre- and post-intervention.

We provide descriptive statistics for the variables in Table 8.1. We observe that the sample firms, on average, are large, old and less export-oriented and have less liquidity and low leverage. Table 8.2 provides the descriptive statistics separately for exporters and non-exporters. It can be seen that exporters tend to have higher sales, are bigger in terms of employment and are more productive than the non-exporters. The table also shows that exporters are mostly the older firms and young firms tend to serve the domestic markets only for many theoretical reasons. Table 8.3 reports the correlations between the variables in this study. Firm size is negatively correlated with the WW index, positively correlated with the HP index, negatively correlated with liquidity and positively correlated with leverage. Thus, the relation between firm size and financial constraints is dependent on the measures of financial constraints. Similar observation appears for all other variables too. However, none of the correlations among the variables raises multicollinearity concerns.

Table 8.1 Descriptive Statistics

Variable	*Obs*	*Mean*	*Std. Dev.*	*Min*	*Max*
Size	88,680	1538.127	17307.405	0	1682856.4
Exports sales	79,942	52.473	4120.652	-8.33	789947.38
Age	88,680	36.2	17.261	10	157
lnsales	64,009	3.636	3.043	-4.773	13.166
lnlabor	74,003	.751	2.797	-4.773	10.885
lnTAssets	80,087	4.109	2.532	-4.773	15.022
TFP	53,243	190.073	431.027	.001	17803.219
HPI	88,680	12980941	6.802e+08	-8.835	1.218e+11
Liquidity	80,087	−152.857	7232.809	−1144741.5	11923.803
Leverage	80,087	26.687	1282.165	0	253421.05
WWI	88,680	-1.368	335.67	-62578.813	54153.094

Source: Authors.

Note: lnsales = log of sales; lnlabor = log of total employees; lnTAssets = log of total assets; TFP = total factor productivity; HPI = Hadlock and Pierce Index; WWI = Whited and Wu Index.

Table 8.2 Descriptive Statistics of Exporters versus Non-Exporters

Variable	*Obs*	*Mean*	*Std. Dev.*	*Min*	*Max*
Non-Exporters					
Size	34,937	1064.149	15282.73	0	1347611
Age	34,937	32.91828	14.07766	10	141
Lnsales	17,566	1.370118	2.978136	−4.773224	9.831215
Emp	6,751	1695.708	8681.966	0	264041
Lnta	34,937	4.208734	2.546759	−4.773224	14.70924
TFP	10,708	106.0342	259.0695	.0021007	9217.309
Exporters					
Size	42,765	964.9845	5985.69	0	338022.2
Age	42,765	38.5534	18.68217	10	157
Lnsales	38,037	4.531211	2.437049	−4.773224	12.96388
Emp	17,072	2583.489	9704.239	0	455685
Lnta	42,765	4.199193	2.416829	−4.773224	15.02153
TFP	35,310	197.3985	408.8836	.0066836	17803.22

Source: Authors.

Note: lnsales = log of sales; lnlabor = log of total employees; lnTAssets = log of total assets; TFP = total factor productivity.

8.5 Empirical estimation

First, we analyse how financial constraints impact the extensive margin of trade. In other words, does the presence of financial constraints hinder a firm's decision to export? Table 8.4 presents the results from the fixed effects estimation of our baseline model, Equation (8.1), on the dummy variable distinguishing between exporters and non-exporters (ExportDummy). The findings show that as a firm's exports increase, the financial constraints measured by the WW index and leverage increase. By comparison, this relationship is negative for the measures HPI and liquidity. However, the coefficients for HPI and leverage are statistically significant only. These imply that, as a firm's exports increase, financial constraints decrease, with respect to the measure HPI. However, the implication is the opposite for the measure leverage. Thus, the effects of exports on financing constraints are dependent on the measure of financing constraints. Thus, we observe that financing constraints assume an important role in influencing firm-level exports. For the firm-specific determinants, we observe most of the results are consistent with our expectations. The number of employees is larger in exporting firms. The size of firms is smaller in exporting firms, and the exporting firms are productive when using the measures HPI and leverage.

Next, we compare ex ante financial health of new exporters and non-exporters, 1 year before the former starts to export. The results are reported in Table 8.5. Such a comparison tells us whether future exports were less financially constrained than their non-exporting counterparts even before entering into the export market. The findings are similar to the findings in Table 8.4 with respect to the variable ExportDummy. The coefficient of this

Table 8.3 Correlation Matrix

	size	*Age*	*Exports sales*	*Lnl*	*lnsales*	*lnta*	*TFP*	*WWI*	*HPI*	*liquidity*	*leverage*
Size	1										
Age	0.123	1									
Export sales	−0.083	−0.002	1								
lnl	0.204	0.288	0.009	1							
lnsales	0.237	0.203	−0.015	0.841	1						
lnta	0.0368	0.0124	−0.005	0.0300*	0.0254*	1					
TFP	0.399	0.0583	−0.006	0.26	0.458	0.0363	1				
WWI	−0.015	−0.0302	−0.001	−0.0485	−0.0492	0.0246	−0.0442	1			
HPI	0.765	0.0296	−0.001	0.0454	0.0774	0.0132	0.243	0.00205	1		
Liquidity	−0.186	−0.108	0.001	−0.252	−0.223	0.22	−0.205	0.185	−0.03	1	
Leverage	0.0389	0.0308	0.001	0.201	0.192	−0.163	0.104	−0.005	0.01	−0.294	1

Source: Authors.

Note: lnsales = log of Sales; lnlabor = log of total employees; lnTAssets = log of total assets; TFP = total factor productivity; HPI = Hadlock and Pierce Index; WWI = Whited and Wu Index.

* Significant at 10%.

Table 8.4 Difference between exporters and non-exporters in terms of financial status

	(1)	(2)	(3)	(4)
	lnWWI	*lnHPI*	*lnliq*	*lnlev*
ExportDummy	0.0085	−0.154***	−0.131	0.0724*
	(0.91)	(−5.68)	(−1.26)	(2.19)
TFP	−0.0292***	0.305***	−0.0108	0.0702***
	(−6.30)	(11.31)	(−0.17)	(3.37)
Lnta (total assets)	−0.154***	−0.00174	−1.004***	−1.000***
	(−58.31)	(−0.88)	(−117.44)	(−335.80)
Lnlabor	0.0313***	1.349***	0.497***	0.295***
	(5.99)	(59.98)	(4.85)	(10.72)
_cons	−0.144***	2.917***	2.380***	1.993***
	(−7.56)	(22.94)	(8.52)	(17.98)
N	43,001	39,184	1107	19,843
R^2	0.294	0.586	0.925	0.865
adj. R^2	0.294	0.586	0.925	0.865

Source: Authors.

Note: t-statistics are in parentheses. lnWWI =log of Whited and Wu Index; lnHPI = log of Hadlock and Pierce Index; lnliq =log of liquidity; lnlev = log of leverage; TFP = log of Total Factor Productivity; Lnta = log of total assets; Lnlabor = log of total employees; _cons = constant.

$^*p < .05$; $^{**}p < .01$; $^{***}p < .001$.

Table 8.5 Ex ante difference between exporters and non-exporters in terms of financial status

	(1)	(2)	(3)	(4)
	lnWWI(−1)	*lnHPI(−1)*	*Lnliq(−1)*	*Lnlev(−1)*
ExportDummy	0.00288	−0.174***	−0.172	0.0690*
	(0.30)	(−6.68)	(−1.82)	(2.25)
TFP(−1)	−0.0292***	0.321***	−0.00185	0.0541*
	(−5.97)	(11.47)	(−0.03)	(2.42)
Lnta(−1)	−0.153***	−0.00105	−1.004***	−0.999***
	(−57.46)	(−0.52)	(−120.15)	(−336.23)
lnlabor(−1)	0.0348***	1.343***	0.496***	0.285***
	(6.44)	(56.79)	(4.87)	(9.70)
_cons	−0.149***	2.855***	2.344***	2.117***
	(−7.27)	(21.59)	(8.67)	(18.22)
N	40,963	37,129	829	17,910
adj. R^2	0.293	0.584	0.927	0.875

Source: Authors.

Note: t-statistics in parentheses. lnWWI = log of Whited and Wu Index; lnHPI = log of Hadlock and Pierce Index; lnliq = log of liquidity; lnlev = log of leverage; TFP = log of total factor productivity; Lnta = log of total assets; Lnlabor = log of total employees; _cons = constant.

$^*p < .05$; $^{**}p < .01$; $^{***}p < .001$.

variable is negatively significant for HPI and positively significant for leverage. It indicates that compared to non-exporting firms, in the cases of exporting firms, the financial health was better, one year before the entry into export markets, according to the measure HPI. However, the results are the opposite for leverage. Moreover, we observe that starters are more productive with respect to the measures HPI and leverage but less productive with respect to the measure WWI. All these coefficients are statistically significant. Furthermore, firm size, measured by the log of total assets, shows that the starters are smaller in size, which contradicts earlier findings by Silva (2011). However, in terms of number of employees, the starters have more employees, irrespective of the measures of financial constraints.

Then we estimate the impact of financial constraints on the extensive margin of exports. The results are reported in Table 8.6. This is based on Equation (8.3) and estimated as a logit model. The results show that the lagged value of HPI has a negatively significant effect on exports. Thus, as the firm becomes more financially constrained, exports decrease, confirming that financial constraints are a significant determinant of a firm's export decision. This finding is as expected. However, the results are not significant with respect to other measures of financial constraints used in this study. The lagged export status dummy is always significant and positive. The lagged value of TFP is also positively significant in all the models. The lagged value of employment is positively significant in Model 1 and Model 2 only. However, the variable age is significant in none of the models.

Table 8.6 Determinants of the decisions to export: Financial constraints

	(1)	*(2)*	*(3)*	*(4)*
	Xd	*xd*	*xd*	*xd*
Expdum(*t* – 1)	4.521***	4.583***	4.576***	4.575***
	(124.05)	(117.91)	(131.05)	(131.05)
L.lnta	–0.00829	0.00354	0.00184	0.00143
	(–0.96)	(0.48)	(0.28)	(0.22)
L.lnl	0.0425***	0.138***	0.0178	0.0181
	(4.00)	(7.61)	(1.84)	(1.87)
L. TFP	0.116***	0.179***	0.114***	0.114***
	(8.76)	(10.25)	(8.97)	(8.98)
Age	0.000287	0.00179	0.00113	0.00112
	(0.28)	(1.77)	(1.20)	(1.19)
L.lnWWI	–0.0470			
	(–1.64)			
1.ownc	0.147	0.0931	0.160	0.159
	(1.47)	(0.95)	(1.74)	(1.73)
L.lnHPI		–0.102***		
		(–10.14)		
L.liquidty			–0.000000175	
			(–0.06)	

(*Continued*)

Table 8.6 (Continued)

	(1)	*(2)*	*(3)*	*(4)*
	Xd	*xd*	*xd*	*xd*
L.leverage				−0.0000106
				(−0.95)
_cons	−2.853***	−2.744***	−2.884***	−2.883***
	(−39.06)	(−31.90)	(−41.66)	(−41.63)
lnsig2u	−10.31*	−13.89	−12.28	−12.27
	(−2.15)	(−1.07)	(−1.55)	(−1.55)
N	40,963	37,129	45,654	45,654

Source: Authors.

Note: t-statistics are in parentheses. Xdn = binary depended variable in a logit model showing export status; Expdum = lagged 'dummy' for export decision, equals 1 if firm exports and zero otherwise; L.lnta = lag of total assets; L.lnl = lag of total employees; L.TFP = lag of total factor productivity; L.lnWWI = log of Whited and Wu Index; 1.ownc = dummy for foreign ownership; L.lnHPI = lag of Hadlock and Pierce Index; L.liquidity = log of liquidity; L.leverage = log of leverage; _cons = constant; lnsig2u = panel-level variance.

$^{*}p < .05$; $^{**}p < .01$; $^{***}p < .001$.

Next, we empirically test the LBE hypothesis, that is, if exporting improves a firm's financial health. Here we are using the DID approach combined with the PSM method, as discussed earlier. Before the estimation from DID, we carry out a balancing test, which assessed the matching quality and the results are reported in Table 8.7. We observe that after matching, the percentage of bias between the treated group and the control group is reduced for all the variables largely. As the percentage of bias is less than 20 for all the variables, it suggests that the matching is done properly (Girma and Gorg, 2007). We also carry out a *t*-test for equality of means between control and treated groups with respect to the variables and reported in Table 8.8. We observe that these differences are significant only for the variables HPI, age and size.

Table 8.7 Assessing the matching quality: Balancing test

Variables 1	*Treated Group*	*Control Group*	*% Bias*	*% Reduction in bias*
Age	3.6189	3.5982	5.1	83.0
TFP	211.28	204.77	1.7	91.2
Total Assets (t − 1)	4.1492	4.2153	−2.7	64.1
Total employees	2.4138	2.4612	−2.3	97.0
Foreign	.05084	.03994	5.9	65.4
Industry dummies	31.943	32.023	−0.4	98.9
N	21,804	24,214	–	

Source: Authors.

Note: Mean reduction in bias from unmatched to matched: 31.8 to 3.0 (<5%). TFP = total factor productivity.

Table 8.8 Two-sample *t*-test

Weighted Variables	*Mean Control*	*Mean Treated*	*Difference*	t-*statistic*
lnHPI	5.903	10.997	5.094	129.03***
age	39.750	41.984	2.234	5.67***
lnTFP	5.446	5.429	−0.016	0.69
lnta	4.848	4.540	−0.309	7.01***
ownc	0.042	0.045	0.003	0.90

Source: Authors.

Note: lnHPI = log of of Hadlock and Pierce Index; lnTFP = log of total factor productivity; lnta = log of total assets; ownc = foreign ownership dummy.

Table 8.9 Propensity score matching–difference-in-difference estimations

Variables	*T + 1/t − 1*	*T + 2/t − 1*	*T + 3/t − 1*	*T + 4/t − 1*
lnHPI	−.358***	−.308***	−.263***	−.195***
	(.028)	(0.0276)	(0.0271)	(0.0273)
WWI	−.545***	−.369***	−.373***	−.301**
	(0.090)	(0.083)	(0.083)	(0.085)
Leverage	−.642***	−.793***	−.816***	−.794***
	(0.080)	(0.078)	(0.075)	(0.075)
Liquidity	.019***	.024***	.018***	.011**
	(.005)	(0.006)	(0.007)	(0.005)

Source: Authors.

Note: Standard errors are reported in parentheses. lnHPI = log of Hadlock and Pierce Index; WWI = Whited and Wu Index.

$^{**}p = .05$; $^{***}p = .01$.

Table 8.9 reports the results for DID estimation between starters and non-exporters (control) for the measures of financial constraints, observed cumulatively from $t - 1$ to that year. By using ln, the values in Table 8.9 are percentage point differences in growth rates between starters and controls for each variable. We observe that the effect of exports on HPI, WWI and leverage are negative and statistically significant from 1 year after export entry up to 4 years later. By comparison, this effect is positive and statistically significant for the measure liquidity. All these findings indicate that financial constraints are relatively less for starters relative to non-exporters in all the years.

Then we estimate Equation (8.4) in order to examine the effect of IBC-2016 on the credit constraints of firms by applying the PSM-DID methodology. The results are reported in Table 8.10. The variable **_diff** represents the β_2 coefficient, that is, the DID effect. It appears that this coefficient is negatively significant for WWI and positively significant for HPI. Therefore, in the post-treatment period, that is, after the implementation of IBC-2016, the financial constraint as measured by WWI decreased whereas it increased for HPI. Therefore, we get opposite results for the two measures of financial

Table 8.10 Difference-in-difference estimates with kernel propensity score matching: Insolvency and Bankruptcy Code intervention

	(1)	*(2)*	*(3)*	*(4)*
	WWI	*Leverage*	*HPI*	*Liquidity*
IBC	1.023***	−0.0317	−0.449***	0.000465
	(9.92)	(−0.20)	(−11.06)	(0.19)
Treatwwi	2.080***			
	(20.70)			
_diff	−0.731***	−0.00220	0.658***	−0.00323
	(−5.13)	(−0.01)	(11.87)	(−0.95)
Treatlev1		7.721***		
		(48.43)		
Treathpi			5.072***	
			(131.76)	
Treatliqi				−0.0460***
				(−19.30)
_cons	−1.094***	0.0654	5.734***	6.845***
	(−15.05)	(0.58)	(209.76)	(4032.15)
N	23,982	23,258	23,329	23,482
R^2	.028	.166	.620	.032
Controls	Yes	Yes	Yes	Yes
Firm-Specific Effects	Yes	Yes	Yes	Yes
Year-Specific Effects	Yes	Yes	Yes	Yes

Source: Authors.

Note: t-statistics are in parentheses. IBC = Insolvency and Bankruptcy Code; Treatwwi = treatment dummy based on Whited and Wu Index (takes the value of 1 if the firm is financially constrained and zero otherwise); _diff =D ID coefficient (β_2 coefficient); Treatlev1 = treatment dummy based on leverage; Treathpi = treatment dummy based on Hadlock and Pierce Index; Treatliqi = treatment dummy based on liquidity; _cons =constant .

*$p < .05$; **$p < .01$; ***$p < .001$.

constraints. It indicates that the findings are sensitive to the measures of financial constraints. Results for all other variables are as expected.

As a next step, we test to see if the financial health of the firms has an impact on the intensive margin of exports, that is, on their ability to export more than before. In Table 8.11, we report the results for Equation (8.5), and we apply the GMM estimation technique here. The findings show that lagged exports have a positive significant effect on the intensive margin. Moreover, HPI has a negative, significant effect and liquidity has a positive significant effect on the intensive margin. These findings indicate that as financial constraints increase, the intensive margin of exports decreases. Therefore, our finding supports the prediction that the financial health of the firms has an important impact on the intensive margin of exports.

Table 8.11 Baseline model (GMM estimator)

	(1)	*(2)*	*(3)*	*(4)*
	lnes	*lnes*	*lnes*	*Lnes*
EXPORTS(–1)	0.664***	0.654***	0.664***	0.664***
	(0.0315)	(0.0274)	(0.0310)	(0.0310)
EXPORTS(–2)	0.113***	0.102***	0.113***	0.112***
	(0.0217)	(0.0213)	(0.0214)	(0.0214)
Lnage	–0.141***	–0.174***	–0.165***	–0.165***
	(0.0357)	(0.0366)	(0.0385)	(0.0385)
TFP	0.00000517	–0.0000428*	–0.0000409	–0.0000390
	(0.0000208)	(0.0000249)	(0.0000262)	(0.0000259)
Lnta	–0.00166	–0.00229	–0.00197	–0.00300
	(0.00276)	(0.00282)	(0.00276)	(0.00287)
Log HPI	–0.0138***			
	(0.00445)			
Foreign	–0.0650	–0.0668	–0.0702	–0.0718
	(0.0474)	(0.0484)	(0.0481)	(0.0482)
WWI		0.00107		
		(0.00130)		
lnliquidity			0.0871***	
			(0.0164)	
Leverage				–0.00145
				(0.00102)
Constant	1.206***	1.287***	0	1.218***
	(0.230)	(0.210)	(.)	(0.228)
Year Dummies	Yes	Yes	Yes	Yes
Observations	14,507	14,507	14,507	14,507
Instruments	26	26	25	26
Firms	1978	1978	1978	1978
AR1 (*p*-value)	2.73e–35	9.55e–38	1.76e–35	1.74e–35
AR2 (*p*-value)	0.549	0.416	0.551	0.554
Hansen J (*p*-value)	0.169	0.194	0.152	0.189

Source: Authors.

Note: Robust standard errors reported; standard errors presented in parentheses. Our specification for the generalized method of moments (GMM) estimation is as follows: Firm age, log of total assets, foreign ownership and year dummies are treated as strictly exogenous; the lagged values of exports and firm productivity are treated as potentially endogenous; and the log of Hadlock and Pierce Index (HPI), Whited and Wu Index (WWI), liquidity and leverage are our measures of the financial constraints, and all are treated as weakly exogenous.

$^{*}p < .10$; $^{**}p < .05$; $^{***}p < .01$.

8.6 Conclusion

This chapter has examined the effect of financing constraints on the extensive and intensive margins of exports for a large sample of manufacturing firms in India during the 2000–2020 period. Using two multivariate indices of financing constraints proposed by WW (2006) and HP (2010), along with conventional measures like liquidity and leverage, we examined whether changes in firms' financial health influence the decision to export, as well as the level of exports. We also examined whether the implementation of the bankruptcy code, IBC-2016, helped reduce the financial constraints of firms in India. We also examined if exports help to promote financial health. We found that an increase in the degree of financing constraints adversely affects the decision to export. Moreover, as the financing constraints increase, the level of exports decreases. These results are consistently observed for alternative measures of financing constraints. Therefore, both extensive and intensive margins of exports are influenced by financial constraints. We also observed that export starters display better financial health than their non-exporting competitors, even before they start to export. Moreover, we also found that exports lead to faster improvements in the financial health of starters, possibly through a signalling effect in financial markets by reducing informational asymmetries (Ganesh-Kumar et al., 2001; Greenaway et al., 2007). Our findings also show that after the implementation of IBC-2016, financial constraint was decreased for the measure WWI whereas it increased for HPI. It indicates that the findings are sensitive to the choice of measures of financing constraints.

This chapter adds to the literature by providing new insights into the role of firm-level determinants of exports in India and bringing into focus the challenges faced by the manufacturing firms. It highlights that inadequate access to external finance is a major challenge for Indian manufacturing firms. Our findings also highlight that after the implementation of IBC-2016, financing constraints on manufacturing firms have been reduced, which has some important policy implications. It suggests that the implementation of IBC-2016 helped ease the credit constraints on exporting firms to reorganize their business. Through the reform of the bankruptcy law, the bargaining position of creditors has been strengthened, which, in turn, helped manufacturing firms get rid of credit constraints, and consequently, it helped improve their exports. This supports the findings from earlier literature that those firms that are more likely to be in distress are more responsive to the design of insolvency and bankruptcy reform (Rodano et al., 2016). Our findings suggest that exporting manufacturing firms in India have benefitted from the bankruptcy reform law, IBC-2016, which helped them have better access to credit and get out of financial constraints. Our findings provide novel evidence of the impact of the bankruptcy reform on the export performance of financially distressed Indian manufacturing firms. Therefore, the implementation of IBC-2016 became effective in enhancing the export promotion policy of the government, particularly for the manufacturing firms in India since 2016. Hence, this is a positive step toward the right direction, which will promote exports further. Existing studies show that there was no speedy resolution mechanism until 2016. The IBC-2016 helped to address the deficiencies in the earlier laws like the DRT Act, 1993 and the SARFAESI Act, 2002 and strengthened the creditor rights which became instrumental in relaxing the financial constraints of exporting firms. We conclude that the results of this study are relevant for policymakers to safeguard and preserve businesses in manufacturing firms in India, especially if they are subject to bankruptcy due to financial distress. Moreover, our study highlights that an effective public policy could play an important role in mitigating the sunk costs involved in exporting in emerging economies like India.

Notes

1 Be it the success of East Asian Tigers, the rise of China or India's growth story, most of it can be attributed to the liberalized trade policies.

2 The DRT Act did not allow creditors to advance their priority claims on a defaulting firm without a court/tribunal, the SARFAESI Act strengthened creditors' rights by allowing them to take possession of the assets of a defaulting firm without a court/tribunal trial (Bose et al., 2020).

3 The main reasons for it are (1) exporting firms benefit from more stable cash flows through international diversification of their sales (Campa and Shaver, 2002); (2) as a result of informational asymmetries and imperfect capital markets, exporting sends a signal about firm efficiency; and (3) exporting increases access to international financial markets. (iv).

4 The investment cash flow sensitivity was based on the assumption that firms' current revenue is uncorrelated with future investment opportunities which Kaplan and Zingales (1997) proved to be wrong.

5 In the finance literature, neither leverage nor liquidity is used as a measure of financial constraints because high liquidity does not necessarily mean good financial health of a firm (see Almeida et al. (2004), Qasim et al. (2020)).

6 Hadlock and Pierce (2010) argue that our measure of financial constraints has many advantages over other indices such as its intuitive appeal, its independence from various theoretical assumptions, and the presence of corroborating evidence from an alternative approach.

7 Rosenbaum and Rubin (1983) defined the propensity score for participant i ($i = 1, \ldots, N$) as the conditional probability of assignment to a particular treatment ($Wi = 1$) versus nontreatment ($Wi = 0$) given a vector of observed covariates, xi (Guo and Fraser 2014).

References

Acharya, V., Almeida, H., and Campello, M. (2007). Is cash negative debt? A hedging perspective on corporate financial policies, *Journal of Financial Intermediation*, 16(4), 515–554.

Acharya, V., John, K., and Sundaram, R. K. (2011). Cross-country variations in capital structure: The role of bankruptcy codes, *Journal of Financial Intermediation*, 20, 25–54.

Acharya, V., and Subramaniam, K. (2009). Bankruptcy codes and innovation, *Review of Financial Studies*, 22, 4949–4988.

Almeida, H., and Campello, M. (2007). Financial constraints, asset tangibility, and corporate investment, *The Review of Financial Studies*, 20(5), September, 1429–1460.

Almeida, H., Campello, M., and Weisbach, M. S. (2004). The cash flow sensitivity of cash, *The Journal of Finance*, 59, 1777–1804.

Banerjee, A., Cole, S. A., and Duflo, E. (2004). Banking Reform in India, Vol. 1, Brookings Institution Press and National Council of Applied Economic Research India, 277–323, Working Paper, Department of Economics, MIT.
Bas, M., and Berthou, A. (2012). The decision to import capital goods in India: Firms' financial factors matter, *World Bank Economic Review*, 26(3), 486–513.
Beck, T., and Levine, R. (2002). Industry growth and capital allocation: Does having a market-or bank-based system matter? *Journal of Financial Economics*, 64, 147–180.
Becker, S. O., and Ichino, A. (2002). Estimation of average treatment effects based on propensity scores, *The Stata Journal*, 2(4), 358–377.
Bellone, F., Musso. P., Nesta, L., and Schiavo, S. (2010). Financing constraints and firm export behaviour, *World Economy*, 30, 347–373.
Bernard, A. B., and Jensen, B. J. (1999). Exceptional exporter performance: Cause, effect or both? *Journal of International Economics*, 47, 1–25.
Bernard, A. B., and Jensen, B. J. (2004). Why some firms export? *Review of Economics and Statistics*, 86, 561–569.
Bernini, M. (2014). Essays on financial factors and firm export behaviour, (Unpublished Doctoral Dissertation), University of Toronto, Canada.
Bharat, Y. (2019). Financial Constraints and Exporting Firms: Evidence from India. Michigan State University *Working Paper*.
Bose, U., Filomeni, S., and Mallick, S. (2020). Does bankruptcy law improve the fate of distressed firms? The role of credit channels, *Journal of Corporate Finance*. https://doi.org/10.1016/j.jcorpfin.2020.101836
Campa, J.-M., and Shaver, J.-M. (2002). Exporting and capital investment: On the strategic behaviour of exporters (Discussion Paper No. 469), IESE Business School, University of Navarra.
Chaney, T. (2005). Liquidity constrained exporters (Mimeograph), *Journal of International Economics*, 1(47), 1–25.
Chaney, T. (2016). Liquidity constrained exporters, *Journal of Economic Dynamics and Control*, 72, 141–154.
Chatterjee, S., Shaikh, G., and Zaveri, B. (2017). Watching India's insolvency reforms: A new dataset of insolvency cases (*RePEc Working Papers* ID 12105).
Cleary, S. (1999). The relationship between firm investment and financial status, *Journal of Finance*, 54, 673–692.
Economic Survey. (2020). Government of India, Ministry of Finance.
Egger, P., and Kesina, M. (2013), Financial constraints and exports: Evidence from Chinese firms, *CESifo Economic Studies*, 59(4), December, 676–706.
Farre-Mensa, J., and Ljungqvist, A. (2016). Do measures of financing constraints measure financing constraints? *Review of Financial Studies*, 29, 271–308.
Fazzari, S. M., Hubbard, R. G., and Petersen, B. C. (1988). Financing constraints and corporate investment, *Brooking Papers on Economic Activity*, l(1), 141–195.
Fernandes, Ana. (2003). Trade policy, trade volumes and plant level productivity in Colombian manufacturing industries, *World Bank Policy Research Working Paper 3064*.
Ganesh-Kumar, A., Sen, K., and Vaidya, R. (2001). Outward orientation, investment and finance constraints: A study of Indian firms, *The Journal of Development Studies*, 37(4), 133–149
Girma, S., and Gorg, H. 2007, Evaluating the foreign ownership wage premium using a difference-in-differences matching approach, *Journal of International Economics*, 72, 97–112.
Greenaway, D., Guariglia, A., and Kneller, R. (2007). Financial factors and exporting decisions, *Journal of International Economics*, 73. 377–395.
Guo, S., and Fraser, M. W. (2014). *Propensity score analysis: Statistical methods and applications*, Second Edition, Sage Publications.

Hadlock, J. C., and Pierce, R. J. (2010). New evidence on measuring financial constraints: Moving beyond the KZ index, *The Review of Financial Studies*, 23, 1909–1940.

Harrison, B. (1994). The dark side of flexible production, *National Productivity Review*, 13(4), 479–501.

Hovakimian, G., and Titman, S. (2006). Corporate investment with financial constraint: Sensitivity of investment to funds from voluntary asset sales, *Journal of Money, Credit and Banking*, 38(2), 357–374.

Jarreau, J., and Poncet, S. (2014). Credit constraints, firm ownership and the structure of exports in China, *International Economics*. http://doi.org/10.1016/j.inteco.2014.04.004

Kaplan, S. N., and Zingales, L. (1997). Do investment-cash flow sensitivities provide useful measures of financing constraints, *Quarterly Journal of Economics*, 112(1), 169–215.

Kapoor, M., Ranjan, P., and Raychaudhuri, J. (2012). The impact of credit constraints on exporting firms: Empirical evidence from India. https://www.poverty-action.org/sites/default/files/publications/paper_92.pdf

Khanna, T., and Palepu, K., (1999). Emerging market, business groups investors and corporate governance, National Bureau of Economic Research working paper No., W6955, Cambridge, MA

Khanna, T., and Palepu, K. (2000). Is group affiliation profitable in emerging markets? An analysis of diversified Indian business groups, *Journal of Finance*, 55(2), 867–891

Kiendrebeogo, Y., and Minea, A. (2012). Financial factors and manufacturing exports: Theory and firm-level evidence from Egypt, Series Etudes Et Documents Du Cerdi. https://halshs.archives-ouvertes.fr/halshs-00710718v2/document

Kiendrebeogo, Y., and Minea, A. (2017). Financial factors and manufacturing exports: Firm-level evidence from Egypt, *Journal of Development Studies*, 53(12), 2197–2213.

La Porta, R., Lopez de Silanes, F., Shleifer, A., and Vishny, R. (1998). Law and Finance, *Journal of Political Economy*, 106, 1113–1155.

Leuven, E., and Sianesi, B. (2003). Psmatch2: Stata module to perform full Mahalanobis and propensity score matching, common support graphing, and covariate imbalance testing, *Statistical Software Components*.

Li, Z., and Yu, M. (2009). Export, Productivity, and Credit Constraints: A Firm-level Empirical Investigation of China (Discussion Paper Series No. 098), December, Hitotsubashi University Research Unit for Statistical and Empirical Analysis in Social Schiences (Hi-Stat).

Manole, V., and Spatareanu, M. (2010). Trade openness and income-A re-examination, *Economics Letter*, 106(1), 1–3.

Manova, K. (2010). Credit constraints and the adjustment to trade reform. In G. Porto & B. Hoekman (Eds.), *Trade adjustment costs in developing countries: Impacts, determinants and policy responses*, The World Bank and CEPR.

Manova, K. (2013). Credit constraints, heterogeneous firms, and international trade, *Review of Economic Studies*, 80, 711–744.

McVanel, D., and Perevalov, N. (2008). Financial constraints and the cash-holding behaviour of Canadian firms (Bank of Canada Discussion Paper 2008–16.), October.

Melitz, M. (2003). The impact of trade on intra-industry reallocations and aggregate industry productivity, *Econometrica*, 71, 1695–1725.

Mukherjee, S., and Chanda, R. (2020). Financing constraints and exports: Evidence from manufacturing firms in India, *Empirical Economics*. https://doi.org/10.1007/s00181-020-01865-9

Musso, P., and Schiavo, S. (2008). The impact of financial constraints on firm survival and growth, *Journal of Evolutionary Economics*, 18, 135–149.
Muûls, M. (2008). Exporters and Credit Constraints. A Firm Level Approach, National Bank of Belgium (Working Paper Research 139)
Muûls, M. (2015). Exporters, importers and credit constraints, *Journal of International Economics*, 95(2), 333–343.
Nagaraj, P. (2014). Financing constraints and export participation in India, *International Economics*, 140, 19–35, https://doi.org/10.1016/j.inteco.2014.07.001
Olley, S., Pakes, A. (1996). The dynamics of productivity in the telecommunications equipment industry, *Econometrica*, 64, 1263–1297.
Padmaja, M., and Sasidharan, S. (2020). Financing constraints and exports: Evidence from India, *Journal of Economics and Finance*. https://doi.org/10.1007/s12197-020-09532-6
Paravisini, D., Rappoport, V., Schnabl, P., and Wolfenzon, D. (2012). Dissecting the Effect of Credit Supply on Trade: Evidence from Matched Credit-Export Data, NBER (Working Paper 16975).
Pavcnik, N. (2002). Trade liberalization, exit, and productivity improvements: Evidence from Chilean plants, *The Review of Economic Studies*, 69(1), January, 245–276.
Qasim, S., Rizov, M., and Zhang, X. (2020). Financial constraints and the export decision of Pakistani firms, *International Journal of Finance and Economics*, 1–17. https://doi.org/10.1002/ijfe.2030
Rodano, G., Serrano-Velarde, N., and Tarantino, E. (2016). Bankruptcy law and bank financing, *Journal of Financial Economics*, 120, 363–382.
Rosenbaum, P., and Rubin, D. (1983). The central role of the propensity score in observational studies for causal effects, *Biometrika*, 70, 41–55
Schaller, H. (1993). Asymmetric information, liquidity constraints and Canadian investment. *Canadian Journal of Economics*, 26, 552–574.
Serti, F., and Tomasi, C. (2008). Self-selection and post-entry effects of exports: Evidence from Italian manufacturing firms, *Review of World Economics*, 144, 660–694.
Silva, A. (2011). Financial constraints and exports: Evidence from Portuguese manufacturing firms, FEP Working Papers No. 402. http://wps.fep.up.pt/wps/wp402.pdf
Silva, F., and Carreira, C. (2012). Do financial constraints threat the innovation process? Evidence from Portuguese firms, *Economics of Innovation and New Technology*, 21(8), 701–736.
Thapa, C., Rao, S., Farag, H., and Koirala, S. (2020). Access to internal capital, creditor rights and corporate borrowing: Does group affiliation matter? *Journal of Corporate Finance*, 62. https://doi.org/10.1016j.jcorpfin
Topalova, P., and Kandelwal, A. (2011). Trade liberalization and firm productivity: The case of India, *Review of Economics and Statistics*, 93, 995–1009.
Tornell, A., and Westermann, F. (2003). Credit market imperfections in middle income countries, NBER Working Paper 9737. http://www.nber.org/papers/w9737
Tybout, J., deMelo, J., and Corbo, V. (1991). The effects of trade on scale and technical efficiency: New evidence from Chile reforms, *Journal of International Economics*, 31, 231–250.
Tybout, J. R., and Westbrook, M. D. (1995). Trade liberalization and the dimensions of efficiency change in Mexican manufacturing industries, *Journal of International Economics*, 39(1–2), 53–78.
Vig, V. (2013). Access to collateral and corporate debt structure: Evidence from a natural experiment, *Journal of Finance*, 68(3), 881–928.
Wagner, J. (2007). Exports and productivity: A survey of the evidence from the firm level data, *World Economy*, 30, 60–82.

Wagner, J. (2014). Credit constraints and exports: Evidence for German manufacturing enterprises, *Applied Economics*, 46, 294–302.
Wagner, J. (2019). Access to finance and exports—Comparable evidence for small and medium enterprises from industry and services in 25 European countries, *Open Economies Review*, 30(4), 739–757.
Whited, T. M., and Wu, G. (2006). Financial constraints risk, *The Review of Financial Studies.*, 19, 531–559.

Part II

Business and Macro Policies

9 Fiscal Policy in India

Trends, Challenges, and Future Directions

Amarendu Nandy and Abhisek Sur

9.1 Introduction

Fiscal policy holds immense significance when it comes to shaping a country's economic path. It serves as a potent instrument for governments to navigate through economic landscapes, foster growth, ensure stability, and tackle a range of socioeconomic issues. A vibrant and rapidly expanding economy like India depends heavily on fiscal policy to steer and accelerate its economic progress.

Over the years, India's fiscal policy framework has undergone a noteworthy transformation. This transformation is intricately linked with the ever-changing sociopolitical dynamics, economic ambitions, and global influences. In this chapter, we aim to provide a comprehensive overview and analysis of the trends and dynamics shaping fiscal policy in India. We delve into its evolution, the strategies employed for its management, the impact of political and economic factors, some recent developments and discuss the challenges and unfinished agenda in fiscal policy implementation in India.

In the years following India's independence, there was a strong emphasis on centralized planning, with the government taking a leading role in making economic decisions. Since 1947, fiscal policy has been instrumental in driving the nation's economic progress, tasked with attaining a range of objectives, including economic growth, poverty eradication, equity, and social justice. The vision was to achieve these goals through state-directed investment, expenditure programs, and a tax policy designed to redistribute income and wealth.

The Planning Commission[1] initially shouldered the responsibility of spearheading these development objectives. It charted development programs, devised revenue generation strategies, and crafted expenditure plans in alignment with the nation's evolving needs and the priorities set by the central government, thus playing a pivotal role in shaping India's fiscal policy landscape.

In the first three decades post-independence, fiscal policy was geared toward the monumental task of nation-building. The era was characterized by significant government intervention, active public sector participation, and a focus on import substitution. The government took a commanding role in

DOI: 10.4324/9781003509721-12

driving economic growth, exemplified by the establishment of public-sector units (PSUs) that formed the cornerstone of the country's industrial infrastructure. During this period, both the union and state governments experienced revenue surpluses, suggesting a reasonably sound fiscal foundation.

However, a turning point emerged in the 1980s when revenue deficits began to surface in the central government's budget, raising concerns about the sustainability of public finances.[2] While the earlier approach of centralized planning and import substitution aimed to foster self-reliance and industrialization, India encountered challenges such as resource constraints, inefficient allocation of resources, and a lack of market-driven incentives. These challenges underscored the need for prompt intervention to address the escalating fiscal predicament.

The Reserve Bank of India (RBI), as the vanguard of monetary policy, assumed a critical role in stabilizing the teetering economy at the time. However, the measures implemented to tackle the burgeoning fiscal imbalances inadvertently stoked inflationary pressures and aggravated the external payments position, culminating in a balance-of-payments (BoP) crisis in the early 1990s.

In response, India initiated an extensive economic reform initiative, adopting liberalization measures under the guidance of the International Monetary Fund (IMF) and the World Bank. Acknowledging the necessity of transitioning from a centrally planned economic system to a market-oriented one, the country embraced globalization and liberalized its markets to foreign trade and investment. This shift in approach brought about significant changes to India's fiscal policy framework. The government acknowledged the importance of fiscal discipline, aiming to reduce fiscal deficits and implement reforms to boost the efficiency and competitiveness of the economy.

In the initial years of the reform era, especially from 1991–92 to 1996–97, there was notable progress in fiscal performance. Deficit indicators saw substantial reductions, showcasing the positive impact of fiscal discipline and prudence on economic stability and growth. However, this favorable trend was reversed in the following years until 2002–03, and fiscal performance deteriorated. Understanding the urgency of sustained fiscal discipline, the Government of India (GoI) introduced the landmark Fiscal Responsibility and Budget Management (FRBM) Act in August 2003 to institutionalize fiscal prudence and accountability.

The early 2000s marked a period of resurgent economic growth for India, with an impressive average gross domestic product (GDP) growth rate of 7.9 percent from 2003 to 2007. Unfortunately, the global financial crisis (GFC) between 2007–09 had a severe impact on the Indian economy, leading to a significant slowdown in GDP growth. In response, the central government implemented countercyclical measures, such as tax cuts and increased spending, to stimulate economic activity. These measures temporarily suspended the FRBM targets, causing the deficit level to rise to 6.6 percent of GDP during this period.

Despite efforts to reign in the fiscal deficit in the years following the GFC, the pace of improvement has slowed ever since, attributable to various factors. Persistent challenges in meeting disinvestment targets, succumbing to fiscal populism, and augmenting allocations for the beleaguered banking sector, particularly to enhance liquidity in public-sector banks (PSBs), all contributed to a deviation from fiscal prudence and impeded progress in fiscal consolidation.

Notably, India's fiscal policy also operates within the fiscal federalism framework, involving the distribution of fiscal powers and responsibilities between the central and state governments.[3] Intergovernmental transfers, such as grants and revenue-sharing mechanisms, play a crucial role in promoting cooperative federalism and addressing regional disparities. However, striking a balance between the need for fiscal autonomy for states and ensuring fiscal discipline at the national level remains an ongoing challenge.

In the past few years, various developments have influenced the fiscal policy scenario in India. The implementation of demonetization in 2016 aimed at tackling corruption and promoting a digital economy, resulting in significant changes. Subsequently, the Goods and Services Tax (GST) introduced in 2017, aimed to simplify the complex system of indirect taxation, fundamentally reshaping the landscape of revenue collection. Embracing technology-driven solutions like e-governance platforms and digital transactions aimed to enhance tax administration, cut compliance costs, and combat tax evasion. Efforts were also made to streamline subsidies, ensuring targeted delivery and minimizing their impact on fiscal resources.

More recently, the global pandemic in the early 2020s posed unprecedented challenges for governments worldwide, including India, leading to increased government expenditure, especially in health care and economic stimulus measures. The COVID-19 pandemic exacerbated existing fiscal concerns in India, including elevated deficit and debt levels compared to other emerging economies. It emphasized the necessity for changes in budget administration and establishing a rule-based fiscal policy to ensure long-term sustainable growth.

As the country focuses on economic recovery and socioeconomic well-being, understanding India's fiscal policy trends and dynamics becomes crucial. This chapter delves into the trends and dynamics shaping fiscal policy in India, providing a comprehensive understanding of its evolution over time. Additionally, the chapter examines how political-economic factors have affected India's public finances and explores the challenges and unfinished agenda in India's fiscal policy landscape.

9.2 Evolution of Fiscal Policy in India: Trends and Dynamics

9.2.1 The First Three Decades Since Independence

As India shook off colonial rule in 1947 and embarked on the journey of nation-building and development, fiscal policy took center stage in shaping the economy. Several key goals steered India's fiscal policy right after gaining independence. *First*, there was a strong push for swift economic growth and industrialization (Mishra & Maheshwari, 2020). The government understood the importance of building an independent economy, reducing import reliance, and supporting domestic industries. Fiscal policy played a crucial role in gathering resources, using them effectively, and offering vital support to key sectors.

Second, there was a commitment to tackling socioeconomic inequalities and championing social justice. India inherited deep-seated gaps in income, wealth, and access to basic amenities. Fiscal policy aimed to narrow these gaps through progressive taxation, increased spending on the social sector, and targeted welfare programs (Rao & Kumar, 2018). The government aimed to uplift the living standards of marginalized sections, alleviate poverty, and provide fundamental education and health care services.

Third, the focus was on promoting agricultural development and transforming rural areas. Agriculture served as the backbone of the Indian economy, and policies were crafted to boost agricultural productivity, offer irrigation facilities, develop rural infrastructure, and ensure fair prices for farmers' produce (Krishna, 2022). The government acknowledged the pivotal role of rural development in achieving overall economic growth and social stability.

To attain these goals, a strategy of planned development was embraced. In 1950, the establishment of the Planning Commission coincided with the adoption of a federal Constitution that granted considerable authority to the Central government for economic planning. Following that, the planning process focused on boosting public-sector firms in order to achieve economic expansion and encourage industrial growth. This approach involved imposing administrative controls, licensing systems, and quotas on private industries. Fiscal policy was pivotal in redirecting private savings toward fulfilling the public sector's investment and consumption requirements. It also aimed to reduce income and wealth disparities through taxation and transfers. Additionally, fiscal policy was instrumental in fostering equitable regional development, supporting small-scale industries, and guiding economic activities toward desired outcomes (Rao, 2005).

Taxation played a pivotal role in fiscal policy during this era, primarily focusing on generating revenue from the private sector to finance the public sector and achieve redistributive objectives. From 1950–51 to 1987–88, there was a notable upswing in the combined ratio of central and state tax revenue to GDP. Initially, the central government relied more on indirect taxes, while direct taxes played a minor role. Conversely, the states had limited direct tax levers and primarily collected indirect taxes (Rao, 2005).

In 1953, the Indian government undertook a thorough review of the tax system and enlisted the assistance of economist Nicholas Kaldor to assess potential reforms. Kaldor identified the restricted tax base, insufficient property income, and tax disclosure as major contributors to inefficiencies and inequalities in the existing system. His suggestions encompassed lowering the top marginal income tax rate from 92 percent to 45 percent, instituting capital gains taxation, imposing a gift tax, a wealth tax, and an expenditure tax (Herd and Leibfritz, 2008).

Notwithstanding Kaldor's suggestions, the highest marginal rate of both income and corporate taxes remained exceptionally high. In the 1970s, the maximum personal income tax rate reached a staggering 97.5 percent for income above a certain threshold, while corporate tax rates varied depending on the ownership structure of companies. Recognizing the complexity of the system, the central government established the Direct Taxes Enquiry Committee in 1971, which pointed out the need for simplification to discourage tax evasion. Subsequently, some simplifications were implemented, such as reducing the number of tax brackets and lowering the highest income tax rate in 1985–86.

A major feature of indirect taxes was the central excise duty, initially imposed on intermediate and raw materials but progressively extended to encompass all manufactured goods. The excise duty structure was complex and had a cascading effect, resulting in double taxation of inputs. The situation was exacerbated by individual sales taxes imposed by the states at different stages of the supply chain. Attempts were undertaken to streamline the system, resulting in the introduction of the modified value-added tax (MODVAT) and customs duty in 1986 as part of broader reform endeavors. However, revenue considerations led to increased tariffs despite some attempts to reduce tariffs and remove quantitative limits on imports in the mid-1980s. The granting of exemptions independently of the budgetary process further added to the complexity of the tax structure (Rao & Kumar, 2018).

Significant changes occurred in the composition of government revenues from 1970–71 to 1990–91. While the share of direct taxes decreased, non-tax revenues remained relatively stable, and the share of indirect taxes increased (Figure 9.1). The era witnessed increased government expenditures, with limited reforms in specific areas such as partial liberalization of the trade and exchange rate systems, relaxation of domestic industrial controls, and the promotion of investments in modern technologies like telecommunications. Notably, fiscal conservatism was replaced by an expansionary approach, relying on increased domestic and international borrowing, despite its rising costs. As a result, although average economic growth accelerated to 5.8 percent throughout the 1980s, macroeconomic imbalances surfaced, including fiscal and current account deficits. These imbalances were further exacerbated in the early 1990s due to external and domestic political factors, ultimately culminating in the BoP crisis in 1991 (Singh and Srinivasan, 2004). These events and the urgent need for economic stabilization paved the way for subsequent economic reforms that brought lasting changes to the Indian economy.

The initial three decades in the post-independence period were not without its challenges in implementing fiscal policy. One of the primary

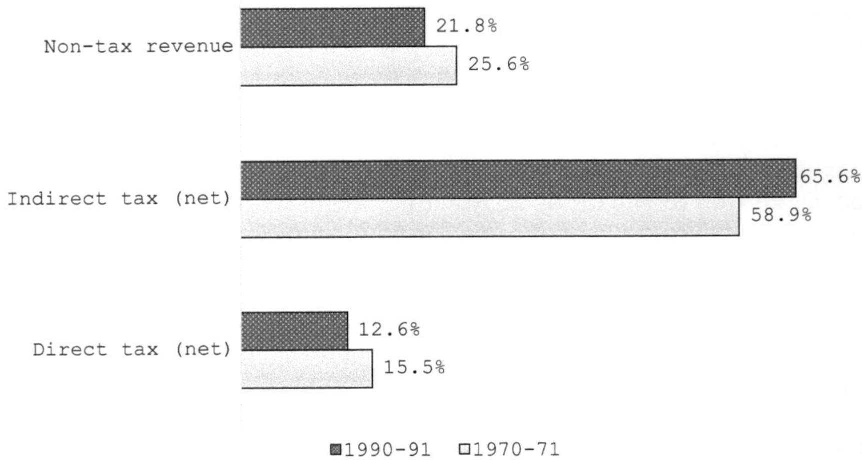

Figure 9.1 Composition of central government revenues from 1970–71 to 1990–91.
Source: Authors' calculations from RBI (2023), DBIE-RBI: Database of Indian Economy (https://dbie.rbi.org.in).

challenges was the scarcity of resources. India was a developing nation facing challenges due to limited capital and budgetary capacity. The task at hand was to mobilize resources for development while addressing urgent social needs, a delicate balancing act (Rangarajan & Subbarao, 2007). The government had to navigate between development spending and social welfare expenditures carefully.

Another hurdle was the inefficiency and leaks in public expenditure. An effective implementation of fiscal policy demanded a robust administrative machinery capable of efficient resource allocation, monitoring, and evaluation. Unfortunately, administrative capacity at the time had limitations, leading to leaks, corruption, and inefficiencies in public spending (Rao & Kumar, 2018). Overcoming these challenges required ongoing institutional reforms and capacity building.

Despite the obstacles, the fiscal policy in this period produced notable outcomes. The emphasis on industrialization and import substitution led to the establishment of crucial industries like steel, heavy machinery, and chemicals. Public investment in infrastructure, including transportation networks and power generation, laid a solid foundation for economic growth (Jha, 2011).

Furthermore, fiscal policy interventions for rural development and agriculture showed positive results. In the mid-1960s, the Green Revolution enhanced agricultural productivity through high-yielding crop varieties, improved irrigation facilities, and better farming practices (Jha, 2011). This significantly increased food production, improving food security and reducing rural poverty.

In terms of social development, fiscal policy initiatives expanded access to education and healthcare. The government invested in constructing schools and colleges, offering scholarships and subsidies, and expanding healthcare facilities.[4] These efforts significantly increased educational opportunities and improved health care outcomes for the population (Dev, 2021).

9.2.2 *The Economic Reforms and Fiscal Policy*

India's economic reforms, which kicked off in 1991, marked a significant turning point for fiscal policy and overall economic path. Unlike other emerging market economies (EMEs), India took longer to jump on the reform bandwagon. By then, the Asian EMEs had already seen substantial economic growth and a significant poverty reduction, thanks to reforms that prioritized increased export orientation and more involvement from the private sector.

In 1991, India embraced the LPG (Liberalization, Privatization, Globalization) policy, ushering in substantial structural changes. The goal was to open the economy to foreign investment and trade, dismantle the existing quota and licensing system, rethink the role and size of the government and PSUs compared to the private sector, and revamp public finances.

A crucial aspect of the fiscal policy reforms was to enhance revenue generation while ensuring equitable distribution of the tax burden. The earlier emphasis on indirect taxes, disproportionately affecting the ordinary citizens, gradually shifted towards direct taxes, targeting the higher income groups. The intention was to create a more progressive tax structure to reduce income and wealth disparities. Consequently, the reforms encompassed comprehensive alterations in both direct and indirect taxes, aiming to reduce the share of trade taxes in total tax revenue. The objective was to stimulate the expansion of domestic consumption taxes by transitioning from excise duties to a value-added tax (VAT) and augmenting the proportion of direct taxes. This holistic strategy aimed to rationalize the tax system, enhance efficiency, and foster economic advancement (Rao, 2005).

The shift in fiscal policy approach did yield some positive outcomes. In the immediate post-reform period, India experienced a notable enhancement in its economic performance. Between 1992–93 and 2001–02, India emerged as one of the fastest-growing EMEs, registering a 6.0 percent growth rate (on average). Notably, the Indian economy displayed remarkable stability in the external sector, even during the Asian financial crisis of the late 1990s. Furthermore, there was a significant improvement in public finances, with the combined fiscal deficit decreasing to 7 percent in 1992–93 from 9.4 percent of GDP in 1990–91 (Ahluwalia, 2002).

In line with the neoliberal reforms, India also adopted a policy of disinvestment of PSUs, with the dual objective of generating additional revenue for the budget and enhancing the commercial orientation and efficiency of the PSUs through private shareholder participation. However, this policy achieved limited success, primarily due to the political fragmentation observed in the latter half of the 1990s and the lack of consensus regarding the disinvestment strategy.

One of the main objectives of the reforms was to enhance public savings, ensuring that essential public investments could be financed without causing an unsustainable fiscal deficit that might hinder private investment. However, this aspect of the reform agenda was not given sufficient attention. Public savings experienced a consistent decline from 1.7 percent to −1.7 percent of GDP between 1996–97 and 2000–01, accompanied by a corresponding reduction in the fiscal deficit, which reached 9.6 percent of GDP in 2000–01. As a result, India's public debt-to-GDP ratio increased to about 80 percent. The fiscal shortcomings of both the union and state governments diminished the fiscal capacity for crucial public investments and led to substantial public borrowings that crowded out private investment (Ahluwalia, 2002).

The issue of fiscal consolidation and debt sustainability became a focal point as the post-reform period saw alarming levels of fiscal deficit and public debt. The government recognized the need to restore fiscal discipline and ensure long-term fiscal sustainability. Measures such as introducing fiscal responsibility legislation and establishing fiscal targets aimed to bring about greater discipline in public finances.

9.2.3 Fiscal Responsibility Legislation and Attempts of Fiscal Consolidation

Recognizing the imperative for fiscal discipline, the central government presented the FRBM Act to Parliament in December 2000. The primary objectives of this act were to achieve fiscal restructuring by enhancing expenditure management, reducing revenue deficits, and improving public debt management. After being passed in 2003, the act officially took effect on July 5, 2004.

The FRBMA set ambitious goals, aiming to eliminate revenue deficit by 2008–09 and reduce the fiscal deficit to less than 3 percent of GDP by the same year. The restructuring initiative demonstrated substantial progress until 2007–08. However, the advancements in fiscal consolidation faced setbacks in 2008–09 due to the GFC. In reaction to the crisis, the government enacted fiscal stimulus measures, resulting in the temporary deferment of the fiscal targets.[5]

The GFC precipitated a steep drop in both domestic and international demand, capital inflows, and economic growth within India. Compounding the effects of the crisis, deficient monsoons in 2008–09 and 2009–10 exacerbated the downturn in GDP growth. In response to these challenges, the government enacted three stimulus packages in December 2008, January 2009, and March 2009. These packages encompassed measures such as tax reliefs, heightened expenditure, and targeted subsidies, aiming to revitalize economic growth and alleviate the repercussions of the global economic downturn.

The government also implemented measures such as farm loan waivers, expanded national rural employment guarantee schemes, and pay increases for government employees. However, the government's unwillingness to hike distillate prices during an election year, combined with the 2008 oil price explosion, led to a significant increase in the petroleum subsidies bill (about 2.5 percent of GDP). These elements presented the fiscal restructuring project with substantial obstacles. These factors posed formidable challenges to the fiscal restructuring endeavor.

As a result, the country experienced a notable escalation in the gross fiscal deficit (GFD), reaching 6 percent of GDP in 2008–09 and further surging to 6.4 percent in 2009–10, surpassing the budget estimate of 2.5 percent for 2008–09. Similarly, the revenue deficit (RD) rose from 1.1 percent to 4.5 percent of GDP in 2008–09, reaching 5.2 percent in 2009–10. These instances clearly indicated a substantial deviation from the FRBM targets (Rao, 2022a).

The fiscal targets were set aside for 2 years, spanning from 2009 to 2011, during which both the fiscal and revenue deficits continued to escalate. In 2010–11, the fiscal deficit reached 4.9 percent of GDP, with the revenue deficit at 3.3 percent. Despite a slight improvement in 2011–12, the actual GFD and RD remained higher than the budget estimates.

The GoI introduced amendments to the FRBM Act in the 2012–13 budget. These changes brought in the idea of an effective revenue deficit and implemented the Medium-Term Expenditure Framework Statement in the FRBMA. These tweaks aimed to bring in more certainty, encourage prioritization of expenditures, and boost the fiscal situation overall.

Subsequent to this, the Fourteenth Finance Commission evaluated the financial conditions of both the union and state governments. The commission made necessary amendments to the FRBM Act and proposed measures to establish a stable and enduring fiscal environment conducive to equitable growth. Its goals included eradicating the revenue deficit by 2019–20 and decreasing the fiscal deficit to 3 percent of GDP by 2016–17. To enhance tax collections, the commission also recommended tax reforms, including the implementation of the GST.

In 2016, a new review committee for the FRBMA was formed to evaluate how its provisions were working. The committee suggested making the fiscal deficit the primary anchor for achieving fiscal consolidation and setting a debt target of 60 percent of GDP to be achieved by 2023–24. It also suggested, taking into account the comparatively low level of household savings, that the union government must strive to lower its debt-to-GDP ratio to 40 percent, and the state governments aim for 20 percent.

Following these suggestions and after extensive discussions involving the central government and all states, India introduced the GST on July 1, 2017. The aim was to create a unified national market, crack down on tax evasion, and make doing business easier. This new tax framework, which included the central (CGST), state (SGST), and inter-state GST (IGST), replaced various domestic trade taxes and operated as a destination-based tax system with a robust input tax credit mechanism. The GST was anticipated to be revenue-neutral in the short term, with the expectation that enhanced compliance, facilitated by the self-policing nature of the tax, would lead to substantial revenue generation over time.

The Fifteenth Finance Commission adopted a comparable approach, although it had to navigate through significant uncertainties and challenges brought about by the outbreak of the COVID-19 pandemic (Fifteenth Finance Commission, 2021). The commission recommended a more lenient indicative fiscal restructuring path, aiming to reduce the consolidated debt to 86 percent of GDP by 2025–26 (Table 9.1). However, achieving debt sustainability without significant adjustments remains uncertain.

The current external environment, marked by the Russian invasion of Ukraine, consequential economic sanctions, supply interruptions, and escalating commodity prices, poses considerable challenges for India. The policy measures, including interest rate increases in developed nations, have prompted capital outflows from emerging economies, including India, affecting exports, exchange rate stability, and the current account deficit. In light of these challenges, there is an urgent requirement that the central and state governments collaboratively devise a fiscal restructuring strategy, as well as a timeline to establish sustainable public finances.

The implementation of rule-based fiscal policy in India has faced challenges. Governments have not shown a sense of urgency in meeting their

Table 9.1 Indicative Deficit and Debt Path for the General Government (% of GDP), 2020–21 to 2025–26

	2020–21	*2021–22*	*2022–23*	*2023–24*	*2024–25*	*2025–26*
Revenue deficit–union	5.9	4.9	4.5	3.9	3.3	2.8
Revenue deficit–states	−0.1	−0.4	−0.8	−1.1	−1.6	−2.4
Revenue deficit–combined	**5.8**	**4.5**	**3.7**	**2.8**	**1.7**	**0.4**
Fiscal deficit–union	7.4	6.0	5.5	5.0	4.5	4.0
Fiscal deficit–states	4.2	3.3	3.3	2.8	2.8	2.8
Fiscal deficit–combined	**11.6**	**9.3**	**8.8**	**7.8**	**7.3**	**6.8**
Total liabilities–union	62.9	61.0	61.0	60.1	58.6	56.6
Total liabilities–states	31.1	30.7	31.3	31.1	30.9	30.5
Netting[a]	4.2	3.4	2.7	2.1	1.7	1.4
Total liabilities–combined	**89.8**	**88.3**	**89.6**	**89.1**	**87.8**	**85.7**

Source: Fifteenth Finance Commission (2021), "Finance Commission in COVID Times", p. 375, (https://nhsrcindia.org).

Note: GDP = gross domestic product. The data in bold represent the sum of the figures for the union and the states for the respective heads.

[a] The union loans to states and the stock of the National Small Saving Fund (NSSF) and treasury bills held by state governments are excluded.

targets, and the quality of adjustment has been unsatisfactory. Unanticipated spending cuts, irrational tax demands, off-budget borrowing, and delayed expenditures have adversely impacted revenue and expenditure efficiency. To put it succinctly, the past 30 years of experience with fiscal legislation has not ensured financial viability.

With deficits and debt levels running relatively high, there is a timely opportunity to craft new rules, drawing insights from our experiences with rule-based policies. It is imperative to not only formulate these regulations but also guarantee their efficient execution within an all-encompassing structure of prudent budgetary management and a pragmatic, medium-range fiscal strategy.

9.3 Revenue and Expenditure Management

9.3.1 Taxation

India has been grappling with a persistent challenge – its relatively low tax-to-GDP ratio, posing hurdles for effective revenue management and fiscal sustainability. Despite taxation being a fundamental source of revenue, India's tax-to-GDP ratio falls short compared to the global average and many other nations. This has significant implications, impacting the government's ability to gather sufficient resources for public expenditure and foster sustainable economic development.

Although there has been some improvement in India's tax-to-GDP ratio in recent years, it still trails behind international standards. According to the IMF, the global average tax-to-GDP ratio in 2020 was 14.3 percent, while India's ratio hovered around 17.5 percent during the same period. To put this in perspective, economies with per capita incomes between US$1000 and US$17,000 had an average tax-to-GDP ratio of about 22 percent in 2000, underscoring the gap India needs to narrow (Rao & Kumar, 2018).

Historically, India's tax-to-GDP ratio has experienced fluctuations. It witnessed an upward trajectory, rising from below 10 percent in the 1970s to 14 percent in the 1990s and further to 16.5 percent after 2008–09. However, it is worth noting that the ratio peaked at 17.5 percent in 2007–08, before falling to 15.5 percent in 2009–2010, due to reduced central tax collections influenced by the GFC (Table 9.2). Since then, the ratio has shown gradual recovery but has not reached the levels observed before the crisis.

One of the key factors contributing to India's low tax-to-GDP ratio is the high prevalence of informality in the economy. A significant portion of economic activity remains unreported and is outside the tax net, resulting in a narrow tax base.[6] Addressing this issue requires comprehensive measures to promote formalization and increase tax compliance. The government has taken several steps in this direction, including implementing the GST, which aims to streamline and unify indirect taxes, reducing complexity and improving tax administration.

Table 9.2 Trends in Tax–Gross Domestic Product Ratio at the State and Union Levels (%), 1951–2020

Year	*Centre*			*State*			*Total*	
	Direct	*Indirect*	*Total*	*Direct*	*Indirect*	*Total*	*Direct*	*Indirect*
1951–60	1.57	2.77	4.34	0.65	1.69	2.34	2.22	4.46
1961–70	1.93	4.49	6.42	0.44	2.48	2.92	2.37	6.97
1971–80	2.21	6.21	8.42	0.26	3.71	3.97	2.47	9.92
1981–90	1.96	7.77	9.73	0.2	4.79	4.99	2.16	12.56
1991–00	2.64	6.21	8.85	0.16	4.97	5.13	2.8	11.18
2007–08	6.26	5.63	11.89	0.13	5.43	5.56	6.39	11.06
2010–11	5.63	4.55	10.18	0.16	5.99	6.15	5.79	10.54
2016–17	5.54	5.65	11.19	5.23	0.68	5.91	10.77	6.33
2017–18	5.85	5.35	11.2	4.35	1.06	5.41	10.2	6.41
2018–19	6.31	5.38	11.69	4.57	1.43	6.00	10.88	6.81
2018–20	6.34	5.34	11.68	4.45	1.67	6.12	10.79	7.01

Source: Rao (2022a).

Another contributing factor to India's low tax-to-GDP ratio is the significant reliance on indirect taxes, particularly sales taxes. Indirect taxes account for a substantial portion of the tax revenue, but they can be regressive, disproportionately affecting lower-income groups. This highlights the need for a balanced approach that emphasizes progressive direct taxes, which can help reduce income inequality.

Furthermore, the composition of tax revenues in India also warrants attention. The proportion of direct taxes in the total central tax revenue has steadily increased over the years (Figure 9.2). This shift is encouraging as direct taxes, such as income and corporate taxes, are generally considered more stable and reliable sources of revenue. However, the share of indirect taxes, particularly customs duties, has declined significantly. This is partly due to trade liberalization policies, which have led to lower tariff rates and reduced reliance on international trade taxes.

The tax-to-GDP ratio has also witnessed fluctuations at the state level, albeit with a gradual upward trend (Table 9.2). Sales taxes, especially on petroleum products, constitute a significant portion of states' own tax revenue. However, the heavy reliance on petroleum taxes presents challenges due to price volatility and the potential cascading effect, as these taxes are not included in the GST framework.

Comparing India's tax-to-GDP ratio with global standards reveals the need for further improvement. To achieve sustainable development goals and enhance fiscal resilience, India should aim for a 19–20 percent tax-to-GDP ratio, as Rao and Kumar (2018) estimated.

Tackling India's challenge of a low tax-to-GDP ratio calls for a well-rounded strategy. *First*, there's a need to broaden the tax base by

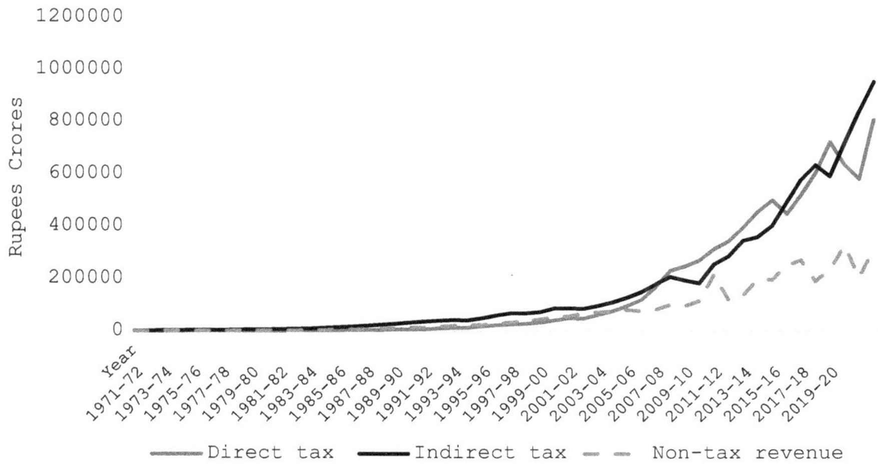

Figure 9.2 Trends in major components of central receipts, 1971–72 to 2019–20.

Source: Authors' calculations from RBI (2023), DBIE-RBI: Database of Indian Economy, (https://dbie.rbi.org.in).

including more economic activities in the tax net. This involves encouraging digital transactions, improving data integration and sharing among government departments, and boosting tax compliance through stricter enforcement.

Second, simplifying the tax structure is crucial to reduce complexity and enhance compliance. This means addressing issues like multiple tax rates, exemptions, and confusing thresholds that can create loopholes.

Third, improving tax administration and building capacity at both central and state levels is critical. This requires investments in technology, training for tax officials, and better coordination among different tax authorities to ensure efficient tax collection and enforcement.

Finally, fostering economic growth and formalizing the informal sector is vital for expanding the tax base and increasing revenues. Policies that encourage investment, entrepreneurship, and job creation and simplify the business environment can stimulate economic growth and motivate businesses to operate within the formal economy.

India's low tax-to-GDP ratio poses challenges to revenue management and fiscal sustainability. To bridge the gap between India's ratio and global standards, a comprehensive approach is necessary, focusing on broadening the tax base, improving compliance, simplifying the tax structure, and encouraging economic formalization. Implementing these measures can boost revenue generation, ensure sufficient funding for public expenditure, and support inclusive and balanced economic growth.

9.3.2 Public Expenditure

The trend of public expenditure over the past decade has been relatively stable (Table 9.3). In 2000–01, the (consolidated) public expenditure–GDP ratio stood at 25.6 percent. The expenditure increased to 28.3 percent in 2009–10, that is, following the GFC, primarily due to the fiscal stimulus provided. With the withdrawal of the stimulus, the ratio decreased to 26.4 percent in the next year. From that point until 2015–16, the expenditure remained relatively stable, accounting for about 26–27 percent of GDP (Table 9.3). From 2016–17 onward, a marginal upward shift in public expenditure is observed. It is worth noting that even during the pre-reform period, particularly since the mid-1990s, the public expenditure–GDP ratio consistently hovered about 25–26 percent.

A closer examination of public expenditure trends since 1990–91 reveals some critical insights.

First, despite the significant increase in per capita income from Rs. 29,971 (at 2011 prices) in 1990–91(Rao, 2022a) to Rs. 108,387 in 2019–20, the public expenditure–GDP ratio has consistently hovered around the 26–28 percent level instead of exhibiting a rising trajectory. This indicates that despite the growth in individual income levels, the proportion of public expenditure in relation to GDP has not experienced a corresponding increase.

Second, there has been a persistent trend of large revenue deficits and a significant decline in capital expenditure. The revenue and capital expenditure gap as a percentage of total expenditure continues to widen (Figure 9.3), limiting the fiscal space for productive investment in crucial infrastructure sectors. In India, the impact of a resource crunch and a need for fiscal correction has usually happened at the expense of capital expenditure through a reduction in capital outlays.

Third, non-developmental expenditure has consistently risen, while developmental expenditure has exhibited fluctuations and generally remained lower than non-developmental expenditure (Figure 9.4). The GoI and the RBI have both categorized spending on social and economic services as developmental expenditure, and administrative services as non-developmental expenditure. Expenditure on social services has been stable, whereas there have been fluctuations in spending on economic services, mainly affecting capital expenditure.

Fourth, decomposing expenditure on social services highlights a concerning area – the government's inadequate spending on the health care and education sectors. The expenditure on education and health care relative to GDP has been abysmally low, hovering around 3 percent and less than 1.5 percent, respectively. This falls far short of global norms, which average around 6 percent for education and 3 percent for health care.[7] Out-of-pocket healthcare expenditure is four times higher than government spending. The health care sector suffers from market failure due to asymmetric information, requiring significant allocation and market regulation. Instead of investing in

Table 9.3 Trends in Public Expenditure in India, 1990–91 to 2019–20

	1990–91	*2000–01*	*2009–10*	*2010–11*	*2011–12*	*2012–13*	*2013–14*	*2014–15*	*2015–16*	*2016–17*	*2017–18*	*2018–19*	*2019–20*
Central Government Expenditure to GDP (%)													
General Services	7.62	7.87	8.22	7.55	7.35	7.21	7.29	7.36	7.62	7.12	6.85	6.43	6.66
Social Services	0.86	0.94	1.52	1.53	1.45	1.34	1.33	0.63	0.69	0.77	0.82	0.68	0.8
Economic Services	3.32	2.17	3.52	3.04	2.45	1.89	3.12	3.12	3.38	2.12	2.4	5.1	4.95
Total Expenditure	**13.68**	**11.9**	**13.85**	**12.76**	**12.41**	**12.37**	**11.91**	**10.54**	**10.88**	**11.04**	**10.65**	**14.03**	**14.86**
State Government Expenditure to GDP (%)													
General Services	4.51	5.94	5.62	5.32	5.56	5.2	5.5	5.43	6.23	6.64	6.66	4.98	4.82
Social Services	4.42	4.3	4.87	4.83	4.98	5.27	5.01	5.17	4.8	5.54	5.59	5.97	5.79
Economic Services	4.02	3.44	3.93	3.47	3.6	3.8	3.87	4.46	5.57	6.11	5.54	1.7	4.48
Total Expenditure	**12.95**	**13.67**	**14.42**	**13.63**	**14.13**	**14.27**	**14.38**	**15.07**	**16.59**	**18.29**	**17.79**	**13.08**	**15.49**
Center and State Consolidated													
General Services	12.13	13.81	13.84	12.87	12.91	12.41	12.79	12.79	13.85	13.76	13.51	11.41	11.48
Social Services	5.28	5.24	6.39	6.36	6.43	6.61	6.34	5.8	5.49	6.31	6.41	6.65	6.59
Economic Services	7.34	5.61	7.45	6.51	6.05	5.69	6.99	7.58	8.95	8.23	7.94	6.8	9.43
Total Expenditure	**26.63**	**25.57**	**28.27**	**26.39**	**26.54**	**26.64**	**26.29**	**25.61**	**27.47**	**29.33**	**28.44**	**27.11**	**30.35**

Source: Authors' calculations from Comptroller and Auditor General of India (2023).

Note: GDP = gross domestic product.

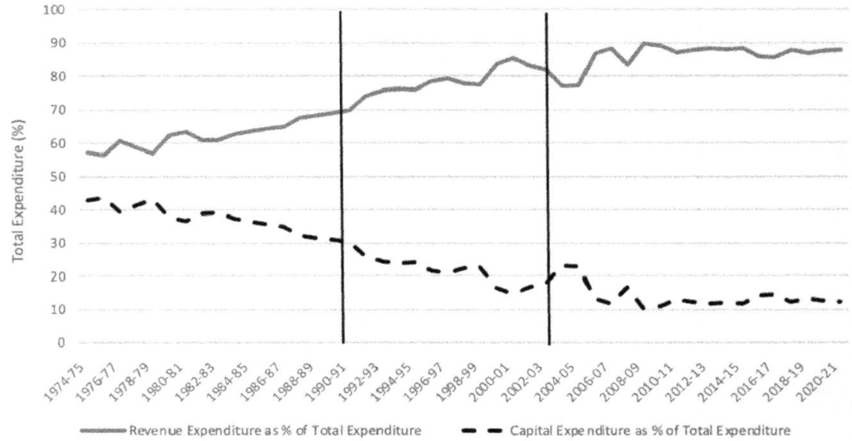

Figure 9.3 Revenue and capital expenditure as a percentage of total expenditure, 1974–75 to 2020–21.

Note: Data for 2021–22 are revised estimates.

Source: Authors' calculations from RBI (2023), DBIE-RBI: Database of Indian Economy (https://dbie.rbi.org.in).

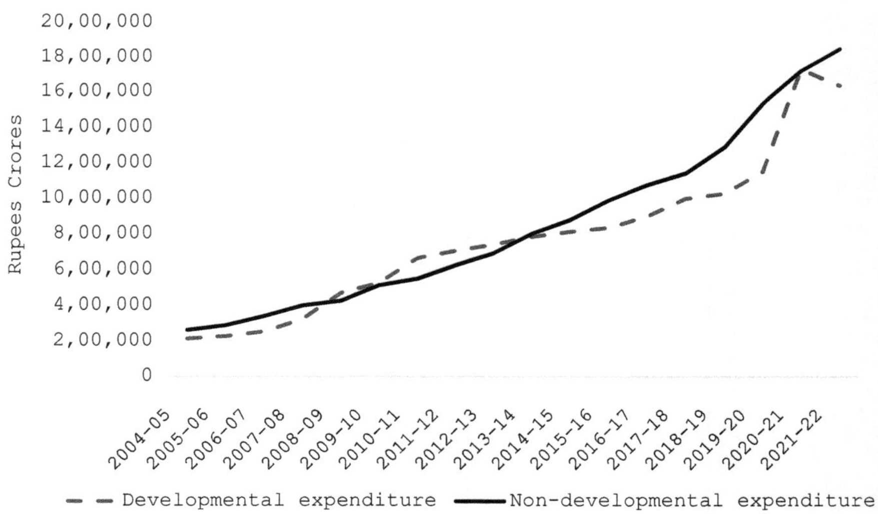

Figure 9.4 Developmental and Non-Developmental Expenditure of the Central Government, 2004–05 to 2021–22.

Note: Data for 2021–22 are revised estimates.

Source: Authors' calculations from RBI (2023), DBIE-RBI: Database of Indian Economy (https://dbie.rbi.org.in).

health infrastructure and training healthcare workers, the government has opted for the easier route of providing insurance through the centrally sponsored *Ayushman Bharat* scheme. However, controlling tertiary care expenses becomes difficult without adequate primary health care, as was evident during the COVID-19 pandemic.

Additionally, the quality and composition of expenditure require attention. Trends in government spending indicate increases in revenue expenditure at the expense of capital outlays and consistent increases in non-developmental expenditure. Furthermore, insufficient investment in social services and physical infrastructure raises concerns about the effectiveness of public expenditure. There has been a focus on spending more to gain public support, often resulting in announcements of new schemes with token allocations or renaming old schemes, especially during elections (Karnam, 2022). The quality of public expenditure has deteriorated over time, highlighting the need for a periodic review of the growth and composition of public expenditure in relation to changing societal needs and preferences.

Time and again, India has appointed several committees to examine issues of tax reforms to enhance tax revenue, the most recent major indirect tax reform being the introduction of GST. On the contrary, the issue of expenditure reform is inadequately addressed, barring some mentions in budget speeches and sporadic establishment of commissions and committees like the Expenditure Reforms Commission in 2000 and the Committee on Efficient Management of Public Expenditure (chairman: Dr C Rangarajan) in 2011. However, expenditure reform should not be a onetime effort but an integral part of the budgeting process, involving periodic evaluation of programs that should inform decision-making.

Furthermore, in terms of expenditure as a tool for fiscal policy, it is essential to acknowledge that mere growth in tax and non-tax revenue will not be enough to manage or optimally utilize expenditure and achieve long-term fiscal sustainability.

As per a study conducted by the IMF (Cordes et al., 2015), the implementation of expenditure rules has shown efficacy in encouraging adherence. Countries tend to demonstrate higher compliance with expenditure rules when the government directly controls the expenditure target and formally establishes the rule in law or a coalition agreement. Furthermore, expenditure rules exhibit superior compliance records when compared to budget balance and debt rules.

Expenditure rules can be applied to total expenditure or specific components. For instance, investments in infrastructure and social sectors essential for human development could be exempted. The government can exercise discretion, guided by expert advice, on which expenditure items should be subject to control and which ones need protection. In nominal or real terms, expenditure targets can be set based on the growth rate or the absolute size. The advantages of expenditure rules lie in their ability to address fiscal correction at the source, unlike deficit targets that pose challenges in the fiscal consolidation process.

As part of implementing expenditure rules, another initiative could be forming a regulatory body, perhaps something like an Expenditure Council along the lines of the current GST Council. The body would develop guidelines and promote consensus among state governments regarding optimal resource allocation practices. With a clear roadmap for expenditures in place, the focus would shift towards rolling out programs that not only drive inclusive growth but also champion sustainable development and maintain fiscal stability.

9.4 Fiscal Management and Political Economy Transitions

9.4.1 A Saga of Economic Populism and Fiscal Profligacy

Since the 1980s, India has witnessed a complex interplay of fiscal management, political economy transitions, economic populism, and fiscal profligacy. Political considerations have often shaped the country's economic policies, leading to a trade-off between populism and prudent fiscal management. One of the significant impacts of economic populism is fiscal profligacy, where governments engage in unsustainable spending, often financed through increased borrowing or printing more money. This results in budget deficits, rising public debt, inflationary pressures, and a potential strain on the economy.

Over the past 40 years, the Indian economy has consistently had a fiscal imbalance, being more pronounced in this century. Despite achieving an average growth rate of over 6.56 percent since the initiation of economic reforms in 1991, and with the consolidated GFD averaging around 7 percent of GDP over the same period, India's fiscal discipline has been inadequate (Table 9.4). India's public debt, at over 82 percent of the GDP, is significantly higher than peer EMEs.

The persistence of the fiscal deficit has been detrimental to the Indian economy. Scholarly work shows that persistent fiscal has a negative impact on growth (Carrère and de Melo 2012; Karnik 2002), consumption (Ghatak and Ghatak 1996), private investments (Rangarajan & Srivastava, 2020), and inflationary risks (Khundrakpam and Pattanaik 2010). It has also made trade deficits worse. India's fiscal deficit reflects a record of fiscal profligacy, regardless of changes in economic growth or political transitions. Besides the major macroeconomic factors, political economy factors have been instrumental in India's tryst with fiscal (mis)management, and fiscal outcomes. Electoral cycles have severely influenced economic policies in India, paving the way for economic populism and fiscal profligacy.

As discussed earlier, in the first 30 years following independence, India embraced a planned development strategy centered on a massive industrialization process led by the public sector. Nonetheless, the stringent tax structure[8] assisted in keeping government deficits within reasonable bounds. Not only did the government successfully restrict the GDF within 3.5 percent of

Table 9.4 India – Key Deficit Indicators and Political Transitions, 1977–2022

Period	*GDP growth rate (average)*	*Average gross fiscal deficit (% of GDP)*	*Average revenue deficit (% of GDP)*	*Average primary deficit (% of GDP)*	*Average central government debt (% of GDP)*	*Election year*	*% of seats held by the single largest party in the parliament*	*% seats of the party to which the prime minister belongs*	*Government Type[a] (S = single party; WC = weak coalition; SC = strong coalition)*	*change in fiscal deficit in preelection and election years[b]*
1977–80	1.01	5.19	−0.11	1.88	41.39	1977	54.43	54.43	S	0.61
1980–84	3.45	5.56	0.84	3.48	43.78	1980	66.73	66.73	S	1.23
1984–89	6.89	7.60	2.19	2.95	55.10	1984	78.60	78.60	S	0.95
1989–91	6.45	7.59	2.77	3.76	60.27	1989	37.24	27.03	WC[c]	-0.28
1991–96	4.91	5.72	2.78	1.48	49.75	1991	44.27	44.27	S[d]	0.51
1996–98	8.32	5.34	2.63	1.01	55.28	1996	29.65	8.47	WC[e]	-0.56
1998–99	8.25	6.48	3.71	1.97	56.14	1998	33.52	33.52	WC	0.96
1999–2004	4.77	5.50	3.84	0.82	62.49	1999	33.52	33.52	WC	-1.11
2004–09	8.13	4.06	2.47	0.37	61.66	2004	26.70	26.70	WC	-0.51
2009–14	7.88	5.38	3.95	2.12	43.88	2009	37.94	37.94	SC	2.95
2014–19	6.77	3.67	2.50	0.52	68.80	2014	51.93	51.93	SC	0.92
2019–Current[f]	3.48	6.75	4.78	3.36	82.45	2019	55.80	55.80	SC	0.37

Source: Adapted from Nandy et al. (2020).

Note: GDP = gross domestic product.

[a] Strong coalition – in which the single largest party of the coalition alone holds three-fourths or more of the seats required to form the government; otherwise, it is a weak coalition.

[b] Equals (average GFD in preelection and election year) – (average GFD of the previous years of the incumbent government).

[c] Two successive coalition governments ran the government at the center for 2 years 126 days and 170 days, respectively.

[d] Indian National Congress ran a minority government although it completed its tenure.

[e] Two weak coalition governments ran the government at the center, and neither completed its tenure.

[f] For the current government, data up to 2022 has been considered.

GDP until the mid-70s, but it also ran a revenue surplus in that period. However, the economic performance remained bleak, with the average annual growth rate from 1950 to 1980 being only a meager 3.75 percent. The budgetary situation was worsened by the political unrest of the 1970s (the India–Pakistan War in 1971 and the declaration of Emergency Rule in 1977[9]), which eventually prompted changes in a few crucial economic areas.

Although the tax code modifications and major industry reforms were started in the initial years of the 1980s, the protectionist policies of the time necessitated large government spending, especially on capital projects. Consequently, the fiscal deficit increased, along with gross debt and non-planned revenue expenditures. The central GFD-to-GDP ratio rose rapidly from 5.7 percent in 1981 to a high of 8.4 percent in 1987. Similarly, the gross debt escalated quickly, rising from 49 percent of GDP in 1981 to 72 percent in 1990. High levels of unplanned revenue expenditure, mostly on interest payments and subsidies, caused the revenue shortfall to increase to 2.9 percent of GDP in 1987 from 1.4 percent of GDP in 1981.

The political landscape in India concurrently witnessed a significant shift as regional political parties emerged to challenge the dominance of the Indian National Congress (INC). Weak coalition governments hindered the implementation of systematic approaches to tackle fiscal imbalances (Joshi and Malcolm, 1994; Singh and Srinivasan, 2004).

As India embarked on the liberalization process in the early 1990s, besides a series of reforms and stabilization programs, the government also initiated the disinvestment of PSUs to reduce capital expenditures and increase capital receipts. The primary deficit improved significantly to 0.5 percent in 1997 from about 4 percent in 1990, and the GFD-to-GDP ratio fell from 7.8 percent in 1991 to 5.4 percent in 2000. Because these economic reforms negatively impacted a sizable portion of the populace, they had political ramifications. Thus, consecutive central governments, particularly those that included regional political parties as coalition members, were reluctant to enforce fiscal reforms, fearing the erosion of popular support. On the contrary, the governments resorted to populist policies and large-scale spending programs to address the political risks brought about by the distorted effects of radical economic reforms (Nandy et al., 2020).

In the latter part of the 1990s, India experienced a series of short-lived multiparty coalition governments, causing significant uncertainty in the political landscape (Table 9.4). The diminishing influence of national parties at the central level and the concurrent rise of regional parties contributed to a lack of agreement on development policies. Moreover, the coalitions' limited capacity to address diverse interests gave rise to competitive electoral populism in India, exacerbating fiscal imbalance at the central and state levels (Bijukumar 2004). Subsequent coalition governments adopted large-scale spending programs to mitigate the political dangers involved. Economic populism in India appeared to exhibit herd behavior tied to the electoral cycles and was especially noticeable when the strength of the opposition matched the strength of the ruling party.

The fiscal deficit resurfaced in the 2000s, resulting from political-economy developments, posing a threat to India's debt sustainability. To tackle this worsening fiscal situation, the FRBMA was introduced in 2000 and finally implemented on July 5, 2004. As a result, the fiscal deficit was decreased despite the center's coalition government, compelling the states to adopt a more prudent budgetary approach. Therefore, by 2007–08, just before the global headwinds resulting from the GFC started to influence India's fiscal and monetary policies, the country's consolidated fiscal deficit was roughly only 4.5 percent of GDP, compared to a target of 6 percent, and the revenue deficit was about 0.5 percent. This resulted in a primary surplus of 1 percent (Rao, 2022a).

However, the FRBMA achieved only limited success, as the prescribed path of fiscal consolidation was notably violated in the subsequent period. The implementation of countercyclical expansionary measures, including tax breaks and fiscal stimulus, was driven by the intent to shield the Indian economy from the GFC of 2007–2009 and rejuvenate the economy amid decelerating growth. Moreover, the increased government expenditure on wages and subsidies in the preelection and election year, under the incumbent government, led to a substantial breach of the fiscal deficit target of 2.5 percent of GDP, resulting in a consolidated fiscal deficit of 10.6 percent of GDP in 2009 – indicative of the presence of political budget cycles (Acharya, 2020; Kanagasabapathy et al., 2013).

We continue to witness instances of financial slippage and profligacy in more recent times. The target rate of 3 percent of GDP was considerably lower than the actual average fiscal deficit during 2019–22, which was 6.75 percent of GDP (Table 9.4). Thus, the competitive electoral populism trend that began with India's political fragmentation continues unabated, seriously endangering the country's fiscal balances as incumbent governments at the national and subnational levels spend extravagantly in an attempt to boost their chances of reelection.[10]

Our earlier study[11] revealed that political and economic issues have played a significant role in triggering India's ongoing fiscal imbalance. Certain critical political-economy factors, like competitive electoral populism (proxied by the expenditure of incumbent governments in the election years to enhance the chances of their reelection), were found to have a major impact on India's fiscal deficit. Our regression analysis reveals that the election year dummy is significant and is positively related to GFD, indicating that with the onset of general elections, there is a tendency toward fiscal populism. To appease various pressure groups and important constituencies, existing governments have typically relied upon large spending programs and populist schemes. This has exacerbated the country's fiscal deficit, especially in the lead-up to general elections.

One of the main factors that is thought to drive good fiscal management is the strength of the government. Research conducted in many contexts has demonstrated that coalition governments did not practice as much fiscal discipline as single-party governments (Woo, 2003; Alesina and Tabellini, 2008;

Roubini and Sachs, 1989). Conversely, our study shows surprising findings, indicating that lower budget deficits did not always result from administrations headed by the single largest party with a comparatively higher seat share.[12] However, given the Indian context, these counterintuitive findings are unsurprising and can be explained by a few significant advancements in the political economy.

There were eight coalition governments, most of which fell short of their full term in office. Five prime ministers could not serve a full year in office, and these partnerships lasted as little as 13 days. Furthermore, at least on two occasions, the single largest party in the Lok Sabha failed to form the government. Because of the inherent instability of coalition governments, regardless of their strength, resulting from ideological disagreements, the current administrations had little political room to pursue fiscal consolidation as they had to balance a number of conflicting interests.

To summarize, both economic and political-economic factors have been instrumental in shaping fiscal policies and fiscal outcomes in India. Indeed, in a democratic setup like India, where the onset of elections heavily influences the incumbent government's fiscal policies, it is difficult to delineate the political-economy factors. Competitive electoral populism and political contestation have led to undesirable fiscal outcomes, with incumbent governments often resorting to fiscally populist stances closer to elections. Strong opposition did not necessarily restrain fiscal profligacy, indicating the increasing propensity toward fiscal populism in India. On the contrary, strong opposition has often led incumbent governments to undertake massive welfare programs in the election or preelection year in an increasingly aggressive attempt to hold onto their political base.

9.5 Fiscal Policy Response to Crisis and Shocks

9.5.1 Lessons Learned from the Experiences of the Recent Past

9.5.1.1 Fiscal Policy Response to the GFC

India's fiscal situation experienced significant improvement following the implementation of FRBM targets by successive governments from 2003–04 until the outbreak of the GFC in early 2008–09. The country's high GDP growth rate, averaging 8.7 percent during the period, contributed to increased revenue and reduced both the revenue and fiscal deficits. In 2007–08, the combined fiscal deficit stood at approximately 4 percent, with the revenue deficit nearing zero and a primary surplus. However, the situation took a drastic turn in 2008–09.

The crisis that unfolded in 2008 significantly impacted economies worldwide, including India. As the crisis reverberated across financial markets and economies, the Indian government faced the challenge of managing its fiscal policies to mitigate the adverse effects and stimulate economic growth.

To combat the effects of the GFC, the Indian government unveiled a stimulus package to boost economic activity and counter the downturn. The package, announced in December 2008, amounted to about 2 percent of India's GDP, totaling approximately INR 1.86 lakh crore (US$40 billion). The stimulus package primarily focused on increasing public spending in key sectors, such as infrastructure, housing, and rural development, to stimulate demand and job creation.[13] Investments in roads, railways, and urban infrastructure were accelerated, creating employment opportunities and boosting economic activity. The increased public expenditure aimed to enhance both short-term demand and long-term growth potential.

To provide relief to businesses and stimulate private investment, the Indian government implemented tax cuts and incentives. Measures such as reducing corporate tax rates (from 30 percent to 25 percent for domestic companies), offering tax holidays for specific sectors, and promoting investment through tax benefits were introduced. These measures aimed to improve the business environment, attract investment, and stimulate economic growth. The government announced a recapitalization plan of INR 20,000 crore (US$4.3 billion) to strengthen PSBs as part of the financial sector reforms. This capital infusion aimed to enhance the lending capacity of banks and support credit flow to the economy.

All of these measures led to a considerable increase in the center's GFD and RD, surpassing the levels prevailing before the enactment of the FRBM Act. However, it is essential to recognize that in a majority of the Advanced G-20 economies, direct fiscal assistance to financial institutions averaging about 5.7 percent of GDP was provided by governments, but the Indian government refrained from offering such support.

Table 9.5 provides an overview of India's stimulus measures. The fiscal deficit indicators reversed during 2008–09 and 2009–10 due to the fiscal stimulus package. The timing of the stimulus package coincided with the payments associated with the Sixth Pay Commission, which acted as an

Table 9.5 Fiscal Stimulus Measures during the Global Financial Crisis

Fiscal Stimulus Measures (% of GDP)	*2008–09*	*2009–10*	
Tax reductions	0.2	0.4	
Expenditure measures	2.2	1.4	
of which Six Pay Commission	0.5	0.3	
Total	2.4	1.8	
Fiscal Deficit 2008–10			
Fiscal deficit	**2007–08**	**2009–10**	**Difference**
Centre	2.5	6.3	3.8
State	1.5	3.3	1.8
Combined center and state	4.1	9.5	5.4

Source: Misra (2011).

additional boost to the economy amidst declining levels of private consumption and demand for investment. In 2008–09, the central government's overall tax collection as a percentage of GDP fell significantly to 10.9 percent, which further dropped to 9.6 percent in 2009–10, primarily due to a sharp decrease in the collection of indirect taxes, particularly excise duties. Consequently, the central government breached the revenue and fiscal deficit goals set forth in the FRBM Act for 2008–09 and 2009–10. This disruption in fiscal consolidation also affected the state governments, leading to deviations from the targets outlined in their respective fiscal responsibility legislation (FRL).

While comprehensive data on the fiscal stimulus measures implemented by the state governments is not readily available, an estimated variation in the fiscal deficit between 2009–10 and 2007–08 offers insights into the effects of the global fiscal crisis on the fiscal positions of both the central government and the state governments (Table 9.5). The difference between the combined fiscal deficit of the center and the state governments in 2009–10 as compared to 2007–08 is significant, amounting to a deviation of 5.4 percent, exceeding the FRBM target of 3 percent for the central government by at least 3.5 percent and the targets of the FRL (3 percent of gross state domestic product (GSDP)) for the state governments.

In coordination with fiscal measures, the central bank of India (RBI) implemented an expansionary monetary policy to support economic recovery. The RBI reduced policy interest rates,[14] eased liquidity conditions, and implemented measures to enhance credit flow to businesses and consumers. These monetary policy actions aimed to lower borrowing costs, boost credit availability, and encourage investment and consumption.

In summary, India's approach to fiscal management in response to the GFC exhibited mixed effectiveness. The fiscal stimulus package and the subsequent increase in public expenditure played a crucial role in bolstering economic growth, sustaining employment levels, and stimulating demand in the short term. Notably, investments in infrastructure contributed to enhanced connectivity and productivity, delivering tangible benefits across various sectors. This coordinated effort resulted in a rebound, with India's GDP growth rate recovering from a slowdown of 6.7 percent in 2008–09 to a commendable 8.6 percent in 2009–10.

However, there were challenges in the effective implementation of fiscal measures. Some infrastructure projects faced delays and cost overruns, hampering the desired impact on economic growth. Additionally, the expansionary monetary policy faced limitations due to global economic conditions and inflationary pressures.

The lessons gleaned from India's fiscal response to the GFC offer valuable insights for future policy formulation. *First*, it highlighted the importance of timely and effective implementation of fiscal measures, particularly infrastructure investments. Swift and precisely targeted fiscal interventions can mitigate the adverse effects of a crisis, providing a much-needed economic boost. Furthermore, strategic investments in infrastructure can trigger a multiplier effect, fostering long-term growth and development.

Second, maintaining fiscal discipline while offering countercyclical support is paramount. Striking a balance between short-term stimulus and long-term fiscal sustainability is crucial to prevent fiscal imbalances and excessive debt accumulation.

Third, collaborative efforts between fiscal and monetary authorities are essential for enhancing policy effectiveness and minimizing potential trade-offs. India's fiscal management during the GFC was complemented by an expansionary monetary policy executed by the RBI. The reduction in interest rates and measures to facilitate credit flow supported fiscal measures by reducing borrowing costs and encouraging investment.

Finally, the crisis highlighted the importance of a resilient financial sector. India's fiscal management included reforms to strengthen the banking sector, improve risk management practices, and enhance regulatory oversight. These measures aimed to boost public trust in the financial system and ensure the smooth functioning of credit markets. Thus, maintaining a robust and well-regulated financial sector is vital for overall economic stability and resilience during a crisis.

9.5.1.2 Fiscal Policy during the COVID-19 Pandemic

During the challenging period of the COVID-19 pandemic, the Indian economy experienced a significant downturn due to the prolonged lockdown policies. The adverse effects were felt across various sectors, leading to a contraction in economic growth. In 2020–21, India's GDP witnessed a substantial decline of 7.3 percent, primarily attributed to the strict lockdown measures that disrupted economic activities.

This economic slump profoundly affected the manufacturing, construction, trade, transportation, hospitality, and tourism industries. Mobility restrictions, supply chain disruptions, and diminished consumer demand resulted in severe disruptions. The aftermath included a surge in unemployment and job losses, especially affecting micro, small, and medium enterprises (MSMEs). Sectors relying heavily on labor, such as construction and informal services, were particularly impacted. Households, grappling with income uncertainties, reduced discretionary spending, while businesses adopted a cautious approach, delaying investments and capital expenditures.

The global disruptions also impacted India's external trade and capital flows. Supply chain disruptions affected export–import activities, and remittances from overseas Indians dwindled, impacting household incomes. Foreign direct investment (FDI) inflows experienced a temporary slowdown as investors exercised caution amid the uncertain economic environment.

The economic strain extended to the government's finances, with tax revenues declining due to reduced economic activity. The GST, income tax, and corporate taxes all saw lower collections. Increased public spending to address the health crisis and provide economic relief further contributed to fiscal pressures (Rao, 2022b).

According to data from the GST Network, the gross GST revenue collected in fiscal year 2020–21 (April 2020–March 2021) stood at INR 19.95 lakh crore (approximately US$268 billion). This represented a decline of 8.2 percent compared to the previous fiscal year. According to the Controller General of Accounts data, India's net income tax collections for the fiscal year 2020–21 stood at INR 4.95 lakh crore (approximately US$66 billion), reflecting a decline of 11.4 percent compared to the previous fiscal year. Corporate tax collections were also affected by the economic slowdown. The net corporate tax collections for the fiscal year 2020–21 amounted to INR 4.57 lakh crore (approximately US$61 billion), witnessing a decline of 26.2 percent compared to the preceding fiscal year.

To counteract the negative economic effects of the crisis, the Indian government implemented various fiscal measures during the COVID-19 epidemic. These measures aimed to provide relief to individuals, support businesses, and stimulate economic activity. The government unveiled an economic stimulus package valued at INR 20 lakh crore, which accounted for about 10 percent of India's GDP (Rangarajan & Srivastava, 2020). This package aimed to support various sectors and included measures such as credit guarantees, liquidity support, and reforms in various sectors, including agriculture, manufacturing, MSMEs, and real estate. For example, the government provided a collateral-free credit guarantee scheme of INR 3 lakh crore (approximately US$40 billion) to enable MSMEs to access working capital and loans.

The government expanded its Direct Benefit Transfer (DBT) program to provide financial assistance directly to individuals and vulnerable sections of society. This included the Pradhan Mantri Garib Kalyan Yojana, facilitating cash transfers to Jan Dhan account holders, farmers, women, and the elderly. Additionally, free food grains and cooking gas cylinders were distributed to ensure food security. The Mahatma Gandhi National Rural Employment Guarantee Act (MGNREGA) was also extended to offer employment opportunities in rural areas, increasing workdays[15] and enhancing wages for immediate income support to rural households.

Various tax relief measures and extended compliance deadlines were introduced to ease the financial burden on businesses and individuals. These measures included the extension of income tax return filing deadlines, reducing tax rates for certain sectors, and suspending certain tax provisions. Credit guarantee schemes, such as the Emergency Credit Line Guarantee Scheme, were introduced to give financial assistance (collateral-free loans) to MSMEs and other troubled industries. Specific support measures were tailored for severely affected sectors like aviation, tourism, and hospitality, including sector-specific loan restructuring, fee waivers, and assistance in meeting working capital requirements.

The fiscal policy approach of the Indian government set it apart from other developed and emerging market countries in several aspects. *First*, the focus was on providing direct support to households and businesses rather than on tax cuts, driven by the belief that direct support would be more effective for those most in need. *Second*, fiscal rules were relaxed more liberally than in other countries, allowing for increased borrowing to finance the stimulus package, albeit with concerns about the country's rising debt burden. *Third*, the emphasis on direct benefit transfers through the DBT program aimed to provide targeted support to vulnerable sections of society and reduce leakages, presenting a relatively unique approach compared to countries primarily focusing on wage subsidies or unemployment benefits.

The fiscal policy approach proved effective in mitigating the immediate economic impact of the pandemic. Despite a 24.4 percent contraction in the first quarter of 2020–21, the Indian economy rebounded by 16.3 percent in the second quarter. The unemployment rate, which surged to 23.5 percent in April 2020, declined to 7.8 percent. While the central fiscal deficit widened to 9.5 percent of GDP in 2020–21, it narrowed to 6.8 percent in 2021–22. The fiscal policy approach of the GoI was effective in mitigating the economic impact of the pandemic. The Indian economy contracted by 24.4 percent in the first quarter of 2020–21 but rebounded by 16.3 percent in the second quarter. The unemployment rate rose to 23.5 percent in April 2020 but has since declined to 7.8 percent. The union fiscal deficit widened to 9.5 percent of GDP in 2020–21 but narrowed to 6.8 percent of GDP in 2021–22.

However, the fiscal policy approach also had its drawbacks. The relaxation of fiscal rules increased the country's debt burden, raising concerns about potential adverse effects on the economy in the long run. The government's debt-to-GDP ratio rose from 67.9 percent in 2019–20 to 89.6 percent in 2021–22, potentially leading to higher interest rates and inflation. Additionally, the focus on direct support to households and businesses meant less funding was available for investment in infrastructure and other long-term projects.

Several critical lessons can be drawn from India's fiscal management during the COVID-19 pandemic. *First*, the importance of prioritizing health and human welfare in fiscal management became evident. India's fiscal response included increased health care spending, provisioning of medical supplies, and the implementation of social welfare programs to provide relief to vulnerable populations. Investing in health care infrastructure, strengthening healthcare systems, and ensuring social welfare measures emerged as essential components for effective crisis management.

Second, well-designed and targeted relief measures that reached the most affected sectors and vulnerable populations were effective in mitigating the socioeconomic impact of the crisis. India's fiscal management involved the implementation of targeted relief measures, such as income support schemes, food distribution programs, and assistance to small businesses.

Third, during the pandemic, India's fiscal management emphasized that fiscal policies should focus on boosting demand through both supply-side and demand-side interventions to reignite economic growth. Measures such as increased public spending, tax incentives, and credit support to businesses were implemented to stimulate consumption and investment.

Fourth, the pandemic underscored the need for a conducive business environment. India's fiscal management included reforms to enhance the ease of doing business, such as simplifying regulatory processes, reducing compliance burdens, and promoting digital governance. Fostering a business-friendly environment through structural reforms was recognized as crucial for attracting investments, stimulating entrepreneurship, and driving economic recovery.

Finally, the crisis highlighted the importance of resilience and contingency planning in fiscal management. India's response involved setting up emergency funds, such as the PM CARES Fund, to address unforeseen contingencies. This underscored the importance of proactive planning, building adequate fiscal buffers, and establishing mechanisms to respond swiftly to future crises or emergencies.

9.6 Challenges and Unfinished Agenda

The process of fiscal adjustment was temporarily halted due to the impact of the pandemic. However, with the situation now under control and economic recovery in progress, it becomes imperative to prioritize fiscal correction. The anticipated real GDP growth is on track to return to pre-pandemic levels this year, although the external environment remains fraught with challenges.

The ongoing Russia–Ukraine conflict and the subsequent economic sanctions have introduced disruptions in the supply chain, contributing to a rise in international commodity prices. Policy responses like interest rate hikes in developed countries have triggered capital flight from emerging market economies like India. The growing possibility of a recession in developed countries has cast a shadow on exports and exchange rate stability, resulting in an increased current account deficit. Addressing these challenges in the fiscal strategy is now crucial as we navigate through the complexities of the post-pandemic economic landscape. These factors emphasize the necessity of cooperation between the federal and state governments on the strategy and timeline for fiscal reform to achieve sustainable public finances.

Two significant aspects are revealed by the experience of executing a rule-based fiscal policy. *First*, governments have not shown a sense of urgency and discipline in meeting the targets they set. *Second*, the quality of the adjustment has been unsatisfactory. Off-budget borrowings and innovative accounting techniques have been employed in an attempt to demonstrate achievements in fiscal consolidation. The cash budget system is still in use, notwithstanding suggestions from several organizations, including the Finance Commission, to switch to accrual accounting. Budgets frequently include aggressive and unachievable goals for lowering revenue and fiscal deficits, often resulting in unforeseen spending cuts, irrational tax demands, borrowing outside of the budget, and delays in bill payment. These practices damage the budgetary process's credibility and have a detrimental effect on income and expenditure efficiency.

India has not had great success implementing rule-based fiscal policy, especially in relation to deficit and debt targets. This issue is not unique to India but is a global phenomenon. Approximately 105 nations have enacted at least one fiscal law by 2021, many of which included restrictions on debt, spending, or the budget balance. Nonetheless, the past 30 years' experiences with fiscal regulations have not been able to guarantee fiscal sustainability. Frequently occurring events include rule modifications, budgetary target deviations, and exceptional clause-based rule suspensions, all of which raise concerns about credibility.

Given the high levels of deficits and debt, this is an opportune time to design new rules that consider lessons learned from the implementation of rule-based policies. These guidelines must be simple, enforceable, and flexible enough to address emergencies. In order to do this, it is necessary to ensure that the budget is managed properly and that an efficient monitoring system is in place. A realistic medium-term fiscal policy and a comprehensive framework for prudent budget management should be incorporated into the successful execution of rule-based fiscal policy (Davoodi et al., 2022).

The Thirteenth Finance Commission emphasized the importance of transparency and comprehensiveness in the FRBM process and the need to address external shocks and enhance monitoring and compliance. They recommended forming a committee to examine FRBM compliance independently and evaluate the financial effects of policy decisions made on the roadmap. Over time, this body was supposed to transform into a Fiscal Council.

The FRBM Review Committee also proposed a similar recommendation, but the council established by the Finance Ministry lacked legislative supervision. Consequently, the Fourteenth Finance Commission suggested amending the FRBM Act to empower Parliament to select a Fiscal Council responsible for overseeing the nation's fiscal management. The Fiscal Council's envisioned role included evaluating budget proposals for conformity and coherence with the Medium-Term Fiscal Plan and regulations, providing multiyear fiscal forecasts, appraising fiscal performance, assessing fiscal targets at the state level, ensuring fiscal sustainability, scrutinizing fiscal policy statements, offering guidance on escape clauses, supporting the Finance Commissions, and sharing their reports and methodologies with the public.

The Fifteenth Finance Commission further emphasized the need to strengthen the institutional process by improving the budgetary process, transitioning to accrual accounting, and standardizing fiscal information across all levels of government. They proposed in-depth suggestions to enhance public finance management and the budgeting process, including establishing an autonomous Fiscal Council. Even though this idea has not gained favor from the government, an independent Fiscal Council seems to be the need of the hour.

Establishing a Fiscal Council in India would strengthen fiscal discipline, promote long-term fiscal sustainability, enhance transparency and accountability, provide independent fiscal analysis, facilitate policy coordination, and contribute to public debate and education on fiscal matters. It would serve as a valuable institution to support responsible fiscal management and ensure the effective and efficient use of public resources.

9.7 Concluding Remarks

Fiscal Policy in India has witnessed a dynamic trajectory since its inception. While the fiscal policy initially facilitated a public-sector-led development process, the fiscal balance remained within manageable limits. However, the tax system was repressive, and fiscal imbalances stemmed in the 1980s due to various domestic and international factors. The inward-oriented policies and the fiscal imbalances triggered the BoP crisis of the early 1990s, and India ultimately adopted the liberalization strategy following the Washington Consensus. India achieved impressive economic growth in the early 1990s, aided by the reforms that helped restore fiscal balance. However, there was a lack of steady progress, being successively hindered by fiscal profligacy, competitive economic populism, and the inability to adhere to fiscal norms.

India continues to face the challenge of high deficits and debt, posing a significant threat to fiscal stability and sustainability. The targets set by the Finance Commissions regarding deficits and debt have frequently experienced deviations, delays and revisions and have often been manipulated using innovative accounting techniques to portray better outcomes than reality. The COVID-19 epidemic further exacerbated the difficulties in achieving debt consolidation and deficit correction. As the economy emerges from the after-effects of the COVID-19 pandemic and the green shoots of recovery become evident, fiscal policy will have a crucial role and significant bearing on fiscal and economic outcomes. Some policy imperatives follow.

First, a long-term credible roadmap for fiscal consolidation must be devised and followed in spirit. Due to the limited tax base and inadequate tax buoyancy, India's high growth periods have not aided the government treasury.[16] The protracted nature of enacting indirect tax reforms serves as a reminder that, in a dispersed democracy like India, attaining fundamental improvements in tax administration and rationalization may be a laborious and politically fraught undertaking. Therefore, in the short term, the government should prioritize bolstering non-tax revenues while implementing adjustments in direct taxes, as exemplified by the Direct Taxes Code. Improvements in fiscal balances can be accomplished by developing better pricing and consumption methods for public resources.

Second, legislators must enhance fiscal responsibility both at the central and subnational levels by ensuring strict adherence to the specified goals in their respective fiscal legislations. The 2003 FRBM Act has fallen short in imposing fiscal restraint, both in terms of flow and stock. A key reason for this failure is that the act set multiple policy objectives, including reducing debt-to-GDP, fiscal deficit-to-GDP, and revenue deficit-to-GDP, which became mutually inconsistent over various stages of the business cycle. Thus, the administration could regularly overshoot the targets with no repercussions. While the N.K. Singh Committee, in its update of the FRBM Act, recommended the establishment of a Fiscal Council to enforce fiscal discipline, it continued with a number of fiscal objectives similar to the previous act.

Given the current growth projections, it may be prudent for India to prioritize lowering the primary deficit, aligning with the country's anomaly compared to other emerging market counterparts. In line with the projected long-term debt trajectory the economy may wish to follow, aiming for the primary balance would also be appropriate. Since sovereign credit rating organizations place substantial significance on fiscal metrics, careful adherence to a stated fiscal plan is imperative, especially in the face of external shocks threatening the fiscal balance.

Third, as previously mentioned, the significance of political-economic issues confirms a strong correlation between India's electoral cycles and supernormal fiscal expenditures, exacerbating the country's budget imbalance. The competitive economic populism and budgetary profligacy of the incumbent administration, especially during election seasons, can be explained by the degree of political contestation and government fragmentation. Legislation alone cannot bring about fiscal virtue. In a fragmented democracy, an approach to achieving it involves self-regulation by developing a shared minimum program that prioritizes fiscal restraint as an essential objective. Additionally, in this context, the proposal of 'One Nation, One Election', envisioning concurrent elections at the center and the states, merits attention and may prove to be an effective way to control fiscal profligacy and competitive populism. By adopting these measures, India can seek to enhance its fiscal structure, increase transparency, and ensure the long-term viability of its finances and economic growth.

Acknowledgement

The authors thank Ms. Abhinanda Mallick for her valuable research assistance.

Notes

1 The Planning Commission held a pivotal role in shaping and executing India's Five-Year Plans (FYPs). Established in 1950, it served as a crucial advisory body to the government, concentrating on economic and social planning. In 2014, the Planning Commission was succeeded by NITI Aayog, a think tank and policy advocacy organization. The stated agenda of the Aayog is to foster cooperative federalism, advocate for sustainable and inclusive development, and embrace a

more participative approach by involving state governments and various other stakeholders in the policymaking process. The shift indicates a move toward a more decentralized and collaborative approach to planning and development in India.

2 Throughout the 1980s, there was a gradual rise in both revenue and fiscal deficits, sparking worries about the growing public debt and interest payments. This, in turn, posed limitations on mobilizing resources to achieve the country's developmental objectives. Between 1980–81 to 1990–91, the revenue deficit increased sharply from a mere 0.4 percent to 4.5 percent of GDP. Moreover, the overall borrowing requirements of the government sector experienced a remarkable surge, averaging approximately 8.5 percent of GDP during the 1980s, in stark contrast to the 5 percent witnessed in the preceding decade.

3 Fiscal federalism involves deciding which functions go to different government levels and how they get their funding, all based on what they are good at. In India, we have a bit of an uneven situation in which the central and state governments do not share revenue sources equally (vertical imbalance) – a typical thing in federal systems. On top of that, each state's ability to generate revenue and its spending needs vary, thanks to differences in their starting conditions, history, and development levels. This creates a bit of a horizontal imbalance. The Finance Commissions (FCs) were established as a way to manage these transfers. Since the formation of the first FC in November 1951 (covering the 1952–57 period), a total of 15 FCs has been constituted. The most recent, FC-XV, submitted its report in November 2020, covering the 2020–26 period.

4 The Indian government put a strong emphasis on growing educational infrastructure, especially in rural areas, with a particular focus on primary schools. From 1950 to 1970, the number of primary schools in India soared from about 240,000 to over 670,000, ensuring improved access to education. During this time, the higher education sector witnessed the establishment of several prestigious institutions, including Indian Institutes of Technology (IITs), Indian Institutes of Management (IIMs), and the All India Institute of Medical Sciences (AIIMS). Concurrently, the government worked towards enhancing pan-India healthcare infrastructure by establishing numerous primary health centers (PHCs) and community health centers. The number of PHCs surged from around 1,800 in 1950 to more than 23,000 by the late 1970s. In the initial 30 years post-independence, India achieved a major milestone in public health by successfully eliminating diseases like smallpox. There were also dedicated efforts to control malaria and tuberculosis through targeted programs and interventions.

5 According to the FRBM Act 2003, the established targets for revenue and fiscal deficit can be surpassed "due to reasons of national security, national calamity, or other exceptional grounds as specified by the Central Government.".

6 According to the latest available data from the Finance Ministry, the number of people filing income tax returns as of 2021–22, is 68 million, and of these, only a meager 16.9 million (1.2 percent of the entire population) paid income tax.

7 The Education Commission, chaired by D. S. Kothari in 1966, initially proposed a requirement to allocate 6 percent of GDP for spending (India). This recommendation was later supported by the Saikia Committee and the Tapas Majumdar Committee. Similarly, the High-Level Expert Group on Universalising Healthcare, appointed by the Planning Commission and led by Dr. Srinath Reddy, recommended increasing public expenditure on healthcare. They suggested raising the expenditure from 1.2 percent of GDP in 2012–13 to 2.5 percent by the end of the 12th Five-Year Plan and further to 3 percent by 2022.

8 The public sector-led industrialization effort and social welfare programs were financed in part by the transfer of resources from the private sector through the

tax system. The corporate income tax varied from 45 to 65 percent for certain widely held enterprises, and the top marginal income tax rate was an abhorrently high 90 percent until the 1980s.

9 Upon the recommendation of then prime minister Mrs. Indira Gandhi, the president of India at that time, Fakhruddin Ali Ahmed, declared a nationwide emergency using the powers outlined in Article 352 of the Indian constitution. This emergency persisted for a duration of 21 months, spanning from 1975 to 1977. During this period, elections were suspended, civil liberties were restricted, and the prime minister was granted the ability to govern through decrees.

10 For instance, the ruling party in the center paid off farmer loans totaling almost US$15 billion before the 2009 general elections, at a cost of 1.2 percent of GDP. The pattern was also visible in other states, especially those controlled by regional parties, which offered freebies to voters in the form of televisions, cell phones, gold for marriage, cars, power, and a waiver of all farm loans. All such populist measures were implemented at the cost of fiscal prudence at the national and subnational levels.

11 For a detailed analysis, refer Nandy et al. (2020).

12 We investigated the correlation between the budget deficit and the government's strength, where the strength of the government is characterized as the ratio of the seats held by the largest party in the lower house of parliament to the overall size of the legislature. Additionally, we explored an alternative hypothesis that defines SEAT as the total size of the legislature divided by the number of seats held by a party to which the prime minister belonged. The results were consistent.

13 Public expenditure on infrastructure increased significantly during the fiscal years 2008–09 and 2009–10. For instance, in 2008–09, the allocation for infrastructure development was INR 1.82 lakh crore (US$39 billion), representing an 87 percent increase from the year before.

14 During the period from October 2008 to April 2009, the RBI implemented a series of policy measures, including a substantial reduction in the policy repo rate. Over this time frame, the RBI lowered the policy repo rate by a cumulative 425 basis points – bringing it down to 4.75 percent.

15 The number of workdays under MGNREGA was increased from 100 to 150 for the financial year 2020–21, providing additional employment opportunities. Additionally, wages were enhanced to provide immediate income support to rural households.

16 India lags significantly behind its peers in tax revenue collection. The tax–GDP ratio in India was reported at 16.8 percent, considerably lower than that of Brazil (33.4 percent), China (24.8 percent), Russia (28.2 percent), and South Africa (27.8 percent). The fact that only 37 million individuals out of a population exceeding 1250 million paid taxes in 2015–16 underscores the limited tax base in India.

References

Acharya, V. (2020). *Quest for Restoring Financial Stability in India*. Sage Publications Pvt. Limited.

Ahluwalia, M. S. (2002). Economic Reforms in India Since 1991: Has Gradualism Worked? *Journal of Economic Perspectives*, 16(3), 67–88. https://doi.org/10.1257/089533002760278721

Alesina, A. F., & Tabellini, G. (2008). Why Is Fiscal Policy Often Procyclical? *Journal of the European Economic Association*, 6(5). https://doi.org/10.1162/JEEA.2008.6.5.1006

Bijukumar, V. (2004). Economic Reforms, Populism and Party Politics in India. *The Indian Journal of Political Science*, 65(2), 161–180.

Carrère, C., & de Melo, J. (2012). Fiscal Spending and Economic Growth: Some Stylized Facts. *World Development*, 40(9), 1750–1761. https://doi.org/10.1016/j.worlddev.2012.04.011

Comptroller and Auditor General of India (2023). Combined Finance and Revenue Accounts-Union & State | Comptroller and Auditor General of India. Cag.gov.in. Retrieved June 19, 2023, from https://cag.gov.in

Cordes, T., Kinda, T., Muthoora, P., & Weber, A. (2015). Expenditure Rules: Effective Tools for Sound Fiscal Policy? *IMF Working Papers*, 15(29), 1. https://doi.org/10.5089/9781498390576.001

Davoodi, H. R., Elger, P., Fotiou, A., Garcia-Macia, D., Han, X., Lagerborg, A., Lam, W. R., & Medas, P. A. (2022). Fiscal Rules and Fiscal Councils: Recent Trends and Performance during the COVID-19 Pandemic. *IMF Working Papers*, 2022(011).

DBIE-RBI: Database of Indian Economy. (2023). Rbi.org.in. https://dbie.rbi.org.in

Dev, S. M. (2021). Beyond India 75. Indira Gandhi Institute of Development Research.

Fifteenth Finance Commission (XVFC). (2021). Report of the 15th Finance Commission for 2021–26. Government of India. https://nhsrcindia.org

Ghatak, A., & Ghatak, S. (1996). Budgetary Deficits and Ricardian Equivalence: The Case of India, 1950–1986. *Journal of Public Economics*, 60(2), 267–282. https://doi.org/10.1016/0047-2727(95)01551-5

Herd, R., & Leibfritz, W. (2008). Fiscal policy in India. OECD Economics Department Working Papers, No.595. https://doi.org/10.1787/244241786035

Jha, P. K. (2011). *Progressive Fiscal Policy in India*. SAGE Publishing India.

Joshi, V., & Malcolm, I. (1994). *India: Macroeconomics and Political Economy, 1964–1991*. World Bank Publications.

Kanagasabapathy, K., Vaidya, D. S., & Tilak, V. G. (2013). Budgeting for Fiscal Consolidation: Myth and Reality. *Economic and Political Weekly*, 48(17), 57–59.

Karnam, G. (2022). Public Expenditure in India: Policies and Development Outcomes. (Oxford, 2022; online edn, Oxford Academic, 19 May 2022), https://doi.org/10.1093/oso/9780192857569.001.0001

Karnik, A. (2002). Fiscal Policy and Growth. *Economic and Political Weekly*, 37(9), 829–831.

Khundrakpam, J. K., & Pattanaik, S. (2010). Fiscal Stimulus and Potential Inflationary Risks: An Empirical Assessment of Fiscal Deficit and Inflation Relationship in India. *Journal of Economic Integration*, 25(4), 703–721.

Krishna, K. L. (2022). Sources of India's Post reform Economic Growth. *Economic and Political Weekly*, 57(31), 36–43.

Mishra, H., & Maheshwari, P. (2020). Achieving Sustainable Development Goals through Fourth Industrial Revolution: An Indian Perspective. *Indian Journal of Commerce & Management Studies*, 11(2). Retrieved from https://ijcms.in/index.php/ijcms/article/view/309

Misra, B. (2011). Fiscal Consolidation and Macroeconomy: India's Experience with Rule-Based Fiscal Policy and Post-Crisis Challenges. *Rules and Institutions for Sound Fiscal Policy after the Crisis*, 11(2), 75–106.

Nandy, A., Sur, A., & Kundu, S. (2020). Persistent Fiscal Deficits and Political Economy Transitions in India: An Empirical Investigation. *Economic and Political Weekly*, 55(8), 34–41.

Rangarajan, C., & Srivastava, D. (2020). India's Growth Prospects and Policy Options: Emerging from the Pandemic's Shadow. *Indian Public Policy Review*, 1(1), 1–18.

Rangarajan, C., & Subbarao, D. (2007). *The Importance of Being Earnest about Fiscal Responsibility*. Madras School of Economics Chennai.

Rao, M. G. (2005). Tax System Reform in India: Achievements and Challenges Ahead. *Journal of Asian Economics*, 16(6), 993–1011. https://doi.org/10.1016/j.asieco.2005.10.003
Rao, M. G. (2022a). *Studies in Indian Public Finance*. Oxford University Press.
Rao, M. G. (2022b). Sustainable Fiscal Policy in India: Post-Pandemic Challenges. *Indian Public Policy Review*, 3(6) (Nov–Dec), 1–15. https://doi.org/10.55763/ippr.2022.03.06.001
Rao, M. G., & Kumar, S. (2018). Envisioning Tax Policy for Accelerated Development in India. *Asia-Pacific Sustainable Development Journal*, 25(1), 85–107.
Roubini, N., & Sachs, J. (1989). Government Spending and Budget Deficits in the Industrial Countries. *Economic Policy*, 4(8), 99–132.
Singh, N., & Srinivasan, T. N. (2004). Fiscal Policy in India: Lessons and Priorities. SSRN Electronic Journal. Retrieved from https://escholarship.org/uc/item/8nx3v467
Woo, J. (2003). Economic, Political, and Institutional Determinants of Public Deficits. *Journal of Public Economics*, 87(3–4), 387–426. https://doi.org/10.1016/S0047-2727(01)00143-8

10 Financial Instability, Credit Growth and Optimal Monetary Policy Design

*Sanjay Basu and Tasneem Chherawala**

10.1 Introduction

Prof. Anindya Sen has always worked at the interface of economic theory and policy. He has used the tools of Industrial Organization to throw light on important macroeconomic issues. For instance, his joint work (Dutt and Sen 1997) provides the microfoundations of the Kaleckian proposition that an increase in the bargaining power of workers increases real wage, aggregate demand, output and employment. In a similar vein, he introduces imperfect competition, in a Gylfason - Lindbeck (1994) model of interaction between monetary policy and wage fixation, to rationalize the simultaneous persistence of involuntary unemployment and inflation in an economy (Sen 1996).

In this chapter, we also follow a game-theoretic approach to address an important problem: should financial stability be an objective of monetary policy? In our simple model, the central bank acts as a Stackelberg leader to set optimal repo rates. In response, the monopoly bank (or a group of oligopolistic banks) sets the equilibrium loan rate. Hence, aggregate loan volume is also determined. We show that, if the central bank tries to balance price stability and financial stability,[1] it will not raise or lower policy rates to the same degree as the change in gross domestic product (GDP) growth and inflation gaps. The fear of financial instability restrains it from a sharp spike or cut in policy rates.

In this chapter, we make the following contributions. First, we present a parsimonious theoretical framework to understand the sharp rise in bank credit (both retail and corporate) during the tight money regime in India, from May 2022 onwards. While the policy repo rate has risen by 250 basis points, between May 2022 and February 2023, credit disbursement has also shot up, especially in the personal loan segment. We state the conditions under which such a counterintuitive result may occur. Hence, we add to the

* This chapter is a tribute to Prof. Anindya Sen, who was the doctoral thesis guide of Sanjay Basu at IIM Calcutta. The hallmark of Prof. Sen's work is simplicity and clarity of exposition. We have tried to retain the same flavour in this chapter. It has benefited from helpful comments and suggestions by Jiji Mathew, Partha Ray and Saibal Ghosh. The usual disclaimer applies.

DOI: 10.4324/9781003509721-13

large literature on the credit channel of monetary policy transmission (e.g., Bernanke and Blinder 1988).

Second, much of the literature treats individual agents as the first mover, while the central bank is the follower. For instance, in the seminal Barro and Gordon (1983) model, wages and prices are higher than they should be, because agents anticipate surprise inflation by the central bank, in future (Gibbons 1992). However, in our story, the central bank decides policy rates at the outset, while banks respond with the equilibrium loan rate. This role reversal gives the central bank some degree of control over the credit channel of monetary policy transmission. This result chimes in well with a world in which the bargaining power and information processing ability of agents is limited relative to the central bank.

Third, we contribute to the recent literature on the changing contours of monetary policy, after the global financial crisis (GFC) of 2008. Before the meltdown, traditional Macroeconomics would treat a bank as a passive conduit of credit from the central bank to the real sector (Dornbusch et al. 1998). However, after the collapse, it was felt that the asset allocation strategies of banks (i.e., the manner in which funds were deployed in loans, bonds and structured products) had aggravated systemic risk. It was also argued that such errant behaviour was triggered by sustained easy money policies of central banks in advanced countries for more than a decade. The allegation was that monetary policy, focused only on the stabilization of price and output, was oblivious to the perils of financial instability. The important question, now, is whether monetary policy should be used to reduce the likelihood of financial crises (in addition to its traditional goals) or whether the management of financial instability should be best left to macroprudential tools like the Countercyclical Capital Buffer (Blanchard 2018). Our model suggests that recognition of the threat of financial instability instils more caution with rate fixation – neither a sharp rise nor a steep cut in policy rates. As we discuss later, a sharp and prolonged decline in policy rates followed by a sudden spike is a strong early warning indicator of financial crises.

Finally, we provide the microfoundations of the Taylor rule, for nominal policy rate determination. The Taylor rule is a famous heuristic, which uses arbitrary coefficients for inflation and output gaps. In our model, the coefficients are derived through an optimization process. They are based on parameters related to financial instability. The most important difference between the original Taylor rule (Taylor 1993) and the one we derive lies in the coefficient of the inflation gap. In the original model, the coefficient is expected to be greater than 1 so that the central bank changes the nominal policy rate more than the change in inflation. The real rate increases, and spending is reduced. In our framework, the response is less than proportionate, given the fear of financial instability.

The rest of the chapter is as follows: Section 10.2 presents some stylized facts on policy rate change, credit growth and economic growth in India. In Section 10.3, we review the existing literature to contextualize our work.

Section 10.4 develops a dynamic game framework in which the central bank sets the policy rate first and the bank reacts with equilibrium loan rates and volumes. In Section 10.7, we discuss the recent US macro-financial trends and monetary policy response in light of our model. Section 10.8 presents our conclusions, with some suggestions for future research.

10.2 Stylized Facts – India

The Indian economy went through a phase of price surge, after the COVID-19 pandemic, which was aggravated by supply shocks created by the Ukraine–Russia war. Retail inflation had breached the target of 4% ± 2% set by the Reserve Bank of India (RBI) and remained elevated after March 2022. In line with other central banks, the RBI started raising the policy repo rate, from 4.00% in May 2022 to 6.5% by February 2023 (Figure 10.1).

There is a potential short-run trade-off between economic growth and inflation. High inflation, i.e. beyond a threshold, can be inimical to growth. Inflation targeting monetary policy authorities have to consider this dilemma when they choose policy rates and liquidity measures. As can be seen from Figure 10.2(a), this trade-off was valid for the Indian economy in the past. Bouts of high inflation slowed down output growth, and benign prices accompanied faster economic growth. However, after the pandemic, this relationship broke down as the economy registered a sharp recovery, in a low-interest rate environment, despite price conflagration. Furthermore, the growth momentum has continued even during the latest tight money regime (Figure 10.2a).

One of the transmission mechanisms of tightening monetary policy is through the credit channel. The lending rates of banks and financial

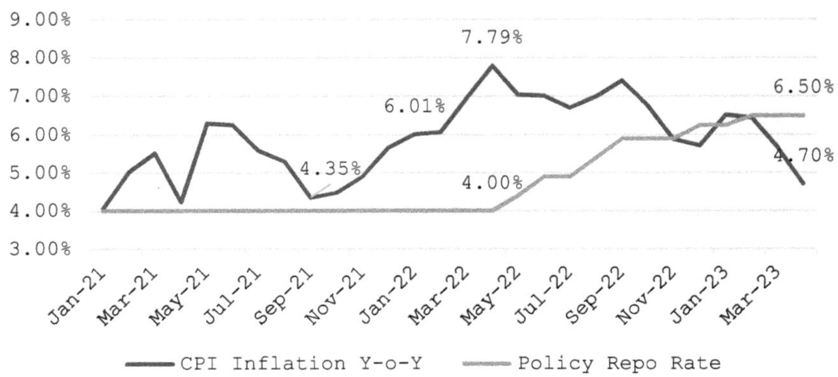

Figure 10.1 Annual Consumer Price Index (CPI) Inflation and Policy Repo Rate.

Note: Y-o-Y = year over year.

Source: The Reserve Bank of India Database on Indian Economy.

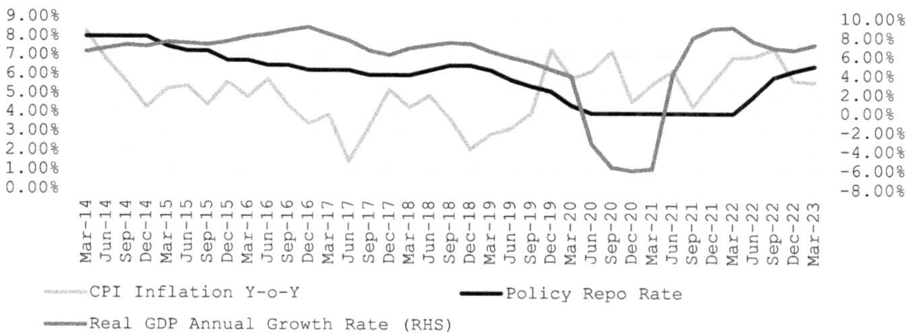

Figure 10.2a Trends in Real Gross Domestic Product (GDP) Growth, Consumer Price Index (CPI) Inflation and Policy Repo Rate.

Note: Y-o-Y = year over year.

Source: RBI Database on Indian Economy and MoSPI.

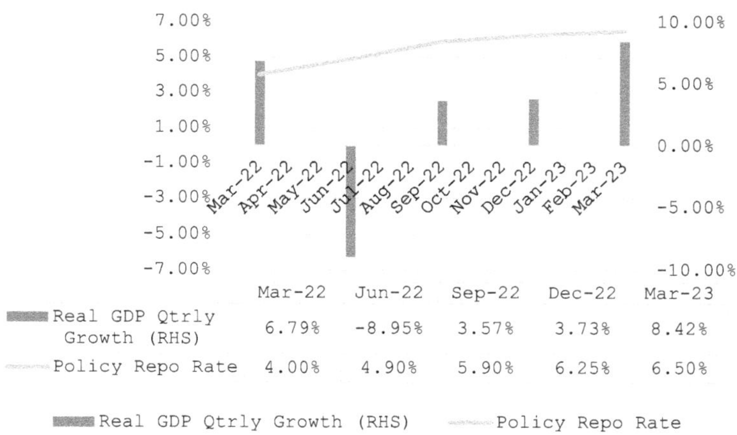

Figure 10.2b Quarter-on-Quarter GDP Growth Rate and Repo Rates during the Latest Tightening Phase.

Source: RBI Database on Indian Economy.

institutions adjust to higher policy rates. Figure 10.3 shows the correlated changes to lending rates (weighted average lending rates on outstanding and fresh loans and the marginal cost of funds–based lending rate – MCLR) as RBI has changed the repo rate. In the latest tightening phase (May 2022–March 2023), banks have passed on 181 bps of the 250-bps rate hike to fresh loans, and the average lending rate on outstanding credit has increased by 100 bps.

An increase in policy rates reduces the supply of bank loans, which, in turn, reduces spending by borrowers (Bernanke and Blinder, 1988).

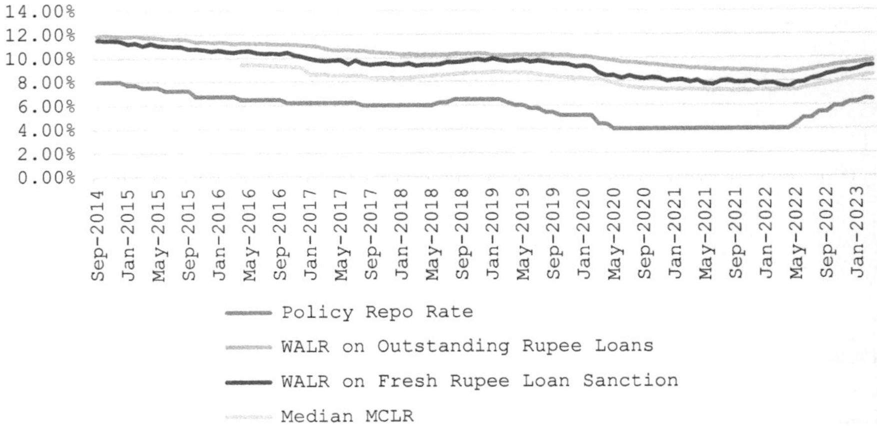

Figure 10.3 Movement of Lending Rates with Policy Repo Rate.

Note: WALR = weighted average lending rate; MCLR = marginal cost of funds–based lending rate.

Source: RBI Database on Indian Economy.

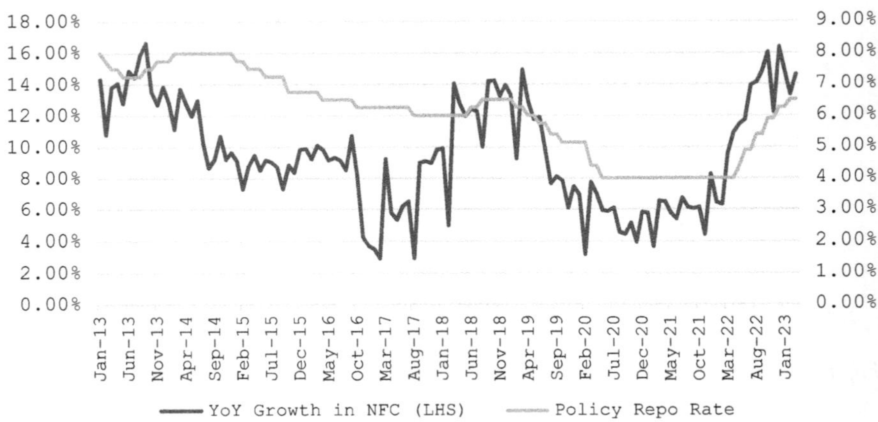

Figure 10.4 Year-over-Year (YoY) Non-Food Credit (NFC) Growth and Policy Repo Rate.

Source: RBI Database on Indian Economy.

Furthermore, higher interest costs weaken corporate balance sheets, reducing their ability to borrow from all sources and creating a potential risk of default. Retail credit-driven consumption can also be expected to fall with rising interest rates. Figure 10.4 not only demonstrates this relationship in the long run but also highlights that in the period after the COVID-19 pandemic, loan volumes continued to spike despite consecutive rate hikes.

During this tight money phase, such paradoxical credit growth has been driven by the spurt in retail loans (Figure 10.5). However, credit to industry has slowed down (Figure 10.6).

There is a strong interdependence between credit expansion and economic growth. (Figure 10.7). The significance of such a positive correlation is clear – if credit continues to rise, despite the increase in rates, economic growth will be boosted. Higher GDP growth, in turn, will accelerate credit growth. A virtuous cycle – between the financial and real sectors – will ensue.

The non-performing loans (NPLs) of the Indian banking sector have also shrunk over the last 4 years (Figure 10.8). For banks, this implies a declining

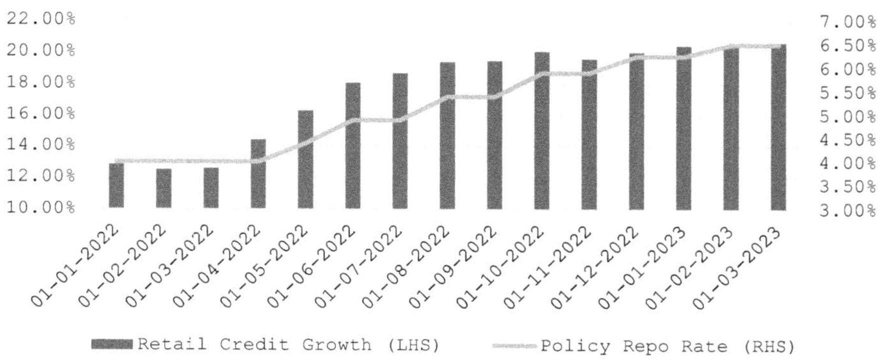

Figure 10.5 Year-on-Year Retail Credit Growth vis-à-vis Policy Rate Hikes during the Rate Hike Period.

Source: RBI Database on Indian Economy.

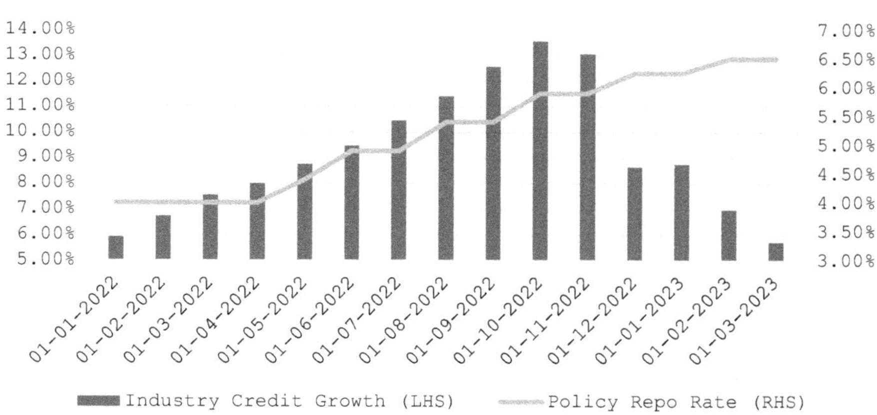

Figure 10.6 Year-on-Year Credit Growth to Industry vis-a-vis Policy Rate Hikes during the Rate Hike Period.

Source: RBI Database on Indian Economy.

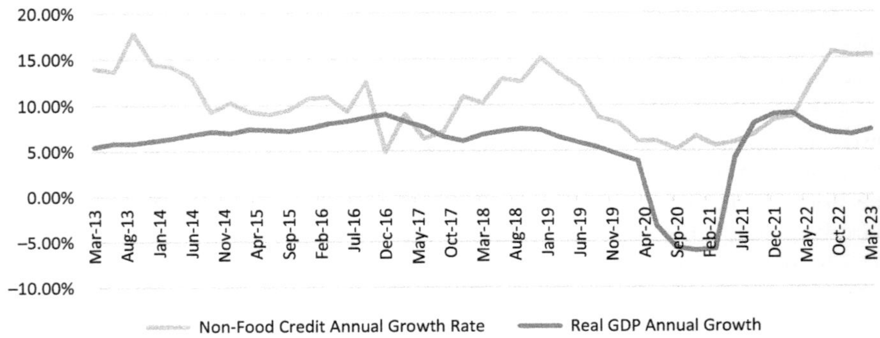

Figure 10.7 Trends in Real Gross Domestic Product (GDP) Growth and Non-Food Credit Growth.

Source: RBI Database on Indian Economy.

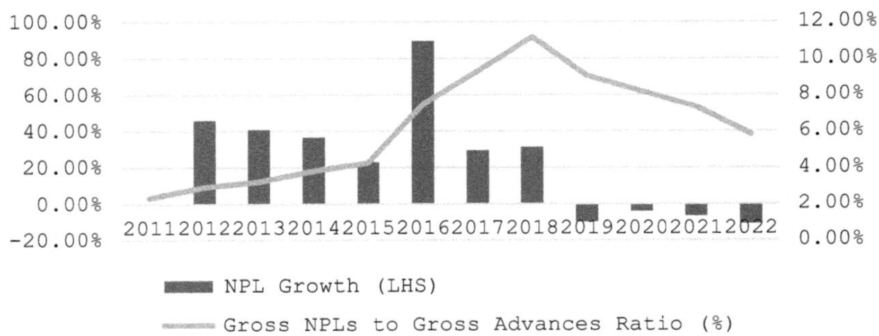

Figure 10.8 Trend in Non-Performing Loans (NPLs) of Indian Banks.

Source: RBI Database on Indian Economy.

probability of default (PD) for their credit portfolios and a corresponding improvement in profitability and capital adequacy.

The main research questions which emerge from these stylized facts are as follows:

1. Under what conditions will credit continue to grow during a tight money regime?
2. How should a rational central bank set policy rates, over time, to ensure adequate credit growth?

We seek the answers to these questions in Section 10.4. The next section provides the backdrop against which we develop our theoretical model on commercial and central bank interactions.

10.3 Literature Review

Our work aims to tie up two strands of literature. The first is on the Credit Channel of Monetary Policy transmission. One of the seminal papers, in this domain, is Bernanke and Blinder (1988). Through the addition of a CC (i.e. Commodities and Credit) curve, to the IS-LM (Investment-Saving and Liquidity Preference-Money Supply) framework, the authors investigate the effects of factors like an increase in bank risk aversion, tight money policy and gross national product (GNP) shocks on credit supply and loan rates. Another important contribution is by Bernanke and Blinder (1992). It provides evidence of the presence of the credit channel based on US data. It establishes that a monetary contraction is followed by a decline in aggregate bank lending. It does not explain further whether the reduced credit volumes are due to demand or supply factors in the credit markets. Kashyap and Stein (2000) analyse a large data set of US banks over 20 years and conclude that the impact of monetary policy on lending is stronger for smaller banks and those with less liquid balance sheets.

Altunbas et al. (2010) examine the impact of monetary policy regimes on bank risk profiles. They find that, in an environment of sustained low short-term interest rates, bank risk increases. This may happen due to the manner in which banks measure risks related to valuations, incomes and cash flows during periods of low interest rates. It may also happen through their search for higher yields. They imply that central banks need to be aware of the financial stability implications of monetary policy actions and the fall-out on longer-term macroeconomic growth. Aikman et al. (2020) infer that the relationship between the credit gap and the monetary policy transmission channel is non-linear. When the credit gap is low, monetary tightening leads to an increase in unemployment, a contraction of GDP and a decline in credit. However, when the credit gap is high, financial constraints do not bind during a tight money regime, and this works against the contractionary effect.

These papers establish that there is a strong linkage between monetary policy actions and the price and quantum of bank credit, which, in turn, has implications for financial stability. We examine the nature of such a relationship, within a theoretical construct, in the next section. However, the more important branch of literature relates to the objectives of monetary policy. The goal will shape monetary policy strategies, which will be transmitted to banks as fluctuations in quantum and the cost of credit.

The traditional goal of the monetary policy authority is to minimize a discounted loss function, which consists of squared deviations of output and inflation from their target levels (Clarida et al. 1999). The weight (i.e., relative importance) of each component need not be the same. This principle – known as Flexible Inflation Targeting – served the discipline well until the GFC. However, in the wake of the collapse, central banks came under increased scrutiny due to their persistence with cheap money policies before the crisis. It was alleged that the single-minded pursuit of recovery from a recession, after the dot-com bubble and 9/11, made them neglect the dangers of sustained easy money policy. It was proposed that monetary policy should be mindful of financial instability concerns as well.

However, an influential body of macroeconomists invoked the separation principle – macroprudential policy for financial booms and busts while monetary policy is appropriate for inflation and output fluctuations (Caruana 2015). Svensson (2010) observes that higher policy rates might not have prevented the crisis, given the global saving glut and free capital mobility. Furthermore, empirical models do not link monetary policy regimes with asset price bubbles. Adrian et al. (2018) point out that the impact of higher rates on credit growth not only occurs with a lag but is also small. Moreover, there may not exist any trade-off between output stability and financial stability – similar monetary policy actions may be recommended in both cases. Finally, the costs of a spike in policy rates, beyond that warranted by inflation levels, may outweigh the benefits. Hence, the appropriate division of labour should be the use of monetary policy for price and output stability and the deployment of macroprudential policy for financial stability.

Caruana (2015) feels that these two policies should operate together to be most effective. Monetary policy affects all interest rates while macroprudential policy targets only bank borrowers. As a result, booms in the capital market (outside banks) may be managed better by monetary, rather than macroprudential, policy. Moreover, monetary and macroprudential policies are interactive and not separable. Hence, the separation argument is not credible enough, and management of financial stability may be a goal of monetary policy design.

Even if financial instability is considered to be a monetary policy objective, how should it be incorporated? Adrian and Duarte (2022) consider a value-at-risk (VaR) constraint, as a limit on tail risk assumed by banks. Due to macro-financial linkages, GDP and monetary policy are affected. Akinci et al. (2022) determine a real interest rate r^{**}, above which financial instability will occur. A sustained cheap money policy is found to lower the threshold.

The debate on price versus financial stability has been reignited in the recent past, after the failure of Silicon Valley Bank in the US and Credit Suisse in Europe. Despite deficiencies in internal risk management practice and loopholes in bank supervision and regulation (Fed Reserve 2023), such a failure has also been blamed on a sharp rise in rates after a prolonged phase of low rates (Rajan 2023). Jimenez et al. (2023) have shown that a U-shaped monetary policy curve (sharp, sustained decline in policy rates, followed by a steep hike) increases banking sector risk, across 17 countries over 150 years. The implication is that central banks should be careful about the trajectory of policy rates, lest financial instability pressures arise.

In light of the preceding discussion, the following questions arise:

1. What is the relationship between bank loan rates and policy rates? This is the credit channel for the transmission of monetary policy.
2. What are the implications for monetary policy if the management of financial instability is an explicit goal for the central bank?

We shall answer both the questions in the next section.

10.4 The Model

We begin with a list of symbols used for subsequent analysis:

Sl. No.	*Symbol*	*Interpretation*
1.	π_B	Profit function of monopoly bank
2.	p	Probability of default (PD) of loans
3.	r_L	Lending interest rate
4.	L	Volume of loans
5.	r	Policy interest rate (repo rate)
6.	M	Investments in market instruments linked to policy rates (government bonds/ money market instruments)
7.	r_D	Deposit interest rate
8.	D	Volume of deposits
9.	$C(D,L)$	Operating costs for loans and deposits
10.	c_D	Marginal operating cost of deposits
10.	c_L	Marginal operating cost of screening/monitoring a loan
11.	ξ	Elasticity of loan demand
12.	b	Constant elasticity of loan demand
13.	$A(=PY)$	Nominal economic output (say nominal gross domestic product) or market size
14.	P	General price level
15.	Y	Real economic output
16.	NPL_1	Level of non-performing loans in Period 1
17.	NPL_e	Target non-performing loans
18.	θ_0/θ_1	Inflation level in period 0/1
19.	θ_e	Target inflation level
20.	a	(Regression) Coefficient of lending interest rate
21.	c	(Regression) Coefficient of market size
22.	$\hat{Y}_0 / \hat{Y}_1$	Real output growth in period 0/1
23.	$\hat{Y}_e$	Target Real output growth

In the following subsections, we develop a simple theoretical model to illustrate how the banking sector may set the optimal loan rate in response to the equilibrium repo rate announced by the central bank. The extensive-form game has to be solved backwards – we determine the optimal loan rate first (Stage 2) and then proceed to fix the equilibrium repo rate for the central bank (Stage 1).

10.5 The Banker's Problem (Stage 2)

We assume a monopoly bank (or a group of oligopolistic banks) in a Monti–Klein framework (Freixas and Rochet 2008, Ch. 3). The profit function of this bank is given by

$$\pi_B = (1-p)r_L L + rM - r_D D - C(L,D), \tag{10.1}$$

where

p = probability of loan default,
r = Policy repo rate,
D = deposit volume, and
M = investments in market instruments (opportunity cost of loans).

We also assume, for simplicity, that the recovery rate is zero. In other words, the bank does not recover any principal after the loan defaults. The introduction of a positive recovery rate will complicate the analysis without any substantive contribution to the results.

If a bank's reserve ratio with the central bank is α, then investments in market instruments by the bank will be to the extent of net deposit funds less the loan volumes. That is,

$$M = (1-\alpha)D - L.$$

Furthermore, if the cost of processing deposits and loans is additive and each segment of credit is independent of others, then the bank becomes a multi-product monopolist. That is,

$$C(L,D) = c_L L + c_D D.$$

Based on the preceding two conditions, the profit function of the bank can be rewritten as

$$\pi_B(L) = (1-p)r_L L - rL - c_L L + r(1-\alpha)D - r_D D - c_D D. \tag{10.2}$$

Optimizing the bank's profit function with respect to loan volumes, we get

$$\frac{\partial \pi_B(L)}{\partial L} = 0 \rightarrow r_L^* = \frac{1}{(1-p)}\left[\frac{1}{\left(1-\frac{1}{\xi}\right)}\right](r + c_L), \tag{10.3}$$

where

ξ is the elasticity of loan demand.

While traditional theories of monetary policy transmission focus primarily on money or bank deposits, i.e. treat bank liability as a driver of aggregate demand, the emphasis of our model is on bank assets, that is credit, à la Bernanke and Blinder (1988). The implicit assumption is that bank deposits are substitutable with bonds and other market instruments. We are agnostic on the source of finance. That is why we do not include equity as well. This approach allows us to develop a direct linkage between lending rates and external benchmarks (such as the policy repo rate).

It follows from Equation (10.3) that the lending rate is computed as a markup over policy rate r (risk-free) and the processing cost c_L. The mark-up consists of the credit spread $\frac{1}{(1-p)}$ and the strategy premium $\frac{1}{\left(1-\frac{1}{\xi}\right)}$, which depends on the elasticity of loan demand. The Janak Raj Committee Report (RBI 2017), which recommended migration to an external benchmark for bank loans, observed that both the credit spread and strategy premiums were manipulated by some banks to keep lending rates unchanged, even as market rates declined during the MCLR regime.

Comparative statics:

$$\frac{\partial r_L^*}{\partial p} = \frac{1}{(1-p)^2}\left[\frac{1}{1-\frac{1}{\xi}}\right](r + c_L) > 0$$

The higher the credit risk (p), the higher the equilibrium loan rate, to offset the losses from future loan defaults. As long as loans continue to perform, the bank earns more than the risk-free rate r.

$$\frac{\partial r_L^*}{\partial \xi} = -\frac{1}{(1-p)}\left[\frac{1}{(\xi-1)^2}\right](r + c_L) < 0$$

The higher the elasticity of loan demand, the lower the equilibrium loan rate. This is the familiar inverse elasticity pricing rule.

$$\frac{\partial r_L^*}{\partial r} = \frac{1}{(1-p)}\left[\frac{1}{1-\frac{1}{\xi}}\right] > 0$$

As the risk-free rate rises, the equilibrium loan rate increases more, given the margin. Therefore, those loans which are linked to the external benchmark (e.g. personal loans in India) become more profitable cet. par. (i.e. ceteris paribus) as the risk-free rate increases. However, those loans which are not priced off the market benchmark (e.g. corporate loans) may not be as profitable after the policy rate is hiked. This may be one reason why personal loan growth has been more robust than corporate credit in India during the rate hike phase since May 2022.

Proposition 1:

The equilibrium loan rate includes the credit spread and strategy premiums. Loans linked to the external benchmark become more profitable after policy rates are hiked.

Loan Demand

For simplicity, we assume an isoelastic loan demand curve, i.e. $\xi = b\forall\ (r_L, L)$

$$L = Ar_L^{-b},$$

where A is the market size (nominal output) and b (>1) is the constant elasticity of demand. Thus, optimal loan volumes can be represented as

$$L^* = \frac{A}{\left(r_L^*\right)^b}, \tag{10.4}$$

from which it follows (after substitution for r_L^*), from Equation (10.3),

$$\widehat{L^*} = \hat{A} + b\widehat{(1-p)} - b\widehat{(r + c_L)}. \tag{10.5}$$

Since b is constant, $\hat{b}$ is zero.

The "hat" symbol denotes proportional change or growth. The use of a proportional change operator was pioneered by Jones (1965).

Equation (10.5) captures a standard debt sustainability condition. Even with a rise in policy rates, loan growth may persist if (1) the market continues to expand and (2) the expected risk of loan defaults reduces at a faster rate.

Proposition 2:

Loan volumes may increase after policy rate hike, with an increase in market size and a reduction in credit risk.

It follows, from Proposition 2, that robust credit growth may be possible even after policy repo rates increase. If margins rise, the market expands and credit risk declines, loan volumes may continue to grow. The intertemporal implications of such a proposition are significant. In Section 10.2, we saw that if credit increases at present, future GDP growth may be higher. As a result, the market size will expand and encourage a sharper increase in loan volumes. The process will be accelerated if credit risk also declines. The rise in interest rates, during this cycle, may be a boon in disguise. It may prevent excessive credit growth or a lending boom which triggers future financial crises. In short, Equation (10.5) presents a condition under which an initial expansion in credit may be self-sustainable.

10.6 The Central Bank's Problem (Stage 1)

In this section, the central bank acts as a Stackelberg leader. It anticipates the equilibrium loan rates chosen by banks and fixes the policy rate, at the outset, to optimize its objective function.

We assume that the central bank tries to strike a balance between financial stability and price stability. It minimizes a quadratic loss function, which features the squared deviation of future NPL and inflation from their target levels. The perils of a high system-wide NPL, for the central bank, are well-documented. Too-low NPL levels (relative to the target) may also be dangerous. Such episodes could imply that banks take inadequate risk and earn low returns. A stream of low returns may erode capital adequacy and increase systemic risk.

At this point, it is important to clarify that NPLs may not constitute the only source of financial instability for an economy. The recent spate of bank failures in the US and Europe (IMF 2023) was triggered by a collapse in bond and deposit markets. However, we have chosen NPLs because we want to focus on the role of lending rates, which, in turn, are affected by policy repo rates.

The current period loss function for the central bank is as follows:

$$\text{Loss}_0 = \left(\text{NPL}_1 - \text{NPL}_e\right)^2 + \left(\theta_1 - \theta_e\right)^2 \tag{10.6}$$

$$\text{NPL}_1 = ar_{L0} - c\widehat{A_0} \tag{10.7}$$

$$\text{NPL}_e = ar_{Le} - c\hat{A}_e \tag{10.8}$$

Assumption 1: $a > c$.

For simplicity, the weights on financial stability and price stability are the same as in Equation (10.6).

In other words, we assume that future NPL is positively related to the current lending rate and declines with faster growth in the current market size or nominal GDP. The reason for the adverse impact of higher loan interest rates on NPL is straightforward. Higher loan interest rates adversely impact the financial positions of borrowers and increase the prospect of default. However, the rationale for the reduction in NPLs, with growth in the nominal GDP, needs some elaboration. First, the increase in real output or GDP will raise national income and reduce future NPLs. Second, a rise in price will, cet. par., improve business profitability and reduce NPLs. We also assume that the marginal impact of a rate hike on NPLs is stronger than the effect of nominal GDP growth (i.e. $a > c$).

We know that since $A_0 = P_0Y_0$

$$\widehat{A_0} = \hat{P}_0 + \hat{Y}_0 \tag{10.9}$$

or

$$\widehat{A_0} = \theta_0 + \hat{Y}_{0,} \tag{10.10}$$

where θ_0 is the current inflation in period 0. A similar derivation follows for $\widehat{A_e}$.

Substituting Equations (10.9) and (10.10) into Equation (10.6), we have

$$\text{Loss}_0 = \left[a\left(r_{L0} - r_{Le}\right) - c\left(\hat{Y}_0 - \hat{Y}_e\right) - c\left(\theta_0 - \theta_e\right)\right]^2 + \left[\theta_1 - \theta_e\right]^2. \tag{10.11}$$

Substituting equilibrium loan rates, from Equation (10.3), we have

$$\text{Loss}_0 = \left[a\left(\frac{1}{(1-p)}\right)\left(\frac{1}{\left(1-\frac{1}{b}\right)}\right)\left(r_0 - r_e\right) - c\left(\hat{Y}_0 - \hat{Y}_e\right) - c\left(\theta_0 - \theta_e\right)\right]^2 + \left[\theta_1 - \theta_e\right]^2. \tag{10.12}$$

After optimization of the loss function *w.r.t* r_0 and simplification we get

$$\frac{\partial \text{Loss}_0}{\partial r_0} = \left[a\left(\frac{1}{(1-p)}\right)\left(\frac{1}{\left(1-\frac{1}{b}\right)}\right)\left(r_0 - r_e\right) - c\left(\hat{Y}_0 - \hat{Y}_e\right) - c\left(\theta_0 - \theta_e\right)\right] = 0; \tag{10.13}$$

that is

$$r_0 = r_e + \left(\frac{c}{a}\right)(1-p)\left(1-\frac{1}{b}\right)\left(\hat{Y}_0 - \hat{Y}_e\right) + \left(\frac{c}{a}\right)(1-p)\left(1-\frac{1}{b}\right)(\theta_0 - \theta_e)$$

$$r_0 = r_e + w_1\left(\hat{Y}_0 - \hat{Y}_e\right) + w_2(\theta_0 - \theta_e), \tag{10.14}$$

where $w_1 = w_2 = \left[\frac{c}{a}\right](1-p)\left(1-\frac{1}{b}\right) < 1$, by Assumption 1.

Equation (10.14) represents a modified Taylor rule, with equal weights on current output growth and inflation gaps. It is noteworthy that Taylor himself had chosen equal weights in his seminal paper (Taylor 1993), to illustrate the eponymous monetary policy rule. The first implication of Equation (10.14) is that, if both inflation and GDP growth exceed their target levels, the central bank should increase the policy repo rate above its target but by less than the change in growth and inflation gaps. The reason is that, unlike the original Taylor proposal, a policy rate hike in our model will increase future NPLs as well. In particular, if (c/a) is low and p is high, the weights on inflation and growth gaps (in Equation (10.14)) will be low. Large deviations from target growth and inflation levels will elicit smaller policy rate responses. Therefore, some degree of price stability may have to be sacrificed at present to ensure financial stability in future.

The second point is that the coefficients of the growth and inflation gaps are no longer arbitrary. The original Taylor rule is a heuristic, with the coefficients chosen by the central bank. In a world where the central bank is as concerned with financial stability as inflation control, Equation (10.14) shows how it could construct optimal weights from macro-financial data. The weights depend on the following factors: (i) relative impact of nominal GDP growth and lending rate on future NPL (ii) probability of default and (iii) elasticity of loan demand. In this paper, we derive the Taylor rule and its coefficients from first principles.

Comparative Statics:

$$\frac{\partial r_0}{\partial\left(\frac{c}{a}\right)} = \left[(1-p)\left(1-\frac{1}{b}\right)\right]\left\{\left(\widehat{Y}_0 - \hat{Y}_e\right) + (\theta_0 - \theta_e)\right\} > 0 \tag{10.15}$$

With a stronger impact of output growth and weaker transmission from lending rate changes to NPL (i.e. higher (c/a)), the policy rate should increase when growth and inflation are above their target levels. The central bank can focus on inflation control rather than the repercussions on financial stability.

$$\frac{\partial r_0}{\partial p} = -\left[(c/a)\left(1-\frac{1}{b}\right)\right]\left\{\left(\widehat{Y}_0 - \hat{Y}_e\right) + (\theta_0 - \theta_e)\right\} < 0 \tag{10.16}$$

As the PD increases, the policy rate should decline, even when growth and inflation are above their target levels. This is another instance of a compromise of the price stability objective, given the threat of financial instability.

$$\frac{\partial r_0}{\partial b} = \left[\left(\frac{c}{a}\right)(1-p)\left(\frac{1}{b^2}\right)\right]\left\{\left(\widehat{Y}_0 - \hat{Y}_e\right) + \left(\theta_0 - \theta_e\right)\right\} > 0 \tag{10.17}$$

As loan demand elasticity (b) increases, the policy rate should also rise. With more elastic loan demand, the impact of a rate increase on positive output and inflation gaps will be stronger.

The moral of the story is summarized as follows:

Proposition 3:

The threat of financial instability will constrain the management of price stability.

The linkage between Stage 1 and Stage 2, of the model, is straightforward. The spectre of financial instability does not allow the central bank to recommend a steep hike in the policy rate, vide Equation (10.14). The consequent rise in loan rates, vide Equation (10.3), is also moderate. As a result, the growth in loan volume, vide Equation (10.4), is not dampened. It continues to support economic activity. As already discussed, if external conditions are favourable (i.e. market size registers healthy growth and credit risk is on the decline), a virtuous cycle of credit and GDP growth may follow.

What happens when growth and inflation are below their target levels? The simple answer is that the rate cut is less than the size of the negative gaps. The same principle applies here as well – the fear of a financial crisis that often follows an extreme easy money policy will prevent the central bank from a large rate cut.

10.7 Recent US Experience

In this section, we analyse recent US macro-financial data to evaluate the impact of its monetary policy response to inflationary pressure. We illustrate the trends below.

Even before real GDP growth in the United States had recovered from the slowdown after the pandemic, inflationary headwinds were visible, which were exacerbated by geopolitical tensions in Europe. The US Fed took delayed but sharp action in consecutive monetary policies starting from March 2022. Within one year, it had administered a 475-bps increase in the Fed Funds rate (Figure 10.9). However, the credit markets in the US had not yet stabilized. In fact, credit growth rates began to decline, after the rebound from the

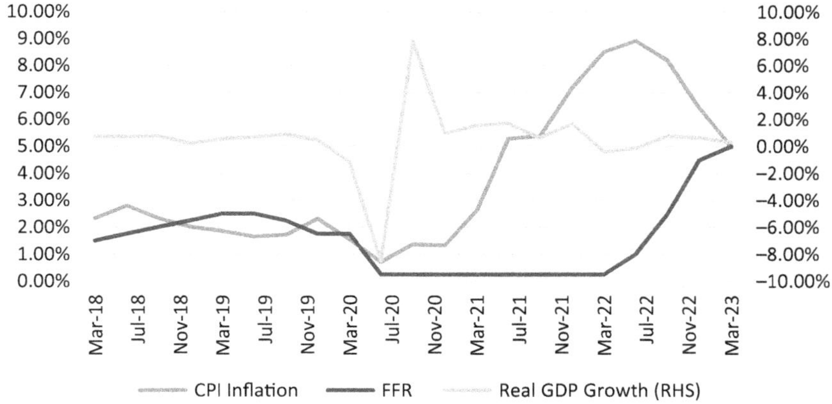

Figure 10.9 Trends in Real Gross Domestic Product (GDP) Growth, Consumer Price Index (CPI) Inflation and Policy Rate in the US.

Note: FFR = federal fund rate.

Source: Federal Reserve Board, US and NY Fed Reserve.

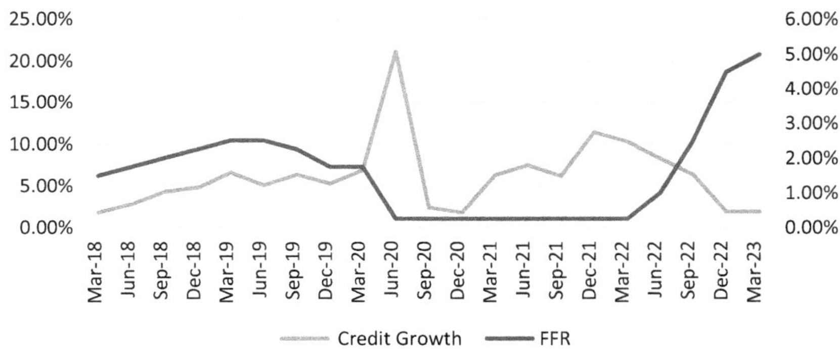

Figure 10.10 Credit Growth and Policy Rate Movements in the US.

Note: FFR = federal fund rate.

Source: Federal Reserve Board, US and NY Federal Reserve.

pandemic, when the monetary tightening started (Figure 10.10). Furthermore, the credit risk (delinquency rates) of different loan segments had also not fallen enough (Figure 10.11). In terms of our model (Equation (10.5)), the conditions were not ideal for large rate hikes targeted at price stability. On an almost one-to-one basis, the rate shocks were passed onto credit (Figure 10.12). Such transmission may trigger potential financial instability, as seen by the escalating delinquencies in consumer loans (Figure 10.11). The policy rate spikes have not only shaken bond and deposit markets since 2022, but may also have sown the seeds of the next credit crisis in the US.

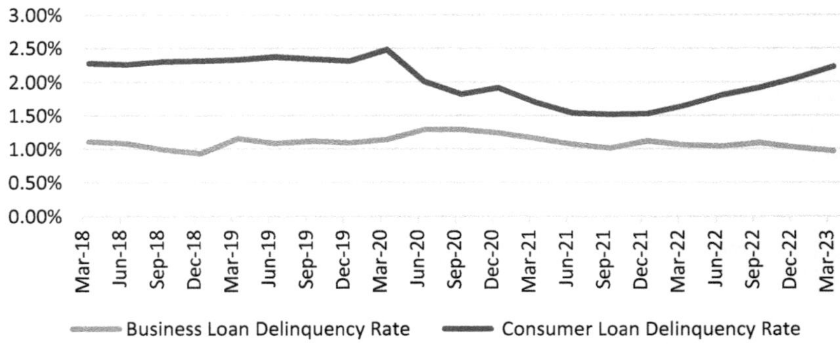

Figure 10.11 Delinquency Rates in US Loan Segments.
Source: Federal Reserve Board, US and NY Fed Reserve.

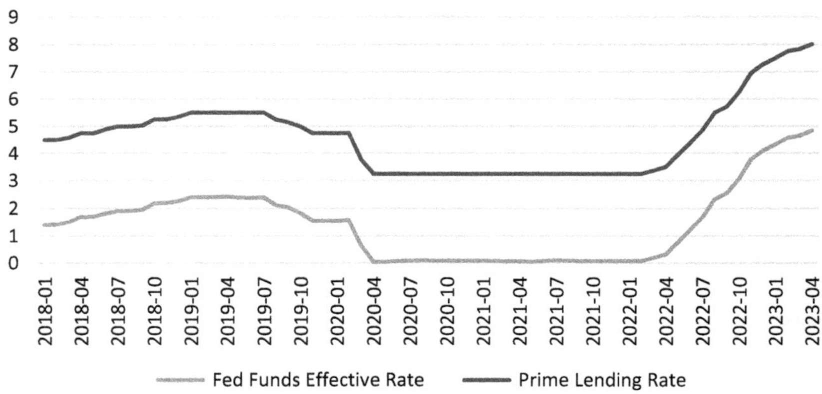

Figure 10.12 Co-movement of Fed Funds Effective Rate and Prime Lending Rate.
Source: Federal Reserve Board, US and NY Fed Reserve.

In short, the US experience offers a stark contrast to the Indian case, discussed in Section 10.2. It also shows that, if initial conditions are not favourable, sharp rate hikes aimed at price stability may instead engender financial instability. This is what our theoretical framework suggests as well.

10.8 Conclusion

In this chapter, we try to understand why robust credit growth may occur, even after sustained rate hikes. We find that such a phenomenon is possible if (1) loans are linked to an external benchmark, (2) the size of the credit market expands and (3) loan quality improves over time. We also investigate the challenges faced by a central bank that aims to manage both price and financial stability, with the policy rate. We observe that such an institution should follow a modified Taylor rule, with equal emphasis on current growth and inflation gaps. It has to monitor the elasticity of loan demand in the economy, the default risk of different loan categories and the impact of GDP growth and lending rates on NPLs. Such macro-financial information will help the central bank improve its monetary policy rules.

There are a few directions in which this work can be extended. First of all, in order to focus on financial stability, the central bank may lose sight of price stability in future. Many central banks have paused rate hikes while others have slowed down in the wake of the recent bank collapse in the US and Europe. This aspect appears in our work as well. Though the future inflation gap ($\theta_1 - \theta_e$) is a central bank target in Equation (10.12), it drops out of the subsequent optimization programme altogether. However, this happens due to the design of our problem. In subsequent analysis, we may examine how financial stability considerations may make the central bank myopic and less attentive to future price stability.

Second, we have used only one instrument – policy rate change – to address both price and financial stability issues. Further ahead, macro-prudential tools like Countercyclical Capital Buffer, for management of financial stability can also be considered. This will allow the central bank more freedom to use policy rates for price stability. In this chapter, we have employed a simple model in which banks are funded only by debt. The inclusion of equity capital (or net worth) in future will enrich the analysis further. It will enable us to study the combined impact of two devices on multiple targets.

Finally, our model should incorporate the oft-documented non-linear relationship between market rates and bank assets. Financial instability may occur – in the loan and bond markets – only when rates are high enough. A preliminary analysis suggests that the task is not simple. We need to assess the objective function of the central bank at low and intermediate market rates as well. We need to identify the location of a possible kink or break in the function and investigate its implications.

The history of financial crises has shown that a meltdown is often preceded by a prolonged decline in policy rates, followed by a sudden rise that acts as the trigger. Such a behaviour needs to be changed. If *unconventional monetary policy* can be used after the global financial crisis and the failure of Silicon Valley Bank (i.e., ex post), why can conventional monetary policy not be employed before crises occur (i.e., ex ante)? Our analysis shows that consideration of financial instability makes traditional monetary policy more conservative. The resultant policy decisions should bode well for the financial sector.

Note

1 We thank Saibal Ghosh for suggesting that management of financial stability, rather than output stability, should be a more appropriate goal of monetary policy at present.

References

Adrian, T., G. D. Ariccia, V. Haksar and T. M. Griffolli (2018): Monetary Policy and Financial Stability, in T. Adrian, D. Laxton and M. Obstfeld eds. *Advancing the Frontiers of Monetary Policy*, Chapter 6, International Monetary Fund, Washington DC.

Adrian, T. and F. Duarte (2022): *Financial Vulnerability and Monetary Policy*, Federal Reserve New York Conference, September.

Aikman, D., A. Lehnert, N. Liang and Michele Modungno (2020): Credit, Financial Conditions, and Monetary Policy Transmission, *International Journal of Central Banking*, Volume 16(1), 141–179.

Akinci, O., G. Benigno, M. Del Negro and A. Queralto (2022): *The Financial (In) Stability Real Interest Rate, R***, Federal Reserve New York Conference, September.

Altunbas, Y., L. Gambacorta and D. Marqués-Ibáñez (2010): Does Monetary Policy affect Bank Risk Taking? *European Central Bank Working Paper Series, No. 1166*, March.

Barro, R. and Gordon (1983): Rules, Discretion and Reputation in a Model of Monetary Policy, *Journal of Monetary Economics*, 12(1), 101–121

Bernanke, B. and A. Blinder (1988): Credit, Money and Aggregate Demand, *American Economic Review*, 78(2), 435–439.

Bernanke, B. and A. Blinder (1992): The Federal Funds Rate and the Channels of Monetary Transmission, *American Economic Review*, 82(4), 901–921.

Blanchard, O (2018): *Macroeconomics*, 7th Edition, Pearson India, New Delhi.

Caruana, J (2015): Revisiting monetary policy frameworks in the light of macroprudential policy, Panel Remarks at the *IMF Seminar on 'Revisiting Monetary Policy Frameworks'*, 10th October, 2015, Bank of International Settlements.

Clarida, R., J. Galí and M. Gertler (1999): The Science of Monetary Policy: A New Keynesian Perspective, *Journal of Economic Literature*, 37(4), 1661–1707.

Dornbusch, R., S. Fischer and R. Startz (1998): *Macroeconomics*, 7th Edition, Irwin McGraw Hill, New York, US.

Dutt, A.K. and A. Sen (1997): Union Bargaining Power, Employment and Output in a Model with Monopolistic Competition and Wage Bargaining, *Journal of Economics*, 65 (1), 1–17

Federal Reserve (2023): *Review of the Federal Reserve's Supervision and Regulation of Silicon Valley Bank*, Board of Governors of the Federal Reserve System, April 28.

Freixas, X. and J-C Rochet (2008): *Microeconomics of Banking*, 2nd Edition, MIT Press, Cambridge, MA.

Gibbons, R. (1992): *Game Theory for Applied Economists*, Princeton University Press, Princeton, NJ.

Gylfason, T. and A. Lindbeck (1994): The Interaction of Monetary Policy and Wages, *Public Choice*, 79, 33–46.

IMF (2023): *Global Financial Stability Report*, Chapter 1, April.

Jimenez, G., D. Kuvshinov, J.-L. Peydro and B. Richter (2023): Monetary Policy, Inflation and Crises: New Evidence from History and Administrative Data, *Barcelona School of Economics Working Paper 1378*, May.

Jones, R. (1965): The Structure of Simple General Equilibrium Models, *Journal of Political Economy*, 73(6), 557–572.

Kashyap, A. and J. Stein (2000): What Do a Million Observations on Banks Say about the Transmission of Monetary Policy? *American Economic Review*, 90(3), 407–428

Rajan, R. (2023): Not Buying Central Banks' Favourite Excuse, *Project Syndicate*, May 26.

RBI (2017): *Report of the Internal Study Group to Review the Working of Marginal Cost of Funds Based Lending Rate System*, September.

Sen, A. (1996): Imperfect Competition and the Interaction of Monetary Policy and Wages: An Extension of Gylfason and Lindbeck, *Indian Economic Review*, 31(2), 235–240.

Svensson, L. (2010): Inflation targeting after the financial crisis, Speech at International Conference, *Challenges to Central Banking in the Context of the Financial Crisis*, February 12.

Taylor, J. (1993): Discretion versus Policy Rules in Practice, *Carnegie-Rochester Conference Series on Public Policy*, 39, 195.

11 Evolving Nature of Women Empowerment in India

Manisha Chakrabarty and Arpita Kundu

11.1 Introduction

The term *empowerment* is described as a process of gaining freedom and power to do what you want or to control what happens to you. The World Bank defines empowerment as "the process of enhancing an individual's or group's capacity to make purposive choices and to transform those choices into desired actions and outcomes". In literature, women empowerment is considered to be an important indicator of a nation's economic growth, poverty reduction and overall well-being of children, thereby having intergenerational impacts (Agarwal, 1994; Duflo, 2012; World Development Report, 2012).

Women empowerment has therefore been included in the Sustainable Development Goals emphasizing gender equality. This includes equal rights in every sphere of life, particularly in the workplace, and the betterment of their health. According to the World Economic Forum's data-based Global Gender Gap Index 2022, constituting four sub-indicators as women's economic participation, political representation, health and survival, and educational attainment, developed countries such as Iceland, Finland, Norway, New Zealand and Sweden secure top five positions in terms of gender gap. Among these countries, Iceland has nearly closed its gender gap by attaining a female health and survival rate of 96.4% and an educational attainment rate of 99.9%. In the corporate sector also, women are representing both the senior positions in the administration as well as board members. According to the Women Business and the Law Index (2020), released by the World Bank in 2020, comprising *eight indicators*: mobility, workplace, pay, marriage, parenthood, entrepreneurship, assets and pension, developed countries such as Belgium, Canada, Denmark, France and Iceland have scored a perfect 100 out of 100 marks, and other high-income-based Organisation for Economic Co-operation and Development (OECD) countries also have pretty high scores as opposed to developing countries. According to the Global Nutrition Report (2016), which uses the WHO Global Database on the Implementation of Nutrition Action (GINA), the top five performers are the US, Chile, Nicaragua, Vietnam and Mexico.

DOI: 10.4324/9781003509721-14

India unfortunately is far away from reaching these objectives, although the principle of gender equality is enshrined in the Indian Constitution in its Preamble. It has ranked 140 out of 156 countries on the list in the World Economic Forum's Global Gender Gap Report (2022). In terms of labor force participation also, India ranks 120 among 131 countries. According to Women Business and the Law Index (2020), India stands at the 117th position out of 190 countries. Not only in terms of workforce participation, India's women are at a grim stage also in terms of nutritional status according to the Global Nutrition Report (2016).

Against this backdrop, several studies attempt to examine women's empowerment and its association with sociodemographic indicators such as fertility rate, children's health and educational outcomes, and women's own health using Indian data. The paper by Singh et al. (2018) shows that there is a strong positive impact of women's household decision-making power on their propensity to use contraceptives. Women's empowerment is not only beneficial for themselves but is also linked to the betterment of a child's nutritional status. A study based on three rounds of the National Family Health Survey (NFHS) by Katsushi et al. (2014) shows that a mother's education is associated with a child's educational outcome in the short run. By comparison, they also find strong associations between women's empowerment and the nutritional status of children in the long run. Donta et al. (2015) have observed that empowered women have a lesser probability of facing domestic violence using a sample of married women aged between 15 and 39 years residing in a slum in Mumbai.

A study by Yadav et al. (2021), using NFHS-IV (2015–16) data, has shown that economically independent women are more likely to get better maternal care and maternity-related assistance from family members as compared to women who are economically dependent on their spouses. Contrary to the previously mentioned findings, the paper by Pathak (2022) using NFHS-III (2004–05) and NFHS-IV (2015–16) unit-level data, shows that "[e]ducation's mitigating effects on intimate partner violence (IPV) are weakening over the decade. It is observed that working women have a higher likelihood of IPV, which has not declined over the decades".

The other thread of studies focuses on the determinants of women's empowerment. A study by Bushra and Aajiha (2015), using a sample of 200 women from renowned universities of Lahore, shows that education, poverty and economic opportunities available for women increase their empowerment. In this study apart from conventional determinants, women having a bank account also turned out to be a significant channel to improve women empowerment. Another paper by Bhatt and Shastri (2018), based on a self-help group of women in the state of Gujarat in India, has described that loan amounts and women's autonomy to spend the borrowed money impact women's empowerment most. We follow this line of investigation in an attempt to find determinants to explain the women's empowerment movement.

Our chapter starts with building a multidimensional Women Empowerment index by using several sub-indices. Second, we investigate the evolution of women's empowerment over a span of 5 years. For our purpose, therefore, we use two rounds of NFHS data, namely, NFHS-IV (2015–16) and the most recent NFHS-V (2019–21), which enable us to examine the trend of women's empowerment post the National Policy for the Empowerment of Women (2001), sufficiently long time to evaluate the goals, stated to be achieved by 2010. Also, this time span experienced the launching of some policies post-2014 aimed at tackling age-old social evils against women, such as Beti Bachao Beti Padhao Yojna, Pradhan Mantri Surakshit Matriva Abhiyan and others at the center level. This is more important given the United Nation's 2030 agenda of Sustainable Development Goals (SDG). Third, given the fact that India is a heterogeneous country with varied socioeconomic backgrounds and compositions along with India's federal structure with different state-level policies, it is imperative to investigate the heterogeneity. Hence, we attempt to examine the heterogeneity at the district level, the lowest identifiable unit for which the data are available.[1] Next, we attempt to build an association between women's empowerment and the socioeconomic and demographic indicators, considered to be important determinants in describing women's empowerment. We also use census data (2011) for several population-related variables in our empirical model. Our results for two rounds separately indicate the dominance of family-level demographics and educational variables in explaining women's empowerment (WEMP) compared to socioeconomic and sociodemographic variables.

The chapter is structured as follows: In Section 11.2, we provide more details of existing work in this area beyond India and the background of our empirical model, Section 11.3 describes the data, and Section 11.4 describes the methodology and the empirical model; results are described in Section 11.5, and our conclusions are given in Section 11.6.

11.2 Literature Review on Women's Empowerment

Recent studies have focused on finding the causal relationship between the Women Empowerment Index on other socioeconomic and demographic outcomes. These studies mostly examined the incidence of the presence or absence of women empowerment across African countries and Asian countries.

Most of these studies consider the impact of women's empowerment on the growth of the economy (Saqib, 2016), children's health and nutritional status (Yaya et al., 2020), fertility rates (Chakrabarty et al., 2022) and the educational status of women (Abbas et al., (2021).

While the previously mentioned studies focus on the explanatory power of women's empowerment, there are quite a few studies that also investigate the explanatory power of several community levels, socioeconomic and demographic factors and policy changes in describing women's empowerment. To name a few, a study by Mason and Smith (2003), using data on 56 communities spanning five Asian countries (India, Malaysia, Pakistan, the Philippines, Thailand), has found that community-level factors such as gender relations, community norms and values are stronger predictors of women empowerment in those communities. A recent study by Anukriti (2020) shows that "co-residence with the mother-in-law is negatively correlated with her daughter-in-law's mobility and ability to form social ties outside the household, especially those related to health, fertility, and family planning". Hence, overall intergenerational power dynamics negatively affect WEMP, especially in the context of rural India.

The major driving forces implied by these studies are government policies such as increasing the age of marriage, implementing flexible hours and workplace allotment in a development program like MGNREGA in India and political representation of women through changing the reservation policy in the electoral process (see Chattopadhyay & Duflo, 2001), gender equality–driven labor market policies, changing community-level values and gender norms and enhancing the opportunities for educational attainment.

Taking the cue from these studies, we develop our model to explain the incidence and variation of women empowerment across districts of the major 19 states of India.[2] Table 11.1 describes the plausible list of variables and associated references for our model described in Section 11.4.

Table 11.1 Plausible set of variables and related literature

Categories	*Variable*	*Source*
Demographic	**Total number of children (fertility)**	Upadhyay et al. (2014): women empowerment was inversely associated with number of children born to a woman.
	Age of first child	Nava et al. (2020): delaying the first childbirth could improve women's educational and economic opportunities and their health.
Sociodemographic	**Age of marriage**	Kishore and Gupta (2004): Early marriage/cohabitation at younger age reduces opportunities for sufficient education and skill formation, impeding proper physical and mental development of women.
Socioeconomic	**Poverty**	Ravindra and Tiwari (2016): empirically establish a negative association between self-help groups of women and poverty within household

(*Continued*)

Table 11.1 (Continued)

Categories	*Variable*	*Source*
Family Structure	**Household head's education**	World Bank Report (2011): a higher level of education of household head positively influences women's autonomy.
	Percentage of joint families in the district	Dyson and Moore (1983), Dixon-Muller (1989), Anukriti (2020): residing in nonnuclear families is likely to affect women's ability to access resources and to exercise decision-making control.
Educational	**Women's level of education**	Kaur (2010): education is the aid for empowering women by helping them respond to the challenges that they have to face and gain status and respect in society

Source: Authors.

11.3 Data Description

This study uses district-level data mainly from two sources, namely, (a) Census data of India for 2011 and (b) the NFHS for 2015–16 (NFHS-IV) and 2019–21 (NFHS-V). For the empirical model, we consider demographic data from Census 2011 that are most recent with the NFHS rounds.[3] These are used in conjunction with the women empowerment and other covariates derived from NFHS rounds.

The NFHS is a large-scale survey conducted in a representative sample of households throughout India that began in 1992–93. The survey provides information for India on fertility, infant and child mortality, the practice of family planning, maternal and child health, nutrition, anemia, utilization and quality of health and family planning services, status of women, domestic violence and more.

The purpose of our main study is to examine the evolution of women empowerment in India and its relationship with covariates. The time period corresponds to several gender-based policy measures adopted both at the center and state levels, such as Beti bachao beti paddao, Ujjwala yojana, Nari Shakti Puraskar and the Women Helpline Scheme from the Ministry of Women and Child Development; similarly, at the state level, different state governments have taken schemes like Kanyashri in West Bengal, Streesakthi in Karnataka and Mahila Sakti Mission by the Uttar Pradesh (UP) government for empowering women. These two rounds of NFHS data also come after the National Policy of Women Empowerment (2001),[4] which stated the target of 2010 to achieve the measurable goals, described within the policy. This decade also experienced social changes caused by the spread of internet usage and social networks,[5] which may have changed the social dynamics and norms. According to Lemire et al. (2008), the internet is widely used for personal empowerment by facilitating health-related awareness, such as using contraceptives, information about maternal health care checkups and other personal hygiene and health care–related information. The paper by Mackey et al. (2021) also reveals that technology played a variety of roles in the development of women's capabilities in the overarching areas of outreach (e.g., health promotion), education (e.g., health literacy opportunities), lifestyle (e.g., peer coaching and planning), prevention (e.g., screening opportunities), health challenges (e.g., intimate partner violence apps) and perceptions of barriers (i.e., uptake, utilization and ubiquity of information and communication technology (ICT) for women).

For our empirical methodology, the major demographic covariates at the district level, such as the percentage of Scheduled Caste & Scheduled Tribe population (%SCST population), the percentage of the population that is Hindu (%Hindu), the percentage of the population that is Muslim (%Muslim population) and female–male sex ratio are taken from Census data of 2011. The household-related variables such as age at cohabitation, number of children ever born, and family structure are obtained using NFHS data. Variables from the individual level data of NFHS are converted into district-weighted averages by taking sample weight, given for each sampled women member in the data. Table 11.A1 in the Appendix describes the data source for each of our relevant variables.

We considered all districts from 19 major states of India covering four regions, namely, North (Uttar Pradesh, Rajasthan, Punjab, Uttarakhand, Himachal Pradesh, and Haryana), Central-East (Madhya Pradesh, Bihar, Assam, West Bengal, Chhattisgarh, Jharkhand, Odisha), West (Maharashtra and Gujarat) and South (Karnataka, Kerala, Tamil Nadu, Andhra Pradesh).

The variations in the level of socioeconomic development and the associated status of several indicators depicting women's health, education and other cultural factors across states of different regions motivate us to consider these states for our analysis.

- According to the report by Jukariya et al. (2018), a state like Rajasthan has a very skewed sex ratio with low literacy status of women. The participation of women in the tertiary sector such as medical, teaching, administrative and other official services is also lower than the male population. According to a report based on 2011 Census data, 42% of women experience spousal violence in Rajasthan. According to the NFHS III, only one-third of the girls aged between 15 and 17 years attend school in rural Uttar Pradesh (UP), and each year the dropout rate in rural areas of UP among women is as high as 72%; in terms of workforce participation rate also, according to the Census 2011, it is only 17% across the districts of UP. In the case of Punjab, although the state is highly developed in terms of assets, discrimination against women is quite prominent (Kaur, 2010). In the case of Uttarakhand, despite the existence of a large number of schemes for women's welfare, mostly women are deprived of such facilities in these development programs due to patriarchal constraints such as restricted movement outside the local territory (Nautiyal, 2003). Similarly, in Haryana, there exists a low level of literacy among women, the incidence of harassment of women in the household, a lack of financial and community-based support and the existing practice of child marriage [Bala & Namita (2015)].

- In the central-eastern zone, we have considered Madhya Pradesh, Bihar, West Bengal, Chhattisgarh, Jharkhand, Assam, and Odisha. According to a report by *Times of India*,[6] in Bihar, the prevalence of the caste system leads to aggravated discrimination against women, and as a result, an average unskilled Dalit woman is paid far less than an upper-caste woman doing the same job. Dowry (Sahay, 2017), domestic violence (Satija, 2013) and sex-selective abortion (Arnold et al., 2004) are some of the crucial menaces of the state of Bihar. In Madhya Pradesh, 38% of the women surveyed during NFHS 2, had body mass index (BMI) <18.5, and the number increased to 42% during NFHS 3, which shows that the percentage of undernourished women is not only higher than the national average but over time it is also increasing (Tiwari, 2009). In the case of West Bengal, although the literacy rate is higher than the national average, the incidence of domestic violence is still very high (40.3%; Sarkar, 2010). According to a report by Niti Aayog's SDG India Index report (2020–21), Chhattisgarh, by comparison, ranks quite high in development measures due to a balanced sex ratio at birth, improvement in equity in wage payment and lower crime rate against women, among others. A report based on the Annual Health Survey (2010–2011), Jharkhand scores poorly on female literacy; only 56.21% of females are literate, with a poor sex ratio of 947 per 1000 males. Moreover, this survey also mentions that this state fares poorly on other development indicators related to women such as 17.6% of women are married before the age of 18 years, and institutional delivery is 37.6% only in Jharkhand (Kumari, 2019). Nayak et al. (2009) have shown that certain indicators of women empowerment like participation of women in government services, and political decision-making bodies are very low in Assam also.
- In the southern region, we have considered Andhra Pradesh, Tamil Nadu, Karnataka and Kerala. According to a study by Shivaleela et al. (2018), Karnataka has improved significantly in terms of women's empowerment and education. Now, women have 3.4% representation in Vidhan Sabha. Kondal (2014), based on the survey of self-help groups of the Medak district of Andhra Pradesh, has found that the involvement of women in self-help groups (SHGs) has a major positive impact on women empowerment. Not only in Andhra Pradesh but also in Tamil Nadu, microfinance has played a very crucial role in improving women's empowerment (Sultana, Abdul Jamal, and Najaf, 2017). In Kerala also, the condition of women working particularly in the informal sector is very poor as they are mostly casual or irregular type of workers who receive lower wages than men working in the same field/factory (Eapen, 2001).

- From the western region, we have chosen two states: Maharashtra and Gujarat. In Gujarat, there exists strong evidence of dowry (Anukriti, 2020). The study conducted by the International Institute of Population Sciences (2006) using Census data of 2001 reveals that in Maharashtra, more than 40% of the women have a BMI of less than 18.5, and more than 48% of women suffer from anemia due to malnutrition.

Such heterogeneity across states is also quite evident in Figure 11.2 in the Result section. However, the figure, across two rounds, indicates an improvement in women's position over the years.

11.4 Description of the Model and Hypothesis Building

We construct an index of WEMP using four dimensions such as knowledge, health, and decision-making process within the household and outside the household.[7] The list of variables within each domain is described in Figure 11.1. This is very similar to the one constructed by Chakrabarty et al. (2022).

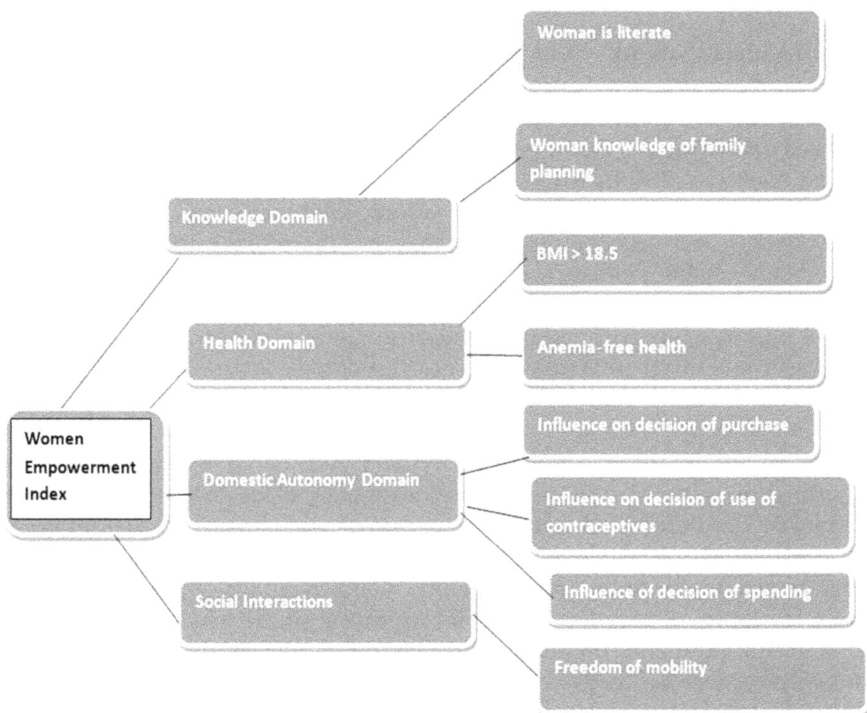

Figure 11.1 Definition of Women Empowerment.

Source: Authors.

We use a simple weighted average of these four components with equal (1/4) weight given for each dimension to avoid any arbitrary weight distribution. The weights for the components within each dimension are distributed accordingly. Hence, our constructed index is derived as follows:

$$\text{WEMP} = \left[\frac{1}{8}^{*}(\text{literacy}) + \frac{1}{8}^{*}(\text{awareness about family plan}) + \frac{1}{8}^{**}(\text{BMI index}) + \frac{1}{8}^{*}(\text{anemia free health}) + \frac{1}{12}^{*}(\text{purchase power}) + \frac{1}{12}^{*}(\text{contraceptive power}) + \frac{1}{12}^{*}(\text{spending power}) + \frac{1}{4}(\text{Freedom of Mobility})\right]$$

Our choice of explanatory variable attempts to capture the channels as described in Akter and Chindarkar to explain the path of women's empowerment. Akter and Chindarkar (2019) describe primarily three channels to explain the path of women's empowerment:

a. **Individual capability** – Women's education, skills and employment increase access to economic opportunities and thereby increase women's empowerment (see also Duflo, 2012; Chen and Chindarkar, 2017).
b. **Asset endowment** – According to several other studies by Agarwal (1994) and Narayan (2005), women's holding of financial assets such as stocks, savings accounts and assets like livestock, land and so on, generate more autonomy and decision-making power for the women in the household and hence help in enhancing woman empowerment.
c. **Formal and informal institutional factors** – It is also observed that social ties and kinship with other women of the community help build self-respect and affect in fertility and health-related outcomes of the woman, thus affecting the status of women (Kabeer, 2000).

Following the described framework, we have considered several variables as described in Table 11.2 in our analysis capturing these channels, at the district level. The variables, such as mean years of schooling of household head, women's highest level of education and female labor force participation, serve as proxies for individual capability. The percentage of poor population and a few other district-level variables capturing social structure such as sex ratio, mean number of children ever born in a family, mean age at marriage and cohabitation act as proxy variables for the other two channels. We also consider some other control variables for our district-level analysis. These variables are the percentage of affirmative category population and the percentages of the population that are Hindu and Muslim. The data source of these variables can be traced from Table 11.A1 in the Appendix.

Table 11.2 Determining Variables in our Empirical Model

X_{1i}	%SCST
X_{2i}	%Hindu
X_{3i}	%Muslim
X_{4i}	Sex ratio
X_{5i}	Average number of children ever born
X_{6i}	Mean marriage to first birth interval
X_{7i}	Mean age of cohabitation
X_{8i}	% of poor population in that district
X_{9i}	Mean years of schooling of household head
X_{10i}	% of joint family
X_{11i}	Female workers' participation
X_{12i}	Women's highest year of education
X_{13i}	Use and intention of contraceptives

Source: Authors.

We use the following empirical model to examine the association between these variables and *WEMP* (Y_i) across districts for two rounds of data. This will not only help us determine the role of these factors in explaining WEMP but also help us examine the evolution of the importance of these factors in the time path of WEMP.

$$Y_i = \alpha + \sum_{k=1}^{13} \beta_k X_{ki} + \varepsilon_i, \tag{11.1}$$

where $i = 1 \ldots 536$ districts for NFHS IV and V.

The following Table 11.3 depicts the expected sign, derived from previous studies, and related mechanisms in explaining women's empowerment.

11.5 Description of Results

11.5.1 Women Empowerment

Before describing the methodology for finding the association between WEMP and covariates, let us focus on the graphical trends in women empowerment across different states of India over NFHS IV (2015–16) and NFHS V (2019–21). Figure 11.2 depicts this variation across states and the improvement in position except for the marginal improvement for the states Bihar, UP and West Bengal and the decline in the state of Punjab. [8] The worsening position of WEMP in Punjab is mainly driven by the decline in the sub-indices such as women's knowledge of family planning, anemia-free health, women's influence on household-related spending and freedom of mobility. [See Table 11.A2 in the appendix].

Table 11.3 Details of the Determining Variables

Independent Variable	*Expected Sign*	*Categories As Described in Table 11.1*	*Channel*	*Intuition*
%SCST	–	Sociodemographic	Formal Institutional Factors	Backward classes like SC/ST may have adverse effects on WEMP (Khubchandani, 2018).
%Hindu	–			Orthodox belief among most of the Hindu community creates adverse circumstances for women, such as early child marriage, dowry system, not educating girl child, etc. (Aggarwal, 2021).
%Muslim	–			Due to the perceived strict social norms imposed on women in that community, women are expected to be adversely affected.
Sex ratio (number of female/per 1000 males)	+	Demographic	Informal Institutional Factor	Sex ratio signifies equal birth status of male and women, the higher number of the girl children born may indicate absence of sex-selective bias, and therefore, the society is perceived to be more open-minded in terms of women's empowerment (Rogers 2007).
Average no. of children born to women	–			Higher number of children to a woman means most of her time is devoted for rearing and caring the child and therefore less time is left for her self- development (Atake & Ali, 2019).
Mean marriage to first birth interval	+			It is often found that in rural regions, females get married at the age of 18 or less and give birth to a child soon after that. This might affect not only her health but also educational achievement. Hence, an increase in this interval is good for enhancing women's capability. The timing of the first birth influences the number of children a woman bears throughout her reproductive period in the absence of any active fertility control, as mentioned by Gyimah (2003).
Mean age of cohabitation	+	Sociodemographic		This is also linked with the lack of educational opportunities and may force women to have early children if they are married at younger age.
% of poor population in that district	–	Socioeconomic	Endowment	Negatively affects WEMP due to lack of opportunities, especially women, to thrive through education, nutrition, and health (Ngoma and Mayimbo, 2017).

Mean yr of schooling of HH head	+	Family structure	Endowment	The more educated the household head, the higher the probability that the household head promotes more gender equality (Rashmi et al., 2022).
% of joint family	–/+		Informal Institutional Factor	This could work in both ways. It could be in a bigger family presence of an older generation may impose stricter norms. On the other hand, the presence of more female members could help in more ties, sharing of activities and therefore more time for self-development (Debnath, 2015).
Female workers' participation (%)	+	Socioeconomic	Capability	The economic power not only enables women to participate in decision-making but may also help in achieving outcomes such as more education for girl children within the family and better health status [(Sen, 1990).
Women's highest years of education	+	Educational	Capability	Overall, women's years of education are presumed to make a woman more empowered with more knowledge and more information. Education reduces inequalities and improves their status within the family and develops the concept of participation
Use and intention of contraceptives	+	Sociodemographic	Interaction between Formal and Informal Institutional Factors	Dhak et al. (2020) by using data on NFHS 4 have shown that the use of contraception among women and men can be critical to improving women's empowerment by controlling family size and birth interval.

Source: Authors.

Note: SC/ST = Scheduled Caste/Scheduled Tribe; WEMP = women empowerment; HH = household; NFHS = National Family Health Survey.

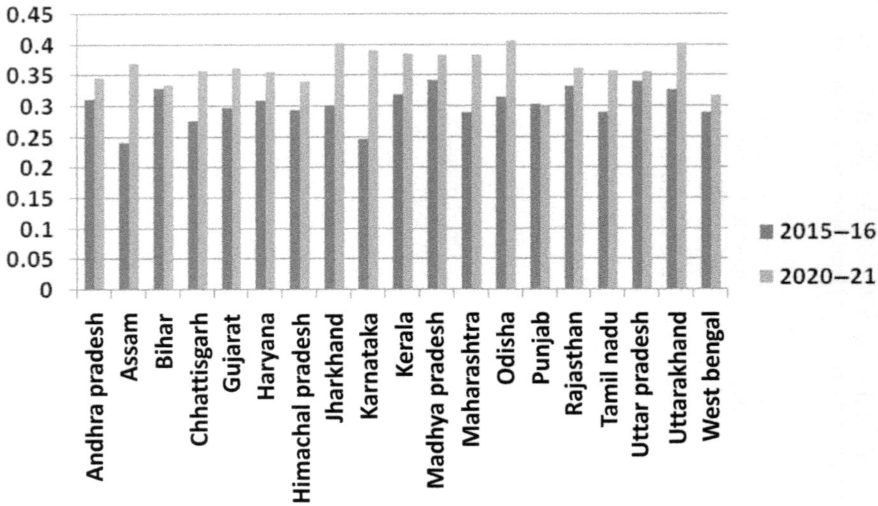

Figure 11.2 Mean WEMP across States for Two Rounds of the National Family Health Survey.

Source: Authors' calculation.

The heterogeneity across regions is quite evident when we construct the WEMP index at the district level. The districts in the southern region not only perform better in terms of empowering women but also remain in the top quintile of the distribution of the WEMP index. However, poor-performing districts in the central-eastern region have made certain improvements during this period, although they remain in the lower quintiles. In our empirical analysis, we attempt to ascertain which factors, as indicated in the literature determining women empowerment, at the district level, explain such variation and contribute more to the evolution of the measure of WEMP.

11.5.2 Descriptive Statistics of Determining Variables

As depicted in Table 11.4, we get an idea of the movement of our major determining variables. The data show that in 2019–21 in our sample, the percentage of Hindu population is 81.33% and about 11% population is Muslim, the sex ratio is 950 per 1000 males and % SCST is 28.37%.

The data shows that while there is an improvement in most of the determining variables during these 5 years, female workforce participation declined significantly during this period.[9] There is a drop in the marriage–to–first birth interval also in 2019–21 as compared to 2015–16. This period also experiences a 27% increase in the use of contraceptives at the district level.

Table 11.4 Descriptive Statistics: Major Determining Variables

Census Variables	*2011*	*NFHS Variables*	*2015–16*	*2019–21*
Hindu	81.333 (17.419)	Total number of children born to a women	2.437 (0.429)	2.323 (0.377)
Muslim	11.638 (12.642)	Marriage to first birth interval	56.037 (19.688)	48.686 (13.403)
Sex ratio	950.103 (54.250)	Age of cohabitation	18.342 (1.175)	18.737 (1.204)
SCST	28.375 (16.748)	Poor	42.179 (25.982)	41.696 (25.175)
		Mean years of schooling of household head	5.859 (1.336)	6.117 (1.309)
		Female workforce participation	32.097 (9.137)	15.013 (10.113)
		Percentage of joint family	27.085 (5.326)	26.565 (6.895)
		Women's highest year of education	4.050 (0.274)	4.141 (0.269)
		Use and intention of contraceptives	52.712 (16.174)	67.058 (10.789)

Source: Authors' calculation.

Note: NFHS = National Family Health Survey; SCST = Scheduled Caste/Scheduled Tribe.

11.5.3 Findings from the Empirical Model

We estimate Equation (11.1) by applying ordinary least squares (OLS) with the white's robust standard error. The Regression results are described in Table 11.5.

From Tables 11.A3–11.A5 in the Appendix, we may conclude that there is no occurrence of multicollinearity. There could be several omitted variables that could affect the incidence of women's empowerment.[10] There could be an endogeneity problem due to reverse causality for some variables such as 'total children ever born', 'age of cohabitation', 'marriage to first birth interval', and 'female workforce participation'. However, the issue of reverse causality is more prominent at the individual household level due to intra-household dynamics that may not be that strong at the aggregated levels such as districts. Therefore, we report OLS-based results to explain the association of WEMP and certain socioeconomic, sociodemographic and institutional variables.

As hypothesized in Section 11.4, most of the signs are as expected except marriage to first birth interval, though insignificant. The variables related to religion, caste composition and poverty do not have any significant impact

Table 11.5 Regression Results of the NFHS IV and NFHS V Rounds

Variables	*NFHS 4(2015–16)*	*NFHS 5(2019–21)*	*Evolution of WEMP*
Hindu	0.0000563 (0.553)	0.0001055 (0.301)	NA
Muslim	−0.0000358 (0.79)	0.0002139 (0.158)	
Sex ratio	0.0000876*** (0.000)	0.0000801*** (0.006)	
Total children ever born	−0.0251671*** (0.000)	−0.0258069*** (0.000)	−0.021** (0.004)
Marriage to first birth interval	−0.0000853 (0.189)	−0.0001572 (0.197)	−0.0001485* (0.042)
Age of cohabitation	0.0038201*** (0.003)	0.0068402*** (0.000)	0.0036948* (0.064)
Poor	−0.0000859 (0.193)	0.000027 (0.754)	−0.0001367 (0.539)
Mean years of schooling of household head	0.0098372*** (0.000)	0.0047413*** (0.000)	0.0052041*** 0.001
% of joint family	0.0000077 (0.97)	0.0007433*** (0.001)	0.0004117 0.213
Female workforce participation	0.0001957 (0.251)	0.0006796*** (0.000)	0.0001509 0.273
%SCST	−0.0000229 (0.801)	−0.0001436 (0.249)	NA
Women's mean years of schooling	0.0095547** (0.035)	0.0234809*** (0.000)	0.0069437 0.532
Use and intention of contraceptives	0.000252** (0.005)	0.0002949* (0.061)	0.0000801 0.509
No. of Observations	536	536	536
R^2	0.6206	0.4215	0.1346
Chi-square (White Test for Heteroscedasticity)	0.52 (.4692)	5.55 (.0185)	6.72 (.0095)

Source: Authors' calculation.

Note: Standard errors are robust. *p*-values are in parenthesis. NFHS = National Family Health Survey; WEMP = women empowerment; NA = not applicable; SCST = Scheduled Caste/ Scheduled Tribe.

* Means significant at 10% level, ** means significant at 5% level and *** means significant at 1% level.

on WEMP. The only significant coefficients we can find from this analysis are sex ratio, total children ever born, age of cohabitation, mean years of schooling of household head, women's mean year of education, female workforce participation, use of contraceptives and percentage of joint family, obtained from the NFHS. For example, in both years, a 1-unit increase in the total number of children will lead to a decrease in mean WEMP by approximately 2.5%. However, as expected, a 1-year increase in the age of cohabitation may lead to 0.38% increase in women's empowerment index in 2015–16, whereas in 2019–21, the effect increases to 0.68% and the effect is highly significant. In the year 2015–16 a 1% increase in mean years of schooling of the household head will lead to a 0.98% increase in the mean WEMP of that district with a 1% level of significance, similarly in the year 2019–21, a 1% increase in mean years of schooling of the household head will lead to 0.47% increase in the mean WEMP of that district. However, as expected, the positive impact of women's education on WEMP is more (1% and 2.3 % in 2015–16 and 2019–21, respectively). The impact of female workforce participation on WEMP is also positive, although not significant, in 2015–16. In this data set, joint family exerts a positive and significant effect, although only in 2019–21.

Another interesting factor affecting women's empowerment is the impact of the use and intention of contraceptives among people. The regression results show a positive and significant impact of this variable on WEMP. This might give us insights into the policy prescription through some interventions and knowledge-spreading activities by government agencies to spread awareness of such birth control mechanisms. Our results for two rounds, separately, therefore, indicate the dominance of family-level demographic, educational and family structure variables in explaining WEMP as compared to socioeconomic and sociodemographic variables.

The last column also corroborates these findings in explaining the evolution of WEMP and emphasizes the role played by the fertility and household head educational status capturing informal institutional factors. Nevertheless, the government can play a role in empowering women, which is also one of the crucial factors in today's SDG goal, by creating opportunities for education for girl children and hence facilitating the environment of more job opportunities for women.

11.6 Conclusion

Our chapter started with building a multidimensional Women Empowerment index by using several sub-indices. We investigated the evolution of women's empowerment over a span of 5 years. For our purpose, therefore, we used two rounds of NFHS data, namely, NFHS-IV (2015–16) and the most recent NFHS-V (2019–21), which enabled us to examine the trend of women's empowerment post the National Policy for the Empowerment of Women (2001), sufficiently long enough to evaluate the goals, stated to be achieved by 2010. We also used Census data (2011) for several population-related variables in our empirical model. This is more important given the United Nation's 2030 Agenda of Sustainable Development Goals. Given the fact that India is a heterogeneous country with varied socioeconomic backgrounds and compositions along with India's federal structure with different state-level policies, it is imperative to investigate the heterogeneity. We attempt to examine the heterogeneity at the district level, the lowest identifiable unit for which the data are available. Our results for two rounds separately indicate the dominance of family-level demographic, educational and family structure variables in explaining WEMP as compared to socioeconomic and sociodemographic variables.

Our analysis shows the significant positive impact of sex ratio, age of cohabitation, mean years of schooling of the household head, female worker's participation, education level and use and intention of contraceptives on mean women empowerment index at the district level.

In this chapter, we did not address the issue of endogeneity due to the aggregate-level analysis. Yet, there could be several unobserved factors explaining gender norms and social stigma that affect women's empowerment. To cite a few, one may mention the role played by the mother-in-law in the house in terms of household spending-related decision-making, fertility decisions, free mobility to health clinic–related decisions and the like. The importance of the Ghunghat or Purdah system (in Hindu and Muslim households respectively; Rao et al., 2004; Coffey et al., 2018) in explaining the attitude toward women and the practice of having meals after the male members, which may adversely affect women health, especially during pregnancy (Desai, 2010). These can be accommodated in the individual-level model using both primary and secondary surveys.

The current work can also be extended in several directions, such as (a) the impact of several gender-specific policies by the government both at the center and state levels and (b) a comparative cross-country analysis for similar developing countries, such as Pakistan, Bangladesh, Myanmar, Sri Lanka and others.

Notes

1 We would like to mention that NFHS-III (2004-05) does not provide district identifier and hence cannot be considered for our analysis, immediately after the National Policy of women Empowerment (2001).
2 These states comprise of 93.12% of total Indian population and 54.89% of female population of India.
3 However, for the 2019–21 round of NFHS, we cannot use Census of 2021 as the data are still unavailable; hence, we use 2011 data for this round of NFHS data also.
4 The immediate round of NFHS (2004–05) post-2001 policy cannot be considered due to unavailability of district identifier in the data.
5 According to internet world statistics, the use of internet jumped from 8% of world population in 2001 to 65% in 2020.
6 Extracted on April 22, 2011. Please see http://timesofindia.indiatimes.com/articleshow/8058458.cms?utm_source=contentofinterest&utm_medium=text&utm_campaign=cppst
7 According to United Nation, women empowerment means elimination of discrimination against women and girls, achievement of equality between women and men as partners and beneficiaries of development, human rights, humanitarian action and peace and security.

8 The corresponding numerical values are described in Table 11.A2 in the Appendix.
9 Note that the year 2019-21 corresponds to the COVID-19-affected period. According to CMIE data, as of December 2021, while the male LFPR was 67.4%, the female LFPR was as low as 9.4%.
10 We address these issues by considering state fixed effects in our model. However, that does not change the main findings of our regression results.

Appendix 11A

Table 11.A1 Variables Considered in Our Analysis

Dependent Variables	Women Empowerment	Education Domain	Women is literate	NFHS
			Woman has knowledge of family planning	NFHS
		Health Domain	BMI > 18.5	
			Anemia-free health	NFHS
		Domestic Autonomy Domain	Woman's influence on decision of purchase	NFHS
			Woman's influence on decision of using contraceptives	NFHS
			Woman's influence on decision of spending	NFHS
		Social Interactions	Women's freedom of mobility	NFHS
Independent Variables		Sociodemographic factors	%SCST	Census
			%Hindu	Census
			%Muslim	Census
		Demographic	Sex ratio (Female/ male)	Census
			Average no. of children born to women	NFHS
			Mean Marriage to first birth interval	NFHS
		Sociodemographic	Mean Age of cohabitation	NFHS
		Socioeconomic	%of poor population in that district	NFHS
		Family structure	Mean yr of schooling of HH head	NFHS
			% of joint family	NFHS
		Socioeconomic	Female worker's participation (%)	NFHS
		Educational	Women's highest years of education	NFHS
		Sociodemographic	Use and intention of contraceptives	NFHS

Source: Authors.

Note: NFHS = National Family Health Survey; BMI = body mass index; SCST = Scheduled Castes & Scheduled Tribes; HH = household.

Table 11.A2 Indicator-Wise Change over the Years

State	*Year*	*1. Knowledge Domain*		*2. Health Domain*		*3. Domestic Autonomy*			*4. Social Interactions*	*Women Empowerment Index*
		1.1. Woman is literate	*1.2. Woman has knowledge of family planning*	*2.1. BMI > 18.5*	*2.2. Anemia free health*	*3.1. Influence on decision on purchase and sales of household resources*	*3.2. Influence on decision on use of contraceptives*	*3.3 Influence on decision on spending*	*4.1 Freedom of mobility without concession*	
Andhra Pradesh	2015–16	0.160	0.702	0.816	0.641	0.021	0.041	0.012	0.013	0.311
	2019–21	0.575	0.467	0.848	0.651	0.012	0.067	0.008	0.012	0.346
Assam	2015–16	0.157	0.622	0.716	0.753	0.005	0.039	0.003	0.006	0.241
	2019–21	0.708	0.645	0.795	0.604	0.008	0.057	0.004	0.008	0.370
Bihar	2015–16	0.115	0.405	0.648	0.632	0.014	0.031	0.005	0.014	0.329
	2019–21	0.453	0.438	0.713	0.629	0.012	0.080	0.004	0.012	0.334
Chhattisgarh	2015–16	0.196	0.689	0.695	0.745	0.006	0.021	0.009	0.012	0.276
	2019–21	0.616	0.668	0.767	0.635	0.006	0.044	0.006	0.006	0.358
Gujarat	2015–16	0.149	0.543	0.737	0.682	0.037	0.041	0.016	0.024	0.298
	2019–21	0.622	0.529	0.764	0.589	0.012	0.054	0.008	0.012	0.362
Haryana	2015–16	0.127	0.761	0.809	0.575	0.007	0.061	0.005	0.010	0.311
	2019–21	0.610	0.715	0.854	0.634	0.007	0.057	0.004	0.007	0.356
Himachal Pradesh	2015–16	0.147	0.663	0.847	0.688	0.021	0.042	0.017	0.040	0.295
	2019–21	0.701	0.750	0.873	0.713	0.026	0.040	0.014	0.026	0.340
Jharkhand	2015–16	0.124	0.466	0.653	0.603	0.006	0.024	0.005	0.007	0.301
	2019–21	0.524	0.512	0.722	0.620	0.008	0.063	0.003	0.008	0.403
Karnataka	2015–16	0.122	0.722	0.791	0.741	0.015	0.063	0.011	0.014	0.248
	2019–21	0.635	0.837	0.834	0.734	0.012	0.090	0.011	0.012	0.391
Kerala	2015–16	0.041	0.768	0.898	0.845	0.024	0.029	0.013	0.017	0.319
	2019–21	0.649	0.716	0.902	0.825	0.015	0.035	0.014	0.015	0.386

Madhya Pradesh	2015–16	0.179	0.622	0.695	0.685	0.006	0.038	0.006	0.010	0.343
	2019–21	0.580	0.638	0.778	0.708	0.009	0.065	0.005	0.009	0.384
Maharashtra	2015–16	0.145	0.717	0.761	0.740	0.009	0.038	0.010	0.018	0.291
	2019–21	0.659	0.736	0.807	0.698	0.016	0.056	0.011	0.016	0.383
Orissa	2015–16	0.169	0.671	0.724	0.723	0.006	0.048	0.004	0.010	0.316
	2019–21	0.656	0.667	0.776	0.623	0.009	0.072	0.005	0.009	0.407
Punjab	2015–16	0.124	0.838	0.876	0.691	0.007	0.033	0.007	0.013	0.304
	2019–21	0.643	0.684	0.895	0.669	0.011	0.058	0.004	0.011	0.300
Rajasthan	2015–16	0.151	0.597	0.712	0.724	0.007	0.042	0.005	0.011	0.334
	2019–21	0.485	0.658	0.798	0.686	0.010	0.043	0.005	0.010	0.363
Tamil Nadu	2015–16	0.136	0.822	0.857	0.667	0.033	0.064	0.016	0.027	0.290
	2019–21	0.644	0.691	0.876	0.689	0.031	0.065	0.014	0.031	0.359
Uttarakhand	2015–16	0.147	0.775	0.799	0.735	0.012	0.053	0.006	0.015	0.327
	2019–21	0.564	0.743	0.850	0.770	0.011	0.074	0.006	0.011	0.403
Uttar Pradesh	2015–16	0.128	0.530	0.722	0.687	0.008	0.050	0.004	0.011	0.340
	2019–21	0.480	0.664	0.803	0.729	0.008	0.093	0.003	0.008	0.357
West Bengal	2015–16	0.210	0.533	0.770	0.646	0.008	0.052	0.011	0.011	0.290
	2019–21	0.697	0.610	0.835	0.562	0.012	0.071	0.008	0.012	0.318

Source: Authors' Calculation.

Table 11.A3 VIF for NFHS IV and NFHS V

Variables	*NFHS IV*	*NFHS V*
Hindu	2.33	2.02
Muslim	2.59	2.41
Sex ratio	1.89	1.45
Total children ever born	2.86	2.58
Marriage to first birth interval	1.41	1.33
Age of cohabitation	2.52	2.22
poor	3.33	2.64
Mean years of schooling of household head	1.56	1.53
% of joint family	1.4	1.53
Female Workforce Participation	2.32	1.43
%SCST	2.27	2.15
Women mean years of schooling	1.66	1.55
Use and intention of contraceptives	1.82	1.27

Source: Authors' Calculation.

Note: VIF = ; NFHS = National Family Health Survey; SCST = Scheduled Caste/Scheduled Tribes.

Table 11.A4 Correlation Matrix (NFHS Round IV)

	MEANWEMP	*Hindu*	*Muslim*	*Sex ratio*	*Total Children born*	*Marriage to first birth interval*	*Age of cohabitation*	*Poor*	*Mean years of schooling of household head*	*% of joint family*	*Female workers' participation*	*SCST*	*Women's highest year of schooling*	*Use and intention of contraceptives*
MEANWEMP	1													
Hindu	–0.082	1												
Muslim	–0.147	–0.570	1											
Sex ratio	0.297	0.065	–0.065	1										
Total children born	–0.644	0.108	0.129	–0.362	1									
Marriage to first birth interval	–0.280	0.226	–0.023	0.002	0.169	1								
Age of cohabitation	0.581	–0.306	–0.056	0.202	–0.559	–0.372	1							
Poor	–0.508	0.088	0.148	–0.031	0.535	0.184	–0.488	1						
Mean years of schooling of household head	0.619	–0.111	–0.039	0.055	–0.424	–0.242	0.543	–0.397	1					
% of joint family	–0.248	0.048	0.062	–0.344	0.431	0.003	–0.154	0.079	–0.110	1				
Female workers' participation	0.078	0.371	–0.375	0.528	–0.098	0.103	–0.150	0.198	–0.077	–0.198	1			
SCST	–0.056	0.074	–0.366	0.158	0.006	0.020	–0.110	0.389	–0.144	–0.007	0.487	1		
Women's highest year of schooling	0.263	–0.176	–0.146	–0.050	–0.047	–0.211	0.359	–0.452	0.278	0.040	–0.156	–0.163	1	
Use and intention of contraceptives	0.352	–0.050	–0.192	–0.042	–0.378	–0.361	0.191	–0.489	0.167	–0.094	–0.017	0.054	0.133	1

Source: Authors' calculations.

Note: NFHS = National Family Health Survey; MEANWEMP = ; SCST = Scheduled Castes/Scheduled Tribes.

Table 11.A5 Correlation Matrix (NFHS round V)

	MEANWEMP	*Hindu*	*Muslim*	*Sex ratio*	*Total Children born*	*Marriage to first birth interval*	*Age of cohabitation*	*Poor*	*Mean years of schooling of household head*	*% of joint family*	*Female workers' participation*	*SCST*	*Women's highest year of schooling*	*Use and intention of contraceptives*
MEANWEMP	1													
Hindu	–0.067	1												
Muslim	–0.057	–0.570	1											
Sex ratio	0.235	0.065	–0.065	1										
Total children born	–0.496	0.122	0.081	–0.352	1									
Marriage to first birth interval	–0.320	0.025	0.072	–0.220	0.438	1								
Age of cohabitation	0.514	–0.202	–0.098	0.182	–0.583	–0.376	1							
Poor	–0.364	0.053	0.159	0.013	0.388	0.203	–0.428	1						
Mean years of schooling of household head	0.440	–0.058	–0.046	0.043	–0.394	–0.275	0.535	–0.345	1					
% of joint family	–0.141	–0.015	0.115	–0.444	0.444	0.296	–0.193	0.073	–0.068	1				
Female workers' participation	0.334	0.0941	–0.228	0.303	–0.418	–0.230	0.192	–0.262	0.181	–0.345	1			
SCST	–0.080	0.071	–0.353	0.177	–0.020	0.017	–0.060	0.429	–0.178	–0.055	0.122	1		
Women's highest year of schooling	0.255	–0.160	–0.129	0.011	0.007	–0.071	0.312	–0.430	0.208	0.051	0.016	–0.112		
Use and intention of contraceptives	0.155	0.187	–0.255	–0.001	–0.183	–0.149	0.063	–0.240	0.059	–0.088	0.147	0.170	0.060	1

Source: Authors' calculation.

Note: NFHS = National Family Health Survey; MEANWEMP =; SCST = Scheduled Castes/Scheduled Tribes.

References

Aggarwal. (1994), Gender and Command over Property: A Critical Gap in Economic Analysis and Policy in South Asia. *World Development*, 22(10), 1455–1478.

Aggarwal. (2021), Impact of SHGs on Social, Economic and Political Women Empowerment: A Case Study of Ghaziabad District, India. *World Review of Entrepreneurship, Management and Sust. Development*, 17(2/3), 276-290.

Akter, S. and N. Chindarkar (2019), An Empirical Examination of Sustainability of Women's Empowerment Using Panel Data from India. *The Journal of Development Studies*, 56(5), 890–906.

Anukriti. (2020). Curse of the Mummy-ji: The Influence of Mothers-in-Law on Women in India. *American Journal of Agricultural Economics*, 102(5), 1328–1351.

Arnold, Fred, Sunita Kishor, and T. K. Roy (2004), Sex Selective Abortions in India. *Population and Development Review*, 28(4), 759–785.

Atake, E. and Pitaloumani Gnakou Ali (2019), Women's Empowerment and Fertility Preferences in High Fertility Countries in Sub-Saharan Africa. *BMC Women's Health*, 19, 54.

Bala A. and Namita C., (2015), The Empirical Study on Strengthening Endeavors for Social and Political Empowerment of Women in Dairy Cooperatives. *International Journal of Scientific Research and Reviews*, 4(1), 1–6.

Bhatt V. and S. Shastri (2018), Measuring the Impact of Microfinance on Women Empowerment among Women of Rural Gujarat. *International Journal of Reviews and Research in Social Sciences*, 6(3), 123–124.

Bushra, A. and N. Aajiha (2015), Assessing the Socio-Economic Determinants of Women Empowerment in Pakistan. *Procedia-Social and Behavioural Sciences*, 177, 3–8.

Chakrabarty, C., A. Majumder and R. Ray (2022), Female Labour Force Participation, Women's Bargaining Power and Fertility Rates in India: Evidence on their Interaction with Some Policy Lessons, mimeo.

Chattopadhya, R. and E. Duflo (2001), *Women's Leadership and Policy Decisions: Evidence from a Nationwide Randomized Experiment in India*. Boston University, Institute for Economic Development.

Chen, Y. and N. Chindarkar (2017), The Value of Skills – Raising the Socio-Economic Status of Rural Women in India. *Development Policy Review*, 35(2), 229–261.

Coffey, D., P. Hathi, N. Khurana and A. Thorat (2018), Explicit Prejudice. *Economic & Political Weekly*, 53(1), 47.

Debnath, S. (2015), The Impact of Household Structure on Female Autonomy in Developing Countries. *The Journal of Development Studies*, 51(5), 485–502.

Desai. (2010), Gender Scripts and Age at Marriage in India. *Demography*, 47, 2010, 667–687.

Dhak, B., N. Saggruti and R. Fajudar (2020), Contraceptive Use and Its Effect on Indian Women's Empowerment: Evidence from the National Family Health Survey-4. *Journal of Biosocial Science*, 52(4), 523–533.

Dixon-Muller, R. (1989), Psychosocial Consequences to Women of Contraceptive Use and Controlled Fertility. In A. Parnell (Ed.), *Contraceptive Use and Controlled Fertility* (pp. 140–159).Washington, DC, National Academy of Sciences.

Duflo, E. (2012), Women Empowerment and Economic Development. *Journal of Economic Literature*, 50(4), 1051–1079.

Dyson & Moore. (1983), On Kinship Structure, Female Autonomy, and Demographic Behaviour in India. *Population and Development Review*, 9(1), 35–60.

Eapen (2001), Women in Informal Sector in Kerala: Need for Re-Examination, January 2001. *Economic and Political Weekly*, 36(26), 2390–2392.

Global Gender Gap Report. (2022), Insight Report, 13th July 2022, World Economic Forum. https://www3.weforum.org/docs/WEF_GGGR_2022.pdf

Gyimah, S. (2003), A Cohort Analysis of the Timing of First Birth and Fertility in Ghana. *Population Research and Policy Review*. 22. 251–266.

T. Jukariya, P. Sharma and S. Singh (2018), Demographic Profile and Nutrition Status of Women in Rajasthan, India. *International Journal of Current Microbiology and Applied Sciences*, 7(05), 1088–1095.

Kabeer, N. (2000), *The Power to Choose: Bangladeshi Women and Labor Market Decisions in London and Dhaka*. Verso.

Katsushi, I., S. Annim, R. Gaiha and V. Kulkarni (2014), Does Women's Empowerment Reduce Prevalence of Stunted and Underweight Children in Rural India? *World Development*, 62, 88–105.

Kaur, R. (2010), Institutional Structure and Women Empowerment. *Asia-Pacific Journal of Rural Development*, 20(2), 103–124.

Khubchandani. (2018), Caste Matters: Perceived Discrimination among Women in Rural India. *Archives of Women's Mental Health*, 21, 163–170.

Kishor, J. and K Gupta (2004), Women's Empowerment in India and Its States: Evidence from the NFHS. *Economic and Political Weekly*, 39, 694–712. 10.2307/4414645

Kumari, S., N. Garg, A. Kumar, P. Guru, S. Ansari, S. Anwar, K. Singh, P. Kumari, P. Mishra, B. Gupta, S. Nehar, S. Sharma and M. Sohail (2019), Maternal and Severe Anemia in Delivering Women Is Associated with Risk of Preterm and Low Birth Weight: A Cross Sectional Study from Jharkhand, India. *One Health*, 8, Article 100098. https://doi.org/j.onehlt.2019.100098

Lemire, M., C. Sicotte and G. Pare (2008), Internet Use and the Logics of Personal Empowerment in Health. *Health Policy*, 88(1), 130–140.

Mackey, A. and P. Pertrucka (2021), Technology as the Key to Women's Empowerment: A Scoping Review. *BMC Women's Health*, 21, Article No. 78.

Mason, K. and H. Smith (2003), Women's Empowerment and Social Context: Results from Five Asian Countries, Gender Development Group, Washington DC.

Narayan, D. (ed.) (2005), *Measuring Empowerment: Cross-disciplinary Perspectives*. World bank.

Nautiyal, A. (2003), Women and Development in the Garhwal Himalayas. *Asian Journal of Women's Studies*, 9(4), 93–113.

Nava, I., V. Choudhury and A. Agardh (2020), Desire to Delay the First Childbirth among Young, Married Women in India: A Cross-Sectional Study Based on National Survey Data. *BMC Public Health*, 20, Article No 350, 1–10.

Nayak, P. and B. Mahanta (2009), Women Empowerment in Assam. University Library of Munich, Germany, MPRA Paper.

Ngoma, C. and S. Mayimbo (2017), The Negative Impact of Poverty on the Health of Women and Children. *Annals of Medical and Health Sciences Research*, 7, 442–446.

Niti Aayog SDG India Index Report. (2020–21). https://www.niti.gov.in/reports-sdg

Pathak, D. C. (2022), Do Women Empowerment and Intimate Partner Violence Go Hand in Hand? Evidence from India. *Review of Development and Change*, 27(2), 238–263.

Rao, L. and L. Rahaman (2004), The Determinants of Gender Equity in India: Examining Dyson and Moore's Thesis with New Data. *Population and Development Review*, 30, 239–268.

Rashmi, R., B. Mallik, S. Mohanthy, U. Mishra and S. V. Subhramanian (2022), Predictors of the Gender Gap in Household Educational Spending among School and College-Going Children in India. *Humanities and Social Sciences Communications*, 9, Article No. 329.

Ravindra, K. and A. Tiwari (2016), Relationship between Poverty, Women Empowerment and SHGs: A Study of Indian State. *International Journal of Managerial Studies and Research*, 4, 1–10.

Rogers (2007), Is Sex-Selective Abortion Morally Justified and Should it be Prohibited? *Bioethics*, 21(9), 520–524.

Sahay, S., A. Kalokhe, C. Rio, K. Dunkle, R. Stephenson and N. Metheney (2017), Domestic Violence against Women in India: A Systematic Review of a Decade of Quantitative Studies. *Global Public Health*, 12(4), 498–513.

Saqib, N, Priyanka Aggarwal and Saima Rashid (2016), Women Empowerment and Economic Growth: Empirical Evidence from Saudi *Arabia. Advances in Management and Applied Economics*, 6(5), 79–92.

Sarkar, M. (2010), A Study on Domestic Violence Against Adult and Adolescent Females in a Rural Area of West Bengal. *Indian Journal of Community Medicine*, 35, 311–315.

Satija, S. (2013), Violence against Women in Rural Bihar: A Case of Four Villages. Working Paper, No. 3, Institute for Human Development.

Sen, A. K. (1990), Individual Freedom as Social Commitment. *India International Centre Quarterly*, 17(1), 101–115.

Shivaleela, F. B., and Gadawale, H. H. (2018), Women Empowerment in Karnataka – An Analysis. *International Journal for Research in Engineering Application & Management*, 4(6), 564–570.

Singh, S., B. Sharma, D. Vishwakarma, G. Yadav, S. Swati and B. Maharana (2018), Women's Empowerment and Use of Contraception in India: Macro and Micro Perspectives Emerging from NFHS-4 (2015–16). *Sexual & Reproductive Healthcare*, 19, 15–23.

Sultana, H., M. Abdul Jamal and D. Najaf (2017), Impact of Microfinance on Women Empowerment through Poverty Alleviation: An Assessment of Socio- Economic Conditions in Chennai City of Tamil Nadu. *Asian Journal of Poverty Studies*, 3(2), 175–183.

Tiwari, A. K. (2009), Nutritional Status in Madhya Pradesh Evidence from NFHS-2 and NFHS-3. *Child Survival and Health*, 237–247.

Upadhyay, U., J. Gipson, M. Withers, S. Lewis, E. Ciaraldi, F. Fraser, M. Huchko and N. Prata (2014), Women's Empowerment and Fertility: A Review of the Literature. *Social Science & Medicine*, 115, 111–120.

"Women Business and the Law." (2020). World Bank, January 14. https://www.worldank.org/en/news/press-release/2020/01/14/40-economies-make-62-legal-reforms-to-advance-womens-economic-participation

World Bank. (2011), World Development Report 2011: Conflict, Security, and Development. © World Bank. http://hdl.handle.net/10986/4389

World Bank. (2012), World Development Report 2012: Gender Equality and Development. © World Bank. http://hdl.handle.net/10986/4391

Yadav, A., B. Sahni, D. Kumar, K. Bala and A. Kalotra (2021), Effect of Women's and Partners' Education on Maternal Health Care Services Utilization in Five Empowered Group Action states of India. An Analysis of 13,423 Women of Reproductive Age. *International Journal of Applied and Basic Medical Research*, 11, 231–237.

Yaya, S. Odusina, E. K. Uthman, O. A. and Ghose, B. (2020) What Does Women's Empowerment Have to Do With Malnutrition in Sub-Saharan Africa? Evidence From Demographic and Health Surveys From 30 Countries. *Global Health Policy*, 5, Article No. 1.

National Policy for the Employment of Women (2001). (2014). *Indian Journal of Public Administration*, 60(3), 730–740.

Kondal, K. (2014), Women Empowerment Through Self-Help Groups in Andhra Pradesh, India. *Innternational Research Journal of Social Sciences*, 3(1), 13–16.

Donta, B., S. Nair, B. Shahina, and C P Prakasam. (2015), Association of Domestic Violence From Husband and Women Empowerment in Slum Community. *Journal of Interpersonal Violence*, 31(12), 2227–2239.

Abbas, S., N. Isaac, M. Zia, Z. Rubeena, and F. Florian. (2021), Determinants of Women's Empowerment in Pakistan: Evidence From Demographic and Health Surveys, 2012–13 and 2017–18. *BMC Public Health* 21, Article No. 1328.

12 Should Climate Change Include a Separate Focus on Loss and Damage?

*Runa Sarkar**

12.1 Introduction

The rise in frequency and intensity of extreme weather events, ranging from floods on one end to forest fires on the other, cyclones and hurricanes hitting the coasts to severe and prolonged droughts in inland areas appear to have become the 'new normal' across the world. While extreme weather events are nothing new, the sharp increase in their frequency and intensity may be attributed to the impact of a sustained increase in average temperatures across the world over the years, loosely referred to as 'climate change'. The recognition that climate change would lead to hardship and an overall decline in the quality of life for the world's population, with different regions being affected differently, led to the setting up of the United Nations Framework Convention on Climate Change (UNFCCC) secretariat in 1992 as the United Nations entity tasked with supporting global response to climate change. The UNFCCC organizes the annual Conference of Parties (COP), the largest annual United Nations conference to facilitate intergovernmental climate change negotiations besides providing technical assistance in analysing climate change information and maintaining a registry for nationally determined contributions of member countries. Since 1992, the primary focus of the UNFCCC has been on mitigation, that is, ameliorating the stressors responsible for climate change, and adaptation, that is, building institutional and human capacity to live with climate change. These focus areas were adequate until the late 1990s, when climate change was a future event that the world recognized and was preparing for.

The 2022 Intergovernmental Panel for Climate Change (IPCC) reports have clearly underlined that greenhouse gas emissions (GHGs; and concentrations in the atmosphere) are continuing to rise along with the number of people exposed to acute food insecurity and reduced water security as a result (IPCC 2022a, 2022b). The United Nations Environment Program's Adaptation Gap Report accuses climate change of "landing blow after blow upon humanity" (UNEP 2022). Sunita Narain of the Center for Science and

* The author is grateful to Ms Swathy S. for research assistance.

DOI: 10.4324/9781003509721-15

Environment calls it "the revenge-of-nature moment that we have brought on ourselves by years of procrastination" (Narain 2022). The prime minister of the Republic of Vanuatu states that "climate change is an existential threat. It is the single greatest threat to our livelihoods, security and well-being" and estimates that economies of the Pacific islands suffer damages of over 50% of gross domestic product (GDP) from climate extremes (Weibur 2022).

Thus, climate change is no longer a threat for the future as it was in the 1990s but is upon us and affecting our daily lives. Moreover, the impact is uneven, with the Pacific islands claiming that the impact is as high as a reduction by half for those nations! The countries most affected by climate change in the context of food security in the recent past are Sudan, Madagascar, Pakistan, Somalia, Burkina Faso, Chad, Mali, Mauritania, Niger, El Salvador, Honduras and Guatemala (World Food Program USA, 2023). Other lists, based on criteria such as the largest number of extreme weather events or the percentage of population vulnerable to climate change yield similar results, sometimes including countries like the US or Australia that have large tracts of land at risk for forest fires. It should not come as a surprise that most of the vulnerable countries represent the 'global South' – low- or middle-income countries located around the equator. The role of these countries in the historical accumulation of GHGs in the atmosphere is negligible, yet they bear the brunt of unhindered economic growth that the developed world benefits from. It is imperative, therefore, that in addition to mitigation and adaptation, the mainstay of the COPs, the world wakes up to a third thread of deliberations and even more urgent action, namely, assessing and compensating for loss and damage (L&D).

Although the UNFCCC has not come up with a formal definition of L&D, for a working definition, we could use that provided by Adelle Thomas, a lead author of several IPCC reports, who states that loss and damage are the "negative impacts of climate change that occur despite, or in the absence of, mitigation and adaptation" (Rao, 2022). That L&D is an additional area to address with respect to the impact of climate change, over and above mitigation and adaptation, is evident from this definition. Authors such as Pinninti (2013) and Roberts and Pelling (2018) have stated that the impacts of climate change that cannot be addressed through adequate mitigation and adaptation strategies are formally regarded as climate change L&D. Figure 12.1 illustrates how L&D fit into the agenda to address climate change.

L&D refers to permanent losses and repairable damage from extreme weather events such as floods, heat waves, cyclones and forest fires and slow onset events like a rise in sea level or land-use change as a result of climate change. Mechler and Schinko (2016) and (Nand 2023) differentiate between the two terms *loss* and *damage*, suggesting that *loss* refers to adverse impacts to which reparation or restoration is impossible, whereas *damage* refers to adverse impacts in relation to which reparation or restoration is possible. Thus, instances such as the loss of freshwater resources, habitat, or, worse still, life, would qualify as loss. Reversible impacts such

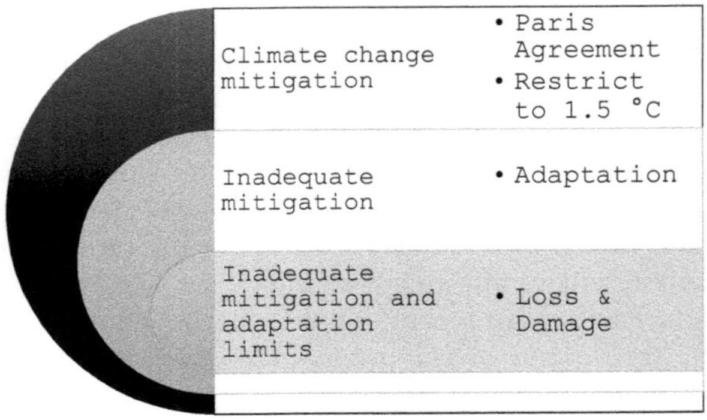

Figure 12.1 The Role of Loss and Damage in Addressing Climate Change.
Source: Adapted from Boyd et al. (2021).

as damage to infrastructure or crops or limited damage to coastal mangrove forests as a result of coastal surges would qualify as damage.

Yet another distinction, useful for operationalisation of L&D costs, comes from classifying them as economic L&D and non-economic L&D. As the name suggests, economic L&Ds related to losses of or damage to those physical and/or financial assets that can be either be assigned a monetary value or be associated with reduced earnings or productivity as a consequence. For example, a flood may result in a loss of crops, buildings and infrastructure, which are measurable. Even harder to measure damage such as the loss of important documents, papers and cash for people living in flood-affected areas is considered economic L&D as it impacts the livelihoods of the communities. Non-economic L&D refers to those impacts that hold significant value, affecting an individual's or community's sense of identity and well-being, that cannot be traded in the market. Loss of life, territory, local and indigenous knowledge, ecosystem services, sense of community and forced displacement are examples of non-economic L&D. Boyd et al. (2021) provide a good overview of NELDs across different countries from different climate events.

Finally, the biggest challenge with L&D is attributing its cause to climate change. Figure 12.2 is a schematic that attempts to link L&D to climate change, illustrating that there are multiple potential causal chains between anthropogenic changes in the concentration of GHGs in the atmosphere, human activity, land-use changes, vulnerability of certain communities and changes in the biosphere and loss and damage to society.

12.2 The Emergence of L&D in Climate Change Parlance: A Brief History

The impact of climate change was first felt by the small island states in the Pacific due to the gradual increase in sea levels. Hence it is hardly surprising that the first indications of an ask for some sort of compensation came from

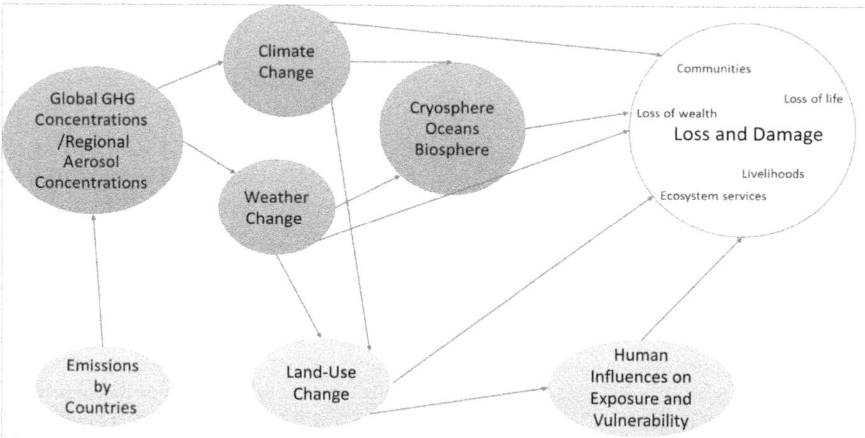

Figure 12.2 A Simplified Causal Network for Loss and Damage.
Source: Adapted from James et al. (2019).

these states. During the formation of UNFCCC in 1991, Vanuatu, on behalf of the Alliance of Small Island States (AOSIS), proposed the creation of an insurance scheme for financial support to nations affected by the rise in sea levels, on the basis of the notion of common but differentiated responsibilities (CBDR; McNamara 2014). The proposed scheme suggested a mechanism for how to use the resources from the insurance pool to compensate the most vulnerable countries for L&D (Wewerinke-Singh & Salili 2019). Unfortunately, the proposal received no traction at that time, with mitigation and, later, adaptation garnering all the attention. Discussions on L&D, if at all, were clubbed with those on adaptation. Another key milestone was reached at the COP 11 in 2005, when Bangladesh, on behalf of the least developed countries, asked for direct compensation rather than insurance for loss and damage. Finally, in the 13th COP in 2007, L&D was recognised officially in the text with the statement that "enhanced action on adaptation, including disaster reduction strategies and means to address loss and damage with climate change impacts in developing countries that are particularly vulnerable to the adverse effects of climate change" (UNFCCC 2008, p. 4). The AOSIS submitted a detailed version of the scheme they had submitted in 1991, proposing three interdependent components of any global response, including insurance, rehabilitation/compensation, and risk management (AOSIS 2008). Three years later, at COP 16 in 2010, an agreement was reached on a work programme on L&D under the Subsidiary Body of Implementation of the UNFCCC (UNFCCC 2011). At the COP15 in 2009, several countries formally included loss and damage in their submitted texts, leading to the recognition of the need (decision 7/CP.17) to explore a wide range of possible approaches and mechanisms to address L&D (UNFCCC 2012).

In 2012, a call by the G77 for a loss and damage mechanism at the COP18, and the sustained pressure over the years led to an assurance of an L&D mechanism being provided for the first time, in addition to a decision to establish a work programme on L&D that included a technical paper on enhancing the formal understanding of non-economic losses (Preston 2017). One hundred ninety-four countries negotiated a best approach to institutionalise arrangements to address the issue of L&D under the UNFCCC at COP 19 in Warsaw, with the G-77 and China proposing that an L&D mechanism be considered as the third pillar of the UNFCCC alongside mitigation and adaptation (McNamara 2014). This led to the establishment of the Warsaw International Mechanism (WIM) to "address loss and damage associated with impacts of climate change, including extreme events and slow-onset events, in developing countries that are particularly vulnerable to the adverse effects of climate change" (UNFCCC 2014, p. 6). The WIM aims to enhance knowledge and understanding of L&D, strengthen dialogue among stakeholders, and enhance action and support to address L&D (James et al., 2014). WIM discussed developing knowledge capacity and strengthening dialogue around action to support L&D, with an executive committee being formed to guide the implementation of the functions of WIM.

The COP21 at Paris marked a major milestone in the journey of L&D as a pillar in global climate change action plans under Article 8 of the Paris Agreement in 2015, where they specifically speak of "averting, minimising and addressing Loss and Damage" (Lai et al., 2022). However, the phrasing of Article 8 of the Paris Agreement was vague, with no mention of whether developed nations would bear greater responsibility for the climate change impacts faced by developing nations. In 2019, at the Madrid COP, the WIM was strengthened with the establishment of the Santiago Network on Averting, Minimising and Addressing Loss and Damage to provide technical assistance through relevant stakeholders to address loss and damage at the local, national, and regional levels. It stressed the principles of coherence, comprehensiveness, and integration to operationalize L&D research into more effective policy (Boda et al., 2021). At the same time, the clamour for funding L&D, along with financial estimates started getting louder, culminating in a proposal by the G77 at the COP 26 for a Loss and Damage Finance Facility. Unfortunately, the setting up of the Glasgow dialogue for discussions on L&D finance dampened the proposal somewhat.

In the run-up to COP 27, several countries and civil society organisations ensured that L&D was part of the provisional agenda for negotiations. During the negotiations, several (non-trivial) pledges for contributions to L&D were received from countries such as Austria, Belgium and New Zealand. Germany led the G7 and climate-vulnerable nations to put forward the Global Shield initiative to support developing countries through climate risk insurance (Rao 2022). Most importantly, a Transitional Committee was set up to operationalise the funding for loss and damage. This committee, composed of 10 members from developed countries and 14 from developing countries, would build on past work to establish an L&D

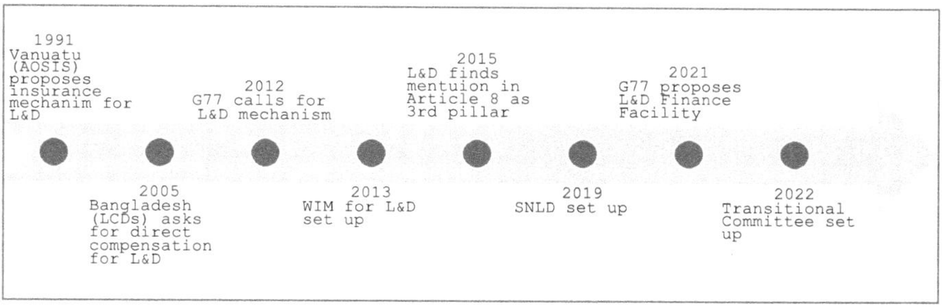

Figure 12.3 The Progression of Loss and Damage Discussion in the UNFCCC.
Source: Authors' own.

fund flow mechanism before COP 28. While it was already evident that this would not be in the form of direct reparations from industrialised nations to more vulnerable ones, it was still a landmark event, because, for the first time UNFCCC financing mechanisms were dealing with the accumulative effects and aftermath of extreme events. It is likely that L&D financing mechanisms would build on and expand existing climate financing challenges (Naylor and Ford 2023). Figure 12.3 summarises this discussion.

There is still a lot of ground to cover with respect to L&D discussions. The quantum of resources to be mobilised for such a financing facility and who would contribute are yet to be identified. Whether the nature of the contribution would be mandatory or not and the parameters to arrive at contributing nations or receiving nations are yet to be identified. Points of contention include whether to include erstwhile developing countries like Saudi Arabia and China, which are large present contributors to climate change as fund contributors, or wealthy nations, such as Singapore and South Korea, as recipients. Even more critical is to arrive at a definition of L&D that all parties would agree to for compensation (Harris 2023). Going forward, L&D should become a permanent agenda item at the COP, and efforts need to be made to include it both in nationally determined contributions and long-term climate strategies and in the global stocktaking as an L&D inventory. Finally, the financial architecture to facilitate L&D flows has to be determined. We explore some of these issues in the rest of the chapter.

12.3 The Contributors and the Recipients: Climate Justice

It is now common knowledge that the cause of climate change is the stock of GHGs in our atmosphere which has been accumulating since the industrial revolution. The developed world is largely responsible for the historical emissions and, to date, dominates per capita emissions of GHGs, although fossil fuel–intensive countries, such as China and Saudi Arabia, are also significant contributors to current emissions. Furthermore, as a nation grows economically, its per capita emissions of GHGs also tend to rise. Thus, while addressing climate change is a challenge for both the developed and developing world, the challenge is two pronged for the developing world because not only is economic growth necessary for sustainable development, but it is also concomitant with increases in GHG emissions which need to be curbed to address (future) climate change. If this were not enough, the impact of climate change is manifested unevenly across nations, with the developing world bearing the brunt of the impact. Although the UNFCCC adopted the notion of CBDR in recognition of this challenge, the implementation of the notion is fraught with difficulties.

L&D is not only an environmental distress, but it also affects the livelihood and very identity of affected communities. Hence, climate justice must also encompass social and economic justice in addition to environmental justice. This implies that the historical socio-political context of communities affected by L&D must first be disentangled and then damages should be addressed across all dimensions (Boyd et al., 2021). Toussaint and Blanco (2020) came up with a human rights–based approach to address loss and damage under the climate change regime, emphasizing the rights and well-being of individuals and communities impacted by climate change. In addressing L&D, they emphasize the significance of involvement, accountability, non-discrimination and equality and underscore the need to prioritize the rights of the most vulnerable and marginalized communities, who often bear the brunt of climate change impacts with limited resources and capacity to adapt.

Boda et al. (2021) point out that sustainable development implicitly presupposes that society can adjust to and lessen the effects of climate change through technology developments, governmental initiatives and economic expansion, which implies that sustainable development, as a notion, did not account for the rising number of situations in which L&D outweighs a nation's capacity for efficient mitigation and adaptation. This understanding then has implications for how countries approach the problem of L&D and can explain, to some extent, the reason for a lack of engagement of the developed world with the concept. Thus, while South Korea and Singapore fall among the climate-vulnerable nations, their ability to cope with L&D surpasses that of Bangladesh or Mauritius. At the same time, as is evident from research related to the recent forest fires in the US and Australia, developed countries are better equipped to assess both L&D for present extreme events and future risks. Addressing L&D from the point of view of who is responsible opens up a completely different set of issues. First, how to attribute the causes of historical emissions is complex. Second, even if one looks at current emissions, whether one should look at per capita emissions, total emissions or rate of change of emissions is a point of contention. Finally, without an updated developed and developing country list, key GHG emitters such as Saudi Arabia and China may not be held responsible for L&D. Little wonder then, why civil society and advocacy play such a pivotal role in every COP event!

To address climate justice in the context of L&D, a coalition of nearly 80 countries set up the Vanuatu International Court of Justice (ICJ) Initiative requesting a non-binding Advisory Opinion from the ICJ to understand what existing international laws may be applied to current climate issues and the rights of independent countries. With respect to L&D, justice involves establishing responsibilities and liability for the loss (itself a contentious issue) and developing adequate reparation and compensation mechanisms, which, in turn, requires an objective assessment of loss value. Toussaint (2021) argues that L&D-related litigation can play a significant role in the UNFCCC process, particularly by giving a voice to climate victims. He identifies several key influence channels, including targeted non-governmental organisation advocacy, encouraging vulnerable country delegations to use litigation as a negotiating tactic and enhancing the contribution of the expert community of climate lawyers through litigation networks, and demonstrates how closely climate litigation and UNFCCC negotiation are related. Despite his optimism, while the Vanuatu ICJ Initiative has the potential to open the L&D discussion on liability and compensation, one is not as hopeful that the discussions will lead to deliberative action, in the short term at least.

Based on the nature of past COP negotiations and current geopolitics in the climate space, it is almost certain that climate change impacts will not be paid as reparations to affected people. Developed countries have made it abundantly clear during negotiations that while they agree that there has been L&D, the L&D has nothing to do with liability or compensation. Under these circumstances, given the immediate nature of the damage suffered across the world, an interim solution is to work towards the establishment of an L&D fund, which the developed world may contribute towards. Hence, the focus of a financial mechanism must be to create an adequate and fit-for-purpose L&D fund that is additional to financial resources allocated for adaptation and mitigation.

12.4 Assessing and Quantifying Loss and Damage and Its Attribution

Measuring and recording L&D is fraught with several challenges ranging from identifying the range of losses to be assessed to developing appropriate methodologies for measurement and capacity building for identification and measurement. To start with, there is no universally accepted definition of L&D, as mentioned earlier, which leads researchers to confine their estimates to nationally developed frameworks which have been developed for disaster relief objectives. Furthermore, losses in sectors such as industry, commerce, tourism and mining have not been studied enough to develop an appropriate methodology (Bahinipati and Gupta 2022). Often, informal workers or migrants, who are the most vulnerable, get left out in such estimates. Furthermore, estimating non-economic L&D concerns conceptualizing, accounting and methods to monetize each L&D indicator, attribution and context-dependence, which can be quite subjective. Worse still, other non-economic L&D such as the sense of identity, dignity and emotional attachment with ancestral property are left out as they are not reported in post-disaster assessment reports. As a result, estimates for L&D vary widely, with the 'best' estimates being made available by developed countries such as the US as they file insurance claims for damage to crops or forest fires.

Some examples of research in L&D measurement in the developing context are as follows. Bhowmik et al. (2021) evaluated the condition of adaptive capability as well as loss and damage associated with extreme climate occurrences in the rural communities of three locations in Bangladesh using an analytical and theoretical framework for 191 incidents between 1999 and 2018. He assessed the perception of people in this region towards extreme events and the non-economic L&D associated with this in three locations in Bangladesh. The study demonstrated that while a lack of resources, such as little financial capacity, poor social capital and place attachment due to land ownership or inheritance, forced the people to stay in those vulnerable locations, relocation does not guarantee limiting loss and damage. Improved livelihoods, strong cultural and kinship connections and access to resources to ensure basic needs enable people to create opportunities to stay well and limit L&D. In the context of disaster management in India, while the actual process of L&D assessment differs across states, the procedure broadly comprises a collection of damage-related data on the ground, which is then verified by the revenue department and disaster management officials at the district level and uploaded to a centralised portal. These data are then re-verified by the state disaster management authority, which then calculates its economic value based on available 'Norms of Assistance'. For slow-onset extreme events like drought, agencies monitor their onset by looking at precipitation and soil moisture levels, and local teams create adaptive capacity. This, while the immediate cost of a disaster is addressed, the more chronic and lingering losses that arise from it are not addressed. Bahinipati and Gupta (2022) identify and enumerate several methodological issues that emerged while assessing post-disaster L&Ds in India from extreme climate events like cyclonic storms, floods and droughts.

Bahinipati (2020) estimated the economic and non-economic L&D incurred by the drought-affected farmers in the Kutch district of Gujarat in 2014 and 2016 using a contingent valuation method. He observed that the intensity of economic L&D was perceived as relatively high as compared to non-economic L&D, and on average, the drought cost a household about INR 8035, of which non-economic L&D is estimated as INR 4597. An alternate mechanism to assess L&D could be by developing indices using social and human development indicators (Boyd et al., 2021).

Wang et al. (2020) estimated the L&D costs in the future associated with changes in agricultural productivity, increased energy demand for cooling, damages to infrastructure from extreme weather events and other relevant factors. They came up with an estimate of global GDP losses due to climate impacts for 2050, and they posit that developing countries are extremely vulnerable and experience up to 85% of global economic losses. Hence, standardising L&D measurement methodologies are essential steps in a global empirical stocktaking of impacts to inform and support governance of climate change. There is a need for a large-scale effort to systematically document a vast number of L&Ds associated with climate change for both extreme and slow-onset events. This is more critical for countries where limited data are available coupled with, perhaps, constrained capabilities in analysing what data there are, where the most vulnerable reside. Developing an integrated and nuanced approach towards assessing L&D can also inform planning to avert, minimise and address L&D (James et al., 2019).

The attribution of L&D is an even more contentious issue. In the political context of climate negotiations, questions about whether L&D can be attributed to anthropogenic climate change are often linked to issues of responsibility, blame and liability. Yet, attribution science, which is advancing rapidly, does not aim to establish responsibility or blame but, rather, to investigate drivers of change, and how the change interacts with other drivers of risk, including socio-economic drivers, to influence L&D. James et al. (2019) explore the role of attribution research to inform the management of climate-related risks through improved understanding of drivers of relevant hazards or, more widely, vulnerability and exposure; with potential benefits regardless of political positions on L&D. Attribution studies can estimate the extent to which certain drivers (such as GHGs) contributed to certain outcomes (such as flooding), but this 'contribution' is very different from 'responsibility', which is a moral or ethical issue. However, too much of a focus on causal links with extreme events may not be desirable, as the approach is impotent when more and more systems are approaching tipping points. Policymakers should not expect attribution science to provide conclusive evidence about the influence of climate variability and change on specific incidences of L&D and, in particular, should not expect the strength of evidence to be equal between events and between countries.

12.5 An Architecture for L&D Financing

Over the years, several options have been proposed to finance L&D. Consistent with the principles of CBDR, it would be expected that the donor base for L&D would be states from the global North, yet the language in the decision text from COP27 opens this up to voluntary funding from larger, developing nations as well (Rao 2022). Two broad approaches to L&D funding are evident in discussions pertaining to the issue. One thread, as originally proposed by the AOSIS, and built on by Germany in this proposal of insurance as a 'global shield' in COP 27, pertains to the use of insurance as a mechanism to address L&D. The other, first proposed by Bangladesh, is the creation of a separate fund for L&D financing. Both these approaches are discussed in the following, starting with a discussion on insurance.

Insurance instruments, including micro insurance, regular insurance and climate risk insurance have been proposed by many (e.g., Linnerooth-Bayer et al., 2019, Nordlander et al., 2020) to finance the recovery from extreme and abrupt climate events, such as floods, windstorms, and droughts. Regional (or macro) risk pools can serve as appropriate risk-reduction strategies and provide financial support for vulnerable communities and countries, while micro-insurance schemes could be applied locally for low-income vulnerable populations. International assistance could be in the form of subsidies, technical assistance, capitalisation of insurance programs, provision of reinsurance and other types of support that make insurance affordable to resource-poor and climate-sensitive clients, a 'global shield', as proposed by Germany. However, insurance can only be effective if communities are conversant with the notion of insurance and its application and appropriate data collection mechanisms are there to operationalise the insurance process. This may not be true of several of the island states and developing countries. Furthermore, because of its very nature, insurance cannot compensate for non-economic L&D. Finally, insurance is not appropriate for managing L&D from gradual changes such as sea-level rise, desertification, loss of habitat, loss of biodiversity, erosion, ocean acidification, and glacial retreat. In addition to all the preceding, the closer one gets to the tipping point; that is, the higher the frequency of climate-related events, the higher the cost of providing insurance. In other words, the more frequent these events, the greater the extent to which insurance premiums will rise. Rising premia will then put it beyond the reach of socio-economically vulnerable families and nations. Thus, while insurance is a useful tool, there is a need for the creation of an L&D fund as well. We turn our attention to such funding mechanisms next.

There has been a lot of research on L&D financing mechanisms for the small island developing states (SIDS). Pill (2022) explored what practitioners consider to be the critical elements of an L&D mechanism and how funds should be collected, administered, and distributed to tailor a financial mechanism specific to SIDS due to their high vulnerability status. The study found that a settlement without any formal administrative obligations or repercussions if it included a solidarity component that acknowledged the effects felt by poor countries notwithstanding their lack of culpability, would be acceptable to the SIDS in lieu of 'compensation'. Furthermore, any L&D financial support must be packaged with capacity-building measures and technology transfer to enhance the resilience of affected regions and communities. Lai et al. (2022) qualitatively analysed the appropriateness of different financial mechanisms based on whether they are (a) fair, (b) dependable, (c) feasible and/or (d) suitable for the special circumstances of SIDS. Specifically, they espoused levies on airline travel, fossil fuel extraction, GHG emissions, bunker fuel usage and financial transactions to conclude that levies on airline travel and fossil fuel extraction may be fair to some extent. They also recommended that cutting-edge technologies, such as cryptocurrencies and non-fungible token trading, may be explored in the context of L&D financing.

Already existent funds, namely, the Green Climate Fund (GCF), the Global Environment Facility (GEF) and the Adaptation Fund, within the financial mechanism of the UN could also be explored as sources for L&D funding. However, the cumbersome processes to qualify for funding for each of them are not conducive to disbursing L&D funding. In addition, each of these funds is also insufficient to meet its own stated goals, and L&D funding cannot be readjusted into the US$100 billion promised under the Paris Agreement. It is salient that funding for L&D is in addition to funds required for mitigation and adaptation, as their objectives are quite distinct and each of them is equally necessary. The Bridgetown Initiative, proposed in September 2022, offered solutions to loss and damage that aimed to provide emergency liquidity through the International Monetary Fund, especially to countries that could not afford additional debt. It suggested expanding multilateral development bank (MDB) lending to governments and a re-channelling of unused special drawing rights (SDRs) to nations that need liquidity to address rapid onset climate events. Franczak (2022) highlights the challenges with the Bridgetown Initiative drawing our attention to where such a fund would be located, who would fund it and its areas of focus. Instead, he suggested that the World Bank provide long-term concessional finance to tackle the slow-onset L&D. Non-UNFCCC mechanisms to finance L&D could include a tax on fossil fuel producers or the creation of bilateral or multilateral solidarity funds. It is important to recognise, however, that in contrast to mitigation and adaptation, returns on investing in L&D are momentarily non-existent, thereby removing private flows from the mix of financing options. Hence, it is important to call on the principle of CBDR to ensure a public source of funding. At the end of the day, the fiscal capacity of nations who are dealing with climate concerns, and the availability of several blended finance options are necessary to have a robust L&D finance mechanism.

12.6 The Way Forward for L&D

By providing sufficient and predictable funding, ensuring equitable distribution, and combining financial support with capacity-building measures, this mechanism can assist vulnerable countries and communities in coping with and recovering from the irreversible consequences of climate change.

L&D research has unambiguously demonstrated the present-day realities of vulnerable communities that are approaching their social and ecological limits, facing irreversible and intolerable risks (Handmer & Nalau 2019; Mechler & Schinko 2016). For the SIDS, there are some estimates that L&D accounts for almost 50% of their GDP already, even as increases in global temperature hover about 1.1 °C, as against an expected increase of about 2°C over the next few decades. The world's political leadership has to take cognisance of the threat to livelihoods, security and well-being brought about by L&D due to climate change and a failure to commit the finances, technology and political will to this cause will prove catastrophic. There is an urgent need to understand and tackle drivers of L&D, informing prevention, recovery, rehabilitation and transformation. The environmental, socio-political and economic nature of the problem, coupled with contentious issues of attribution suggest that multiple mechanisms to provide for L&D is the best way to proceed.

Enabling factors of finance, governance and capacity of knowledge sharing must be generated by involving affected communities in decision-making processes, as their perspectives and experiences are crucial for developing effective policies and strategies. Empowering vulnerable populations and integrating their knowledge and traditional practices into climate change risk reduction efforts, especially to address non-economic L&D is critical. A deeper understanding of the information and concepts national policy players use to conceptualize the L&D issue, how political agendas at various scales get shaped by a lack of L&D data and knowledge and the conflicts caused or exacerbated by L&D would be useful in developing policy solutions at the national level (Vanhala and Calliari, 2022).

At the international level, securing additional finance, whether through L&D funding arrangements within the UNFCCC; funding from MDBs and international financial institutions; innovative financing through taxes, debt forgiveness or using an insurance mechanism; or some combination of some of these is salient. While fears persist on attribution and the extent of liabilities of the developed world, enabling conditions of governance and knowledge for addressing L&D can be developed and strengthened through the Santiago Network, as part of the WIM. COP28, in 2023 will be a crucial year to operationalise and answer the where, who and what of L&D funding arrangements, without sacrificing commitments toward mitigation and adaptation.

References

AOSIS (2008). *Multi-window mechanism to address loss and damage from climate change impacts*, Submission to UNFCCC accessed on 24 May 2023 from https://unfccc.int/files/kyoto_protocol/application/pdf/aosisinsurance061208.pdf

Bahinipati, C. S. (2020). Assessing the costs of droughts in rural India: A comparison of economic and non-economic loss and damage. *Current Science* 110(11). https://doi.org/10.18520/cs/v118/i11/1832-1841

Bahinipati, C. S., & Gupta, A. K. (2022). Methodological challenges in assessing loss and damage from climate-related extreme events and slow onset disasters: Evidence from India. *International Journal of Disaster Risk Reduction*, 83, 103418. https://doi.org/10.1016/j.ijdrr.2022.103418

Bhowmik, J., Irfanullah, H. M., & Selim, S. A. (2021). Empirical evidence from Bangladesh of assessing climate hazard-related loss and damage and state of adaptive capacity to address them. *Climate Risk Management*, 31, 100273. https://doi.org/10.1016/j.crm.2021.100273

Boda, C. S., Faran, T., Scown, M., Dorkenoo, K., Chaffin, B. C., Nastar, M., & Boyd, E. (2021). Loss and damage from climate change and implicit assumptions of sustainable development. *Climatic Change* 164, 1–18 https://doi.org/10.1007/s10584-021-02970-z

Boyd, E., Chaffin, B. C., Dorkenoo, K., Jackson, G., Harrington, L., N'Guetta, A., ... & Stuart-Smith, R. (2021). Loss and damage from climate change: A new climate justice agenda. *One Earth*, 4(10), 1365–1370 https://doi.org/10.1016/j.oneear.2021.09.015

Franczak, M. (2022). Options for a Loss and Damage Financial Mechanism, International Peace Institute, October 14, 2022, Accessed on 24 May 2023 from https://www.ipinst.org/wp-content/uploads/2022/10/2210_Options-for-a-Loss-and-Damage-Financial-Mechanism.pdf

Handmer, J., Nalau, J. (2019). Understanding loss and damage in pacific small island developing states. In: Mechler, R., Bouwer, L., Schinko, T., Surminski, S., Linnerooth-Bayer, J. (eds) *Loss and Damage from Climate Change. Climate Risk Management, Policy and Governance*. Springer, Cham. https://doi.org/10.1007/978-3-319-72026-5_15

Harris, P. G. (2023). COP27: From preventing dangerous climate change to salving loss and damage. *PLOS Climate*, 2(1), e0000150. https://doi.org/10.1371/journal.pclm.0000150

IPCC (2022a). Summary for Policymakers [H.-O. Pörtner, D.C. Roberts, E.S. Poloczanska, K. Mintenbeck, M. Tignor, A. Alegría, M. Craig, S. Langsdorf, S. Löschke, V. Möller, A. Okem (eds.)]. In: *Climate Change 2022: Impacts, Adaptation and Vulnerability. Contribution of Working Group II to the Sixth Assessment Report of the Intergovernmental Panel on Climate Change* [H.-O. Pörtner, D.C. Roberts, M. Tignor, E.S. Poloczanska, K. Mintenbeck, A. Alegría, M. Craig, S. Langsdorf, S. Löschke, V. Möller, A. Okem, B. Rama (eds.)]. Cambridge University Press, Cambridge, UK and New York, NY, pp. 3–33, https://doi.org/10.1017/9781009325844.001

IPCC (2022b). Summary for Policymakers. In: *Climate Change 2022: Mitigation of Climate Change. Contribution of Working Group III to the Sixth Assessment Report of the Intergovernmental Panel on Climate Change* [P.R. Shukla, J. Skea, R. Slade, A. Al Khourdajie, R. van Diemen, D. McCollum, M. Pathak, S. Some, P. Vyas, R. Fradera, M. Belkacemi, A. Hasija, G. Lisboa, S. Luz, J. Malley, (eds.)]. Cambridge University Press, Cambridge, UK and New York, NY. https://doi.org/10.1017/9781009157926.001

James, R., Otto, F., Parker, H. et al. (2014). Characterizing loss and damage from climate change. *Nature Climate Change* 4, 938–939 https://doi.org/10.1038/nclimate2411

James, R. A. et al. (2019). Attribution: How Is It Relevant for Loss and Damage Policy and Practice?. In: Mechler, R., Bouwer, L., Schinko, T., Surminski, S., Linnerooth-Bayer, J. (eds) *Loss and Damage from Climate Change. Climate Risk Management, Policy and Governance*. Springer, Cham. https://doi.org/10.1007/978-3-319-72026-5_5

Lai, M., Robinson, S., Salas, E., Thao, W., & Shorb, A. (2022). Climate justice for small island developing states: identifying appropriate international financing mechanisms for loss and damage, *Climate Policy* 22, (9–10), 1213–1224. https://doi.org/10.1080/14693062.2022.2112017

Linnerooth-Bayer, J., Surminski, S., Bouwer, L.M., Noy, I., Mechler, R. (2019). Insurance as a Response to Loss and Damage? In: Mechler, R., Bouwer, L., Schinko, T., Surminski, S., Linnerooth-Bayer, J. (eds) *Loss and Damage from Climate Change. Climate Risk Management, Policy and Governance*. Springer, Cham. https://doi.org/10.1007/978-3-319-72026-5_21

McNamara, K.E. (2014). Exploring Loss and Damage at the International Climate Change Talks. *International Journal of Disaster Risk Science* 5, 242–246. https://doi.org/10.1007/s13753-014-0023-4

Mechler, R., & Schinko, T. (2016). Identifying the policy space for climate loss and damage. *Science* 354, 290–292 https://doi.org/10.1126/science. aag2514

Nand, M. M. (2023). *Policy options for climate change loss and damage: A case study from Fijian agriculture* (Doctoral dissertation). Accessed on 24 May 2023 from https://hdl.handle.net/2440/137297

Narain, S. (2022). Only Together can we win, Down to Earth 1-15 November 2022, pp. 10–11. Accessed on 24 May 2023 from https://cdn.downtoearth.org.in/library/0.78368000_1666845082_11---november-1-15-2022.pdf

Naylor, A. W., & Ford, J. (2023). Vulnerability and loss and damage following the COP27 of the UN framework convention on climate change. *Regional Environmental Change* 23, 1, 38. https://doi.org/10.1007/s10113-023-02033-2

Nordlander, L., Pill, M., & Romera, B. M. (2020). Insurance schemes for loss and damage: fools' gold? *Climate Policy* 20(6), 704–714. https://doi.org/10.1080/14693062.2019.1671163

Pill, M. (2022). Towards a funding mechanism for loss and damage from climate change impacts. *Climate Risk Management* 35, 100391. https://doi.org/10.1016/j.crm.2021.100391

Pinninti, K. R. (2013). Approaches for assessing loss and damage. In *Climate Change Loss and Damage: Economic and Legal Foundations* (pp. 11–24). Springer Berlin Heidelberg, Berlin, Heidelberg. https://doi.org/10.1007/978-3-642-39564-2_2

Preston, C. J. (2017). Challenges and opportunities for understanding non-economic loss and damage. *Ethics, Policy & Environment* 20(2), 143–155. https://doi.org/10.1080/21550085.2017.1342962

Rao, A. S. (2022). The overdue climate justice of loss and damage. *Journal of International Affairs* 75(1), 389–402. https://www.proquest.com/scholarly-journals/overdue-climate-justice-loss-damage/docview/2799234154/se-2

Roberts, E., & Pelling, M. (2018). Climate change-related loss and damage: translating the global policy agenda for national policy processes. *Climate and Development* 10(1), 4–17. https://doi.org/10.1080/17565529.2016.1184608

Toussaint, P. (2021). Loss and damage and climate litigation: The case for greater interlinkage. *Review of European, Comparative & International Environmental Law* 30(1), 16–33. https://doi.org/10.1111/reel.12335

Toussaint, P., & Martinez Blanco, A. (2020). A human rights-based approach to loss and damage under the climate change regime. *Climate Policy* 20(6), 743–757. https://doi.org/10.1080/14693062.2019.1630354

UNEP (2022). Adaptation Gap Report 2022a: Too little, too slow – climate adaptation failure puts world at risk. Nairobi. Accessed 24 May 2023 from https://www.unep.org/resources/adaptation-gap-report-2022

UNFCCC (2008). *Report of the Conference of the Parties on its thirteenth session, held in Bali from 3 to 15 December 2007*. Accessed May 24 2023, from https://unfccc.int/resource/docs/2007/cop13/eng/06a01.pdf

UNFCCC (2011). *Report of the Conference of the Parties on its sixteenth session, held in Cancun from 29 November to 10 December 2010*. Accessed May 24, 2023, from https://unfccc.int/resource/docs/2010/cop16/eng/07a01.pdf

UNFCCC (2012). *Report of the Conference of the Parties on its seventeenth session, held in Durban from 28 November to 11 December 2011*. Accessed May 24, 2023 https://unfccc.int/resource/docs/2011/cop17/eng/09a01.pdf

UNFCCC (2014). *Report of the Conference of the Parties on its nineteenth session, held in Warsaw from 11 to 23 November 2013*, Vol 31, No 11. Accessed May 24, 2023, from https://unfccc.int/resource/docs/2013/cop19/eng/10a01.pdf

Vanhala, L., & Calliari, E. (2022). Governing people on the move in a warming world: Framing climate change migration and the UNFCCC task force on displacement. *Global Environmental Change* 76, 102578. https://doi.org/10.1016/j.gloenvcha.2022.102578

Wang, T., Teng, F., & Zhang, X. (2020). Assessing global and national economic losses from climate change: a study based on CGEM-IAM in China. *Climate Change Economics* 11, 03, 2041003. https://doi.org/10.1142/S2010007820410031

Weibur, B.L., (2022). Loss and Damage, Guest Column, Down to Earth, 1–15 November 2022, pp. 8–9. Accessed on 24 May 2023 from https://cdn.downtoearth.org.in/library/0.78368000_1666845082_11---november-1-15-2022.pdf

Wewerinke-Singh, M., & Salili, D. H. (2019). Between negotiations and litigation: Vanuatu's perspective on loss and damage from climate change. *Climate Policy* 20(6), 681–692. https://doi.org/10.1080/14693062.2019.1623166

World Food Program USA (2023). The 8 Countries most affected by Climate Change, April 21, 2023. Accessed May 24, 2023, from https://www.wfpusa.org/articles/countries-most-affected-by-climate-change/

13 India beyond *jugaad*

The opportunities and pitfalls of R&D-based innovations

Partha Ray and Balram Avittathur

13.1 Introduction

From ancient times, regions with new ideas or technologies dominated other regions on trade and military might. This hastened further with the arrival of the Industrial Revolution. While abundant natural resources, past conquests or an imperial past could explain the wealth of developed economies, a greater explainer of the wealth of a nation in recent times is the extent of research and development (R&D) activities and the resulting scientific knowledge. In 1978, China opened its economy to foreign investors with the aim of achieving prosperity by migrating its workforce from less productive agricultural activities to more productive manufacturing activities. Much of its early investments then were in the making of labour-intensive low-end products like textiles and toys. However, in recent times, as it transits towards becoming a high-income nation, it views itself as a producer of everything, including high-technology products. Many millions of Chinese have emerged out of poverty in the last four decades. In the last 25 years, Chinese spending on R&D has increased substantially from less than 1 per cent of the gross domestic product (GDP) to now close to 2.5 per cent of GDP.

India spends less than 1 per cent of its GDP on R&D activities, and this figure has been stagnant for a long time. The advent of economic liberalisation in the early 1990s hardly contributed to increased R&D expenditure in the country, and many of the R&D activities are still funded by the government only. Many educated and qualified Indians are compelled to explore employment opportunities abroad owing to the insignificant job opportunities in R&D and high-end knowledge sectors. While economists and politicians in India and abroad have been exalting about India being the next economic miracle, the country has seen only sporadic bouts of economic growth exceeding 8 per cent annually after its economy was opened in 1991. In this chapter, we explore whether R&D-based innovations could be the next growth driver for the Indian industry. We also examine why R&D activities have so far been a non-existent or insignificant activity in many Indian manufacturing firms.

DOI: 10.4324/9781003509721-16

13.2 Contribution of R&D to economic growth – What does economic theory tell us?

Traditional economic models of Solow's variety seek to look at economic growth in terms of capital accumulation and total factor productivity growth (i.e., essentially the residuals from the estimate of the production function relating output with labour and capital). The endogenous models of economic growth in this context have attempted to explain productivity growth in terms of innovation and technology (Arrow, 1962), accumulation of human capital (Lucas, 1988), or profit-seeking R&D (Romer, 1990).

Romer (1990), in particular, emphasised the importance of profit-seeking research in the growth process. An extended version of Romer's model has been provided by Jones (2019). In the following, a synoptic presentation of Jones's model is given to capture the role of R&D in the growth process, in line with Jones's (2019) formulation.

13.2.1 The basic endogenous growth model

Consider an aggregate production function of the following Cobb–Douglas form (with L, K, and A as labour, capital, and ideas/R&D, respectively, as the three inputs of production):[1]

$$Y = K^{\alpha}\left(AL_Y\right)^{1-\alpha}. \tag{13.1}$$

By its very construction, the production function exhibits constant returns to labour and capital. However, the presence of ideas (A) leads to increasing returns overall. Capital accumulation $\left(\dot{K} = \dfrac{dK}{dt}\right)$ is given by the following equation of motion:[2]

$$\dot{K} = s_K Y - dK. \tag{13.2}$$

Labour force grows at a fixed rate, n; that is,

$$\frac{\dot{L}}{L} = n. \tag{13.3}$$

Technological progress is no longer exogenous, but it is a function of the number of researchers (L_A) and their average productivity ($\underline{\delta}$); that is,

$$\dot{A} = \underline{\delta} L_A. \tag{13.4}$$

Aggregate labour can be sub-divided into two types, those who produce new ideas, researchers (L_A) and those who produce output(L_Y); that is,

$$L_A + L_Y = L. \tag{13.5}$$

The productivity of researchers is conceived as a function of the current stock of ideas; that is,

$$\underline{\delta} = \delta A^{\theta}; \text{where } \theta(<1) \text{ is a knowledge spillover parameter.} \tag{13.6}$$

Assuming that research output can be duplicated (at the rate of ρ, lying between zero and one) and combining Equations (13.6) and (13.4) we get,

$$\dot{A} = \delta L_A^{\rho} A^{\theta}. \tag{13.7}$$

How do we conceive the ideas/R&D generation process? The production function for R & D can be given by

$$\frac{\dot{A}}{A} = \frac{\delta L_A^{\rho}}{A^{1-\theta}}. \tag{13.8}$$

Along a balanced growth path, the growth rate of the number of researchers must be equal to the growth rate of the population so that we get

$$g_A = \frac{\rho n}{1-\theta}. \tag{13.9}$$

As far as the R&D production function is concerned, there are two formulations.

First, Romer's (1990) original formulation is given by

$$\frac{\dot{A}}{A} = \delta L_A, \tag{13.10a}$$

where δ is the productivity of each researcher and L_A is the number of researchers.

Second, on the contrary, Jones's formulation of the production process of R&D is given by

$$\dot{A} = \delta L_A^{\rho} A^{\theta}, \tag{13.10b}$$

where θ is the returns to the stock of ideas and ρ is the degree of congestion in current research.

Note that $\theta > 0$ implies increasing returns to ideas 'standing on shoulders' or $\theta < 0$ decreasing returns to ideas 'over-fishing', while $\rho < 1$ would imply 'stepping on toes' and $\rho > 1$ would mean 'network externality'.

Thus, new growth theory goes beyond the 'black box' of technological progress and seeks to explore the factors that influence technical progress and growth rate. Three key factors stand out: R&D, openness to foreign ideas, and human capital.

What is the upshot of such models? It is pertinent to turn to Jones (2019), who, in the context of Romer's Nobel Prize, captured the essential idea of endogenous growth and the role of R&D in economic growth in the following manner:

> Here is the key insight: ideas – designs or blueprints for doing something or making something – are different from nearly every other good in that they are nonrival. Standard goods in classical economics are rival: as more people drive on a highway or require the skills of a particular surgeon or use water for irrigation, there are fewer of these goods to go around.... Ideas, in contrast, are nonrival: as more and more people use the Pythagorean theorem or the Java programming language or even the design of the latest iPhone, there is not less and less of the idea to go around. Ideas are not depleted by use, and it is technologically feasible for any number of people to use an idea simultaneously once it has been invented.... How does the nonrivalry of ideas explain economic growth? The key is that nonrivalry gives rise to increasing returns to scale. The "standard replication argument" is a fundamental justification for constant returns to scale in production. If we wish to double the production of computers from a factory, one way to do this is to build an equivalent factory across the street and populate it with equivalent workers, materials, and so on. That is, we replicate the factory exactly. This means that production with rival goods is, at least as a useful benchmark, a constant returns process.... Once you have increasing returns, growth follows naturally. Output per person then depends on the total stock of knowledge; the stock does not need to be divided up among all the people in the economy.
>
> (Jones, 2019, pp. 860–861)

13.2.2 Imitation versus innovation

How does innovation take place? Does it happen via trade? The basic model of innovation is due to Grossman and Helpmann (1990), who, in one of the early papers on trade, innovation, and growth, pointed out several channels. First, countries tend to specialise in the creation of knowledge and in the production of goods that make intensive use of human capital and new technologies in line with the principle of comparative advantage. Second, trade allows exporting countries to exploit the large scale of the world economy of research successes. Third, the spillover effects of technology get transmitted at a fast pace in a world of rapid and cheap communication. However, there is a flip side. While countries stand to "benefit from the spillovers generated by investments in knowledge in trade partner countries, but also may lose from the lack of ability to appropriate all of the benefits from their own investments" (Grossman and Helpman, 1990). Finally, since countries tend to participate in international capital markets, the set of opportunities for financing knowledge capital also gets extended. Notwithstanding such channels, it has been pointed out that the technology flows between the advanced and the emerging countries are anything but automatic.

What is the role of imitation in innovation? Segerstrom (1991) developed a model in which there is a steady-state equilibrium, where some firms spend to discover qualitatively improved products and others devote resources to copying these products. Three crucial results of his model deserve special mention. First, rates of both innovation and imitation are endogenously determined on the basis of the outcomes of R&D races between firms. Second, innovation subsidies tend to promote growth. Third, welfare is enhanced only if the steady-state intensity of innovative effort exceeds a critical level.

However, Aghion et al. (2001) demonstrated that in the presence of imitative innovation, the Schumpeterian effect innovation from a more intense product market competition (PMC) could be almost always outweighed by the increased incentive for firms to innovate in order to escape competition so that PMC has a positive effect on growth. However, there are limits to imitation. While a little imitation is almost always growth-enhancing (through increased competition), too much imitation is unambiguously growth-reducing. The model, thus, emphasises complementary roles for competition (anti-trust) policy and patent policy.

Collins (2015) analysed the process in which imitation can be a catalyst for innovation in which a process of learning to innovate occurs as technology diffuses from a more advanced country to a less developed country. A key result from Collins (2015) is that "[d]eveloping countries that have a healthier and more educated workforce can benefit the most from technology diffusion and are more likely to transition from imitating to innovating … countries that have less efficient R&D workers will continue to imitate products from more developed countries instead of inventing new products". Interestingly, both the level and growth rate of output and total factor productivity increases if a country manages to transition from imitation to innovation.

Thus, while imitation could legitimately be an engine of growth, it has its limitations. However, what have been the experiences in this regard? Towards this, we now turn to cross-country trends in innovation, as proxied by R&D.

13.3 Cross-country trends in R&D and growth

World Bank (2007), in its Growth Report, noted the following loose categories of factors influencing growth, namely, (a) accumulation, (b) innovation, (c) allocation, (d) stabilisation, and (e) inclusion. Of these, strictly speaking, the role of innovation falls within the domain of this chapter. But how do we measure expenditure on innovation? The Organisation for Economic Co-operation and Development (OECD 2003) defined investment in innovation as the sum of (a) R&D expenditure, (b) expenditure for higher education, and (c) investment in software. These indicators are associated not only with growth but also with productivity. What have been the cross-country trends in innovation, in general, and R&D, in particular? Is there an observable feature in the considerable share of high-technology exports in China that could be attributed to R&D investments?

13.3.1 Cross-country trends in innovation and R&D

Table 13.1 reports expenditure on account of R&D as a percentage of GDP. Israel is the only country that spends more than 5 per cent of GDP on account of R&D. Israel Innovation Authority's Annual Report on *the State of High Tech 2022* mentioned that while Israel used to occupy the last place in terms of *government R&D expenditure* (as a percentage of GDP) among OECD countries in 2019, currently it tops the list in terms of *total R&D expenditure* (as a percentage of GDP) indicating the primacy of the private sector in R&D. OECD countries like Korea, Belgium, United States, Japan, Austria, Switzerland, and Germany tended to spend more than 3 per cent of GDP on R&D.

Using national data from 1995 to 2014, Li and Jiang (2016) report that R&D expenditures and patents contributed significantly to the growth of the Chinese GDP. In general, they highlight that "both R&D expenditures and patents granted are significantly positive[ly] correlated with GDP and the growing output elasticity to GDP is in leaps and bounds after 2000 and 2005" and "comparing to patents granted, R&D expenditures account for a higher share of contribution to economic growth".

13.3.2 High-technology exports: China versus other BRICS nations

A key indicator of the R&D or patents is reflected in their role in exports. The OECD has developed a four-way classification of exports: high, medium-high, medium-low and low-technology.[3] In particular high-technology exports, which are products with high R&D intensity, such as aerospace, computers, pharmaceuticals, scientific instruments, and electrical machinery, indicate technological capability of a country. Expectedly, among the BRICS countries (Brazil, Russia, India, China, South Africa), China with a 30 per cent plus share of high-technology exports in total exports tops the list (Figure 13.1). Brazil is a distant second, with a similar share of 15 per cent. While India's share is much lower, in recent times, India is about to touch the share of Brazil.

The surge in R&D expenditure as a share of the GDP in China is evident in the figures shown in Table 13.1. From just 0.9 per cent, it has grown significantly to 2.05 per cent in 2014, the latest year for which the R&D data on

Table 13.1 Research and Development Expenditure (percentage of GDP)

No.	*Country*	*2000*	*2010*	*2020*
1	Israel	3.93	3.92	5.44
2	Korea	2.13	3.32	4.81
3	Belgium	1.94	2.06	3.48
4	USA	2.63	2.74	3.45
5	Japan	2.86	3.1	3.26
6	Austria	1.89	2.73	3.2
7	Switzerland	2.26	2.64	3.15
8	Germany	2.41	2.73	3.14
9	France	2.09	2.18	2.35
10	Norway	n.a.	1.65	2.28
11	China	0.90	1.73	2.05[a]
12	Australia	1.57	2.37	1.83
13	Canada	1.86	1.83	1.70
14	Italy	1	1.22	1.53
15	Poland	0.64	0.72	1.39
16	Brazil	1.05	1.16	1.21
17	Thailand	0.24	0.23	1.14
18	Russia	1.05	1.13	1.10
19	Malaysia	0.47	1.04	1.04
20	India	0.76	0.79	0.66
21	South Africa	n.a.	0.66	0.62
22	Mexico	0.31	0.49	0.3
23	Indonesia	0.07	0.08	0.28
24	Kuwait	0.13	0.10	0.19
25	Sri Lanka	0.14	0.14	0.13
	Memo:			
26	*North America*	*2.58*	*2.65*	*3.32*
27	*High income*	*2.31*	*2.37*	*2.97*
28	*OECD members*	*2.25*	*2.34*	*2.96*
29	*World*	*2.05*	*2.01*	*2.63*
30	*Euro area*	*1.81*	*2.00*	*2.36*
31	*Middle income*	*0.65*	*1.12*	*1.86*

Source: World Development Indicators, World Bank.

Note: Regions shown in italics. GDP = gross domestic product; OECD = Organisation for Economic Co-operation and Development.

[a] China data available only until 2014.

China is available in the World Bank database. From being slightly ahead of India and behind Brazil and Russia in 2000, China is way ahead of the other BRICS countries. The higher expenditure on R&D by China is now reflected in the outcomes as well. Table 13.2 reports the number of patent applications by residents and non-residents with respect to the BRICS countries.[4] China is clearly an exception among the BRICS countries. Illustratively, with 152,000 patent applications by resident Chinese (compared to 270,000 for the US) and 1.3 million applications (compared to 327,000 for the US) by non-resident

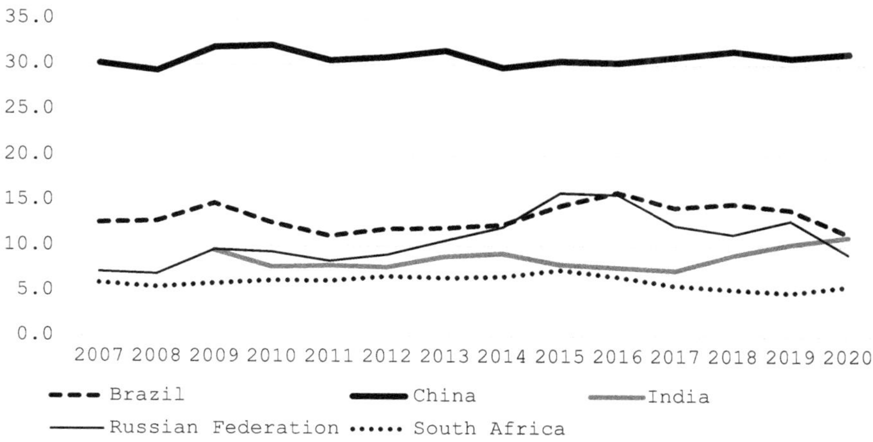

Figure 13.1 High-technology exports (percentage of manufactured exports).
Source: World Bank.

Chinese, the number of patents in China are multiples of the nearest comparator economy, India; others lag far more. There are, however, issues with Chinese patent trends. Illustratively, Long and Wang (2019) found that notwithstanding the explosion of Chinese patents, the overall innovation content of Chinese patents has not achieved proportional growth. After all, Chinese patent promotion policies, which have prompted the quantitative expansion of patent applications and approvals, had negative effects on the average patent quality.

A similar trend is reflected in the number of scientific and technical journal articles across BRICS countries (Table 13.3).

13.4 Evolution of Indian industry and R&D success stories

It would be interesting to understand at this point whether there are any unique aspects to the Indian context regarding R&D investments and their outcomes. Why have R&D expenditure and research activities in firms been historically low? Have R&D investments paid off as well in India compared to any other parts of the world? This is best answered by looking at instances of significant expenditures on R&D activities over a long time and the ultimate benefits obtained because of these investments. We also look at instances of Indian firms not having spent sufficiently on R&D, which ultimately led to their decline and exit from industries they once dominated.

13.4.1 Evolution of Indian industry post-independence

Undoubtedly, independent India commenced its economic journey at a great disadvantage regarding various human development measures. Much of the population was illiterate with little access to proper healthcare. Exposure to

Table 13.2 Number of Patent Applications in BRICS Countries (in thousands)

	Patent Applications, Non-Residents					*Patent Applications, Residents*				
	Brazil	*China*	*India*	*Russia*	*South Africa*	*Brazil*	*China*	*India*	*Russia*	*South Africa*
2000	14.1	26.6	6.3	9.0	2.4	3.2	25.3	2.2	23.4	0.9
2001	14.4	33.4	8.2	9.3	5.4	3.4	30.0	2.4	24.8	1.0
2002	13.2	40.4	8.8	9.6	5.6	3.5	39.8	2.7	23.7	1.0
2003	12.5	48.5	9.2	9.9	5.3	3.9	56.8	3.4	25.0	0.9
2004	12.7	64.6	13.5	7.2	5.8	4.0	65.8	4.0	23.0	1.0
2005	14.4	79.8	19.7	8.6	6.0	4.1	93.5	4.7	23.6	1.0
2006	15.9	88.2	23.2	9.8	6.7	4.0	122.3	5.7	27.9	0.9
2007	17.5	92.1	28.9	11.9	7.4	4.2	153.1	6.3	27.5	0.9
2008	18.9	95.3	30.4	14.1	7.1	4.3	194.6	6.4	27.7	0.9
2009	18.1	85.5	27.0	13.0	5.9	4.3	229.1	7.3	25.6	0.8
2010	20.8	98.1	30.9	13.8	5.6	4.2	293.1	8.9	28.7	0.8
2011	24.0	110.6	33.5	14.9	6.6	4.7	415.8	8.8	26.5	0.7
2012	25.6	117.5	34.4	15.5	6.8	4.8	535.3	9.6	28.7	0.6
2013	25.9	120.2	32.4	16.1	6.7	5.0	704.9	10.7	28.8	0.6
2014	25.7	127.0	30.8	16.2	6.8	4.7	801.1	12.0	24.1	0.8
2015	25.6	133.6	33.1	16.2	6.6	4.6	968.3	12.6	29.3	0.9
2016	22.8	133.5	31.9	14.8	6.5	5.2	1,205.0	13.2	26.8	0.7
2017	20.2	135.9	31.6	14.1	6.8	5.5	1,245.7	15.0	22.8	0.7
2018	19.9	148.2	33.8	13.0	6.3	5.0	1,393.8	16.3	24.9	0.7
2019	19.9	157.1	34.2	12.2	6.3	5.5	1,243.6	19.5	23.3	0.6
2020	19.1	152.3	33.6	11.2	6.1	5.3	1,344.8	23.1	23.8	0.5

Source: World Bank.

Note: BRICS = Brazil, Russia, India, China, and South Africa.

modern manufacturing methods was confined to a small share of the population residing in cities like Ahmedabad, Chennai, Kanpur, Kolkata or Mumbai, where much of the modern Indian industry, such as textile mills, was based. In line with the developments in many parts of the world after the Second World War, free India too opted for an economic model where the government got involved extensively in the production of various goods like iron and steel, oil refining, power generation, machine tool manufacturing, and so on. The emphasis was on the creation of a strong indigenous manufacturing industry that would be self-sufficient in the production of most goods.

To support the fledgling Indian industry, the government embarked on many protectionist policies like import restrictions and the need for licences to produce anything and everything. India had become a heavily protected and regulated economy by the late 1970s, with the need to obtain a licence to start or expand a business turning out to be a significant barrier to competition (Kotwal et al., 2011). At the same time, regulations meant difficult times even for the existing entrepreneurs and managers with lengthy and complicated processes for various aspects of running a firm. These restrictions also meant that typically there were shortages in many industries that had to be

Table 13.3 Scientific and Technical Journal Articles (in thousands)

	Brazil	*China*	*India*	*Russia*	*South Africa*
2000	12.8	53.3	21.4	32.7	4.0
2001	13.9	70.7	22.5	36.6	4.2
2002	16.2	75.2	24.3	36.3	4.5
2003	17.6	87.8	26.8	34.7	4.3
2004	19.8	120.9	28.8	35.0	4.9
2005	22.3	165.4	32.9	34.4	5.2
2006	28.5	192.4	38.1	29.9	5.8
2007	31.0	213.2	42.6	30.8	5.9
2008	35.4	247.5	48.1	32.4	6.3
2009	38.3	285.5	53.6	33.3	7.1
2010	41.5	308.8	60.6	33.9	7.6
2011	44.0	323.1	71.8	36.0	8.3
2012	47.9	328.1	77.7	35.8	8.9
2013	50.0	356.4	82.8	38.3	9.5
2014	51.8	385.2	91.3	43.8	10.2
2015	52.9	405.8	97.8	51.1	10.9
2016	55.0	436.1	107.2	60.2	11.9
2017	58.1	468.0	112.5	67.4	12.9
2018	61.8	531.1	127.5	76.1	13.4
2019	64.4	610.5	129.5	87.2	15.0
2020	70.3	669.7	149.2	90.0	15.9

Source: World Bank.

overcome through imports, often through surreptitious channels. Managing these day-to-day challenges meant that developing new products and processes was hardly the concern of firms, a concern that already was diluted owing to the assurance of a domestic market that was protected from competition and imports. By the 1970s, limited job opportunities in more exciting R&D activities and low salaries in other industrial functions led young Indians, particularly engineers, to look for better opportunities in foreign countries like the US. Simultaneously, firms discovered that adopting technologies that succeeded in other parts of the world was a shortcut solution to the challenges faced in running firms because of regulations and the inability to attract talent. In fact, many Indian firms started promoting their own products based on the foreign origin of their technology.

The economic liberalisation that commenced in the 1980s and gathered momentum in the 1990s saw an increase in competition in various sectors. The opening of the economy and trade liberalisation that followed meant that Indian firms could now tap foreign markets more easily. However, after more than 30 years of economic liberalisation and the removal of the licence raj, many of the benefits seem to be in the service sector, comprising information technology, banking, education, electronic media, health care, housing, insurance, hospitality, and tourism. While India has performed well in sectors like automobiles, pharmaceuticals, steel, petrochemicals, and oil refining post-liberalisation, it has conceded ground significantly in many other manufacturing sectors to its Asian neighbours (Piramal, 2017). Piramal (2017) cites many instances of Indian firms outsourcing the production of parts and components to suppliers from China and other countries. India continues to be a big importer of high-technology defence and industrial equipment. Forbes (2017) argues that the continued low R&D investments and innovations in post-liberalisation India are because most firms have identified an advantage that is based on competing on cost, particularly in labour-intensive sectors. R&D expenditure as a share of the GDP has remained stuck at below 1 per cent before and after the economic liberalization.

13.4.2 R&D and innovation success stories

While we lament the low importance accorded by Indian firms to R&D and innovations, it would be unfair not to highlight the few R&D and innovation success stories. As the government share of Indian Gross Expenditure on Research and Development (GERD) is greater than the business share, it is logical that some of the R&D success stories in the country turn out to be government scientific organizations. Top among these organizations is the Indian space organization ISRO. Goswami (2020) highlights the various achievements of India's space program, which apart from various civilian and military capacities for the country also include commercial satellite launches for clients across the world and various scientific missions in space. With an annual budget close to US$2 billion in 2019, the organisation has over the last half century grown into one employing more than 15,000 scientists and engineers. Another organization that has benefited from substantial government spending in R&D and has contributed significantly to the indigenization of defence technologies and weapons systems in India is the Defence Research and Development Organisation (DRDO). Bhushan and Madhusudan (2019) describe the evolution of DRDO from a small organisation to one that was supplying significantly to the Indian armed forces (about INR 1 trillion over a 2-year period ending in 2017). Presently, their programmes include developing battle tanks, combat aircraft, airborne early warning and control systems, indigenous submarines, artillery rocket systems, radars, electronic warfare systems, assault bridges, and underwater systems, among others. Yet another technological initiative by the Indian government is the Unified Payments Interface (UPI), which has now established itself as one of the best payment systems and is designed to offer availability at all times, transparency, ease of use, and instantaneous transfer of money (Shahid, 2022). According to Rastogi et al. (2021), UPI has enabled a higher level of financial literacy and contributed significantly to the financial inclusion as well as economic development of Indians, particularly the poor. UPI was launched in 2016 and is according to the authors a technology based on an open application programming interface platform that runs on a mobile phone and is linked to Aadhar (biometric unique identity number for

Indian citizens). Today, India has become the world's largest real-time payments market with over 83 billion transactions in the 2023 financial year.[5]

There are exceptions to the broad observation that Indian firms incur low expenditure on R&D. One such organization is Mahindra & Mahindra (M&M), a leader in tractor and utility vehicle business. While Indian firms are notorious for their low spend on R&D, M&M has made a mark as a firm spending considerably on R&D. In the 2020 financial year, R&D expenditure was 6.5 per cent of its revenue. In an interview in 2008, its then CEO Anand Mahindra explained the great emphasis laid by the firm on innovations and R&D (Stewart & Raman, 2008). While discussing his focus on innovations, Mr Mahindra argues that "what's going to distinguish us in the future is our ability to make products and services that capture the customer's imagination" and "if M&M is going to compete with the world's best companies, it has to become an innovation factory" (Stewart &Raman, 2008). Mr Mahindra undoubtedly was arguing about serious R&D and not *jugaad*-based innovations. Another organization that has benefitted from sustainable R&D efforts is Aravind Eye Care, the leading eye hospital chain in India. According to Sharma (2022), Aravind Eye Care developed a low-cost, high-quality eye care and cataract surgery model by incorporating various innovations like an assembly-line technique for boosting surgeon productivity, recruiting and training a paramedical service that would take care of much of the non-surgery tasks, and designing and manufacturing intraocular lens implants that brought down the cost from US$150 to just US$10. This example is again of an organization that depends highly on science-based innovations and not just on simple improvisations.

From these examples, it is abundantly clear that as in other parts of the world, Indian organizations that invested in R&D have also adequately benefitted through new products, services, or process innovations.

13.4.3 Indian businesses hit by innovative competitors

At the other end of the spectrum are firms that were at one time the pride of the nation but faded once they were subjected to a higher level of competition when the Indian market opened to foreign investors. Firms like BPL and Videocon dominated the white goods product market until the turn of the century but could not withstand the competition from Korean brands like Samsung and LG, which developed products that were better suited for the Indian conditions based on Indian customer needs. Similarly, Hindustan Motors, maker of the iconic Ambassador brand of cars that were ubiquitous until the arrival of Maruti Suzuki and other competitors, ceased production in 2014 owing to lack of demand.[6] Many Indian manufacturing firms, particularly in the small and medium-sized enterprises category, have been hit hard by lower cost and often good-quality Chinese imports. These firms would have spared their ill fate if they had invested sufficiently in R&D and innovations and improved their products and processes continuously.

13.5 R&D-based growth: Opportunities and pitfalls

Post-independence India has seen considerable progress in the various sectors of its economy. The economic liberalisation and reforms of the last three decades have seen an acceleration in economic growth. However, India has grown at a slower pace than other Asian countries like China, South Korea, and Taiwan. While these countries were similar to India regarding prosperity at the end of the Second World War, they are presently much ahead of India on various economic measures like per capita GDP. Indian firms, too, would have to adopt the R&D strategies followed by firms in these countries to ensure the transition from a low-middle-income country to a high-middle-income or rich industrialised nation. What are the various opportunities that Indian firms should exploit, and what are the pitfalls of not adopting an R&D and innovation-based growth model?

13.5.1 Opportunities

As India marches strongly towards becoming a middle-income nation, there are sufficient worries regarding sustaining rapid economic growth. A slowing population growth and the saturation of markets for many products and services are serious threats to fast growth. This is noticeable, for instance, in fast-moving consumer good products, where annual growth used to be very high until recently. In this context, firms have to sufficiently innovate new products or services and processes as a means of driving growth. Fortunately, many global factors are presently in India's favour, and we elicit various opportunities that have emerged as a result to Indian firms.

13.5.2 Opportunity 1: Demographic shifts

Much of the developed world now comprises countries that have a growing proportion of old-age population. Many countries like Japan and South Korea are already witnessing a reduced labour force as those joining the workforce are fewer than those leaving. While fertility levels have reduced in India too, its workforce numbers are still increasing. However, this increase is not expected to continue for many years, and India, too, will soon start witnessing a shortage of manpower. The abundance of cheap blue-collar labour that has been a striking feature of growth in the previous decades could very well be a luxury in the coming years. This is already visible in the better-developed parts of the country that now depend on cheaper migrant labour from the lesser-developed states. As observed in many other parts of the world, a shortage of blue-collar labour could encourage firms to innovate processes that require less manpower and improve labour productivity. Firms that fail to innovate will carry the risk of inferior business performance or getting disrupted by smarter competitors.

13.5.3 *Opportunity 2: Changing aspirations of the youth and talent availability*

The aspirations of the Indian youth have increased over the years, and they are no more content with traditional jobs like farming or blue-collar, low-paying jobs in manufacturing, retailing, or logistics. Across various communities and states, India today is witnessing higher ambition and an urge to seek better employment opportunities. The surge in coaching institutes or the availability of online tutorials is now enabling the youth to train themselves better in cracking competitive examinations. The growing number of good-quality technical education institutes that are either government-owned or in the private sector is contributing to a huge supply of engineering graduates. This is already recognised by multinational firms, which are affected by a shortage of talent in their home countries, and many are setting up R&D facilities in India to tap the talent available. This could have a rub-off effect on Indian firms too and help in developing an R&D-based innovations ecosystem.

13.5.4 *Opportunity 3: The changing international order*

The international order has shifted drastically in the past few years with geopolitical tensions between Western democracies and China. The Ukraine war has also contributed to changes in the international order. As labour gets costlier and restrictions on Western firms increase in China, there is pressure on these firms to identify alternate supply sources. Also, the COVID-19 pandemic has taught the business world the perils of relying on supplies from China. Hence, multinational firms with a large China footprint are now focusing on reducing their supply chain risks by developing alternate supplies. Being a democracy with mature institutions is enabling India to attract these firms. Many of these firms have a strong R&D and innovation culture in their DNA. Collaborating with such firms is a great opportunity for Indian firms to climb the value chain through higher expenditure in R&D, which could eventually lead to India becoming an important sourcing hub for the world.

13.5.5 *Opportunity 4: Recent tax initiatives and production incentives*

While the economic reforms of the 1990s and 2000s focused on liberalisation and easing trade barriers, India continued to lag countries in East and Southeast Asia in manufacturing. In 2019, the government reduced corporate tax rates so that they were like the tax rates in other manufacturing countries. This was soon followed by the introduction of the Production Linked Incentive scheme, whereby companies are provided incentives on incremental sales for production based out of their Indian manufacturing units.[7] These measures are expected to increase investments in manufacturing that would lead to reduction of component and finished product imports and increase in manufacturing exports. However, constant innovation in products and processes is mandatory for making inroads in international markets that are currently being served by Chinese and other Asian manufacturers.

13.5.6 Opportunity 5: Climate change and the green economy

Narrowing the knowledge lead of technology leaders that are primarily based out of the developed world in a short period is a monumental challenge. The inherent nature of innovations and the resource advantages possessed by the R&D leaders often result in efforts of emerging world challengers turning out to be just catch-up innovations. Instead, creating a niche for oneself in drab domains where there are few players has been a successful R&D strategy of Japanese firms.[8] Climate change and the need to invest more in a green economy are compulsions faced by the world. Owing to the nascency of the field, no country in the world can, at the present, claim to be the pioneer and technology leader in the various green technologies that are emerging. This offers many opportunities for Indian firms to tap through investments in serious R&D activities.

13.5.7 Opportunity 6: Digitization and other new technologies

Policy initiatives, such as Aadhar and UPI mentioned in the previous section, have indeed catapulted India to the status of a digital technologies leader, particularly in the digital finance domain. The driving force behind these policies has been the objective of improving the lives of millions of Indians with moderate means. Owing to the omnipresence of various digital technologies in day-to-day business for many firms, it would be natural to extend the digital competence acquired to various other aspects of running a firm. This is already visible in such aspects like production planning and logistics, where many Indian start-ups like Delhivery, an Indian courier and logistics firm, have established a strong technological presence. The abundant availability of talent in information technology is also attracting technology leaders from other countries to set up R&D facilities in India. These developments contribute immensely to the creation of a strong R&D ecosystem which could again be a great opportunity for other Indian firms to exploit and build a strong technological competence.

13.5.8 Pitfalls

Indian firms should be strongly vigilant against the pitfalls of not migrating to a strong R&D and innovations-based ecosystem and, hence, miss the opportunity to grow rapidly in the coming years. This has been emphasized by the Indian commerce and industry minister Mr Piyush Goyal at a recent business event.[9] Failure to innovate has been a threat to firms' continued existence as described in the previous section. The inability to seize the opportunities described earlier is the biggest pitfall facing any organisation. In addition, we list a few other pitfalls that firms should be cautious about.

13.5.9 Pitfall 1: Competing on cost and the curse of jugaad

The greatest risk to the creation of a strong R&D- and innovations-based ecosystem has been the tendency of Indian firms to accord too much importance to competing on cost. When firms identify cost as the most important competitive advantage, they accord lesser importance to other competitive dimensions like relevant usage features, quality, delivery, and service aspects. In the process, they end up serving markets that are intensely competitive on price, which, in turn, induces them to look for more and newer means of saving costs. It is in such a context that the imitation that we discussed in Section 13.2 becomes a more attractive strategy for the firm than true R&D-based innovation. Many believe that R&D is a luxury that most Indian firms cannot afford, given the low purchasing power of its customers and constrained resources. Instead, they are overwhelmed by the power of *jugaad*, a Hindi word that translates as "makeshift" or "solving problems" through improvisations that come with very little investment. Radjou, Prabhu, and Ahuja (2011) glorify *jugaad* as a faster and cheaper way to innovate. While the examples cited by this article are indeed very relevant and impressive in the context of India, it carries the risk of trivialising R&D. It may, even by deductive reasoning, convey that serious R&D investments are wasteful. While pointing out the need for the GERD in India to increase from 0.7 per cent to 2.0 per cent so that the country could move to a higher growth trajectory, the Economic Survey 2020–21 of India highlighted the need for the business sector's contribution to GERD to increase from 37 per cent presently to 68 per cent, which was the average business contribution in GERD of the top ten economies in the world barring India.[10] In effect, the survey was exhorting Indian businesses to increase their R&D expenditure over fivefold their 2020 level. The low share of business contribution in GERD is a testimony of the low importance Indian businesses accord to innovation and R&D, which is the price paid for an unrelenting focus on cost minimisation and competing on cost.

13.5.10 Pitfall 2: Risk of staticism

The second risk to the creation of a strong R&D and innovations-based ecosystem is the tendency to be content with the status quo. When a business is booming at a given point in time, there is a tendency to assume that the good fortune owes to smart business decisions, and it is best not to alter the status quo. Such thinking carries a big risk in fostering a strong R&D and innovation culture. However, in today's global economy, shocks and disruptions to a currently well-run business model are often with little notice. The uncertainties in running a business and the constant threats they face reinforce the need for firms to constantly innovate their products and processes as a means of hedging the business risks. It is very important for firms to not live on the past laurels nor fall in the trap of staticism.[11]

13.6 Concluding remarks

No country has grown on a sustained basis without critical levels of R&D. It is, therefore, legitimate to assess the role of R&D in India's growth phase. Notwithstanding a low R&D expenditure – GDP ratio – India has shown very impressive performance on growth. Often it is hypothesised that such growth could be the outcome of frugal innovation, or what is popularly called *jugaad*. Such *jugaad*, despite having played its role in the Indian growth trajectory, has its limitations. A time has come when the potential of serious R&D needs to be appreciated among policymakers and industry leaders. There are immense opportunities. Demographic shifts, changing aspirations of the youth and talent availability, the changing international order, recent tax initiatives and production incentives, climate change and the green economy, digitization, and other new technologies – can all, in principle, play catalytic roles in the Indian growth process. In the process, the pitfalls of increased costs and risks of staticism cannot be ruled out. Nevertheless, the path of R&D is the only way to give a solid foundation for a sustainable growth process in India. It is in this context that the recent proposal of the Government of India (on June 29, 2023) to set up a National Research Foundation as an apex body to promote, fund and mentor scientific research in higher education institutions across the country, with the focus on cultivating the culture of research in universities and colleges is a welcome development.

Notes

1 Throughout this section, the process of generating ideas has been referred to as research, or R&D.
2 A dot above a variable typically a denotes time derivative in the model.
3 The classification is based on the importance of expenditures on research and development relative to the gross output and value added of different types of industries that produce goods for export. Examples of high-technology industries are aircraft, computers, and pharmaceuticals; medium-high-technology includes motor vehicles, electrical equipment and most chemicals; medium-low-technology includes rubber, plastics, basic metals and ship construction; low-technology industries include food processing, textiles, clothing and footwear. The date is derived from United Nations, Comtrade database through the WITS platform. See https://data.worldbank.org/indicator/TX.VAL.TECH.CD for details.
4 Per the World Bank classification, "[n]on-resident patent applications are from applicants outside the relevant State or region. Patent data cover applications and grants classified by field of technology. International applications series distinguish four subcategories: a) patents taken out by residents of a country in that country; b) patents taken out in a country by non-residents of that country; c) total patents registered in the country or naming it; d) patents taken out outside a

country by its residents". Moreover, a patent provides protection for the invention to the owner of the patent for a limited period, generally 20 years.

5 J. Anand, UPI: Replicating UPI's success abroad will be tough, *The Economic Times*, May 12, 2023. https://economictimes.indiatimes.com/prime/fintech-and-bfsi/replicating-upis-success-abroad-will-be-tough-think-high-card-penetration-reluctant-banks/primearticleshow/100168038.cms.

6 Hindustan Motors suspends production of India's once iconic Ambassador car, *News 18*, May 25, 2014. https://www.news18.com/news/auto/hindustan-motors-suspends-production-of-indias-once-iconic-ambassador-car-690224.html.

7 Aashish Aryan, Prabha Raghavan, Explained: What is PLI scheme, and which sectors will be under it? Indian Express, November 8, 2020. https://indianexpress.com/article/explained/what-is-pli-scheme-which-sectors-will-be-under-it-7001985.

8 Invisible but indispensable, The Economist, November 5, 2009. https://www.economist.com/briefing/2009/ 11/05/invisible-but-indispensable.

9 Union Minister Piyush Goyal highlights India's focus on innovation, quality & talent as catalysts for unlimited growth at CII Annual Session 2023, NewsOnAIR, May 24, 2023. https://newsonair.com/2023/05/24/union-minister-piyush-goyal-highlights-indias-focus-on-innovation-quality-talent-as-catalysts-for-unlimited-growth-at-cii-annual-session-2023/.

10 Economic Survey: India needs to up its gross expenditure on R&D from 0.7 per cent to 2 per cent of GDP, The Economic Times, January 29, 2021. https://economictimes.indiatimes.com/small-biz/sme-sector/economic-survey-india-needs-to-up-its-gross-expenditure-on-rd-from-0-7-to-2-of-gdp/articleshow/80577225.cms.

11 Mani (2018) noted, "India's GERD (gross domestic expenditure on R&D) to GDP ratio has remained less than 1 per cent of the GDP from 1996 to 2015. The share of private-sector enterprises in overall R&D performance may have increased, but India's payments on royalty and licence fees have also been rising, pointing to the country's increased reliance on foreign technology imports. The government's generous R&D incentive scheme has not promoted the culture of innovation across the country, as R&D remains concentrated in a limited number of industries".

References

Aghion, P., Harris, C., Howitt, P., and Vickers, J. (2001). "Competition, imitation and growth with step-by-step innovation" *The Review of Economic Studies*, *68*(3), 467–492.

Arrow, K. J. (1962). "The economic implications of learning by doing" *Review of Economic Studies*, *29*(3): 155–173.

Bhushan, G., and Madhusudan, M. (2019). "DRDO and Expectations of Stakeholders" *Defence Science Journal*, *69*(6), 613–618.

Collins, T. (2015). "Imitation: A catalyst for innovation and endogenous growth" *Economic Modelling*, *51*, 299–307.

Forbes, Naushad (2017). "India's National Innovation System: Transformed or Half-formed?" Chapter 26, pp. 508–540, in Mohan (2017).

Goswami, N. (2020). "India's space program, ambitions, and activities" *Asia Policy*, *15*(2), 43–49.

Grossman, Gene M., and Helpman, Elhanan. (1990). "Trade, Innovation, and Growth", *American Economic Review*, *80*(2): 86–91.

Jones, Charles I. (2019). "Paul Romer: ideas, nonrivalry, and endogenous growth", *Scandinavian Journal of Economics*, *121*(3): 859–883.

Kotwal, A., Ramaswami, B., and Wadhwa, W. (2011). "Economic liberalization and Indian economic growth: What's the evidence?" *Journal of Economic Literature* 49(4): 1152–1199.
Li, J., and Jiang, Y. (2016). "Calculation and empirical analysis on the contributions of R&D spending and patents to China's economic growth" *Theoretical Economics Letters*, *6*(6): 1256.
Long, C. X., and Wang, J. (2019). "China's patent promotion policies and its quality implications" *Science and Public Policy*, *46*(1): 91–104.
Lucas, R. E. (1988). "On the mechanics of economic development" *Journal of Monetary Economics*, *22*: 3–42.
Mani, Sunil (2018). "What is happening to India's R&D funding? *Economic and Political Weekly*, *53*(14).
OECD (2003). *Research and Development Expenditure in Industry 2003*, Paris: OECD.
Piramal, Gita. (2017). "Animal Spirits: Stray Thoughts on the Nature of Entrepreneurship in India's Business Families after Liberalization", Chapter 25, pp. 485–507, in Mohan (2017).
Radjou, N., Prabhu, J., and Ahuja, S. (2011). "Use jugaad to innovate faster, cheaper, better" *Harvard Business Review*, *8* (Digital Article).
Rastogi, S., Sharma, A., Panse, C. and Bhimavarapu, V. M. (2021). "Unified Payment Interface (UPI): A digital innovation and its impact on financial inclusion and economic development" *Universal Journal of Accounting and Finance*, *9*(3): 518–530.
Romer, P. M. (1990). "Endogenous technological change" *Journal of Political Economy 98*: S71–S102.
Segerstrom, Paul S. (1991). "Innovation, imitation, and economic growth" *Journal of Political Economy*, *99*(4): 807–827.
Shahid, M. (2022). "Exploring the determinants of adoption of Unified Payment Interface (UPI) in India: A study based on diffusion of innovation theory" *Digital Business*, 2(2): 100040.
Sharma, D. C. (2022). *Indian Innovation, Not Jugaad-100 Ideas that Transformed India*. Delhi: Roli Books Private Limited.
Stewart, T. A., and Raman, A. P. (2008). The HBR interview-finding a higher gear - Anand G Mahindra, *Harvard Business Review*: 68.
World Bank (2007). *The Growth Report: Strategies for Sustained Growth and Inclusive Development*, Washington DC: World Bank.

14 India and the recent wave of regionalism in Asia-Pacific

Parthapratim Pal

14.1 Introduction

One of the major features of international trade is that countries are increasingly using bilateral trade agreements to boost their international trade. The pace of forming these regional trade agreements has definitely picked up as the Doha round of trade talks in the World Trade Organization (WTO) has virtually stalled. India has always been a strong proponent of multilateralism. India's involvement in regionalism was traditionally for geopolitical and strategic reasons. Economics and trade were seen as possible catalysts for improved regional cooperation. The stagnation in the Doha round and the proliferation of preferential trade agreements among India's major trade partners forced India to embrace regionalism in a major way.

One of the areas which has received significant policy focus from India in the last decade is the South-East Asian region. India is increasing its economic and strategic presence in South-East Asia. India has signed a free trade agreement with the Association of Southeast Asian Nations (ASEAN). It has also signed bilateral trade deals with Thailand, Singapore, Korea (comprehensive economic partnership agreements [CEPAs]), the India–Japan CEPA and the India–Malaysia CECA. (Comprehensive Economic Cooperation Agreement).

This region is important for a number of reasons. Culturally and geographically, this region is close to India, and there is significant trade complementarity between India and Southeast Asian countries. However, due to a number of of historical and geopolitical reasons, India's footprint in these countries is relatively small. Second, the Southeast Asian region is in a very important strategic zone which is becoming very complicated due to geopolitical tensions between China and other countries of this region. Having a number of allied countries in this region gives India some leverage in terms of diplomatic and economic power in this part of the world. Third, Southeast Asian countries are one of the first set of countries to participate in global production relocation. As India is seeking more participation in global value chains (GVCs), better trade and investment relations with Southeast Asian countries can help India achieve its goal. In this context, it is notable that most of

DOI: 10.4324/9781003509721-17

India's trade agreements with Southeast Asian countries are comprehensive economic cooperation agreement which covers trade investment and services.

Given this context, this chapter looks into India's engagement in Southeast Asian countries against the backdrop of India's overall policy orientation towards regionalism.

14.2 Theoretical Arguments for Regional Trade Agreements

The theoretical justification for regionalism emanates from several international trade theories, starting from the absolute advantage and comparative advantage models. These classical trade models argued that countries should open up and trade with each other even if they can produce all the goods needed for their domestic consumption. The Ricardian arguments regarding trade openness and 'gains from trade' suggest that countries can focus on products with a comparative advantage and move their resources away from inefficient industries in international trade. Ricardo argued that this relocation of resources within the countries should allow them to consume beyond their production possibility frontiers (PPFs) and result in a win–win scenario for both trade partners. These theoretical arguments and technological development since the Industrial Revolution led to the first unbundling of production and consumption and helped countries specialize (Baldwin 2006). The discovery of steam engines significantly reduced the cost and time of moving goods. This allowed production to happen in locations different from consumption. This spatial separation of production and consumption allowed countries to specialize, opening up mutually beneficial international trade among countries, including neighbouring countries. Opening up international trade among neighbours helped producers produce goods efficiently, and it also helped consumers purchase from the most efficient suppliers, thereby improving overall efficiency.

Viner first questioned this traditional view of gains from trade among nations in his 1950 book *The Customs Union Issue*. Viner distinguished between selective and general trade opening and argued that selective opening of trade through regional trade agreements may not necessarily enhance welfare. Viner suggested that trade opening on a preferential basis may allow domestic consumers to switch from inefficient domestic producers to more efficient producers from the preferential trade partners. He called this 'trade creation,' and he recognized that trade creation might enhance welfare. However, he also acknowledged that opening up trade on a preferential basis may not allow domestic consumers to purchase from the most efficient producer if the most efficient producer is not from the preferential trade partner but from the rest of the world. Viner calls this effect 'trade diversion' and argues that trade diversion is not welfare enhancing. Based on these two concepts, Viner suggested it is difficult to say *a priori* whether regionalism will be welfare-enhancing. It will depend on the more dominant effect between trade creation and trade diversion.

Notably, Viner's analysis is mainly from the consumers' side. One primary justification for preferential trade agreements has been to provide greater market access to domestic producers. A preferential trade arrangement with another country allows domestic producers to compete in that market on better terms. Therefore, domestic producers may gain from preferential trade agreements. On the flip side, such trade arrangements exclude some countries from the preferential trade block. Producers of such excluded countries are likely to suffer market access losses due to the formation of preferential trade agreements or PTAs. Therefore, while specific positive theoretical justifications exist for PTAs, the possibility of increased discrimination in the global trading system cannot be ruled out.

Since the 1960s, international trade and international trade theory and policy have undergone massive changes. In post–World War II, economists were experiencing difficulties in explaining global trade patterns using the existing theories. These so-called classical trade theories, which evolved from the pioneering models by Adam Smith and David Ricardo to Heckscher Ohlin and specific factors models, assumed perfect competition and full employment of factors of production. However, these theories could not explain massive intra-industry trade and trade among countries with similar factor endowments. A new breed of trade theories emerged to explain these trade patterns. Intra-industry trade in similar products implied that the assumption regarding market structure in international trade theories should be relaxed. The introduction of different market structures like monopolistic competition and oligopoly changed trade theory significantly. It became amply clear that scale economies, product differentiation and imperfect competition in international trade may allow multiple countries to specialize in different types of a given commodity from within the same industry. It also highlighted that the existence of scale economies benefits countries or blocks with larger markets and hence the theoretical justification for creating a large market using PTAs became important.

It was also recognized that within intra-industry trade, there is an important distinction between horizontal and vertical intra-industry trade. Horizontal intra-industry trade happens when countries engage in trade within an industry when the products traded are of similar quality and somewhat similar price band. By comparison, vertical intra-industry trade implies trade within the same industry but in differentiated products based on different attributes and different price brands. Horizontal and vertical intra-industry trade also justifies the creation of trade blocs among developed and developing countries. As intra-industry trade mostly happens in manufacturing, horizontal and vertical intra-industry trade (IIT) allowed PTA partners to change their production structure according to their comparative advantage. According to some literature, IIT may pose less threat to domestic producers as imports of products of different quality and price bands (vertical product differentiation) may not directly compete with domestic goods. This somewhat moderates the negative distributional impact of inter-industry trade. However, once imperfect competition, scale economies and product differentiation are simultaneously introduced in multi-country preferential trade models, the welfare impact of PTAs becomes complex and ambiguous.

The next significant change that happened in international trade theory literature is around the development of the GVCs. During the 1980s and 1990s, improvements in telecommunication technology reduced coordination and monitoring costs and allowed companies to break down their production into different activities and tasks and relocate these various activities across different countries based on certain comparative or competitive advantages of each of the countries. GVCs allow countries at different stages of development to participate more easily in international trade as it requires countries to engage at various stages of the value chain. The growth of GVCs has been very sharp over the last 30 years, and according to the World Development Report 2020 (WDR), presently, GVCs account for about 50 per cent of global trade. It also suggests that the participation of countries in the GVC has helped poorer countries grow faster and helped these countries reduce poverty. The emergence of GVCs has become a significant trigger for countries to participate in regional value chains through the creation of regional trade blocs. Participation in GVCs requires improving trade facilitation, connectivity and logistics in participating countries. As goods and services can potentially crisscross borders multiple times, participation in global and regional value chains induced countries to come together and form regional blocs to reduce trade costs and trade barriers.

At a policy level, the rise of regionalism coincided with the spread of multilateralism through the establishment of GATT (General Agreement on Tariff and Trade) and, subsequently, the WTO. This raised a considerable debate about the desirability of preferential and regional trade agreements in the global trading system. There are some strong critics of regional trade agreements (RTAs)/PTAs, like Bhagwati (2003, 2008), who believe that in a multilateral trading system, the RTAs/PTAs undermine the transparency and fair play of the system, and the prevalence of these regional trade agreements can destroy the multilateral trading system by acting as "Termites in the Trading System". He also highlighted that countries have signed multiple and overlapping PTAs/FTAs, (free-trade agreements) which may lead to a complex system of regulatory structures and preferences where imports will attract different trade measures depending on their origin. Bhagwati calls this the "spaghetti bowl problem" and warns that it might create opacity in the global trading system. These views form the 'stumbling-block' hypothesis, which suggests that PTAs/FTAs slow down multilateral trade liberalization (Panagariya 2000, Bhagwati 2008). However, there is also a counter-view which argues that regionalism may not hinder multilateralism. If countries are allowed to choose trade partners and gradually liberalize trade through the PTAs and FTAs, in the longer run, these countries would feel more comfortable in reducing tariffs at the MFN level or global level. This is the basic argument for the 'building block' hypothesis. Over the years, several authors, including Riezman (1985), Kennan and Riezman (1990), Levy (1997), Krishna (1998), Freund (2000),

Limão (2006) and Baldwin and Seghezza (2007), have investigated the building-block versus the stumbling-block hypothesis.

However, since the conclusion of the Uruguay round of trade talks, it became apparent that multilateral trade negotiations have not brought the desired results for many countries. The imbalances of the global trading system persisted. And most developing countries believed that they did not get a fair deal in the WTO. Also, as the number of WTO members swelled up to 160-plus, trade negotiation based on the consensus approach preferred by WTO has made the progress of the Doha round of trade talks excruciatingly slow. Consequently, many countries started looking to liberalize trade outside the ambit of the WTO. Also, as discussed before, the nature of international trade has become much more complex over the years. With the servicification of manufacturing, global production networks, emergence of environmental and sustainability issues and widespread use of modern Non-tariff measures in international trade, traditional WTO mechanisms often do not provide policymakers with the right tools to manage trade. In fact, over the years, trade in goods, trade in services and investment have become so intertwined that conventional WTO rules (at the core of which is still the GATT rules of the 1960s and 1970s) are often inadequate. The slow pace of WTO trade talks and the inadequacy of WTO trade tools have pushed many countries to look for regional trade agreements as possible alternate trade liberalization and expansion routes. The problem with the WTO system has been exacerbated in recent years, with the US virtually nullifying the WTO dispute settlement system by not allowing the appointment of members to fill the vacancies on the WTO's Appellate Body. All these factors have made regionalism an attractive alternative for many countries.

Other factors have also driven regionalism. For example, during the 1960s, technological development led to the 'flying geese' model of regionalism, in which Japan and other Southeast Asian countries together climbed up the value chain with Japan as the leader. Regionalism has also been used to forge political ties and geopolitical alliances. One possible reason behind this can be that increased economic linkages between two countries can increase the cost of conflict and may lead to more comprehensive economic cooperation among countries. Recent developments in BRICS (Brazil, Russia, India, China, South Africa) summits also highlight that increasing South–South cooperation in global finance may become another justification for increased regionalism.

14.3 India and its Engagement with RTAs

India has actively participated in multilateral trade negotiations and was among the 23 founding members of GATT when it was established in 1947. Post-independence, India followed inward-looking economic policies, and international trade was not one of the primary focus areas for Indian policymakers during the early planning period. However, India participated in the Bangkok Agreement, which was signed in 1975. Seven countries from the

Asia Pacific signed this agreement.[1] This was Asia's first preferential trade agreement. India is also part of the Global System of Trade Preferences among Developing Countries, which was signed in 1988. This is a large preferential trading bloc involving 42 countries. This preferential block was created to foster South–South cooperation in international trade.

During the 1990s, India continued its pursuit of trade liberalization using both multilateral and preferential channels. In PTAs, India mainly focused on forming trade blocs with other developing countries. India negotiated free trade agreements with its South Asian neighbours and signed the South Asian Free Trade Agreement (SAFTA) under the South Asian Association for Regional Cooperation (SAARC) framework. In the 1990s, India signed RTAs with other developing countries, including the MERCOSUR[2] trade bloc and Chile. India also signed four separate trade agreements with Afghanistan, Bhutan, Sri Lanka, Nepal, and Bangladesh.

In 1991, India adopted the Look East policy, and under this policy, India negotiated several trade agreements with East and Southeast Asian countries. India signed an FTA with ASEAN and separate regional cooperation agreements with Thailand, Malaysia, Singapore, Japan and Korea.[3] Since 1997, India has also been involved in the Bay of Bengal Initiative for Multi-Sectoral Technical and Economic Cooperation (BIMSTEC). BIMSTEC involves seven South Asian and Southeast Asian nations. Along with economic and regional cooperation, India's Look East Policy has geopolitical and strategic considerations, primarily focused on managing China's massive influence in this region. As a continuation of India's outreach towards Asia-Pacific, in December 2022, India signed an economic cooperation and trade agreement with Australia. Negotiations with New Zealand and Taiwan are also in progress.

It is notable that since the start of the Doha round in 2001, India's approach towards regional trade agreements has undergone a significant change. India started negotiations with developed countries. The talks began with the European Union and then post-BREXIT with the UK. The scope of these negotiations is broader than simple trade agreements and involves trade, investment and other aspects of economic cooperation. India is also in talks with the US for a possible economic cooperation agreement. As mentioned before, India has signed comprehensive economic cooperation agreements with other developed countries like Japan and Australia. It can be safely said that India's move towards North–South FTAs is primarily driven by the slow pace of trade negotiations in the WTO, plus the fear of missing out in some of its major markets.

India has generally been quite proactive in pursuing regionalism in Asia and globally. However, India opted out of a mega-trade bloc called the RCEP (Regional Cooperation Economic Partnership) Agreement in 2019. We have discussed this issue elsewhere[4] and concluded that India had strong reasons to move away from the RCEP negotiations as India had little to gain from RCEP; however, there were specific threats from joining the RCEP. Thus, that move should not be interpreted as India's withdrawal from the process of trade liberalization.

14.4 Trade Agreements with Some Asian Countries and India's Performance in International Trade

14.4.1 Merchandise Trade Exports

India has signed a plethora of trade agreements since the 1990s. In nominal terms, India's exports show a positive and steady growth (except during the COVID-19 period). But India's share in global merchandise trade has not shown a perceptible increase (Figure 14.1). India's exports have gone up since its joining in WTO in 1995, but India's share in global merchandise exports is still below 2 per cent (1.8 per cent in 2022). For the fifth-largest economy of the world, that is a low number. The ASEAN countries, which have an aggregate gross domestic product (GDP) slightly larger than India, had a share of 7.9 percent in global merchandise exports in the same year. China's share was 14.4 percent in 2022.

Similarly, in ASEAN, India has a very small market share. Out of its total imports of US$1287 billion in 2021, India accounted for only US$37.7 billion, implying a market share of only 2.9 percent. ASEAN's imports from China, by comparison, was US$388 billion, which indicates that China had a market share of close to 30 percent in ASEAN[5]. In the other two countries with which India has signed free-trade agreements, India's market shares are low and stagnant. In Japan, India has a market share of 0.73 percent in 2022. It was 0.79 percent in 2017 and 0.85 percent in 2013.[6] India's share in South Korea's total imports was 1.02 percent in 2021. It has remained below 1 percent for most of the years after the signing of the trade agreement.

If we look at India's export performance to these countries from the point of view of India's export composition, one expects that these countries will

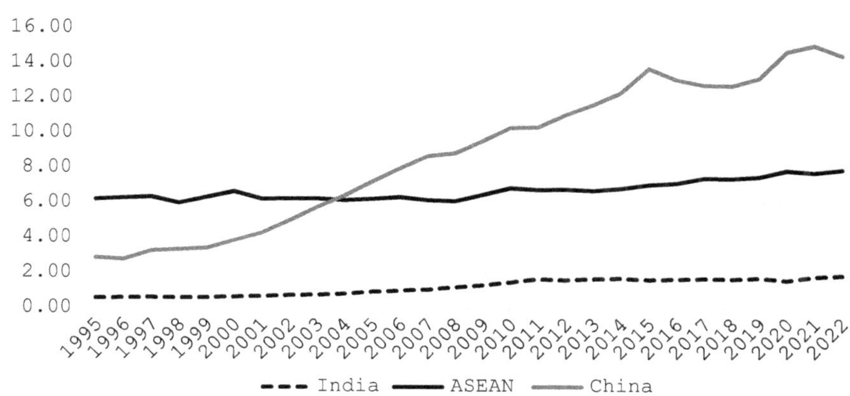

Figure 14.1 Share in Global Merchandise Exports (in percentages).

Source: WTO Trade Statistics.

Note: ASEAN = Association of Southeast Asian Nations.

Table 14.1 Share of South Korea, Japan and ASEAN in India's Total Exports

	S Korea	*Japan*	*ASEAN*	*ASEAN + South Korea + Japan*
2009–10	1.91	2.03	10.13	14.08
2010–11	1.49	2.04	10.26	13.79
2011–12	1.45	2.11	10.99	14.54
2012–13	1.37	1.99	12.01	15.38
2013–14	1.34	2.17	10.54	14.04
2014–15	1.48	1.74	10.25	13.47
2015–16	1.34	1.78	9.58	12.70
2016–17	1.54	1.39	11.22	14.16
2017–18	1.47	1.56	11.27	14.30
2018–19	1.43	1.47	11.35	14.25
2019–20	1.55	1.44	10.07	13.06
2020–21	1.61	1.52	10.79	13.91
2021–22	1.92	1.46	10.03	13.41
2022–23	1.48	1.21	9.76	12.44

Source: Ministry of Commerce, Government of India.

Note: ASEAN = Association of Southeast Asian Nations.

gain shares in India's export basket. This is because one of the major economic motivations for signing FTAs is opening up preferential market access for domestic exporters. The data in Table 14.1 indicate that since the signing of several trade agreements with ASEAN countries, Japan and South Korea, India's exports to these countries have increased in nominal terms. However, the share of these countries in India's total exports shows declining or flat trends. It does not appear that the trade agreements with these countries have resulted in significant market access gains for Indian exporters.

Therefore, to summarize our findings, India's market share in ASEAN, Japan and South Korea has remained low. Signing the FTAs has not resulted in a sizeable increase in India's market share. Even in India's export basket, these countries have not gained any share. In fact, as the table shows, the shares of these countries have contracted even in India's total exports.

There may be a number of reasons why signing several free trade agreements has not increased market access for India globally as well as in ASEAN. If India has a market share of less than 2 percent in global exports, then it is possible that India does not face demand constraints for most of its exports. Although there may be sectors, where India's market share is high and hence some demand constraints may be there, but overall, with less than 2 percent of the market share, it is unlikely that India's exports are low due to demand-side issues. Supply-side issues must be playing a role as well. Therefore, even if the bilateral agreements open up market access, the Indian exporters should be able to be in a position to take advantage of the increased market access. Using the same logic, as India's market share is very low in these countries, it is possible that India may not have the right products to export at the right quality and competitive prices in these markets. In such cases, a preferential tariff may not help Indian exporters.

Moreover, for the countries under consideration, three things are important to consider. First, most of the countries in ASEAN, Japan and South Korea are countries with low most-favoured nation (MFN) tariffs, and hence, the advantage due to tariff preferences will be low. Secondly, in most of these countries, Indian exporters may face non-tariff measures which generally are not covered under the preferential trade agreements. In fact, as these preferential trade agreements go beyond WTO-negotiated areas (like environmental issues, labour standard, etc.), exports through the preferential routes may face more stringent norms as well. In some cases, market access gain will also depend on the exporters' ability to comply with the SPS and TBT standards. There are likely to be certain sectoral gains; for example, India is likely to gain a larger market in textiles and garments in Japan, but the overall extent of additional market access is unlikely to be high in merchandise exports. Finally, historically China is the biggest source of imports for the ASEAN countries, Japan and South Korea. It is not very easy for Indian exporters to break into these markets.

14.4.2 Merchandise Imports

However, the import side of the picture has some interesting facets. Economists argue that trade agreements can bring benefits to countries because they can allow domestic producers access cheap raw materials and intermediate goods from preferential trade partners. If this happens, it should result in improved competitiveness of domestic products. Cheaper and availability of a wider variety of final goods can also improve choices for consumers and can keep domestic inflation low. However, it can lead to increased competition for some domestic producers who compete with foreign producers in the domestic market. It is also expected that sources of imports will move away from countries which are not part of FTAs towards countries which are members of FTAs. Consequently, there was an expectation that signing these trade agreements with countries of Asia Pacific would lead to a shift away from China. It is also notable here that India withdrew from the RCEP before signing a deal and consequently, there is no FTA between India and China right now.

Table 14.2 shows the share of ASEAN, Japan, South Korea and China (with and without Hong Kong). The table indicates that there has not been any perceptible shift away from China and in certain years, shares of China and Hong Kong have actually gone up in India's total imports. This is something apparently counterintuitive. Since the COVID-19 crisis, China is experiencing a slower GDP growth rate, and it is also facing a number of issues related to its supply chain. Moreover, India has not only signed a number of FTAs with several East and Southeast Asian nations, but it has also increased MFN tariff rates on a large number of products. International trade theory

Table. 14.2 Share of Different Countries in India's Total Imports

	Share of ASEAN	*Share of ASEAN + Japan + South Korea*	*Share of China*	*Share of China + Hong Kong*
2009–10	8.95	14.26	10.69	12.33
2010–11	8.28	13.44	11.76	14.30
2011–12	8.62	13.69	11.30	13.43
2012–13	8.74	13.93	10.65	12.26
2013–14	9.17	14.04	11.34	12.96
2014–15	9.98	15.26	13.48	14.73
2015–16	10.47	16.48	16.20	17.78
2016–17	10.57	16.38	15.94	18.08
2017–18	10.12	15.99	16.41	18.70
2018–19	11.54	17.28	13.68	17.18
2019–20	11.66	17.58	13.75	17.32
2020–21	12.02	18.03	16.53	20.38
2021–22	11.11	16.31	15.43	18.54
2022–23	12.27	17.55	13.80	16.35

Source: Ministry of Commerce.

Note: ASEAN = Association of Southeast Asian Nations.

suggests that the combined impact of these two policies should take away some market share from China. Despite this, China has managed to increase its market share in India, and its total trade (export + imports) with India has shown a steady rise in the post-COVID-19 era.

To add to this, India's FTA utilization ratio has not been very high for the FTAs under discussion. The government does not publish exact data about FTA utilization, but a Ministry of Commerce press release has this to say:

> While there has been growth rate in both imports from and exports to these FTA partners, the utilization rate of FTAs both for India and its partners has been moderate. The economic impact assessment of FTAs is a continuous process which is undertaken both in terms of data analysis and stakeholder consultations. An analysis of preferential import data for some of these agreements indicates that the FTA utilization rates have been moderate to high in the case of some sectors like iron and steel for the India Korea Comprehensive Economic Partnership Agreement (CEPA) and India Japan CEPA. Plastics in the case of India Singapore Comprehensive Economic Cooperation Agreement (CECA) and auto-motives in the case of India Malaysia CECA.[7]

This essentially implies that some of the possible benefits from FTAs are not availed by domestic producers as they are not using the FTA channels for imports. It must be kept in mind here that even if the government has signed an FTA, importers still have the option to import through the MFN channel. Some possible reasons for why some producers are not availing the FTA route can be the complex Rules of Origin requirements, complex paperwork, non-substantial benefits from preference margins or simply a lack of awareness. It is also worth highlighting here that for importers in special economic zones (SEZs) or importers who are importing intermediate goods to add value and exporting, FTAs do not matter. Importers in SEZs do not pay any import duty regardless of the origin of the product. Exporters who are importing intermediate goods for their exports get duty drawbacks as long as they are exporting the final good and not selling in the domestic market. These two factors may have also led to a low FTA utilization ratio in India. These facts suggest that on the import side of merchandise trade, these FTAs have not been utilized optimally by domestic producers.

14.4.3 Trade in Services and Investment

India's performance in trade in services is better than its merchandise part. India's export share has reached close to 4.4 percent of global trade in services in 2022. As India is globally competitive in services, it is expected that India will gain an advantage in services exports to these countries. Some of the countries in the Asia-Pacific region are big players in global trade in services. Singapore, Japan and South Korea have big markets for exporting different kinds of services. Table 14.3 shows the market size of some leading countries in global trade in services.

Table 14.3 International Trade in Services, Selected Countries

	Exports		*Imports*		*Share of World Total, 2020*	
	(€ billion)				*(%)*	
	2011	*2021*	*2011*	*2021*	*Exports*	*Imports*
World	2,598.1	3,519.4	2,514.0	3,345.5	100.0	100.0
EU	610.3	1,027.0	511.3	894.4	25.9	26.2
Australia	37.5	38.2	44.8	34.0	1.2	1.0
Brazil	26.6	28.0	53.3	42.5	0.7	1.3
Canada	61.3	87.8	77.2	88.7	2.3	2.6
China	144.4	286.2	178.0	370.6	5.7	10.0
Hong Kong	65.6	64.6	53.3	52.2	1.7	1.4
India	99.5	203.5	55.9	116.7	5.1	3.0
Japan	101.1	143.8	126.3	176.2	4.1	5.2
Mexico	11.4	23.0	22.6	32.7	0.4	0.7
Russia	41.7	47.3	65.7	63.8	1.2	1.7
Singapore	85.7	194.4	84.7	189.0	5.2	5.3
South Africa	12.6	7.7	14.8	11.5	0.2	0.3
South Korea	65.1	102.5	73.7	105.1	2.2	2.7
Turkey	29.6	49.2	15.1	26.7	0.9	0.6
United Kingdom	242.4	352.9	143.1	205.3	9.6	5.5
United States	463.1	652.1	329.2	457.6	17.6	12.0

Source: Eurostat, available at https://ec.europa.eu/eurostat/statistics-explained/images/c/cb/1.3_World_trade_in_services_GL2022.xlsx

Although these market sizes are large, services exports, especially in areas like medical, legal, accounting, architecture and others, are highly dependent on domestic regulations and how much benefit accrues to India will depend on the process of implementation of the preferential trade rules in the partner countries. Also, some of the ASEAN countries have large populations of people of Indian origin. There is demand for specific soft services like Yoga, music and movies in these countries. Japan, by comparison, is a big market for maintenance and repair services and these can open up market access for India.

There is one area where India can have a very strong potential for collaboration with these countries in the Indo-Pacific zone. Countries in ASEAN, Japan and South Korea are very strong in the area of science and technology and are among the top exporters and importers of high-technology related services. In a recent report, Mukherjee and Mukherjee (2023) point out that there is a very large scope for collaboration between India and South Korea in technology-driven areas like the Internet of Things, artificial intelligence, big data, smart factories, and 3D printing. As South Korean firms are adopting automation in manufacturing it can emerge as a strong market for information technology products. Similar opportunities are also there in countries like Singapore and Japan. One country with which India is negotiating an FTA and which has a very high potential of becoming the leading country in hardware related to artificial intelligence in Taiwan. These possible collaborations in the areas of high-technology goods and services can spill over into investments; also, India is trying to attract foreign investment in these areas.

If one looks at India's investment data, it shows that there has been a significant amount of foreign direct investment (FDI) coming from the countries of the Indo-Pacific region. Mauritius and Singapore are the top two sources of India's FDI. For the period April 2000 to March 2023, 25.8 and 23.3 percent of India's total FDI has come from these two countries. Japan is also a big source of FDI in India with a share of more than 6 percent (Table 14.4). Shares of other countries are small. However, these data are of limited use as many of the FDIs from the countries may have come though Mauritius or Singapore.

14.5 Conclusion

The stalling of WTO trade negotiations and, even more importantly, disruptions in the functioning of the WTO appellate body have made regional trade agreements an obvious way to promote trade liberalization. Most regional trade agreements these days go much beyond simple liberalization of merchandise trade. These agreements also include aspects of trade liberalization in various services, investments and other aspects of bilateral economic cooperation. However, the merchandise trade aspect receives the maximum attention as it is easier to comprehend and capture with data.

Table 14.4 Country-Wise FDI Inflow to India (April 2000–March 2023) in USD Million

	Country	*FDI in USD Million*	*Share of the Country (%)*
1	Mauritius	163,876	25.8
2	Singapore	148,169	23.4
3	USA	60,196	9.5
4	Netherland	43,759	6.9
5	Japan	38,740	6.1
6	United Kingdom	33,875	5.3
7	UAE	15,578	2.5
8	Cayman Islands	14,924	2.4
9	Germany	14,138	2.2
10	Cyprus	12,644	2.0
11	France	10,545	1.7
12	Switzerland	9,780	1.5
13	South Korea	5,467	0.9
14	Hong Kong	4,720	0.7
15	Luxembourg	4,393	0.7
16	Spain	3,742	0.6
17	Italy	3,333	0.5
18	Canada	3,306	0.5
19	Saudi Arabia	3,206	0.5
20	Belgium	2,786	0.4
21	China	2,462	0.4
22	Sweden	2,260	0.4
23	British Virginia	2,176	0.3
24	Ireland	1,364	0.2
25	Russia	1,276	0.2
26	Bermuda	1,221	0.2
27	Thailand	1,209	0.2
28	Malaysia	1,175	0.2
29	Australia	1,105	0.2
30	Denmark	1,097	0.2
31	Taiwan	826	0.1
32	Poland	701	0.1
33	Indonesia	648	0.1

Source: dpit.gov.in.

Note: FDI = foreign direct investment; USD = US dollars; UAE = United Arab Emirates.

India's Look East policy led to India signing multiple and sometimes overlapping trade agreements with countries in the Asia-Pacific region. We looked at some of these trade agreements, and it does not appear that so far there is a very strong impact of these trade agreements on the merchandise trade of India. We see that merchandise exports to these countries have increased but that the market shares of India in these countries remain abysmally low. Even within India's export basket, the share of these countries has gone down.

From the import side, imports from these countries to India have increased. But data suggest that China still is the biggest source of imports for India. Taken together, China and Hong Kong have very large and growing shares in India's total imports. This is remarkable because oil is India's biggest import item and China or Hong Kong are not oil-exporting countries. These trade agreements, for whatever reason, have resulted in an increase in imports from these countries, but it has not resulted in a significant switch of imports away from China.

In trading services, the picture is not as clear as country-level data on trade in services are not available on a consistent basis. But given India's better global performance in trades in service, it is possible that India will gain from increased trade with its eastern neighbours. India is presently the second-biggest exporter of services from developing countries (only behind China) and is gaining market share globally. Many Asian countries, especially Singapore, Malaysia, Japan and South Korea, have large and growing potential markets for exporting services. It is possible that India will gain if these countries open up meaningful market access for services exports for India. But the liberalization of trading services is often determined by domestic regulations in the target countries. It remains to be seen how much benefit India can carve out of these economic cooperation agreements in terms of trade in services. However, one can remain hopeful about the potential gains for India in this area. The potential for mutual gain is very strong in high technology areas as there seems to be some mutual synergy. While some of the countries of Asia-Pacific are leading producers of cutting-edge hardware, India has the manpower to supplement the services side of these high-technology goods and services.

As far as FDI is concerned, the data are unclear. It shows a huge amount of FDI from Mauritius and Singapore. Japan and South Korea have decent amounts of direct investments in India. But FDIs from other countries in Southeast Asia are minuscule. However, the nature of the data is such that it is difficult to draw any strong observations as some of these countries may have investments through Singapore and Mauritius. In this context, it is important to point out that the countries of Southeast Asia are established players in GVCs, and as rising wages and growing uncertainty in China are forcing many firms to look for alternate production bases, India can be in a situation where it will have to compete and collaborate with these countries to attract players in GVCs. India can emerge as a possible alternative destination for these large firms. Already India has attracted some large contract manufacturing firms from Taiwan and bilateral economic cooperation agreements will possibly help India to get integrated into GVCs.

Overall, the Look East policy is much more than an economic policy as strategic considerations play a very important role in overall geopolitics and strategy. The South China Sea is at the heart of a major global flashpoint right now. That is an important area because the Strait of Malacca is one of the busiest trade channels. A dispute with China will totally disrupt the economic equilibrium in that area. China and other countries in this region have uneasy diplomatic relations, and Taiwan and Australia are already facing a more direct economic and strategic conflict with China. In the case of escalated tensions in this region, countries need to cooperate to tackle China economically and politically. Given the size, clout and economic power of China, it will be impossible unless countries of this region come together under some form of a broader framework of geopolitical-economic cooperation. These bilateral economic cooperation agreements can be a step towards that bigger goal. India's latest trade agreement with Australia will also help with that. India is also negotiating an economic cooperation agreement with Taiwan possibly with the same broader goal in mind.

Notes

1 These countries are India, Bangladesh, Sri Lanka, Laos, South Korea, Thailand and the Philippines.
2 The Southern Common Market, commonly known by Spanish abbreviation Mercosur, and Portuguese Mercosul, is a South American trade block with Argentina, Brazil, Paraguay and Uruguay.as the full members.
3 The full list of countries is available here: Trade Agreements – Mcommerce.
4 https://www.forbesindia.com/blog/economy-policy/recent-traits-of-indias-trade-strategy-protectionism-or-pragmatic-globalisation/.
5 ASEAN Secretariat.
6 Japanese Trade and Investment Statistics | Reports and Statistics - Japan External Trade Organization – JETRO.
7 A 7.1 percent compound annual growth rate (CAGR) was recorded in trade with India's FTA and PTA partner countries (pib.gov.in).

References

Baldwin, R. (2006): 'Globalisation: The Great Unbundling(s).' Report for the Project "Globalisation Challenges for Europe and Finland Organised" by the Secretariat of the Economic Council. Available at: https://repository.graduateinstite.ch/record/295612/files/Baldwin_06-09-20.pdf

Baldwin, R., and Seghezza, E. (2007): 'Are Trade Blocs Building or Stumbling Blocks? New Evidence.' CEPR Discussion Paper No. DP6599. Available at: https://papers.ssrn.com/sol3/papers.cfm?abstract_id=1140528

Bhagwati, J. (2003): *Trade, Tariffs & Growth: Essays in International Economics*. MIT Press, Cambridge, MA.

Bhagwati, J. (2008): *Termites in the Trading System*. OUP, Oxford, UK.

Freund, C. (2000): 'Multilateralism and the Endogenous Formation of Preferential Trade Agreements.' *Journal of International Economics*, 52, 359–376.

Kennan, J. and Riezman, R. (1990): 'Optimal Tariff Equilibria with Customs Unions.' *Canadian Journal of Economics*, 90, 70–83.

Krishna, P. (1998): 'Regionalism and Multilateralism: A Political Economy Approach.' *The Quarterly Journal of Economics*, 113(1), 227–250.

Levy, P. (1997): 'A Political-Economic Analysis of Free Trade Agreements.' *Americcan Economic Review*, 87(4), 506–519.

Limão, N. (2006): 'Preferential Trade Agreements as Stumbling Blocks for Multilateral Trade Liberalization: Evidence for the U.S.' *American Economic Review*, 96(3), 896–914.

Mukherjee, A. and Mukherjee, E. (2023): Enhancing Trade, Investment, and Cooperation Between India and South Korea, in India-Korea Relations in the Emerging Dynamics of the Indo-Pacific, Special Report, ORF, July 2023.
Panagariya, A. (2000): 'Preferential Trade Liberalization; the Traditional Theory and New Developments', *Journal of Economic Literature*, 2, 287–331.
Riezman, R. (1985): 'Sucstoms Unions and the Core.' *Journal of Internatinoal Economics*, 19, 355–365.

15 Global Supply Chains

Which Way Now?

Preetam Basu and Partha Ray

15.1 Introduction

To say that global supply chains have played a significant role in enhancing the forces of globalization is perhaps stating the obvious without being analytical or informative. With the reduction in transport costs and tariffs and the entry of China to the World Trade Organization (WTO) in 2001, international trade has become the engine of global growth. Interestingly, with the spread of global supply chains, as a particular product represented bundling of various sub-components, processes, and intellectual property rights, the brand "made in country x" has started appearing to be a misnomer. The *World Development Report 2020* has given an illustration of a simple product like a cycle, where its different parts could come from countries as diverse as China, Japan, Vietnam, Singapore, Italy, Spain, and France.

Notwithstanding such diversity of supply chains, China has emerged as the most important hub of global supply chains. While in some sense, China's high growth performance for an extended period might appear to be an enigma, it is in line with the three major strands of economic growth and development, namely, (a) the classical Harrod–Domar type of growth model (whereby high domestic savings and productivity were contributing to rapid growth), (b) the Solow-type growth model (highlighting the role of labor-augmented technical progress), and (c) the standard Lewis model of economic development (whereby labor gets relocated from low-productivity agriculture to high-productivity industry; Raiser, 2019; World Bank, 2019). Apart from China, the story is valid, perhaps to a varying degree, for various other countries of emerging Asia as well.

Is this story of China-based global supply chains being diluted in the current context of the trade war, de-globalization, and the post-COVID-19 effects? If the global supply chains move out of China, where can they be relocated? Will firms adopt a diversifying strategy that is increasingly known as China-Plus-One? This chapter probes some of these questions.

The present research specifically examines the allure of the main rising Asian economies as potential and existing business destinations. Two dimensions are anticipated to be clarified by such research. It could first explain

DOI: 10.4324/9781003509721-18

how different Asian economies came into existence. Second, it could provide some insight into potential places for diversions if the current situation calls for leaving China. In focusing on this issue, we looked at different existing ratings/indicators of various global agencies/think tanks like the World Bank, the Global Economic Forum, or Harvard University and tried to capture the relative attractiveness of different economies in terms of a single grand rank that can form the basis of preference of global corporations.

The rest of the chapter is organized as follows: Section 15.2 is in the nature of a big picture of the emergence of Asia and globalization. The implication of the COVID-19 pandemic and the fault lines of global supply chains is discussed in Section 15.3. Section 15.4 probes into the data and methodology, and in Section 15.5, the results of our construction of a catch-all index of the attractiveness of an emerging Asian economy are discussed. Concluding the chapter, Section 15.6 puts forward a few conjectures about the shape of things to come in global supply chains.

15.2 The emergence of Asia and globalization: The big picture

15.2.1 Asia and the globalization

With hindsight, it does not seem to be an exaggeration that the story of globalization has been one of Asia. This story comes out very clearly from the long time-series data constructed by the Organisation of Economic Cooperation and Development (OECD), led by economic historian Angus Maddison. The OECD has released the distribution of global gross domestic product (GDP) over 1,000 years, 1000–2001, according to certain country groupings. While the absolute numbers of GDP may have various limitations, for our purpose, we look at the country-group=wise composition of global GDP (Table 15.1).

A look at Table 15.1 allows one to discern an interesting big-picture trend in Asia. Asian economies (excluding Japan), which had a near-secular decline in their share over 1000–1973, could nearly double their share over 27 years, 1973–2001. There is no other instance of any group of countries experiencing such a spectacular rise in their global share.[1] What happened in Asia? With the benefit of hindsight, three significant developments may be highlighted.

First, several East Asian countries experienced a quantum leap in their GDP growth as part of a process that is now known as the "East Asian miracle" since the 1970s. Stiglitz (1996) identified eight East Asian countries behind the phenomenon of the "East Asian Miracle", namely, Hong Kong, Japan, South Korea, Singapore, Taiwan (China), Indonesia, Malaysia, and Thailand. Of these Hong Kong, Japan, South Korea, Singapore, and Taiwan are classified as advanced countries by the International Monetary Fund (IMF). Despite the temporary setback in the East Asian crisis during the late 1990s, the comparative advantage of these East Asian countries remained intact.

Table 15.1 Country-Group-Wise Distribution of Global Gross Domestic Product (%)

	1000	*1500*	*1820*	*1870*	*1913*	*1950*	*1973*	*2001*
1. Western Europe	8.7	17.8	23.0	33.0	33.0	26.2	25.6	20.3
2. Western offshoots	0.7	0.4	1.9	10.0	21.3	30.7	25.3	24.6
3. Japan	2.7	3.1	3.0	2.3	2.6	3.0	7.8	7.1
4. Asia (excluding Japan)	67.6	61.9	56.4	36.1	22.3	15.4	16.4	30.9
5. Latin America	3.9	2.9	2.2	2.5	4.4	7.8	8.7	8.3
6. Eastern Europe & former USSR	4.6	6.1	9.0	12.0	13.4	13.0	12.9	5.6
7. Africa	11.7	7.8	4.5	4.1	2.9	3.8	3.4	3.3
8. World	100.0	100.0	100.0	100.0	100.0	100.0	100.0	100.0

Source: Maddison (2004).

Second, China emerged as a global growth pole since the late 1980s. The success of the grand strategy of economic opening up in China since the 1980s has been reflected in the fact that over the last 100 years, China became the only economy that grew at an average rate of 10 percent per annum during the 27 years, 1980–2007 (Luo, 2014; Bruton et al., 2019). It has now become the world's second-largest economy. It is interesting to note that the engines of Chinese growth have been investment and foreign trade and not consumption (like the US or India). Three related developments seemed to have shaped the emergence of foreign trade as an engine of growth in China: (a) its entry to the World Trade Organization (WTO) in 2001, (b) its emergence as a preferred hub of global supply chains and the advent of a "made in China" model, and (c) establishment of several different types of successful special economic zones along the coastal regions.

Third, India opened its economy in the early 1990s and got integrated with the global economy while dismantling the cobweb of a control regime that used to be known as "license-permit raj" (Ahluwalia, 2002). The Indian model of economic growth has been distinct from the Chinese model in several ways, namely, (a) the late opening up in India after a lag of little more than ten years than China, (b) the predominance of consumption and services sector as engines of Indian growth, and (c) India having a huge trade deficit, which has turned into a manageable current account deficit due to a substantial surplus on account of services (primarily information technology) and inward remittances.

Over the years, China has emerged as the global leader in manufacturing in which global value chains have played a key role.[2] China's prime position in the global supply chain is most evident from its share of global exports and imports. In this context, McKinsey (2019) has used an interesting taxonomy. Depending on the extent of involvement with global supply chains, the manufacturing sector of the Chinese economy has been divided into five archetypes, namely, (1) high level of integration, (2) high exposure to Chinese exports, (3) high exposure to Chinese imports, (4) global chain with little trade exposure to China, and (5) local production for local consumption. Interestingly, in sectors like computer, electronics and optical products, or electrical equipment, China is highly integrated with global supply chains, whereas in sectors like textiles, apparel, or furniture, the world has been dependent on Chinese imports (Table 15.2).

Over the past forty years, China's manufacturing dominance has had a profound impact on global trade and supply chains. Many multinational companies have established production facilities or outsourced manufacturing to China to take advantage of its competitive advantages. This has resulted in China becoming an integral part of global value chains, with components and products often traversing multiple countries before reaching the end consumer. However, now Chinese firms face severe competition from other low-cost countries, such as Malaysia, Thailand, and Vietnam. Thus, to pursue the cost-leadership strategy, Chinese firms have to pay continuous attention to cost control and seek new ways to improve production efficiency. In this context, theories of "strategic trade policy" may be helpful (Brander and Spencer, 1985). It is by now well known that "government policies such as export subsidies and import restrictions can, under the right circumstances, deter foreign firms from competing for lucrative markets ... government policy here serves much the same role that 'strategic' moves such as investment in excess capacity or research and development (R & D) serve in many models of oligopolistic competition" (Krugman, 1987).[3] China's trade policy precisely followed this path and emerged as a trading superpower. Empirical investigations revealed that nearly three-fourths of China's industries are dynamic and registered very high growth because of market liberalization, falling trade barriers, and a favorable exchange rate (Fetscherin et al., 2010).

On the contrary, India started attracting the world's interest because of its impressive economic performance, brought about by the liberalization process that started in the early 1990s. A significant driver of the Indian growth story has been information technology (IT) and IT-enabled services (ITeS), providing remote services to clients across the world (Sheth, 2008). Riding of the spectacular dynamism shown by the IT services sector, India became the outsourcing epicenter of the world. Indian IT companies such as TCS, Infosys, and Wipro rode high on the growth wave and joined the billion-dollar club in the early 2000s. The manufacturing sector in India, however, has traditionally lagged China in cost, quality, and contribution. This lag was also reflected in terms of exports. However, with government initiatives such as Make in India that aim to make India an integral part of the global supply chain, the Indian manufacturing sector is in the process of catching up to some extent. Multinational giants such as Apple, Mercedes-Benz, BMW,

Table 15.2 China's Share of Global Exports and Imports (percentage)

		China's Share of Global Exports (%)		*China's Share of Global Imports (%)*	
Archetype	Sector name	2003–07	2013–17	2003–07	2013–17
High level of integration	Computer, electronic, and optical products	15	28	12	16
	Electrical equipment	16	27	7	9
	Other machinery and equipment	7	17	8	9
High exposure to Chinese exports	Textiles, apparel, and leather	26	40	5	5
	Furniture, safety, fire, other	17	26	2	4
	Other non-metallic mineral products	11	22	5	8
	Rubber and plastics	10	19	5	7
	Basic metals	8	13	8	8
High exposure to Chinese imports	Mining and quarrying	1	1	7	21
	Chemicals	4	9	9	12
	Paper and paper products	3	9	6	12
Global chains with little trade exposure to China	Other transport equipment	3	6	3	5
	Pharmaceuticals	2	4	1	3
	Motor vehicles and trailers	1	3	2	7
	Coke and refined petroleum products	2	4	4	6
Local production for local consumption	Food, beverages, and tobacco	3	4	3	6
	Fabricated metal products	14	23	3	5
	Wood and wood products	11	22	2	3
	Printing and media	8	18	2	4
	Agriculture, forestry, and fishing	5	5	7	19

Source: McKinsey (2019).

Hyundai, Honeywell, and OnePlus have started investing heavily in terms of developing their manufacturing bases in India (Saranga et al., 2017). While today India lags China by a considerable margin in this sector, going forward, India has the potential to become a global manufacturing and supply chain hub in the days to come.

15.2.2 Constituents of emerging Asia

Aside from China and India, numerous other Asian nations merit consideration in this perspective. Not all of Asia is the subject of our attention in this chapter; rather, it is the growing and developing Asian nations. Among the Asian economies, the following countries are treated as advanced economies, namely, Japan, South Korea, Hong Kong, Macao, Singapore, and Taiwan by the IMF. Apart from these six economies that account for 7.4 percent of global GDP (at purchasing power parity [PPP]), thirty countries in Asia are classified as "emerging and developing economies" (EMDEs) accounting for 34.2 percent of global GDP. Of these, thirty countries, the share of GDP of twenty-two countries is less than 0.5 percent of global GDP (at PPP). In the rest of this chapter, we exclusively focus our attention on these remaining eight countries, namely, China, India, Indonesia, Thailand, Malaysia, Philippines, Bangladesh, and Vietnam. Thus, our quest for the "Plus-One country" has been confined to seven countries in this list. Note that while these eight economies account for nearly one-third of global GDP, in per capita terms, these are much poorer than the advanced Asian economies (Table 15.3).

15.2.3 Global supply chain potential in Asia

While trade in global supply chains proliferated during the 1990s and the initial years of the new millennium, it stagnated after the 2008 global financial crisis (World Bank, 2020). Thereafter, threats of a trade war and the COVID-19 pandemic have put some sand in the wheels of global supply chains.[4] The origin of the feared Coronavirus in Wuhan has seriously harmed China's reputation as the "factory of the world." Multinational companies with offices and factories in China were the first to face disruption in their supply chains. Several multinational brands are now questioning their supply chain dependence on just one country – China.

According to a recent Gartner survey, approximately one-third of supply chain executives have already relocated or plan to relocate parts of their supply chain out of China by 2023. Apple has stated that certain iPad and MacBook assembly will be moved from China to Vietnam, in collaboration with its supplier Foxconn. Samsung has announced plans to relocate most of its computer monitor manufacturing units to Vietnam. Reportedly, Samsung also intends to invest approximately $660 million in India to build a new manufacturing facility. Hasbro, an American toy company, has begun shifting production from China to Mexico, India, and Vietnam. Hyundai Motors

Table 15.3 Size of the Asian Economies: 2019 (percent)

	No.		*Share (% of GDP at PPP in Global GDP)*	*GDP (at MER; USD billion)*	*GDP (at PPP; USD billion)*	*Per Capita GDP (at MER; USD)*
				(Percent)		
Advanced Asia	1	Japan	4.05	5,154	5,747	40,847
	2	Korea	1.64	1,630	2,320	31,431
	3	Singapore	0.41	363	585	63,987
	4	Taiwan (Province of China)	0.92	586	1,300	24,828
	5	Hong Kong SAR	0.35	373	491	49,334
	6	Macao SAR	0.06	55	78	81,152
	7	Total	7.42			
Emerging & Developing Asian	1	China	19.25	14,140	27,309	10,099
	2	India	7.98	2,936	11,326	2,172
	3	Indonesia	2.64	1,112	3,737	4,164
	4	Thailand	0.98	529	1,383	7,792
	5	Malaysia	0.76	365	1,079	11,137
	6	Philippines	0.72	357	1,026	3,294
	7	Bangladesh	0.59	317	838	1,906
	8	Vietnam	0.54	262	770	2,740
	9	Others	0.74			
	10	Total	34.20			

Source: World Economic Outlook Database, IMF, October 2019.

Note: SAR: Special Administrative Region; PPP: Purchasing Power Parity; MER: Market Exchange Rate.

Others include Myanmar, Sri Lanka, Nepal, Cambodia, Lao P.D.R., Mongolia, Brunei Darussalam, Papua New Guinea, Fiji, Bhutan, Maldives, Timor-Leste, Samoa, Solomon Islands, Vanuatu, Kiribati, Marshall Islands, Micronesia, Nauru, Palau, Tonga, and Tuvalu.

wants to shift its global supply base to India to decouple its dependence on China. Google is also looking at producing the Pixel4A, a low-cost smartphone, and the Pixel5A, a flagship smartphone, in Vietnam rather than China. Microsoft has stated that it intends to move the manufacturing of its Surface notebooks and desktops to Vietnam.

So, as supply chain leaders look at viable alternatives to shift their production base out of China, a diversifying strategy – China-Plus-One is gaining momentum. The "China-Plus-One" strategy refers to the diversification of manufacturing and sourcing options by companies that traditionally relied heavily on China. This strategy aims to mitigate risks associated with overdependence on a single country and take advantage of emerging opportunities in other locations. Several countries, including India, Thailand, Vietnam, Bangladesh, Philippines, Malaysia, and Indonesia, have been identified as potential beneficiaries of this strategy. In the following, we present a brief overview of the opportunities they offer:

India: India has a large and growing consumer market, a skilled workforce, and a robust service sector. The government has been implementing initiatives to promote manufacturing, such as the "Make in India" campaign, which aims to attract foreign investment and boost domestic manufacturing capabilities.

Thailand: Thailand offers a strategic location at the heart of Southeast Asia, well-developed infrastructure, and a strong manufacturing base. It has a skilled workforce, particularly in the automotive, electronics, and machinery industries. The country also has free-trade agreements with several major economies, providing preferential access to various markets.

Vietnam: Vietnam has emerged as an attractive manufacturing destination, particularly for labor-intensive industries such as textiles, garments, electronics, and footwear. The country offers competitive labor costs, a young workforce, improving infrastructure, and favorable investment policies. It has also benefited from various free trade agreements, including the Comprehensive and Progressive Agreement for Trans-Pacific Partnership and the EU–Vietnam Free Trade Agreement.

Bangladesh: Bangladesh has a significant presence in the textile and garment industry, being one of the world's largest exporters of apparel. It offers low labor costs, a large labor force, and preferential trade agreements with several countries. The government has been focused on attracting foreign investment and improving infrastructure to further develop the manufacturing sector.

Philippines: The Philippines has a skilled English-speaking workforce, making it attractive for industries such as business process outsourcing (BPO) and electronics manufacturing. The government has implemented policies to encourage investment, including tax incentives and economic zones. The country's proximity to major markets and its participation in free-trade agreements also contribute to its appeal.

Malaysia: Malaysia has a well-developed manufacturing sector, particularly in electronics, electrical products, and automotive components. The country offers a skilled workforce, advanced infrastructure, and a business-friendly environment. It has also positioned itself as a regional hub for high-tech industries.

Indonesia: Indonesia has a large domestic market, abundant natural resources, and a young workforce. The government has been implementing economic reforms to attract investment and promote industrial development. The country has a strong presence in sectors, such as textiles, automotive, and electronics.

These countries present opportunities for companies seeking to diversify their manufacturing bases or explore new markets. However, it is important to consider factors such as infrastructure, labor costs, regulatory environment, logistics, and market access when evaluating the suitability of each location for specific industries and business needs. Additionally, geopolitical considerations and trade policies can impact the attractiveness and competitiveness of these countries as manufacturing destinations (Table 15.4).

Thus, as global supply chains grapple with the challenges of restructuring their value propositions, we try to identify possible relocation options for these global players. The aggregate ranking of the East Asian countries based on the various metrics provide critical pointers towards relocation opportunities.

15.3 Selecting "Plus One" in the China-Plus-One strategy

15.3.1 Comparing select Asian economies based on aggregate ranking

As already indicated, our focus in this essay is the potential of eight countries (viz., China, India, Indonesia, Thailand, Malaysia, Philippines, Bangladesh, and Vietnam) in emerging Asia. In the absence of any pan-Asian survey data, while assessing the supply chain potential and attractiveness of these economies, we looked at a few standard indices assessing the strength of an economy.

15.3.2 Selection of the indices

Specifically, to begin with, we considered the following four popular indices to understand the potential of these eight economies to become/maintain their position in global supply chains.

World Bank's Logistic Performance Index (LPI): The LPI is an interactive benchmarking tool "created to help countries identify the challenges and opportunities they face in their performance on trade logistics and what they can do to improve their performance". Six indicators are used for the construction of LPI: (1) efficiency of customs and border management clearance, (2) quality of trade- and transport-related infrastructure, (3) the ease of arranging competitively priced international shipments; (4) competence and quality of logistics services, (5) ability to track and trace consignments, and (6) frequency with which shipments reach consignees within the scheduled or expected delivery time.[5]

World Bank's Ease of Doing Business Index (DBI): The DBI takes into account information based on the following ten indicators for any country: (1) Starting a Business, (2) Dealing with Construction Permits, (3) Getting Electricity, (4) Registering Property, (5) Getting Credit, (6) Protecting Minority Investors, (7) Paying Taxes, (8) Trading across Borders, (9) Enforcing Contracts, and (10) Resolving Insolvency.[6]

World Economic Forum's Global Competitiveness Index (GCI): *The Global Competitiveness Report* series was first launched in 1979. The GCI is the product of an aggregation of 103 individual indicators, derived from a combination of data from international organizations as well as from the

Table 15.4 Major Trading Products and Partners of Select Countries in Emerging Asia

Country	*CAB (US$ billion – 2018)*		*Major Products*	*Major Exporter/Importer*
China	49.1	Export	Electrical and other machinery (including computers and telecommunications equipment), Apparel, Furniture, Textiles	US 19.2%, Hong Kong 12.2%, Japan 5.9%, South Korea 4.4%
		Import	electrical and other machinery, including integrated circuits and other computer components, optical and medical equipment, metal ores, motor vehicles;	South Korea 9.7%, Japan 8.6%, US 7.3%, Germany 5%, Australia 4.9%
India	–57.2	Export	petroleum products, precious stones, vehicles, machinery, iron and steel, chemicals, pharmaceutical products, cereals, apparel	US 15.6%, UAE 10.2%, Hong Kong 4.9%, China 4.3%
		Import	crude oil, precious stones, machinery, chemicals, fertilizer, plastics, iron and steel	China 16.3%, US 5.5%, UAE 5.2%, Saudi Arabia 4.8%, Switzerland 4.7%
Indonesia	–31.1	Export	mineral fuels, animal or vegetable fats (including palm oil), electrical machinery, rubber, machinery and mechanical appliance parts	China 13.6%, US 10.6%, Japan 10.5%, India 8.4%, Singapore 7.6%, Malaysia 5.1%, South Korea 4.8%
		Import	mineral fuels, boilers, machinery, and mechanical parts, electric machinery, iron and steel, foodstuffs	China 23.2%, Singapore 10.9%, Japan 10%, Thailand 6%, Malaysia 5.6%, South Korea 5.3%, US 5.2%
Thailand	32.4	Export	automobiles and parts, computers and parts, jewelry and precious stones, refined fuels, electronic integrated circuits, chemical products, rice, fish products	China 12.4%, US 11.2%, Japan 9.5%, Hong Kong 5.2%, Vietnam 4.9%, Australia 4.5%, Malaysia 4.4%
		Import	machinery and parts, crude oil, electrical machinery and parts, chemicals, iron & steel and products, jewelry	China 20%, Japan 14.5%, US 6.8%, Malaysia 5.4%

Malaysia	7.5	Export	semiconductors and electronic equipment, palm oil, petroleum and liquefied natural gas, wood and wood products, palm oil, rubber, textiles,	Singapore 15.1%, China 12.6%, US 9.4%, Japan 8.2%, Thailand 5.7%, Hong Kong 4.5% (2017)
		Import	electronics, machinery, petroleum products, plastics, vehicles, iron and steel products, chemicals	China 19.9%, Singapore 10.8%, US 8.4%, Japan 7.6%, Thailand 5.8%, South Korea 4.5%, Indonesia 4.4%
Philippines	−8.7	Export	Semiconductors and electronic products, machinery and transport equipment, wood manufactures, chemicals, processed food and beverages, garments,	Japan 16.4%, US 14.6%, Hong Kong 13.7%, China 11%, Singapore 6.1%, Thailand 4.3%, Germany 4.1%, South Korea 4%
		Import	electronic products, mineral fuels, machinery and transport equipment, iron and steel, textile fabrics, grains, chemicals, plastic	China 18.1%, Japan 11.4%, South Korea 8.8%, US 7.4%, Thailand 7.1%, Indonesia 6.7%, Singapore 5.9%
Bangladesh	−7.8	Export	garments, knitwear, agricultural products, frozen food (fish and seafood), jute and jute goods, leather	Germany 12.9%, US 12.2%, UK 8.7%, Spain 5.3%, France 5.1%, Italy 4.1%
		Import	cotton, machinery and equipment, chemicals, iron and steel, foodstuffs	China 21.9%, India 15.3%, Singapore 5.7%
Vietnam	5.8	Export	clothes, shoes, electronics, seafood, crude oil, rice, coffee, wooden products,	US 20.1%, China 14.5%, Japan 8%, South Korea 6.8%
		Import	machinery and equipment, petroleum products, steel products, raw materials for the clothing and shoe industries, electronics, plastics, automobiles	China 25.8%, South Korea 20.5%, Japan 7.8%, Thailand 4.9%

Sources: The Word Factbook, https://www.cia.gov/library/publications/the-world-factbook/; The World Economic Outlook Database, International Monetary Fund.

Note: Percentage of distribution of exports and imports pertains to 2017 for most of the countries except for China for which it pertains to 2018. CAB = Current Account Balance = Exports of Goods & Services – Imports of Good & Services.

World Economic Forum's Executive Opinion Survey. Indicators are organized into twelve pillars: institutions, infrastructure, ICT adoption, macroeconomic stability, health, skills, product market, labor market, financial system, market size, business dynamism, and innovation capability.[7]

Economic Complexity Index (ECI) of Harvard University: The economic complexity of a country is calculated based on the "Lin and Ding" of exports a country produces and their "ubiquity", or the number of the countries able to produce them (and those countries' complexity). Diversity and ubiquity are, in some sense, "crude approximations of the variety of capabilities available in a country or required by a product". While diversity measures how many different types of products a country can make, ubiquity measures the number of countries that can make a product.[8]

How to determine the attractiveness of an economy in terms of these indices? After all, each of these indicators may have some specific information and may follow a distinct methodology. Hence, instead of looking at the index values, we looked at the ratings and tried to arrive at some sort of aggregate rating, using the following methodology.

15.4 Methodology of aggregate ranking

Our objective is to capture the relative attractiveness of different economies in terms of a single grand rank that can form the basis of preference of global corporations. Hence, we need to apply a rank aggregation method in terms of deriving a single grand ranking that aggregates and combines all the different rankings.

Rank aggregation (RA) is the process of combining multiple ranked lists into a single ranking. RA has been traditionally applied in the fields of information retrieval, applied psychology, social choice, and political election studies. Recently, it has found novel applications in genomic studies and web search applications for integrating information from individual genomic studies that address the same biological question or determining the relative efficacy of search engines in response to a given query (Aslam and Montague, 2001; Li et al., 2019).

Optimization-based RA methods are one of the most popular methods and have a long history dating back to the 1950s (Mallows, 1957; Fligner and Verducci, 1986). They are designed to minimize some distance measures so that the aggregated rank is as close as possible to all base ranks. Two commonly used measures are Kendall's tau and Spearman's foot rule distances. When initially proposed, these methods were computationally challenging because of the large number of comparisons the algorithm had to perform amongst the different rankings. However, with the advancement in technology and computational horsepower, these methods have become much more usable in practical problems.

The optimization-based RA methods are explained in the following. We first define the objective function that would determine a "super" list, which would be as "close" as possible to all individual ordered lists simultaneously.

$$\varnothing(\delta) = \sum_{i=1}^{n} w_i d(\delta, L_i), \tag{15.1}$$

where L_i is the ith ranked list, δ is a proposed ordered list of length $k = |L_i|$, w_i is the importance weight associated with the list L_i and d is a distance function.

Our objective is to derive δ^* that would minimize the distance between L_i' s.

$$\delta^* = \operatorname{argmin} \sum_{i=1}^{n} w_i d(\delta, L_i). \tag{15.2}$$

There are two choices for finding the appropriate distance function d, which would measure the distance between the ranked lists: Spearman foot rule distance and Kendall's tau distance.

15.4.1 *Spearman's footrule distance*

Spearman's footrule distance is an intuitive generalized distance metric for comparing two ordered lists that calculate the summation of the absolute differences between the ranks of all unique elements from both ordered lists.

Let $r^{L_i(A)}$ be the rank of A in the list L_i (rank 1 denotes the best ranking) and $r^{\delta(A)}$ be the rank of A in the list in any ordered list δ. The Spearman's footrule distance between L_i and any other ordered list δ is defined as

$$S(\delta, L_i) = \sum_{t \in L_i \cup \delta}^{n} \left| r^{\delta}(t) - r^{L_i}(t) \right|. \tag{15.3}$$

As we observe from the definition, Spearman's footrule distance is the summation of the absolute differences between the ranks of all unique elements from both ordered lists combined. The smaller the value of the metric, the more similar the lists.

15.4.2 *Kendall's tau distance*

The Kendall's tau distance utilizes pairs of elements from the union of two ranked lists to calculate the distance and is defined as follows:

$$K(\delta, L_i) = \sum_{t \in L_i \cup \delta}^{n} K_{tu}^{p}, \tag{15.4}$$

where

$$K_{tu}^{p} = \begin{cases} 0 \,\text{if}\, r^{\delta}(t)\langle r^{\delta}(u), r^{L_i}(t)\langle r^{L_i}(u) \,\text{or}\, r^{\delta}(t)\rangle r^{\delta}(u), r^{L_i}(t)\rangle r^{L_i}(u) \\ 1 \,\text{if}\, r^{\delta}(t)\langle r^{\delta}(u), r^{L_i}(t)\langle r^{L_i}(u) \,\text{or}\, r^{\delta}(t)\rangle r^{\delta}(u), r^{L_i}(t)\rangle r^{L_i}(u) \\ p \,\text{if}\, r^{\delta}(t) = r^{\delta}(u) = k+1 \,\text{or}\, r^{L_i}(t) = r^{L_i}(u) = k+1. \end{cases} \quad (15.4a)$$

Here, $p \in [0, 1]$ is a parameter that needs to be specified for Kendall's tau. Intuitively, Kendall's tau calculation works in the following way: if the two elements t and u have the same ordering in both lists, then no penalty is incurred (a good scenario). If the element t precedes u in the first list and u precedes t in the second list, then a penalty of 1 is imposed (a bad scenario). A case in which both t and u do not appear in either one of the lists (their ranks are $k + 1$) can be handled by selecting p on a spectrum ranging from very liberal (0) to very conservative (1).

The main distinction between the distance measures is that Kendall's tau only accounts for discordant pairs, while Spearman's foot rule accounts for the magnitude of the rank differences. To solve the optimization problem and determine the aggregate rank combining the various ranked lists with either the Spearman's footrule distance metric or Kendall's tau distance metric, two methods are applied in practice. One is based on the cross-entropy Monte Carlo simulation approach that works in the context of rare event simulation and combinatorial optimization (; Rubinstein and Kroese, 2013). This method uses importance sampling to iteratively search for the ranked list that minimizes the overall distance. The other is based on a genetic algorithm (Goldenberg, 1989). In our chapter, we considered both optimization methods by using the *RankAggreg* package in the *R* Programming language. The *RankAggreg* package provides an easy and convenient interface to handle complex rank-aggregation problems. It provides the user with two choices of optimization methods for aggregation as well as two different distance functions, as explained earlier.

15.5 Results and discussion

15.5.1 Baseline results

To begin with, we looked at the rankings of the eight countries as per these four indices and derived their relative ranking among these eight economies (Table 15.5).

How close are these rankings? We calculated the Spearman rank correlation coefficients of the relative rankings of the eight countries based on the four indices; some of the correlations are not that high (Table 15.6). The relatively low values of the Spearman correlation coefficients (e.g., 0.738 between LPI and GCI rankings, 0.736 between GCI and ECI rankings) indicate that there exist different rankings of the countries across the different

Table 15.5 Rankings of Eight EMDEs of Asia per Select Indices/Ratings

		World Bank's Logistic Performance Index (LPI): Ranking (2018)		*World Bank's Ease of Doing Business Index (DBI): Ranking (2020)*		*World Economic Forum's Global Competitiveness Index (GCI): Ranking (2019)*		*Harvard University's Economic Complexity Index (ECI): Ranking (2019)*	
		Ranking	*Relative Ranking*	*Ranking*	*Relative Ranking*	*Ranking*	*Relative Ranking*	*Ranking*	*Relative Ranking*
1	China	27	1	31	3	28	2	19	1
2	India	42	4	63	4	68	6	45	5
3	Indonesia	51	6	73	6	50	4	63	7
4	Thailand	34	2	21	2	40	3	25	2
5	Malaysia	35	3	12	1	27	1	28	3
6	Philippines	64	7	95	7	64	5	33	4
7	Bangladesh	100	8	168	8	105	8	104	8
8	Vietnam	45	5	70	5	67	7	57	6

Source: Authors' calculations from different indices.

Table 15.6 Pairwise Rank Correlation between the Six Indices

	LPI	*DBI*	*GCI*	*ECI*	*CPI*	*FSR*
Logistic Performance Index (LPI)	1.000	0.905	0.738	0.857	0.012	−0.238
Ease of Doing Business Index (DBI)		1.000	0.786	0.762	0.107	−0.429
Global Competitiveness Index (GCI)			1.000	0.736	0.298	−0.238
Economic Complexity Index (ECI)				1.000	0.227	0.119
Corruption Perceptions Index (CPI)					1.000	−0.036
Financial Strength Ranking (FSR)						1.000

indices. Hence, an aggregate ranking that combines the individual rankings under each index would be useful in this context.

As explained in Section 15.3, we used the *RankAggreg* package available in the *R* Programming language to determine the aggregate ranking of the eight countries based on the individual ranking across these four indices. In the aggregate ranking, we find that China ranks first followed by Thailand, Malaysia, India, Vietnam, Indonesia, Philippines, and then Bangladesh (Figure 15.1). Insofar as global supply chain management is concerned, this sequence gives us some idea of the possible shifts, however marginal, from China to any of these seven countries of emerging Asia.

15.5.2 Adding two more indices

How do business leaders choose their destinations? In this menu of ideal attributes, we have selected four significant criteria that in our judgment would constitute the core decision-making in zeroing in on a business destination. Towards a robustness check, we looked at two more rankings, namely, *The Economist* magazine's Country Rating of Financial Strength (FSR), and Transparency International's Corruption Perceptions Index (CPI).

The FSR is based on four measures of financial strength, namely, public debt, foreign debt, cost of borrowing, and reserves cover. The ranking is for sixty-six emerging economies.[9] Transparency International complies CPI by aggregating data from several different sources that "provide perceptions by business people and country experts of the level of corruption in the public sector"; the CPI 2019 is calculated using thirteen different data sources from twelve different institutions that capture perceptions of corruption within the past 2 years for 140 countries.[10] The rankings, as well as the relative rankings of these eight economies as per FSR and CPI, are presented in Table 15.7.

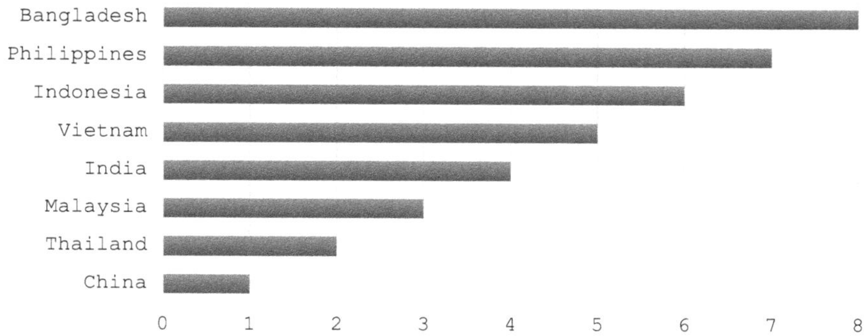

Figure 15.1 Aggregate Ranking of Eight Asian Economies per Four Indices.
Source: Authors' Calculation.

Table 15.7 Rankings of Eight EMDEs of Asia as per Select Indices/Ratings

		Transparency International's Corruption Perceptions Index (CPI): Ranking (2018)		*Economist Magazine's Country Rating of Financial Strength (FSR): Ranking (2020)*	
		Absolute Ranking	*Relative Ranking*	*Absolute Ranking*	*Relative Ranking*
1	China	87	3	10	4
2	India	78	2	18	7
3	Indonesia	89	4	16	6
4	Thailand	99	5	7	2
5	Malaysia	99	5	25	8
6	Philippines	61	1	6	1
7	Bangladesh	149	8	9	3
8	Vietnam	117	7	12	5

Source: Authors.

We calculated the Spearman rank correlation coefficients of the relative rankings of the eight countries based on the six indices; some of the correlations are now very low (e.g., 0.107303 between the DBI and the CPI, 0.298063 between the GCI and the CPI), and some are even negative (e.g., –0.238095 between the LPI and the FSR, –0.428571 between the DBI and the FSR; Table 15.6). Hence, the importance of an aggregate ranking that combines the individual rankings under each index becomes more useful in this context.

When these two additional rankings are taken into account, the grand rankings of the eight countries look slightly different (Figure 15.2). While the ranking of the first three countries in Asia, namely, China, Thailand, and Malaysia, as well as the eighth ranking for Bangladesh, remain unaltered, in between, there is some change in the relative positions of the other four countries.

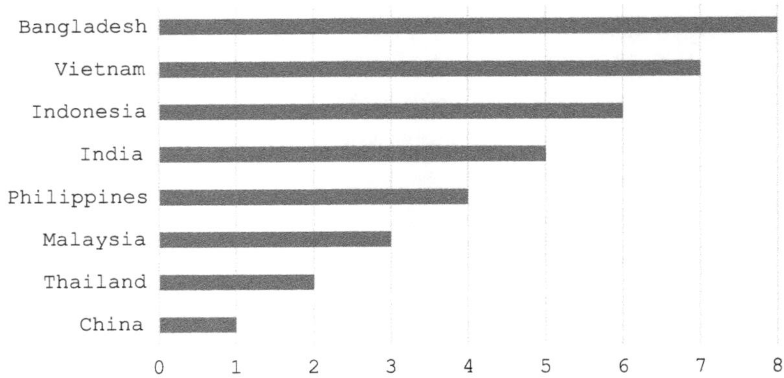

Figure 15.2 Aggregate Ranking of Eight Asian Economies per Six Indices.
Source: Authors' calculation.

15.6 Concluding observations

Asia, in general, and China, in particular, had played a significant role in globalization. In this process, China emerged as the undisputed leader of global supply chain management. Admittedly, several countries in emerging Asia also played vital roles. However, since the global financial crisis of 2008, there has been some drop in the ever-increasing pace of China's production and supply chain activities. Later, with the US–China trade war and the COVID-19 pandemic, there may have been some thinking, however nascent, in multinational corporations in terms of moving away from China.

Insofar as the pursuit of this diversifying strategy from China is concerned, our conclusions are as follows: First, it is challenging to move away from China in the short run. Second, in all likelihood, corporations will pursue a China-Plus-One strategy, whereby they may move marginally from China and relocate part of their supply chain elsewhere. Third, in looking for alternative locations, corporations in all likelihood may look for the following countries in emerging Asia, namely, Thailand, Malaysia, India, Vietnam, Indonesia, Philippines, and then Bangladesh. Aggregating different rankings per different indices, we have indicated a grand ranking of these seven countries indicating their attractiveness as "Plus One" countries in that diversification initiatives.

The relationship between geography and management success is complex. Geopolitics, institutions, cultural factors, and the availability of cheap land, labor, and finance – all could play a role in that. In this chapter, at the current juncture of de-globalization, we have tried to develop a macro approach (and a methodology) of the relevant metrics that could be relevant in making that decision. Admittedly, our menu of attributes of various rankings is far from being exhaustive, and these can be extended depending on the context of the business.

While at this time of uncertainty, we have no way to infer the shape of things to come in the near future, the strategic role of Asian corporations and countries in future global growth and development can hardly take a back seat in the post-pandemic world. To conclude, we echo the sentiments of Lawrance Summers (2020), who said, "If the 21st century turns out to be an Asian century as the 20th was an American one, the pandemic may well be remembered as the turning point".

Notes

1 Peter Drucker was apt when in the context of the changing contours of the world economy, as early as in the mid-1980s, he remarked, "The greatest increases, both in absolute and in relative terms, however, have been in developing countries: in India, in post-Mao China and in the rice-growing countries of Southeast Asia" (Drucker, 1986).
2 Per the United Nations data, as of 2018, China's share in global manufacturing had been close to 30 percent, next to the US, whose share was around 17 percent.
3 Illustratively, it has been documented that in crystalline silicon photovoltaic industry, the Chinese government heavily intervened through several non-WTO-compliant trade and investment measures. Specifically, these measures were employed in such a way that upstream price differentials, midstream subsidization, and downstream export promotion were created effectively favoring China (Kümmerle, and Schmidkonz, 2014).
4 For example, employing a dynamic supply chain model, Walmsley and Minor (2020) found that while both the US and China would be losers, the rest of the world could gain as they fill the gaps left by the US and Chinese producers.
5 The LPI 2018 allows for comparisons across 160 countries and is available at https://lpi.worldbank.org/.
6 The DBI 2020 covers 190 countries and is available at https://www.doingbusiness.org/en/rankings.
7 The GCI-2019 covers 141 countries and is available at http://www3.weforum.org/docs/WEF_TheGlobalCompetitivenessReport2019.pdf.
8 ECI-2019 is available for 133 countries and is available at https://atlas.cid.harvard.edu/rankings.
9 Available at https://www.economist.com/briefing/2020/05/02/which-emerging-markets-are-in-most-financial-peril.
10 Available at https://www.transparency.org/en/cpi/2019.

References

Ahluwalia, Montek S. 2002. Economic Reforms in India Since 1991: Has Gradualism Worked? *Journal of Economic Perspectives*, 16(3): 67–88.
Aslam, J. A., & Montague, M. 2001. Models for Metasearch. In *Proceedings of the 24th annual international ACM SIGIR conference on Research and development in information retrieval* (pp. 276–284).
Brander, James A., and Barbara J. Spencer. 1985. Export Subsidies and International Market Share Rivalry. *Journal of International Economics*, 18: 83–100.
Bruton, G. D., Ahlstrom, D., & Chen, J. 2019. China Has Emerged as an Aspirant Economy. *Asia Pacific Journal of Management*, 38, 1–15.
Drucker, Peter. 1986. The Changed World Economy. *Foreign Affairs*, Spring.

Fetscherin, M., Alon, I., & Johnson, James P. 2010. Assessing the Export Competitiveness of Chinese Industries. *Asian Business & Management*, 9(3), 401–424.

Fligner, M. A., & Verducci, J. S. 1986. Distance Based Ranking Models. *Journal of the Royal Statistical Society: Series B (Methodological)*, 48(3), 359–369.

Goldenberg, D. E. (1989). *Genetic Algorithms in Search, Optimization and Machine Learning*. Boston, MA: Addison-Wesley Longman Publishing Co. Inc.

Krugman, Paul R. 1987. Is Free Trade Passé?, *Economic Perspectives*, 1(Fall): 131–144.

Kümmerle, D., & Schmidkonz, C. 2014. China's Strategic Trade Policy Industry-Specific Trade and Investment Measures in the Value Chain of the Crystalline Silicon Photovoltaic Industry in the Age of WTO Legislation, *Munich Business School Working Paper 2014–02*. Available at https://www.munich-business-school.de/fileadmin/user_upload/forschung/working_papers/mbs-wp-2014-02.pdf

Li, X., Wang, X., & Xiao, G. 2019. A Comparative Study of Rank Aggregation Methods for Partial and Top Ranked Lists in Genomic Applications. *Briefings in bioinformatics*, 20(1), 178–189.

Luo, Xiaopeng. 2014. From a Manipulated Revolution to Manipulated Marketisation: A Logic of the Chinese Model. In Fan, Shenggen, Ravi Kanbur, Shang-Jin Wei, and Xiaobo Zhang (eds.): *Oxford Companion to the Economics of China*. Oxford: Oxford University Press.

Maddison, Angus. (2004). Contours of the World Economy and the Art of Macro-Measurement 1500–2001. Ruggles Lecture, IARIW 28th General Conference, Cork, Ireland August 2004. Available at http://citeseerx.ist.psu.edu/viewdoc/download;jsessionid=211141CFCFBA1A3F757C04E56DA38B04?doi=10.1.1.694.2406&rep=rep1&type=pdf

Mallows, C. L. 1957. Non-Null Ranking Models. *Biometrika*, 44(1–2): 114–130.

McKinsey. 2019. China and the World: Inside the Dynamics of a Changing Relationship. *McKinsey Global Institute Report*. Available at https://www.mckinsey.com/~/media/mckinsey/featured%20insights/china/china%20and%20the%20world%20inside%20the%20dynamics%20of%20a%20changing%20relationship/mgi-china-and-the-world-full-report-june-2019-vf.ashx

Raiser, Martin. 2019. China's Rise Fits Every Development Model. Brookings Blog, available at https://www.brookings.edu/blog/future-development/2019/10/17/chinas-rise-fits-every-development-model/

Rubinstein, R. Y., & Kroese, D. P. (2013). *The Cross-Entropy Method: A Unified Approach to Combinatorial Optimization, Monte-Carlo Simulation and Machine Learning*. New York: Springer Science & Business Media.

Saranga, H., Mudambi, R., & Schotter, A. P. 2017. Mastering the Make-in-India Challenge. *MIT Sloan Management Review*, 58(4), 59.

Sheth, J. N. (2008). *Chindia Rising: How China and India Will Benefit Your Business*. New Delhi: Tata McGraw-Hill Education.

Stiglitz, Joseph E. 1996. Some Lessons from the East Asian Miracle. *World Bank Research Observer*, 11(2), 151–177.

Summers, Lawrence H. (2020. COVID-19 Looks Like a Hinge in History. *Financial Times*, May 14.

Walmsley, Terrie, & Peter Minor. 2020. US Trade Actions against China: A Supply Chain Perspective. *Foreign Trade Review*, 55(3), 337–371.

World Bank. 2019. *Innovative China: New Drivers of Growth*. Washington, DC: World Bank. Available at https://openknowledge.worldbank.org/handle/10986/32351

World Bank. 2020. World Development Report. *Trading for Development in the Age of Global Value Chains*. Washington DC: World Bank.

Index

Pages in *italics* refer to figures and pages in **bold** refer to tables.

For Product Safety Concerns and Information please contact our EU representative GPSR@taylorandfrancis.com
Taylor & Francis Verlag GmbH, Kaufingerstraße 24, 80331 München, Germany

www.ingramcontent.com/pod-product-compliance
Ingram Content Group UK Ltd.
Pitfield, Milton Keynes, MK11 3LW, UK
UKHW022318250926
475702UK00046B/939

9781032670942